Stating the Obvious, and Other Database Writings

Still More Thoughts and Essays on

Database Matters

C. J. Date

Published by:

2 Lindsley Road, Basking Ridge, NJ 07920 USA
https://www.TechnicsPub.com

Cover design by Lorena Molinari

First Printing 2020

Printed in the United States of America.

ISBN, print ed.	9781634629034
ISBN, Kindle ed.	9781634629041
ISBN, ePub ed.	9781634629058
ISBN, PDF ed.	9781634629065

Library of Congress Control Number: 2020949860

In science what is obvious is not necessarily true.

—Max Perutz:
"The Second Secret of Life" (1998)

It requires a very unusual mind to undertake
the analysis of the obvious.

—Alfred North Whitehead:
Science and the Modern World (1938)

The statements was interesting, but tough.

—Mark Twain:
The Adventures of Huckleberry Finn (1884)

———— ♦ ♦ ♦ ♦ ♦ ————

To my friends and personal heroes,
past, present, and future

About the Author

C. J. Date is an independent author, lecturer, researcher, and consultant, specializing in relational database technology. He is best known for his book *An Introduction to Database Systems* (8th edition, Addison-Wesley, 2004), which has sold some 900,000 copies at the time of writing and is used by several hundred colleges and universities worldwide. He is also the author of numerous other books on database management, including most recently:

- From Trafford: *Database Explorations: Essays on The Third Manifesto and Related Topics* (with Hugh Darwen, 2010)

- From Apress: *Date on Database: Writings 2000-2006* (2007); *Database Design and Relational Theory: Normal Forms and All That Jazz* (2nd edition, 2019)

- From Morgan Kaufmann: *Time and Relational Theory: Temporal Databases in the Relational Model and SQL* (with Hugh Darwen and Nikos A. Lorentzos, 2014)

- From O'Reilly: *Relational Theory for Computer Professionals: What Relational Databases Are Really All About* (2013); *View Updating and Relational Theory: Solving the View Update Problem* (2013); *SQL and Relational Theory: How to Write Accurate SQL Code* (3rd edition, 2015); *The New Relational Database Dictionary* (2016); *Type Inheritance and Relational Theory: Subtypes, Supertypes, and Substitutability* (2016)

- From Lulu: *E. F. Codd and Relational Theory: A Detailed Review and Analysis of Codd's Major Database Writings* (2019)

- From Technics: *Logic and Relational Theory: Thoughts and Essays on Database Matters* (2020); *Fifty Years of Relational, and Other Database Writings: More Thoughts and Essays on Database Matters* (2020)

Mr Date was inducted into the Computing Industry Hall of Fame in 2004. He enjoys a reputation that is second to none for his ability to explain complex technical subjects in a clear and understandable fashion.

Contents

Preface

This book is the third in a series. The two previous ones were:

- *Logic and Relational Theory: Thoughts and Essays on Database Matters* (Technics Publications, 2020)

- *Fifty Years of Relational: More Thoughts and Essays on Database Matters* (Technics Publications, 2020)

And what I had to say in the preface to the second of these books applies pretty much unchanged to this third one:

> As the subtitle indicates, this book is basically "more of the same"—but the point is, I found while putting the earlier books together that there was so much I wanted to say that to have put it all in one volume would simply have been overwhelming. Thus, although each of the books can certainly stand on its own, they're really all part of the same overall project as far as I'm concerned.

Structure of the Book

The book is divided into four parts:

   I. Stating the Obvious

  II. Saying It Twice, or Not Clearly

 III. Objects and Objections

 IV. Not So Obvious After All?

Part I takes a close look at certain concepts (e.g., equality) that are so well understood—or so you might think—that we don't usually bother to spell them out, and considers some of the consequences of this state of affairs. Part II consists of a detailed examination of two rather unfortunate aspects of SQL, viz., the fact that the language is highly redundant (in several different ways), and the fact that it permits expressions whose semantics aren't even fully defined.

Part III contains, first, a series of chapters on aspects of object orientation (OO) that aren't as widely or properly understood as they should be; second, a detailed, critical review and analysis of the proposals of the Object Data Management Group, ODMG. Finally, Part IV discusses a variety of database topics (relational and otherwise) that, again, don't seem to be as well understood in the community at large as they might be.

The book doesn't have to be read in sequence; most of the chapters are fairly independent of one another. Because they're independent, however, many of the chapters contain references and examples and figures whose numbering is unique only within the chapter in question. For the same reason, there's also a small amount of overlap among certain of the chapters; I apologize for this fact, but I felt it was better to preserve the independence of each individual chapter as much as possible.

Prerequisites

My target audience is database professionals. Thus, I assume you're somewhat familiar with both the relational model and the SQL language. However, certain relational and/or SQL concepts are reviewed briefly here and there (basically wherever I felt such explanations might be needed, or helpful).

Some Technical Issues

On reviewing the text, it occurred to me that there are a few technical terms that appear ubiquitously and that it would therefore be worth defining right up front, as it were. The terms in question are *relvar*, **Tutorial D**, and *commalist*.

Relvar: "Relvar" is short for *relation variable*. What all too many people still call just "relations" (meaning constructs in the database, that is) are indeed really variables; after all, their value does change over time as INSERT, DELETE, and UPDATE operations are performed, and "changing over time" is exactly what makes them variable. In fact, *not* distinguishing clearly between relation values and relation variables—or table values and table variables, in SQL—has led to an immense amount of confusion in the past, and indeed continues to do so. In our work on *The Third Manifesto*, therefore, Hugh Darwen and I decided to face up to this problem right from the outset. To be specific, in that *Manifesto* we framed all of our remarks in terms of relation values when it really was relation values that we meant, and in terms of relation variables when it really was relation variables that we meant, and we abided by this discipline rigorously (indeed, one hundred percent). However, we also introduced two abbreviations: We allowed "relation value" to be abbreviated to just *relation* (exactly as we allow, e.g., "integer value" to be abbreviated to just *integer*), and we allowed "relation variable" to be abbreviated to *relvar*. Please understand, therefore, that throughout this book, I use these terms very carefully and correctly in full accordance with what I've just been saying; in other words, relation means relation, and relvar means relvar.

Tutorial D*:* I mentioned *The Third Manifesto* in the previous paragraph. Now, *The Third Manifesto* (the *Manifesto* for short) isn't a language definition; rather, it's a prescription for the functionality that its authors, Hugh Darwen and myself, claim a language must provide in order to be considered truly relational. But we did need a way of referring generically to any such language within that *Manifesto*, and we used the name **D** for that purpose. Note carefully, therefore, that **D** isn't a language as such, it's a family of languages; there could be any number of individual languages all qualifying as a valid member of that family. **Tutorial D** is one such.[1] **Tutorial D** is based on the relational algebra; it's defined more or less formally in the *Manifesto* book,[2] and it's used throughout that book and elsewhere—the present book included—as a basis for examples. In fact, I and others have been using that language for such purposes in books and presentations for many years now, and I think our experience in that regard has shown that it's both well designed and fairly self-explanatory.

Note that the names **D** and **Tutorial D** are always set in boldface as shown.

Commalist: This term is used heavily in syntax definitions and the like. It's short for "comma separated list." It can be defined as follows: Let *xyz* be some syntactic construct (for example, "attribute name"); then the term *xyz commalist* denotes a sequence of zero or more *xyz*'s in which each pair of adjacent *xyz*'s is separated by a comma. Within a given commalist, spaces appearing immediately before the first item or any comma, or immediately after the last item or any comma, are ignored. For example, if *A*, *B*, and *C* are attribute names, then the following are all attribute name commalists:

---

[1] By contrast, SQL isn't.

[2] *Databases, Types, and the Relational Model: The Third Manifesto*, by Hugh Darwen and myself (3rd edition, Addison-Wesley, 2007). See also the website *www.thethirdmanifesto.com*.

```
A , B , C

C , A , B

B

A , C
```

So too is the empty sequence of attribute names.

Suppliers and parts: Many examples in the body of the book makes use of the familiar suppliers-and-parts database. Here's the usual sample value:

S

SNO	SNAME	STATUS	CITY
S1	Smith	20	London
S2	Jones	10	Paris
S3	Blake	30	Paris
S4	Clark	20	London
S5	Adams	30	Athens

P

PNO	PNAME	COLOR	WEIGHT	CITY
P1	Nut	Red	12.0	London
P2	Bolt	Green	17.0	Paris
P3	Screw	Blue	17.0	Oslo
P4	Screw	Red	14.0	London
P5	Cam	Blue	12.0	Paris
P6	Cog	Red	19.0	London

SP

SNO	PNO	QTY
S1	P1	300
S1	P2	200
S1	P3	400
S1	P4	200
S1	P5	100
S1	P6	100
S2	P1	300
S2	P2	400
S3	P2	200
S4	P2	200
S4	P4	300
S4	P5	400

And here are definitions, expressed in **Tutorial D**, of the three relvars in this database:

```
VAR S BASE RELATION    /* suppliers */
  { SNO    CHAR ,
    SNAME  CHAR ,
    STATUS INTEGER ,
    CITY   CHAR }
  KEY { SNO } ;
```

```
VAR P BASE RELATION    /* parts */
  { PNO     CHAR ,
    PNAME   CHAR ,
    COLOR   CHAR ,
    WEIGHT  RATIONAL ,
    CITY    CHAR }
  KEY { PNO } ;

VAR SP BASE RELATION   /* shipments */
  { SNO     CHAR ,
    PNO     CHAR ,
    QTY     INTEGER }
  KEY { SNO , PNO }
  FOREIGN KEY { SNO }
        REFERENCES S
  FOREIGN KEY { PNO }
        REFERENCES P ;
```

Publishing History

- Chapter 1, "Equality"; Chapter 2, "Assignment"; and Chapter 3, "Naming": Previously unpublished—and here let me thank and acknowledge my friend and colleague Hugh Darwen for his review of, and helpful comments on, these three chapters.

- Chapter 4, "Redundancy in SQL": Heavily revised version of a series of articles that originally appeared in the magazine *Data Base Programming & Design* and/or on the website *www.dbpd.com* in May, June, and July, 1998.

- Chapter 5, "Indeterminacy in SQL": Previously unpublished, though certain portions did appear, in rather different form, in *A Guide to the SQL Standard*, by Hugh Darwen and myself (4th edition, Addison-Wesley, 1997). The portions in question are reused here by permission of Hugh Darwen.

- Chapter 6, "Thinking Clearly about Persistence"; Chapter 7, "Thinking Clearly about Encapsulation"; and Chapter 8, "Thinking Clearly about Decapsulation": Heavily revised versions of a series of articles that originally appeared in the magazine *Data Base Programming & Design* and/or on the website *www.dbpd.com* during the period September 1998 – January 1999.

■ Chapter 9, "An Overview and Analysis of ODMG": Heavily revised version of (a) Appendix I of *Foundation for Future Database Systems: The Third Manifesto*, by Hugh Darwen and myself (2nd edition, Addison-Wesley, 2000) and (b) Chapter 27 of *Date on Database: Writings 2000-2006* (Apress, 2006). Reprinted here by permission of Hugh Darwen.

■ Chapter 10, "Types, Units, and Representations: A Dialog, of a Kind": Based in part on a series of exchanges in *DBMS* magazine over the period from June 1995 to February 1996.

■ Chapter 11, "Dropping ACID": Heavily revised version of material from (a) a section from Chapter 8 ("SQL and Constraints") of my book *SQL and Relational Theory: How to Write Accurate SQL Code*, 3rd edition (O'Reilly, 2015) and (b) a section from Chapter 16 ("Concurrency") of my book *An Introduction to Database Systems*, 8th edition (Addison-Wesley, 2004).

■ Chapter 12, "Relational Trumpery" and Chapter 13, "Leonardo Was Right": Previously unpublished.

C. J. Date
Winooski, Vermont
2020

Part I

STATING THE OBVIOUS

Some while ago I received a note from a reader containing among other things the following complaint concerning something I'd written a little earlier:

> I had great difficulty in grasping *The Principle of Orthogonal Design* ... and when I finally did manage to understand it, I was *incensed!* Surely it's so obvious—I might even say trivial—that it's not worth even bothering to articulate it, is it?

Actually there are two points here. The first and more important is the general point—the suggestion, rather—that if something's obvious, there's no need to state it explicitly. I do *not* agree with this suggestion. Rather, I believe that explicitly spelling out assumptions is worthwhile, even when whatever it is that's being assumed does seem "obvious." (You probably know the old saying: *Never assume anything—"assume" makes an ass of u and me.*) In this part of the book, therefore, I want to consider a few assumptions that usually aren't spelled out explicitly but I think should be. To be specific, I want to examine equality, in Chapter 1; assignment, in Chapter 2; and naming, in Chapter 3.

My second point has to do with *The Principle of Orthogonal Design* specifically, which (like the familiar principles of normalization) is a principle that's intended for use as a formal guideline in database design. Here's an example. Consider the usual suppliers relvar S, with its attributes SNO, SNAME, STATUS, and CITY, and sample value as shown here:

SNO	SNAME	STATUS	CITY
S1	Smith	20	London
S2	Jones	10	Paris
S3	Blake	30	Paris
S4	Clark	20	London
S5	Adams	30	Athens

Consider also these two projections of S:

SNO	SNAME	CITY
S1	Smith	London
S2	Jones	Paris
S3	Blake	Paris
S4	Clark	London
S5	Adams	Athens

SNO	STATUS	CITY
S1	20	.London
S2	30	Paris
S3	30	Paris
S4	20	London
S5	30	Athens

Well, it's pretty obvious that it wouldn't be a good idea to design the database in such a way as to replace S by these two projections (basically because if we did, then the fact that any given supplier has a given city would be stated twice). Note, however, that such a design certainly abides by all of the usual principles of normalization; in particular, note that both projections are needed in the process of reconstructing the original relvar. It follows that those principles by themselves aren't enough—we need something else to tell us what's wrong with the design (something else *formal*, that is; we all know what's wrong with it informally).

Now, it's clear that the principle we need must be something like: *Don't do that!*—i.e., don't design the database in such a stupid way. It turns out, though, that pinning that principle down precisely is much harder than it might look. Here for the record is a precise definition:

Definition (*The Principle of Orthogonal Design*): There must not exist relvars *R1* and *R2* (not necessarily distinct) such that

a. There exists a join dependency $\bowtie\{X1,...,Xn\}$ that's irreducible with respect to *R1*, and

b. There exists some *Xi* ($1 \le i \le n$) and some possibly empty set of attribute renamings on the projection, *R1X* say, of *R1* on *Xi* that maps *R1X* into *R1Y*, say, and

c. *R1Y* has the same heading as some subset *Y* (distinct from *Xi*, if *R1* and *R2* are one and the same) of the heading of *R2*, and

    d.   There exist restriction conditions *c1* and *c2*, neither of which is a contradiction in the logical sense of that term, and

    e.   The following equality dependency holds:

```
( R1Y WHERE c1 ) = ( R2Y WHERE c2 )
```

(where *R2Y* is the projection of *R2* on *Y*).

Perhaps it's not surprising that the reader who wrote me that note originally had "great difficulty in grasping" this definition! Of course, I certainly don't want to explain that definition in detail here, since I've already done that elsewhere;[1] however, I do hope the manifest complexities it involves will serve to convince you of the truth of my claim—viz., that the principle turns out to be much more complicated than might have been expected, given only simple examples of its violation like the one shown above. (As usual, the devil is in the details. In fact, both I and other writers got the definition wrong the first several times we tried to state it accurately.)

So my second point is this: Just because something seems obvious, it still might be worth spelling it out explicitly—not least because the effort involved in doing so might make one realize on closer examination that what originally seemed "obvious" isn't all that obvious after all, and might even be wrong. The following is one of my all time favorite quotes:

"Obvious" is the most dangerous word in mathematics.

It's from Eric Temple Bell's book *Mathematics: Queen and Servant of Science (*1938), and it's well known, I think. But what's perhaps not so well known is the sentence that precedes it in Bell's original text:

The so called obvious was repeatedly scrutinized from every angle and was frequently found to be not obvious but false.

A personal anecdote here: I well remember one particular mathematics lecture I attended at university in the early 1960s, during the course of which the lecturer wrote something on the chalkboard and said "That, of course, is

---

[1] See my book *Database Design and Relational Theory: Normal Forms and All That Jazz*, 2nd edition (Apress, 2019).

obvious." Then he stopped for a moment and said "At least, I think it's obvious." Then he stared at what he'd written for a minute or two. Then he left the room ... After a few minutes, however (during which nothing happened of any significance!), he came back into the lecture room and stated categorically "Yes, it *is* obvious."

Chapter 1

Equality

Two things are identical
if one can be substituted for the other without affecting the truth.
—Gottfried Wilhelm von Leibniz:
L. Couturat (ed.), Opuscules et fragments inédits de Leibniz (1903)

As explained in the introduction to this part of the book, this chapter is the first of three on concepts that are often taken for granted because they're "obvious." So it's the first installment in a kind of miniseries, in a way, and I'm devoting it to an easy one (?): *equality*.

Now, everyone knows what equality means—right? But if that's really true, then how come SQL makes such a mess of it? Could it be precisely because the meaning is indeed so "obvious" that the SQL language designers never bothered to spell it out? Let's take a closer look.

I'll begin by setting a stake in the ground: To me, two values are equal if and only if they're one and the same value. In fact, that's the way I defined equality in my book *The New Relational Database Dictionary* (O'Reilly, 2016):

> **Definition (equality):** A truth valued or logical operator ("="). Two values are equal if and only if they're the very same value; that is, the comparison *v1* = *v2*, where *v1* and *v2* are values, evaluates to TRUE if and only if *v1* and *v2* are the very same value. *Note:* The equality operator (which is defined for every type, necessarily) is also known, especially in logic contexts, as *identity*.

Points arising from this definition:

■ First, note that the definition does assume that the things that can sensibly be tested for equality are, specifically, values. Of course, the values in question can be—in fact, must be—denoted by some *expression* (possibly just a literal, possibly a variable reference, possibly something more complex), and the actual comparands are determined by evaluating those expressions. Thus, when I say something like "the comparison $v1 = v2$, where $v1$ and $v2$ are values," it must be understood that I'm talking about the semantics of the situation and not the concrete syntax (unless the context demands otherwise).

> *Aside:* Regarding contexts demanding otherwise, please note that I'll often say (in the next chapter in particular) things like "the comparison $V = v$, where V is a variable," meaning that the expression that denotes the first comparand in that comparison is supposed to be a variable reference specifically. And perhaps I should say here too just what I mean by the term "variable reference"! A variable reference is simply a variable name, syntactically speaking; however, the name in question is understood to denote not the pertinent variable as such but, rather, the value of that variable at the time the reference is evaluated. *End of aside.*

■   Second, note that it follows from the definition that if $v1 = v2$ evaluates to TRUE, then $v1$ and $v2$ must certainly be of the same type—because if they're of different types, they're different values by definition.[1] By way of example, the integer 3 is equal to the integer 3 and not to the integer 4 or any other integer, and not to anything else either.

■   Third, it also follows from the definition that if

    a.   There exists an operator Op (other than "=" itself) with a parameter P such that

    b.   Two successful invocations of Op—invocations that are identical in all respects except that the argument corresponding to P is the value $v1$ in one invocation and the value $v2$ in the other—are distinguishable in their effect, then

    c.   The equality test, or comparison, $v1 = v2$ must evaluate to FALSE.

---

[1] This sentence is 100 percent correct as stated, but it needs some elaboration in the context of type inheritance. For simplicity, I propose to ignore type inheritance in this chapter from this point forward, barring explicit statements to the contrary.

■   Finally, observe that without equality as just defined we couldn't even tell whether some given element *e* is contained in (i.e., is a member of) some given set *S*! To be specific, the boolean expression

$e \in S$

("*e* is a member of *S*") is defined to be shorthand for the expression

FALSE OR $e = e1$ OR $e = e2$ OR ... OR $e = en$

where *e1*, *e2*, ..., *en* are all of the elements of *S*.[2] Equality is *fundamental*.

SQL VIOLATIONS

So what does SQL do with—perhaps I should say, what does it do *to*—this very simple notion of equality as I've now defined it? Sad to say, its support for that simple notion is hugely defective. To summarize briefly, SQL's "=" operator:

1. Sometimes gives TRUE when the comparands are definitely distinct

2. Sometimes gives TRUE when the comparands are probably distinct[3]

3. Sometimes has user defined, and hence arbitrary, semantics

4. Isn't supported at all for (a) tables, (b) certain user defined types, (c) the system defined type XML, and—at least in some products—(d) certain other system defined types as well

In the next four sections I'll examine each of these four cases in turn. Before I do that, however, there's something else I need to say. The fact is, it's in the nature of SQL that it's virtually impossible to make a plain statement about any aspect of the language at all without immediately having to hedge that statement about with all kinds of ifs and buts. We'll encounter examples of this

---

[2] Of course, I'm assuming here that set *S* is finite, as indeed sets always are in the computing context. The "iterated OR" definition of set membership isn't valid otherwise.

[3] In previous writings I've stated this case in the form "Can fail to give TRUE when the comparands aren't clearly distinct." I realize now that this formulation is muddled at best; certainly it doesn't properly capture the nature of the problem, and I apologize to anyone who might have been misled by it.

phenomenon all through these three chapters (indeed, that's one reason—in fact, the main reason—why those chapters have such an inordinate number of footnotes). And one such example occurs immediately. To be specific, I've claimed that the SQL language designers never bothered to define the notion of equality. However, in Subclause 3.1.6 of the standard (a section devoted to definitions),[4] we find the following:

> **equal (of a pair of comparable values):** Yielding *True* if passed as arguments in a <comparison predicate> in which the <comp op> is <equals operator>.

Now, this might look like a definition of equality, but I don't think it is. If we compare it with the definition I gave earlier, what do we find? Simplifying and paraphrasing considerably for the sake of the parallel, what we find is this:

- My definition says: If *v1* and *v2* are equal, then *v1* = *v2* gives TRUE.

- SQL's definition says: If *v1* = *v2* gives TRUE, then *v1* and *v2* are equal.

In other words, SQL's definition puts the cart before the horse: It defines equality in terms of an "=" comparison. My own definition, by contrast, defines equality as such, and then explains the implication for "=" comparisons. Not to mention the fact that SQL's definition appeals to the notion of "comparable values," which, as the standard tells us elsewhere, merely means that the values in question can be the operands in an "=" comparison ... Well, I don't know about you, but I can't help feeling there's something circular going on here.

What's more, the SQL standard also includes a section, Subclause 9.9, with the title "Equality operations," and a section with such a title might be expected to contain a definition of such operations. But this one doesn't. Rather, what it does do is (to quote) "Specify the prohibitions and restrictions by data type on operations that involve testing for equality." In other words:

---

[4] All SQL quotes in this book are taken from the 2003 version of the standard ("SQL:2003"), and references to sections of the standard by number, as in, e.g., "Subclause 9.9," apply to that version specifically (unless otherwise noted in both cases). Of course, SQL:2003 isn't the most recent version, but I seriously doubt whether later versions depart from SQL:2003 in any significant respect on the particular issues I reference. (In any case, standards are standards, and they're supposed to live forever; in particular, later versions aren't supposed to reverse earlier decisions—though in the case of SQL, I know that a few decisions *have* been reversed over time. Make of that what you will.)

a. It gives a list, presumably intended to be exhaustive, of contexts in which "operations that involve testing for equality" are performed, either explicitly or implicitly.

b. It then defines what the operands are allowed to be in those various contexts.

c. Finally, it imposes certain additional rules—regarding, e.g., collations, in the case of character string comparisons (see Example 3 in the section immediately following)—in certain specific cases.

Caveat lector.

> *Aside:* Actually I think the situation in SQL is even worse than the foregoing text might suggest. Here again is that definition I quoted earlier:
>
> > **equal (of a pair of comparable values):** Yielding *True* if passed as arguments in a <comparison predicate> in which the <comp op> is <equals operator>.
>
> But if we take a look at SQL's <comparison predicate> construct, we find that the "arguments" referred to in the foregoing definition are quite specifically *rows*. Here's the pertinent part of the grammar:
>
> ```
> <comparison predicate>
>     ::= <row value predicand>
>             <comparison predicate part 2>
>
> <comparison predicate part 2>
>     ::= <comp op> <row value predicand>
> ```
>
> I don't want to have to explain the exact syntax in detail here for those two <row predicand>s; suffice it to say that they do indeed denote rows, not scalars. (Indeed, the "Function" portion of Subclause 8.2 ("<comparison predicate>") of the standard reads as follows: "Specify a comparison of two row values.") As for that <comp op>: One legal <comp op> is, of course, <equals operator>, or in other words the equality symbol, "=".[5]

---

[5] The others are "<>" (not equals), "<" (less than), ">" (greater than), "<=" (less than or equals), and ">=" (greater than or equals). Of course, the whole idea that one row might somehow be (e.g.) "less than" another raises a whole host of further questions!—but questions that, by definition, are beyond the scope of the present chapter. Further discussion can be found if you're interested in the book *A Guide to the SQL Standard*, 4th edition, by Hugh Darwen and myself (Addison-Wesley, 1997).

So how does the standard deal with what's surely the most common case in practice, viz., a comparison of the form *v1 = v2* where *v1* and *v2* are scalar values (scalars for short)? *Answer:* It coerces those scalars to rows! (See later in this chapter regarding my use of the term "coerces" here.) In other words, there's actually no such thing as a scalar comparison, in SQL—there are only row comparisons. Of course, the grammar does allow a <row value predicand> to be a scalar expression, syntactically speaking; however, the scalar value denoted by that expression is automatically and implicitly converted to a *row*, a row that contains exactly one "field." And the standard then goes on to say the following (these are all extracts from the standard's Subclause 8.2):

- (*Syntax Rule 1*) The two <row value predicand>s shall be of the same degree.

- (*Syntax Rule 5, simplified*) Let *Xi* and *Yi* be the *i*th field of the first <row value predicand> and the second <row value predicand>, respectively.

- (*General Rule 1, simplified*) Let *X* and *Y* be [the row values] represented by the first <row value predicand> and the second <row value predicand>, respectively. Then *X* = *Y* is *True* if and only if *Xi* = *Yi* is *True* for all *i*.

In the case we're interested in, of course, *i* is equal to one (i.e., the rows in question were derived from scalars), and so what the foregoing all boils down to saying is this: The original two scalars are equal if and only if the rows containing them are equal—and the rows containing them are equal if and only if the two scalars they contain are equal. In other words, the standard *nowhere actually defines* what it means for two scalars to be equal!

Incidentally, it follows that the standard doesn't define what it means for two rows to be equal, either. Thus, it seems to me that what we have here is another (different, but related) example of circularity. *End of aside.*

Well, never mind, let's soldier on. As I've said, what I want to do in the next four sections is examine, one by one, each of SQL's four major kinds of failures in connection with equality comparisons. *Note:* If you've forgotten by now just what those "four major kinds of failures" are, then I can hardly blame you; but they were summarized on page 7, and I refer you back to that page if you need to refresh your memory.

CASE 1 ("=" true with distinct comparands)

The root of the problem in this first case is SQL's support for *implicit data type conversion*, also known as *coercion*, which—at least in the context that concerns us here, and at least until further notice (see Example 4 and elsewhere)—works as follows. Let *T1* and *T2* be different types,[6] and let *v1* and *v2* be values of types *T1* and *T2*, respectively. Then the boolean expression

```
v1 = v2
```

is syntactically legal in SQL if[7] values of one of the two types (*T1*, say, without loss of generality) can be coerced to values of the other (*T2*)—in which case the semantics are that:

a. The value *v1'* of type *T2* that's *v1*'s counterpart, under the applicable coercion rule, is determined, and then

b. The value of the original expression is defined to be the same as the value of the following expression:

```
v1' = v2
```

Aside: Another way to state the foregoing as follows (you might like this better if you happen to be familiar with the SQL CAST operator): Given *T1*, *T2*, *v1*, and *v2* as defined above, the SQL expression

```
v1 = v2
```

is defined to be shorthand for the SQL expression

```
( CAST v1 AS T2 ) = v2
```

End of aside.

---

[6] Here's a question for you to ponder: What's involved in pinning down, precisely, the notion of types *T1* and *T2* being different (i.e., not equal)? In other words, how is equality of *types* defined?

[7] It's not completely clear (at least to me) whether this "if" can beefed up to "if and only if." Again, see Example 4, later.

Example 1: Let *T1* and *T2* be CHAR(3) and CHAR(5), respectively,[8] and let *v1* and *v2* be 'ABC' and 'ABC ', respectively (note the two trailing spaces in *v2*). Then *v1* and *v2* are definitely distinct—observe in particular that CHAR_LENGTH(*v1*) and CHAR_LENGTH(*v2*) give different results, viz., 3 and 5, respectively[9]—and yet the comparison *v1* = *v2* gives TRUE, just so long as the pertinent "collation" specifies PAD SPACE. (See Example 3 below for further discussion of collations. Here just let me note that I'll assume until further notice that collations always do have PAD SPACE specified.) In this example, in other words, the value 'ABC' is padded with two spaces—i.e., is effectively coerced to the value 'ABC '—before the comparison is done.[10]

Note: The foregoing explanation in terms of coercion is *not* the way such comparisons are explained in the SQL standard, but I think it's a logically clean way to think about the issue. Indeed, the concept of coercion provides a kind of unifying and general principle that can be used to explain all sorts of strange behavior in connection with SQL's treatment of equality, as we'll see many times over as this chapter proceeds.

Now I'd like to consider a variant form of the foregoing example, to illustrate another point. Specifically, I'd like to consider what happens if we're dealing with VARCHAR instead of CHAR types. So let *T1* and *T2* be VARCHAR(3) and VARCHAR(5), respectively, and let *v1* and *v2* be 'ABC' and 'ABC ', respectively (i.e., let *v2* now have just a single trailing space). Note, therefore, that CHAR_LENGTH(*v2*) is 4, not 5—the "5" in VARCHAR(5) denotes a maximum length, of course, not a fixed length. Again, then, *v1* and *v2* are definitely distinct, and yet the comparison *v1* = *v2* gives TRUE (again, so long as the pertinent collation specifies PAD SPACE). In this case, in other words, the value 'ABC' is padded with a single space—i.e., is effectively coerced to the value 'ABC '—before the comparison is done.

---

[8] I'm assuming here that "the length is part of the type," and hence that CHAR(3) and CHAR(5) are indeed different types. Actually, though, these are pretty big assumptions. The SQL standard is ambivalent on the issue, referring sometimes to CHAR(*n*) as a type and sometimes to just CHAR, unqualified, as a type. The issue is explored in depth in Chapter 15, "Values, Variables, Types, and Constraints," of my book *Fifty Years of Relational, and Other Database Writings* (Technics Publications, 2020).

[9] I note here for the record that a character string literal in SQL implicitly has as its declared type "fixed length character string of length *n*," where *n* is the number of characters in the literal in question. Thus, the declared type of the literal 'ABC ' (with its two trailing spaces) is CHAR(5). However, please understand that I'm not assuming in this first example that the comparands *v1* and *v2* are denoted by literals. *Note:* A similar remark applies to Examples 2-4 also, q.v.

[10] By the way, note that with *v1* and *v2* as defined here, while the comparison *v1* = *v2* does indeed give TRUE, the comparisons *v1* LIKE *v2*, *v1*||*v1* = *v2*||*v2*, and *v1*||*v2* = *v2*||*v1* all give FALSE! SQL apologists, please justify.

Now, the interesting thing about this example (and what makes it different in kind from the previous one) is that in this case type *T1* is effectively a proper subtype of type *T2*.[11] To spell the point out, every value of type VARCHAR(3) is necessarily also a value of type VARCHAR(5), and indeed a value of every type VARCHAR(n) for $n \geq 3$. In particular, therefore, *v1* is already of the declared type of *v2*, and so coercing it to that type before doing the comparison doesn't help much with the problem at hand (i.e., the problem of pinning down the semantics of the comparison).[12] Instead, what happens is that *v1* is coerced to the *actual* type—what I would have called the *most specific* type, if we really were talking about subtyping—of *v2*, which is effectively "fixed length character string of length 4."

As a matter of fact, exactly the same is true with CHAR types instead of VARCHAR types: namely, that *v1* is coerced to the *actual* type, not the declared type, of *v2*, even in the fixed length case. But in the fixed length case the actual type and the declared type are always the same, and so whether we talk of coercion to the actual type or to the declared type makes little practical difference. Strictly speaking, however, it must be understood that as far as SQL is concerned such coercions are always to the actual type, not the declared type.

To close discussion of Example 1 (and its variant), let me remind you of the following: If (a) there exists an operator *Op*, other than "=" itself, with a parameter *P* such that (b) two successful invocations of *Op*—invocations that are identical in all respects except that the argument corresponding to *P* is *v1* in one invocation and *v2* in the other—are distinguishable in their effect, then (c) the comparison *v1* = *v2* must evaluate to FALSE. Well, in Example 1 and its variant, if we take *Op* to be CHAR_LENGTH, we can see that the comparison *v1* = *v2* ought to give FALSE—but it doesn't, thanks to SQL's support for coercions.

Example 2: Let *T1* and *T2* be INTEGER—which SQL allows to be abbreviated to just INT—and FLOAT, respectively, and let *v1* and *v2* be 5 and 0.5E1, respectively. Again, then, *v1* and *v2* are definitely distinct, and yet the comparison *v1* = *v2* will give TRUE (*v1* will be coerced to type FLOAT before the comparison is done).

---

[11] What I'm claiming here is certainly true, but SQL doesn't recognize the truth of that claim. To be specific, the SQL concept of subtyping applies only to user defined types (and not even to all of those); in particular, it doesn't apply to system defined types, or what SQL calls "predefined" types. See my book *Type Inheritance and Relational Theory: Subtypes, Supertypes and Substitutability* (O'Reilly, 2016) for further explanation.

[12] Note the tacit assumption here that it makes sense to talk of a value being coerced to a type it already has. I'll revisit this assumption later in this section, in the subsection "Coercion Considered Harmful."

Note: Given *v1* and *v2* as just defined, I'm not aware of any existing SQL operator *Op* with the property that *Op*(*v1*) and *Op*(*v2*) give different results; however, such an operator could clearly be defined. An example might be an operator NEXT, defined to give the "next" value of the pertinent type; NEXT(*v1*) would then give 6, while NEXT(*v2*) would presumably raise an exception (because given a FLOAT number *x* there's no FLOAT number *y* that can sensibly be said to be next after *x* in arithmetical order).

Example 3: My next example concerns character strings again. The fact is, I didn't tell the whole truth in connection with Example 1 above; SQL's support for character strings is extremely complex in its full generality, much more complex than it would be appropriate to explain in detail here. However, one thing I do need to explain is this: Two character strings *v1* and *v2* can be compared—in particular, they can be tested for equality—if and only if (a) they consist of characters from the same *character set* and (b) they have the same *collation* (or can at least be coerced to have the same collation). Now, I'm going to assume for present purposes that we all know what a character set is, though as a matter of fact even that familiar notion isn't quite as straightforward as might be expected, in SQL. But what's a collation? *Answer:* It's a rule that's associated with a specific character set—thus, if *v1* and *v2* have the same collation, they certainly "consist of characters from the same character set" as required[13]—that governs the comparison of strings of characters from that character set. So let *C* be a collation for character set *S*, and let *a* and *b* be any two characters from *S*. Then *C* must be such that exactly one of the comparisons *a* < *b*, *a* = *b*, and *a* > *b* evaluates to TRUE and the other two to FALSE, under *C*.
So much for the basic idea. However, there are complications:

- One complication arises from the fact that if *C* is a collation, then *C* must be defined to have either the PAD SPACE or the NO PAD property. To elaborate: Let *v1* and *v2* be character strings such that *v1* is shorter than *v2*, and consider the comparison *v1* = *v2*. If PAD SPACE applies to the pertinent collation, *v1* will conceptually be padded at the right with spaces to make it the same length as *v2* before the comparison is done (as in Example 1 above). By contrast, if NO PAD applies, then if *v1* "compares equal" to that leading substring of *v2* that's the same length as *v1*, then *v1*

---

[13] But see footnote 14.

will be considered to be less than *v2* even if all remaining characters of *v2* are spaces.

■ A second complication arises from the fact that the comparison *a = b* might evaluate to TRUE under a given collation even if the characters *a* and *b* are distinct. For example, we might define a collation called CASE_INSENSITIVE in which each lowercase letter is defined to "compare equal" to its uppercase counterpart. As a consequence, again, character strings that are definitely distinct will sometimes compare equal.

Note: This effect too can be explained in terms of coercion, though I won't attempt any such explanation here.

Aside:[14] It won't have escaped your notice that I referred on the previous page to the possibility of some character string being "coerced" to have a particular collation. However, this notion has nothing to do with coercion as I've been using that term (nor indeed as that term is usually understood in the programming language context). Rather, it has to do with the question of deciding which particular collation to use for a given character string comparison. That question, not surprisingly, turns on the question of which collations if any are associated with the comparands; and *that* question leads to the question of determining which collation if any is associated with the result of evaluating an arbitrary character string expression. To this end, SQL introduces its notion of "coercibility" (using that term, to repeat, in a specialized and unusual sense). The basic idea is that every character string has a "coercibility" property, the possible values of which are *explicit, implicit, coercible,* and *no collating sequence.*[15]

---

[14] The text of this aside is based on material from the book mentioned in footnote 5 (viz., *A Guide to the SQL Standard*) and thus applies specifically to the version of the standard described in that book, viz., SQL:1992 (also to SQL:1999, as a matter of fact). In SQL:2003, however, some of the details and some of the associated terminology were changed. In particular, (a) what SQL:1992 called the "coercibility" property is now called the "collation derivation" property (hardly an improvement, in my opinion, but I wasn't consulted), and (b) where SQL:1992 had four possible values for that property, SQL:2003 seems to have only three (the *coercible* option seems to have been dropped) What's more, it's now possible for a given collation to be associated with two or more character sets. The detailed implications of all of these changes are unclear.

[15] I say "every character string" has such a property, but I'm being—I hope uncharacteristically—sloppy here. To be specific, that statement needs to be understood as meaning rather that every character string *expression* has such a property. After all, two distinct expressions, with different coercibility properties, might both evaluate to the same character string as such. For exampe, when I say (see later) that a *no collating sequence* string can be a comparand only if the other comparand has an *explicit* collation, what I really mean is that a *no collating sequence* expression can be used to denote a comparand only if the expression used to denote the other comparand is an *explicit* expression. My apologies if you find this all very confusing, but I really don't think the blame is entirely mine.

Before we go any further, I have to say that calling this property "coercibility" doesn't exactly help the cause of understanding—especially since one of the four possible values of that property is *coercible*, implying rather strongly that each of the other three means the character string in question is *not* "coercible"! Moreover, the connection between (a) the intuitive interpretations of the terms *explicit*, *implicit*, and so forth, on the one hand, and (b) their actual significance in the present context on the other, is tenuous at best—which is why I set the terms in italics throughout this discussion, in order to stress the fact that they're being used in a formal sense only.

Now, I certainly don't want to explain these concepts in detail here. However, I would at least like to give a brief informal description of them, if only to bear out what I said earlier regarding SQL's "extreme complexity" in this whole area. Briefly, then:

■ I remind you that for the comparison even to be feasible in the first place, the comparands must have the same associated character set. So let's assume for the remainder of this discussion that such is indeed the case. Also, let me abbreviate "character string" to just "string" for the remainder of this aside, for simplicity.

■ A *no collating sequence* string can be a comparand only if the other comparand has an *explicit* collation (in which case the *explicit* collation governs the comparison). An example of a *no collating sequence* string is the result produced by concatenating two strings, *v1* and *v2* say, where *v1* and *v2* are string values with different collations. (Note, however, that a *no collating sequence* string can easily be given an *explicit* collation by means of the COLLATE operator, which I won't bother to describe further here.) I'll ignore *no collating sequence* strings for the purposes of the next three bullets.

■ A *coercible* string is always a legal comparand; its collation will be "coerced" to that of the other comparand, if necessary. (For reasons beyond the scope of the present discussion, it turns out that if both comparands are *coercible* they'll necessarily have the same collation; thus, no "coercing" will be necessary in this case.) An example of a *coercible* string is the string resulting from evaluation of a string literal. I'll ignore *coercible* strings for the purposes of the next two bullets.

■ A string with an *implicit* collation can always be compared with one with an *explicit* collation (the *explicit* collation taking precedence); it can be compared with one with an *implicit* collation only if the two *implicit* collations are the same. Strings from columns of base tables always have *implicit* collations. I'll ignore *implicit* strings for the purposes of the next bullet.

■ Finally, two strings both having an *explicit* collation can be compared only if the *explicit* collations are the same.

In those cases where the comparison is valid, of course, we also need to know what the pertinent collation actually is. More generally, we need to know, given some specific string, what collation applies to that string, and also what coercibility property. SQL includes a long list of rules that answer these questions. But your patience with all of this complexity is probably exhausted by now—well, I know mine is—so I think I'll stop here. At least for now. *End of aside*.

Example 4: For my final example of Case 1, let *T1* and *T2* be NUMERIC(5,2) and NUMERIC(4,3), respectively,[16] and let *v1* and *v2* be 000.00 and 0.000, respectively. Then *v1* and *v2* are definitely distinct—in particular, they have distinct precisions (5 and 4, respectively) and distinct scale factors (2 and 3, respectively)—and yet I'm pretty sure the comparison *v1* = *v2* will give TRUE, in SQL. What do I mean, "pretty sure"? Well, my apologies, but I've tried, and failed, to find anything in the standard that explains exactly how SQL handles comparisons like this one. Note that with *T1* and *T2* as here defined:

■ A value of type *T1* can't be coerced to type *T2*, in general, without losing information. For example, there's no way to represent the value 123.45 as a value of type NUMERIC(4,3) without losing information (in fact, losing the two most significant digits).

■ Nor can a value of type *T2* be coerced to type *T1*, in general, without losing information. For example, there's no way to represent the value 1.234 as a

---

[16] Considerations with respect to NUMERIC types analogous to those mentioned in footnote 8 with respect to CHAR types apply here also, mutatis mutandis. (In fact a similar remark applies to FLOAT types as well—see Example 2.)

value of type NUMERIC(5,2) without losing information (admittedly only the least significant digit, but information nonetheless).

One way to handle the example, therefore, would be for *v1* and *v2* both to be coerced to a third type, viz., NUMERIC(6,3): The values *v1* (= 000.00) and *v2* (= 0.000) would then both be coerced to 000.000, the original comparison would thus effectively be replaced by the comparison 000.000 = 000.000, and so the final result would be TRUE.

So does SQL actually behave as just described? Almost certainly not—but what it does do is far from clear, at least to me. The only pertinent, or possibly pertinent, text I could find in the standard is as follows (in Subclause 3.1.6):

> **comparable (of a pair of values):** Capable of being compared, according to the rules of Subclause 8.2, "<comparison predicate>" ... For the specification of comparability of individual data types, see Subclause 4.2, "Character strings", through Subclause 4.10, "Collection types".

So I checked Subclause 8.2 and Subclauses 4.2 through 4.10, but they didn't help much. The pertinent text from Subclauses 4.2 through 4.10 is in Subclause (or Subsubclause?) 4.4.1, "Introduction to numbers." Here's the totality of what it has to say regarding numeric comparisons:

> **comparable (of a pair of values):** Any two numbers are comparable.

And the pertinent text from Subclause 8.2 ("<comparison predicate>") says the following. First, Syntax Rule 3:

> The [types of the comparands] shall be comparable.[17]

Second, General Rule 2:

> Numbers are compared with respect to their algebraic value.[18]

---

[17] The standard doesn't seem to define anywhere what it means for *types* to be comparable. It does explain, in various places, what it means for *values* to be comparable, though as already indicated I don't think it does so in anything close to a watertight fashion.

[18] I'm not sure that "algebraic value of a number" is a very respectable notion, either. No such term is used in mathematics, as far as I know. Nor does the standard define it; in fact, the only place it appears in the standard is in the text just quoted. PS: I presume "algebraic value" doesn't just mean "numeric value," because if it did, then don't you think this latter phrase would have been used?

Now, we do find, in Subclause 4.4.2 ("Characteristics of numbers"), the following description of how *assignment* of a value of some numeric type to a target of "exact numeric" type works:[19]

> A number is assignable only to [targets] of numeric type. If an assignment of some number would result in a loss of its most significant digit, an exception condition is raised. If least significant digits are lost, implementation defined rounding or truncating occurs, with no exception condition being raised ...
>
> Whenever [a] numeric value is assigned to an exact numeric [target], an approximation of [that] value that preserves leading significant digits after rounding or truncating is represented in the ... type of the target. The value is converted to have the precision and scale of the target. The choice of whether to truncate or round is implementation defined.
>
> An approximation obtained by truncation of a numeric value *N* for an <exact numeric type> *T* is a value *V* in *T* such that *N* is not closer to zero than is *V* and there is no value in *T* between *V* and *N*.
>
> An approximation obtained by rounding of a numeric value *N* for an <exact numeric type> *T* is a value *V* in *T* such that the absolute value of the difference between *N* and the numeric value of *V* is not greater than half the absolute value of the difference between two successive numeric values in *T*. If there is more than one such value *V*, then it is implementation defined which one is taken.
>
> All numeric values between the smallest and the largest value, inclusive, in a given exact numeric type have an approximation obtained by rounding or truncation for that type; it is implementation defined which other numeric values have such approximations.

To repeat, however, the foregoing text has to do with assignment. To what extent it also applies, mutatis mutandis, to equality comparisons I have no idea. As I've indicated, I couldn't find anywhere in the standard that addresses the issue.

Some Consequences

Needless to say, the state of affairs illustrated by Examples 1-4 above (and others like them) has numerous serious implications. In order to discuss some of those implications, let me use the phrase *distinct but considered equal* to describe pairs

---

[19] "Exact numeric" refers to any or all of the types NUMERIC, DECIMAL, SMALLINT, INT, and BIGINT. Types *T1* and *T2* in Example 4 are exact numeric types (if they're types at all, that is—see footnote 16).

of values *v1* and *v2* that are indeed distinct but are such that the comparison *v1* = *v2* gives TRUE, in SQL.

Now, equality comparisons are performed, often implicitly, in numerous SQL contexts—examples include DISTINCT, LIKE, GROUP BY, UNION, and JOIN—and the kind of equality involved in all such cases is indeed the "distinct but considered equal" kind. For example, let collation CASE_INSENSITIVE be as defined under Example 3 above, and let PAD SPACE apply to that collation. Given the familiar suppliers-and-parts database, then:

- If comparisons involving PNO values from tables P and SP are done using that collation, and

- If 'P2' and 'p2 ' are PNO values in some row of P and some row of SP, respectively, then

- Those two rows will be regarded as satisfying the referential constraint from SP to P, despite the lowercase p and trailing spaces in the foreign key value.

What's more, when evaluating expressions involving operators such as DISTINCT, LIKE, GROUP BY, UNION, and JOIN, the system might have to decide which of several "distinct but considered equal" values is to be chosen as the value of some column in some row of the overall result, or of some intermediate result. Unfortunately, SQL itself fails to give complete guidance in such situations. As a consequence, certain SQL expressions are *indeterminate*— the SQL term is "possibly nondeterministic"—in the sense that SQL doesn't fully specify how they should be evaluated; indeed, they might give different results on different occasions. For example, if collation CASE_INSENSITIVE applies to column *C* of table *T*, then SELECT MAX(*C*) FROM *T* might well return 'ZZZ' on one occasion and 'zzz' on another, even if *T* hasn't changed in the interim.

Note a further consequence of the foregoing state of affairs: namely, that certain SQL queries and certain SQL updates can actually have unpredictable results! Personally, I find it almost unbelievable that somebody would design a language—let alone standardize it—that possesses such horrible properties. But somebody did, and we're stuck with it.[20]

---

[20] A detailed discussion of this whole business of possibly nondeterministic SQL expressions and their consequences can be found in Chapter 5.

I feel obliged to hammer a few more nails into the coffin[21] ... Observe now that another consequence of the "distinct but considered equal" notion is that two rows can be regarded as duplicates even though they're not identical. And a further consequence of *that* fact is that the definition of SQL's UNION operator has to look something like this:[22]

> **Definition (SQL union):** Let tables *t1* and *t2* be the union operands; let *r* be a row that's both a duplicate of some row in *t1* and a duplicate of some row in *t2*; then the result table contains (a) exactly one duplicate of every such row *r* and (b) no row that's not a duplicate of some such row *r*.

Even this byzantine definition is far from complete ... For one thing, additional rules are needed to specify the column names and types of that result table. For another, given that any specific row can have a huge number of "distinct but considered equal" duplicates, each of which is distinct from all of the others, additional rules are also needed to specify *which particular* duplicate of each such row *r* appears in the result![23]

By contrast, the relational definition of union is extremely simple (and note that this definition, in sharp distinction to the SQL "definition" given above, is complete instead of being full of loose ends):

> **Definition (relational union):** Let relations *r1* and *r2* be of the same type *T*; then the union of *r1* and *r2* is the relation of type *T* with body the set of all tuples *t* such that *t* appears in at least one of *r1* and *r2*.

A still further consequence of the SQL "definition" is that the SQL UNION operator applied to tables *t1* and *t2* can quite legitimately produce a result

---

[21] The coffin of what, you might reasonably ask—clearly not SQL, because languages live forever, even bad ones. *Your answer here.*

[22] Analogous remarks apply to intersection and difference as well, of course. By the way, please understand that the "definition" I'm about to give is very far from being the end of the story!—as my subsequent text goes on, unfortunately, to make all too clear.

[23] What's more, if the operator being defined is SQL's UNION ALL instead of (as here) UNION DISTINCT, still more rules are required to specify *how many* duplicates of each such row *r* the result contains, as well as which particular duplicate of *r* each such duplicate of *r* might be. Indeed, given such a row *r*, do the corresponding duplicates in the result all have to be the same? In fact, can such a notion as "the same duplicate" even be defined in such a context? How? Answers on a postcard, please—but don't send them to me, send them to the SQL standardizers instead. Thank you.

containing—even consisting entirely of!—rows that appear in neither *t1* nor *t2*.
By way of example, suppose SQL tables ST1 and ST2 look like this:

ST1	X	Y
	0	1.0
	0	2.0

ST2	X	Y
	0.0	0
	0.0	1
	1.0	2

Further, let the column called X be of type INT in ST1 but type
NUMERIC(2,1) in ST2, and let the column called Y be of type NUMERIC(2,1)
in ST1 but type INT in ST2. Then the SQL expression

```
SELECT * FROM ST1
UNION     /* means UNION DISTINCT by default */
SELECT * FROM ST2
```

produces the following result (let's call it ST3):[24]

ST3	X	Y
	0.0	1.0
	0.0	2.0
	0.0	0.0
	1.0	2.0

In this result:

a. Columns X and Y are both of type NUMERIC(2,1);

b. The process of determining the values to appear in those result columns
    involves a preliminary coercing of every INT value in ST1 and/or ST2 to
    type NUMERIC(2,1); and

---

[24] In the interest of accuracy, I need to add that X is the first column, and Y the second, in both ST1 and
ST2, and hence in ST3 as well. I need to say this because (a) tables in SQL do have a left to right ordering
to their columns, and (b) the unqualified version of UNION shown in the given SQL expression works by
"lining up" columns of the operands in accordance with their ordinal position.

c. The overall result thus consists exclusively of rows that appear in neither ST1 nor ST2—a very strange kind of union, you might be forgiven for thinking.[25]

Aside: Perhaps I should explain what a "clean" version of the foregoing example would look like—where by "clean" I simply mean that where type conversions are necessary they should be made explicit, thereby avoiding surprises. (Type conversions should always be avoided if possible, for performance reasons. Where they can't be avoided, though, they should always be explicit.) Thus, I would (re)write the original UNION expression like this:

```
SELECT CAST ( X AS NUMERIC(2,1) ) AS X , Y FROM ST1
UNION
SELECT X , CAST ( Y AS NUMERIC(2,1) ) AS Y FROM ST2
```

The two "SELECT – FROM" expressions here produce intermediate result tables looking like this (the tables are unnamed, of course, but the columns aren't, thanks in part to the explicit specifications AS X and AS Y):

X	Y
0.0	1.0
0.0	2.0

X	Y
0.0	0.0
0.0	1.0
1.0	2.0

And now the UNION result (already shown above) is "respectable," containing as it does *all* and *only* rows that appear in either or both of these (unnamed) operand tables. *End of aside.*

Coercion Considered Harmful

There are a few more points that I think are worth making in connection with coercions in general. The fact is, there's a widespread opinion—one that I share—that coercion in general is a bad idea and should at least be avoided if

---

[25] In fact I'd go further; I'd say that SQL is of course at liberty to define an operator that behaves as described in the example, if it really wants to (though I think I would have to question the wisdom of its doing such a thing)—but what it's *not* at liberty to do is call that operator "union." The operator in question simply *isn't* union, as the term "union" is (very well) defined and understood both in mathematics in general and in the relational world in particular.

possible, if not outright prohibited.[26] Why? Because it's a rich source of errors, errors that (to make matters worse) probably won't be detected until run time. The by now somewhat antiquated language PL/I is an extreme case, perhaps, but it does illustrate some of the pitfalls very well.[27] *Note:* The first two examples below are taken from *An Introduction to Data Types*, by J. Craig Cleaveland (Addison-Wesley,1986); the other two are my own.

1. `IF 1 < X < 5 THEN CALL Q ;`

   Surprise: Q is always called, even if X is outside the range one to five. Why? Because 1 < X yields either TRUE or FALSE, which are represented in PL/I by the bit strings '1'B and '0'B, respectively. These values are then coerced to 1 and 0, respectively, both of which are less than 5.

2. `DO J = 1 , J = 2 ;` *loop* `; END ;`

   Surprise: The second iteration of *loop* is executed with J = 0, not 2. Why? Because J = 2 is a comparison which (thanks to the assignment of 1 to J, which holds during the first iteration of *loop*) returns FALSE ('0'B), which then gets coerced to 0.

3. `A = B & C ; IF A = B & C THEN CALL Q ;`

   Surprise: Q isn't necessarily called. Why not? Well, assume A, B, and C are bit string variables, each just one bit in length. Then the first statement assigns the value of the expression B & C to A. But the IF statement *doesn't* then compare the value of A with the value of that expression B & C; instead, it evaluates the expression (A = B) & C, and goes on to call Q if and only if *that* expression evaluates to TRUE! E.g., suppose B and C are both '0'B; then A becomes '0'B as well, and the expression (A = B) & C

---

[26] Unless we're talking about a situation in which (a) a value *v* is "coerced" to a type it already has and (b) is thereby "coerced" to itself, in which case the coercion in question might be called trivial. Trivial coercions are presumably harmless and I see no need to prohibit them, even if nontrivial ones are prohibited. *Note:* I don't mean to suggest by the foregoing that coercing a value *v* to a type it already has necessarily means coercing *v* to itself. See the next couple of pages for further elaboration of this point.

[27] One of the design goals for PL/I was "Freedom of expression: If a particular combination of symbols has a reasonably sensible meaning, that meaning is made official" (this is a quote from G. Radin and H. P. Rogoway, "NPL: Highlights of a New Programming Language," *Communications of the ACM 8*, No. 1, January 1965). This "anything goes" objective—which might be stated in the form "anything that might make sense is forced to make sense"—is surely one of the reasons why PL/I (originally called NPL, until the U.K. National Physics Laboratory objected) applies coercion so liberally.

thus becomes ('0'B = '0'B) & '0'B, or in other words effectively TRUE AND FALSE, which is FALSE.

4.
```
DECLARE A FIXED DEC(3,1)  INIT (    9.1 ) ;
DECLARE B BIT(3)          INIT ( '101'B ) ;
DECLARE C CHAR(4)         INIT ( '+12.' ) ;
```

Surprise: A > B, B > C, and C > A are all TRUE. Why? Well, A > B is TRUE because the bit string '101'B is coerced to the value 5, and 9.1 is greater than 5; B > C is TRUE because the bit string '101'B is coerced to the character string '101' and that character string is greater than the character string '+12.';[28] and C > A is TRUE because the character string '+12.' is coerced to 12 and 12 is greater than 9.1.

As a friend of mine once remarked to me—this must have been sometime in the late 1960s—whatever else you might say about it, there's one thing that PL/I is most definitely not, and that's "the language of least astonishment."

Now, it's a little bit of a digression from my main purpose in this chapter, but there's something else I want to say about coercions while we're on the subject. Coercion is, of course, implicit type conversion—but *type conversion* is a slightly strange term, when you stop to think about it. For example, suppose we start with the integer 3, and suppose we "convert" that integer to the character string '3'. But, of course, that integer and that string are two different things! It's true that we tend to talk of them, informally, as somehow being just different "versions" of "the same" thing, but such talk is really pretty sloppy. (Note in particular that nothing has actually been done to the integer 3 in the example—it remains the integer 3 after the "conversion" has been done.) The fact is, there simply are two different values, the integer and the string, and what the "conversion" process does is simply map from one of those values to the other. In other words, "type conversion" is, precisely, a process that, given some value *v1* of some type *T1*, returns the value *v2* of some type *T2* that corresponds to, or is the counterpart to, that value *v1* according to some prescribed mapping.

My next point is this: Why shouldn't those types *T1* and *T2* be one and the same? With mappings in general, we certainly don't impose a rule that the domain and codomain be distinct; so why should we do so now? *Note:* In case you're unfamiliar with the terminology I'm using here, I should explain that, by

---

[28] At least this was true in the original IBM implementation of PL/I, where character strings were represented using EBCDIC. The EBCDIC codes for "1" and "+" are hexadecimal F1 and 4E, respectively.

definition, a mapping is basically just a rule that pairs values in one set with values in another, the pairing being such that each value in the first set is paired with exactly one value in the second. The first set is called the *domain* and the second the *codomain.*

I have a particular reason for wanting to mention this possibility (i.e., that the two types involved be one and the same): namely, as follows. Let *bx* be an SQL boolean expression. As is well known, then, *bx* can evaluate in general to any of the three SQL truth values TRUE, FALSE, and UNKNOWN. In other words, SQL is based, at least internally, on three-valued logic, 3VL. (Or on some version of 3VL, at any rate, though as a matter of fact the version in question doesn't seem to be fully specified anywhere—but I don't want to get into detail on that particular point here, nor do I need to.) However, if *bx* does in fact evaluate to "the third truth value" UNKNOWN, then SQL does its best to conceal that fact from the outside world! To elaborate:

- If *bx* is the boolean expression in an SQL WHERE clause, that UNKNOWN is treated as FALSE. Thus, for example, the result of evaluating the expression

  ```
  SELECT  *
  FROM    S
  WHERE   CITY = 'London'
  ```

  won't contain rows for which the boolean expression CITY = 'London' evaluates to UNKNOWN.

- If *bx* is the boolean expression in an SQL CHECK constraint, that UNKNOWN is treated as TRUE. Thus, for example, if the following CHECK constraint is specified for the parts table P—

  ```
  CHECK ... ( WEIGHT > 0.0 )
  ```

  —then, other things being equal,[29] an attempt to insert a row with a null weight (for which the boolean expression specified in the CHECK constraint evaluates to UNKNOWN) will succeed.

---

[29] Interesting phrase, in the present context!

Well—quite apart from whether you consider SQL's behavior in these examples to be correct—it seems to me that the clean way of describing that behavior is to say that the UNKNOWN is being *coerced* to either FALSE or TRUE, as the case may be.

CASE 2 ("=" true with probably distinct comparands)

The root of the problem in this second case is, as you might have guessed, SQL's concept of *null*: more particularly, the fact that SQL treats two nulls as equal for certain purposes (e.g., duplicate elimination), despite the fact that (a) it *doesn't* treat them as equal for other purposes, and despite the fact also that (b) it's possible, even probable, that the nulls in question denote two different things. (After all, we already know that if *x* and *y* are both null, then the boolean expression *x* = *y*—in a WHERE clause, for example—doesn't evaluate to TRUE, it evaluates to UNKNOWN.) But this inconsistent behavior (nulls sometimes equal and sometimes not), weird enough though it certainly is, isn't the end of the story. Let's take a closer look.

Now, the first thing to say—and to say loud and clear!—is that it's utterly impossible to explain how nulls are supposed to work in a way that stands up to careful logical analysis. The plain fact is, *nulls make no sense.* Please bear this point in mind as you read what I have to say on the subject below; naturally I've tried my best to make the arguments as coherent as I can, but I frankly don't believe such an objective—giving a coherent explanation of the behavior of nulls, I mean—is fully achievable.

That said, the crucial point about nulls is that, whatever else they might be, they're certainly not values.[30] But SQL thinks they are. Here's a quote from the standard, Subclause 3.1.1 ("Definitions provided in this standard"):

null value: A special value that is used to indicate the absence of any data value.

I love this definition, by the way; what it says, to paraphrase, is that null is a value that means there isn't a value. Right?

---

[30] I've explained this point in detail in many places (see, e.g., my book *SQL and Relational Theory: How to Write Accurate SQL Code*, 3rd edition, O'Reilly, 2015). By the way, Codd, who was the original advocate for the entire concept of nulls, would certainly agree with me here (see, e.g., his book *The Relational Model for Database Management Version 2*, Addison-Wesley, 1990, page 173).

Anyway, the standard then goes on to elaborate on its concept of "null values" in Subclause 4.4.2 ("The null value"), as follows:

> Every data type includes a special value, called the *null value*, sometimes denoted by the keyword NULL. This value differs from other values in the following respects:
>
> — Since the null value is in every data type, the data type of the null value implied by the keyword NULL cannot be inferred; hence NULL can be used to denote the null value only in certain contexts, rather than everywhere that a literal is permitted.
>
> — Although the null value is neither equal to any other value nor not equal to any other value — it is *unknown* whether or not it is equal to any given value — in some contexts, multiple null values are treated together; for example, the <group by clause> treats all null values together.

Naturally I have a few comments on this text! To elaborate:

■ "Every data type includes a special value, called the *null value*": This statement reads, at least arguably, as if "every data type" has its own, unique "special value."[31] Of course, that's not what it means, but it's what it says. At least arguably.

■ "This value differs from other values": Surely, if null "differs from other values," and if *v* is one of those "other values," then this statement implies that the expression *v* = NULL evaluates to FALSE. But of course it doesn't, it evaluates to UNKNOWN.

■ "[The] null value is neither equal to any other value nor not equal to any other value": First, the latter part of this sentence contradicts the sentence quoted in the previous bullet. Second, note that what this sentence carefully doesn't say is that "the null value" is neither equal nor not equal to itself; thus, I think we'd be well within our rights if we took it to imply that "the null value" *is* equal to itself. But, of course, that's not the SQL position—the SQL position, rather, is that *we don't know whether* null is equal to itself. At least sometimes.

---

[31] Especially since (a) every value is a value of just one type, generally speaking, and (b) the text quoted also uses the phrase "*the* data type of the null value" (emphasis added).

One of the foundational principles of logic—actually it's one of the so called "Laws of Thought"—is what's called the *Law of Identity*, which states that everything is equal to itself. One consequence of this law is that (as Wikipedia puts it) "we cannot use the same term in the same discourse while having it signify different senses." But using the same term in different senses in the same discourse is *exactly* what SQL does, with its nulls. Again, at least sometimes.

■ "[In] some contexts, multiple null values are treated together": This statement is simply a rather inelegant way of saying that null is sometimes considered as being equal to itself after all. (By the way, it would be helpful if the contexts in question could be precisely characterized. Is there some fundamental principle involved, or is the question—i.e., as to whether two nulls are equal or not—decided on an ad hoc, case by case basis?)

All in all, not a very auspicious beginning, I'd say. Still, never mind, let's struggle on ... Suppose we're given an SQL base table STN with current value[32] as follows (columns X and Y both of type INT, and I assume for definiteness that the key constraint UNIQUE (X,Y) has been specified for the table):

STN	X	Y
	7	NULL
	NULL	4
	NULL	NULL

Now, according to SQL, no two of the rows shown "compare equal"; that is, the SQL comparisons

```
ROW (    7 , NULL ) = ROW ( NULL ,    4 )

ROW ( NULL ,    4 ) = ROW ( NULL , NULL )

ROW ( NULL , NULL ) = ROW (    7 , NULL )
```

---

[32] Forgive my use of the term "current value" here—that "current value" isn't really a value, as such, at all, because it includes nulls. This stuff is *really* hard to talk about in any kind of precise manner.

all evaluate to UNKNOWN. (So what's the current cardinality of STN? Justify your answer![33])

What's more, none of the rows in question is equal to itself; that is, the comparisons

```
ROW (    7 , NULL ) = ROW (    7 , NULL )

ROW ( NULL ,    4 ) = ROW ( NULL ,    4 )

ROW ( NULL , NULL ) = ROW ( NULL , NULL )
```

also all evaluate to UNKNOWN. And yet, e.g., the following INSERT—

```
INSERT INTO STN ( X , Y ) VALUES ( 7 , NULL ) ;
```

—will succeed, and the table will now contain two (7,NULL) rows![34] So in this context the (implicit) comparison

```
ROW (    7 , NULL ) = ROW (    7 , NULL )
```

—which must be done as part of the key constraint checking for table STN— apparently now gives FALSE, not UNKNOWN. (Or perhaps it gives UNKNOWN and that UNKNOWN is then coerced to FALSE, even though in other constraint checking contexts—and after all, constraint checking is what we're talking about here, as I've already said—UNKNOWN is coerced to TRUE, as explained earlier.)

Suppose we now ask for the following expression to be evaluated:

```
SELECT DISTINCT * FROM STN
```

Then the row (7,NULL) will appear in the result once, not twice, and so now that row *is* considered to be equal to itself! So here's a very clear example of "=" giving TRUE, even though (a) the comparands are possibly, and even probably, distinct, and in any case (b) that very same comparison gave FALSE just a moment ago. What *are* we to make of such a muddle?

---

[33] Of course, SQL's COUNT operator would say it's three. In other words, that operator resembles the SQL WHERE clause inasmuch as it treats the expression $x = y$ as FALSE if x is null or y is null or both (or as I'd prefer to put it, the UNKNOWN that such comparisons return is effectively coerced to FALSE in this situation).

[34] See Appendix B for further discussion of this state of affairs.

Aside: Following on from the foregoing example, let *K* be a key for SQL base table *T*, and suppose we attempt to introduce a "new" value for *K*, *k2* say, into *T* (via some INSERT or UPDATE operation). That INSERT or UPDATE will be rejected if *k2* is the same as some value for *K*, *k1* say, that already exists in some other row in *T*. What then does it mean to say the two values *k1* and *k2* are "the same"? It turns out that *no two* of the following three statements are equivalent:

1. *k1* and *k2* are the same for the purposes of a comparison condition

2. *k1* and *k2* are the same for the purposes of key uniqueness checking

3. *k1* and *k2* are the same for the purposes of duplicate elimination

Number 1 is defined in accordance with the rules of SQL's three-valued logic; Number 2 is defined in accordance with the rules for the truth valued operator UNIQUE (see later); and Number 3 is defined in accordance with the rules for the truth valued operator IS DISTINCT FROM (again, see later).

By way of concrete illustration, suppose for simplicity that *K* involves just one column, and suppose further that *k1* and *k2* are both null. Then Number 1 gives UNKNOWN; Number 2 gives FALSE; and Number 3 gives TRUE.[35] *End of aside.*

Actually there's another point I need to discuss here. It has to do with that "all null" row in base table STN—i.e., the row

```
ROW ( NULL , NULL )
```

The truth is, it's not clear whether SQL would allow this row to appear in base table STN in the first place, though personally I think it would. Why might it not? Well, General Rule 1 of Subclause 7.3 of the standard ("<table value constructor>") states, in effect, that if any row that's offered for insertion into some named table "is the null value, then an exception condition is raised: *data exception — null row not permitted in table*." In order to understand this rule, of course, we need to understand what a null row is, or equivalently (?) what it means for a row to be null. In fact the standard doesn't seem to define that "null

---

[35] However, it is at least the case that if Number 1 gives TRUE, then Number 2 gives TRUE, and if Number 2 gives TRUE, then Number 3 gives TRUE.

row" concept anywhere,[36] but it seems to me that a row containing nothing but nulls and a null row are, logically, two different things. (The difference might be analogous, somewhat, to the difference between (a) a set that contains nothing—i.e., the empty set—and (b) no set at all.) So I would say it seems reasonable to take it that the "all null" row is OK for insertion after all but "the null row" isn't.

Evidence that the foregoing distinction is indeed what the standard intends is provided by the following. First, as we saw earlier, Subclause 4.4.2 of that standard says "the null value" is part of every type. Now, row types are certainly types—Subclause 4.4.5.2 ("Row types") makes that clear, and so if *RT* is a row type, then *RT* certainly contains "the null value." And it seems reasonable to assume that "the null value," in a context where the types we're talking about are row types specifically, is surely the same thing as—i.e., is equal to (?!?)—"the null row."

Second, in Subclause 8.7 ("<null predicate>"), the standard states the following (paraphrasing fairly liberally):

> Let *X* be the expression *r* IS NULL, where *r* is a row value. If *r* is the null value, then *X* evaluates to TRUE; otherwise, if the value of every field in *r* is the null value, then *X* evaluates to TRUE; otherwise *X* evaluates to FALSE.

This text indicates rather clearly that SQL considers a null row and a row containing only nulls as two different things, even though they both give TRUE if they're compared with NULL.[37] (Incidentally, it also indicates very clearly that a row such as ROW (7,NULL) is definitely *not* considered to be null.[38])

All of which raises yet another issue, or set of issues ... I assume that base table STN, with "current value" as depicted on page 29, is supposed to be SQL's analog of a relation, and hence that the columns and rows depicted are supposed

---

[36] Indeed, the sole appearance in the standard of the term "null row" is in the rule just quoted. By the way, this is as good a place as any to note that although the standard apparently does support "the null row," it explicitly *doesn't* support "the null table." Here's the pertinent text: "No table can be null, though a table may have no rows." PS: As so often with SQL, this quote raises more questions than it answers. In fact, it's strictly ambiguous!—the phrase "may have no rows" could be understood to mean either "can have no rows" or "might have no rows." *Why* is the standard so full of rabbit holes?

[37] Provided the comparison takes the form *r* IS NULL, that is. If by contrast it takes the form *r* = *r'*, where *r'* IS NULL gives TRUE, it gives UNKNOWN. I hope that's clear.

[38] Nor is it considered to be not null ... That is, if *Z* denotes the row ROW (7,NULL), then *Z* IS NULL and *Z* IS NOT NULL both return FALSE, in SQL! Haven't the SQL designers ever heard of *The Principle of the Excluded Middle*? PS: I remind you, incidentally, that the row ROW (7,NULL) doesn't "compare equal" to itself. Since we've just discovered that the row ROW (7,NULL) isn't considered to be null, we now see that null isn't the only thing in SQL that's considered not to be equal to itself. Where, oh where, does this madness end?

to be SQL's analogs of the corresponding attributes and tuples. Now, relations have predicates,[39] and each tuple in a given relation represents a proposition— viz., a proposition that's (a) obtained from the pertinent predicate by substituting attribute values from that tuple for the parameters of that predicate and (b) is understood by convention to be true. So what's the predicate for STN?

Well, of course you can't answer this question, because I haven't given you enough information. But one at least superficially plausible suggestion might be "X is greater than Y" (and if that's indeed the predicate, tuples or rows such as (7,2) and (5,4) would then represent the corresponding true propositions "7 is greater than 2" and "5 is greater than 4," respectively). However, given that columns X and Y in base table STN both "permit nulls," can the predicate truly be "X is greater than Y"? What true proposition does the row (7,NULL) represent?[40] *Note:* If you say it's the proposition "7 is greater than something," then I ask you further: How does that proposition differ from the one represented by the row (7), which appears in the projection of STN on X? And when you've answered these questions to your own satisfaction, let me ask you analogous questions in connection with the row (NULL,NULL).

> *Aside:* I concluded above that a row of all nulls is OK for insertion. I note, however, for what it's worth, that Codd certainly wouldn't have agreed with that conclusion. On page 175 of his book *The Relational Model for Database Management Version 2* (Addison-Wesley, 1990), he says the following:
>
> > Any row containing nothing but [nulls] can and should be discarded by the DBMS from the [table] in which it appears.
>
> (Though I suppose for it to "appear" before it can be "discarded," that row had to get into the table in the first place, somehow (?).)
> Now, Codd's stated reason for wanting to discard such a row is that the row in question is "devoid of information." However, such is not the case. Suppose that (a) the projection of the parts table P on COLOR contains just one row, and (b) that row "contains a null." The interpretation is "There exists at least one part, but no part with a known color," which is clearly not devoid of

---

[39] I refer here to predicates in the general logical sense, not in the rather limited sense in which SQL uses the term.

[40] You might be tempted to say the predicate isn't "X is greater than Y" but, rather, "X is null or Y is null or X is greater than Y." However, this suggestion is almost certainly not correct, and I'll leave it as an exercise for you to figure out why.

information.[41] By contrast, if that row were discarded, the resulting table would be empty, and the interpretation—given that rows that are all null are indeed discarded—would be the logically distinct "There exists no part with a known color." *End of aside.*

I haven't finished with the STN example. In what seems to me nothing more than an attempt to get around the mess—or part of the mess, at any rate—caused by its ill conceived embrace of nulls in the first place, in 1999 SQL introduced a new comparison operator called IS DISTINCT FROM. Of course, IS DISTINCT FROM is distinct from equality—I choose my words carefully—inasmuch as two nulls are considered to be "not distinct," even though they're not equal.[42] Consider the following comparisons:

```
ROW (    7 , NULL ) IS DISTINCT FROM ROW ( NULL ,    4 )

ROW ( NULL ,    4 ) IS DISTINCT FROM ROW ( NULL , NULL )

ROW ( NULL , NULL ) IS DISTINCT FROM ROW (    7 , NULL )


ROW (    7 , NULL ) IS DISTINCT FROM ROW (    7 , NULL )

ROW ( NULL ,    4 ) IS DISTINCT FROM ROW ( NULL ,    4 )

ROW ( NULL , NULL ) IS DISTINCT FROM ROW ( NULL , NULL )
```

Of these, the first three give TRUE and the other three give FALSE (an IS DISTINCT FROM comparison never gives UNKNOWN). Here's the standard's definition:

---

[41] I'm assuming here for definiteness that the intended interpretation of that null is "value unknown"—i.e., a row in the parts table for which COLOR is null denotes a part whose color is unknown. For the purposes of the projection operator specifically, I'm also assuming that (a) two such nulls are considered to be equal to one another, and (b) such a null is considered not equal to any nonnull value. (Note that assumptions (a) and (b) here are certainly consistent with the way SQL's DISTINCT operator behaves.)

[42] You see once again how difficult it is even to talk about this stuff coherently. In ordinary discourse, two things are distinct if and only if they're not equal. But not in SQL! Can you imagine the likely breakdowns in communication?—breakdowns that could have been avoided if only nulls had been rejected at the outset, but are now all but inevitable. (By the way, note that earlier we had the concept "distinct but considered equal"; now we apparently also have the concept "not equal but not considered distinct." These two concepts are distinct and not equal.)

distinct (of a pair of comparable values):[43] Capable of being distinguished within a given context. Informally, not equal, not both null. A null value and a nonnull value are distinct.

So I suppose we might say, loosely (?), that IS DISTINCT FROM is a version of "=" for which two nulls *are* considered to be equal. Thus, it might be nice if we could simply use IS DISTINCT FROM in place of "=" everywhere. But we can't, because so many of those uses of "=" in SQL are implicit (consider, e.g., SQL's NATURAL JOIN operator).

And then there's UNIQUE ... UNIQUE is used (to quote the standard) to "test for the absence of duplicate rows." Of course, no such test would ever be needed in the relational world, but we're not in the relational world, we're in the SQL world. The syntax is:

```
UNIQUE ( exp )
```

Let *T* be the table denoted by *exp*. Then, as the standard puts it, "if there are no two rows in *T* such that the value of each column in one row is nonnull and is not distinct from the value of the corresponding column in the other row, then the result [is TRUE; otherwise it's FALSE]".[44] Note, therefore, that UNIQUE sometimes gives TRUE when it might have been expected—since null isn't supposed to be equal to itself—to give UNKNOWN. (Contrast EXISTS in SQL, which sometimes gives FALSE when it might have been expected to give UNKNOWN.)

Now (in case you've forgotten!), the present section is supposed to be all about situations in which SQL treats two nulls as equal. So far I've discussed two such situations: one involving SELECT DISTINCT, and the other involving IS DISTINCT FROM.[45] A third is provided by GROUP BY. Here again is base table STN, shown now as it looks after that second (7,NULL) row has been inserted:

---

[43] By the way, there's that notion of "comparable values" again, a notion I've already complained about.

[44] How many times did you have to read that sentence? Perhaps the following example will help. Let table *T* contain five rows, and let column *C* of that table contain 1, 2, 3, NULL, and NULL; then the expression UNIQUE (SELECT *C* FROM *T*) gives TRUE. See also Appendix B.

[45] SQL apologists will claim that these two "situations" are really only one, because SELECT DISTINCT is defined in terms of IS DISTINCT FROM. Maybe—but IS DISTINCT FROM wasn't added to the standard until 1999, whereas SELECT DISTINCT was there right from the outset, in 1986. So defining the latter in terms of the former was obviously a retrofit, intended (as I've more or less said already) to shore up what always was, and remains, a very suspect state of affairs.

```
STN    X        Y
       7      NULL
     NULL       4
     NULL     NULL
       7      NULL
```

Now consider this expression:

```
SELECT  Y , COUNT(*) AS Z
FROM    STN
GROUP   BY Y
```

Here's the result:

```
    Y    Z
    4    1
 NULL    3
```

Clearly, "NULL = NULL" (not intended to be legal SQL syntax) is regarded as TRUE in this context. And the same is true for ORDER BY ... Again given STN as shown above, the result of

```
SELECT  *
FROM    STN
ORDER   BY X , Y
```

looks like one of the following:[46]

```
    X        Y              X        Y
    7      NULL          NULL     NULL
    7      NULL          NULL        4
 NULL        4             7      NULL
 NULL     NULL             7      NULL
```

---

[46] These pictures might look like pictures of SQL tables (or relations), but of course they're not—the top to bottom order of the rows is significant.

(By default, whether nulls "sort high" or "sort low" is implementation defined—that's why there are two possible results—but at least they're required to "sort equal.")

Two further important contexts in which nulls are considered equal are provided by SQL's MATCH operator and the related issue of referential constraint checking, each of which involves several additional situations in which the expression $x = y$ gives TRUE even if x is null or y is null or both. See Appendix A for further discussion.

CASE 3 ("=" user defined)

SQL allows users to define their own types. Such types are of two kinds, viz., DISTINCT types and structured types; here, however, we need consider only structured types. Here's a slightly simplified example—a definition for a structured type called POINT, representing, let's agree, geometric points in two-dimensional euclidean space (note, incidentally, that STRUCTURED doesn't appear as a keyword in the definition):

```
CREATE TYPE POINT
   AS ( X FLOAT , Y FLOAT ) ;
```

X and Y here are *attributes* of the user defined type POINT.

Now, the only aspect of a type such as POINT that concerns us here is: How does equality work for values of that type? Believe it or not, the answer to this question is tied up with a statement called CREATE ***ORDERING***—despite the fact that equality doesn't have very much to do with the concept of ordering as such. Here's an example of a possible CREATE ORDERING statement for type POINT:

```
CREATE ORDERING FOR POINT EQUALS ONLY BY STATE ;
```

Explanation:

- ■ EQUALS ONLY means that "=" and "<>" (not equals) are the only valid comparison operators for values of type POINT (surely implying, I would have thought, that there's no possibility of "ordering" such values at all—but let's not worry about that). The alternative to EQUALS ONLY is

FULL, meaning that "<", "<=", etc., are allowed in addition to "=" and "<>" (but "<", "<=", etc., don't make sense for geometric points).

■ BY STATE means that two values *v1* and *v2* of type POINT are equal if and only if every attribute of *v1* has the same value as the corresponding attribute of *v2*—i.e., if and only if the X attribute of *v1* has the same value as the X attribute of *v2* and the Y attribute of *v1* has the same value as the Y attribute of *v2*.[47]

■ *Note very carefully, however, that alternatives to BY STATE are possible.* Details of those alternatives are beyond the scope of this discussion, but what they all boil down to is this: How the comparison operators work, if one of those alternatives is specified, is defined by user supplied code. Thus, the semantics of "=" in particular are effectively arbitrary in such a situation![48]

Let me now remind you of something I've said in this chapter already: namely, that "=" comparisons are performed, implicitly, in all kinds of situations—DISTINCT, LIKE, GROUP BY, UNION, JOIN, key constraint checking, referential constraint checking, and on and on. And if the semantics of "=" are arbitrary, SQL's behavior in all such cases will be arbitrary in turn—even unpredictable, possibly, from the user's point of view. *Why* is this a good idea? In fact, how can it possibly be?

Let me say too that if a given structured type has no associated CREATE ORDERING—a state of affairs that's certainly permitted—then no comparisons at all, *not even equality comparisons*, can be performed on values of that type. Which brings me to Case 4 ("=" not supported).

CASE 4 ("=" not supported)

As noted near the beginning of this chapter, "=" isn't supported by SQL at all for any of the following:

---

[47] In case you were wondering, "has the same value as" here is defined to mean "=", not "is not distinct from" (and note the recursive nature of the definition, too, given that attributes of a given structured type might themselves be of some previously defined structured type).

[48] But can probably be explained in terms of yet another form of coercion.

- *Certain user defined types:* The types I have in mind here are the ones mentioned at the end of the previous section—that is, structured types that have no associated CREATE ORDERING.

- *The system defined type XML:* Values of this type are XML documents, the structure and inner details of which are rightly of no concern to SQL—but this fact, it seems to me, is no excuse for failing to support "=" for such values.

- *(In some products) certain other system defined types:* I have in mind here the types BLOB and CLOB. Values of type BLOB ("binary large object") are strings of octets (yes, octets, not bits); values of type CLOB ("character large object") are strings of characters; and the maximum length of all such "large objects" is implementation defined, but will presumably be quite large in any real implementation. Now, the standard does support "=" for such values, but certain products don't. (At least, they didn't the last time I looked, which was admittedly quite a while ago. Maybe they do now.)

- *Tables:* This is the most important case, and I'll discuss it further below.

Of these four possibilities, I really don't have much more to say about the first three. I'd just like to remind you of the following general point. Let *T* be any SQL type for which "=" isn't supported, and let *C* be a column, within some SQL table, that's defined to be of type *T*. *Then C can't be used in any context that relies, either explicitly or implicitly, on equality comparisons.* Such contexts include at least all of the following: key constraints; referential constraints; DISTINCT; JOIN; UNION; INTERSECT; EXCEPT; comparisons (in an ON or WHERE or HAVING or CHECK clause); GROUP BY; BETWEEN, LIKE, IN, MATCH, UNIQUE, and IS DISTINCT FROM conditional expressions; and ORDER BY. The full implications of this state of affairs I'll leave as something for you to meditate on.[49]

Let me get back to tables. As I've said, SQL has no "=" operator for tables; in fact, it has no proper table comparison operators, as such, at all. Why not? Well, I'm only guessing here, but it seems to me that the reason these things

---

[49] Here's yet another little weirdness: Again let *T* be any SQL type for which "=" isn't supported; let *V* be a SQL variable that's defined to be of type *T*; and suppose we assign the value *v* to *V*. Then we can't turn around the very next moment and test whether the comparison *V* = *v* gives TRUE! (Or any other truth value, come to that.) *Note:* This state of affairs constitutes a violation of *The Assignment Principle*, which I'll be discussing in detail in the next chapter.

aren't supported is because—amazingly!—SQL doesn't regard tables as what some people like to call "first class objects." Certainly they don't have types, in the sense that (e.g.) integers, character strings, etc., and even rows, have types. In fact, this last contrast, with rows, is instructive. Let me elaborate.

First of all, SQL does support a ROW type generator (it doesn't call it that, though), which can be used in the definition of an SQL variable or column to specify that the data type of the variable or column in question is some specific row type. For example:

```
DECLARE SV ROW ( SNO    VARCHAR(5)  ,
                 SNAME  VARCHAR(25) ,
                 STATUS INTEGER     ,
                 CITY   VARCHAR(20) ) ;
```

In this example, the text from the keyword ROW to the final closing parenthesis, inclusive, constitutes an invocation of the ROW type generator, and SV is thereby declared to be an SQL variable of a certain specific row type—to be specific, the same type as the rows of the suppliers table S from the suppliers-and-parts database. As a consequence, e.g., the following SQL assignment is legitimate—by which I mean both (a) that the assignment is syntactically valid, and also (b) that it will execute successfully at run time:

```
SET SV = ( SELECT SNO , SNAME , STATUS , CITY
           FROM   S
           WHERE  SNO = 'S1' ) ;
```

Various row comparison operations—including row equality comparisons ("=") in particular—involving variable SV are likewise also legitimate.

> *Aside:* Note the coercions involved in the foregoing example! The expression on the right side of the assignment is what SQL calls a subquery, and it evaluates to a table. However, the table in question contains just one row, and so it can be (and is) coerced to a row. That row in turn contains just one field, and so it can be (and is) coerced to a scalar. Thus, the overall assignment succeeds at run time only because a double coercion is done.[50] *End of aside.*

---

[50] In fact SQL supports three semantically different constructs that it calls <table subquery>, <row subquery>, and <scalar subquery>, respectively. Syntactically, however, these three constructs are identical!—each is defined to be just a <subquery> (which is to say, it's just a <query expression> enclosed in parentheses), and they can be told apart only by context. Thus, SQL would say in the example that we can tell from the context that the expression on the right side of the assignment must be a <scalar subquery> specifically. Well, maybe so; but I prefer my explanation in terms of coercion.

What's more, these row assignment and row comparison operations are all *generic*, in the sense that they're associated with the ROW type generator; hence, they're available for use in connection with rows of any type produced using that type generator.

So rows in SQL are "first class objects." But tables aren't; there's no TABLE type generator, and hence no generic operations associated with that type generator a fortiori.[51] And so the SQL designers never thought to approach the matter systematically and define an assignment operation for tables, comparison operations for tables, and so on.

So how can we test two SQL tables for equality?[52] To say it again, there's no direct "=" support; however, workarounds are available. By way of example, consider the relational comparison (a boolean expression with relation operands)

```
S { CITY } = P { CITY }
```

This expression represents an equality comparison between the projections on CITY of the suppliers table (S) and the parts table (P). Here now is one rather longwinded way to do the same comparison in SQL:

```
NOT EXISTS ( SELECT CITY FROM S
             EXCEPT
             SELECT CITY FROM P )
AND
NOT EXISTS ( SELECT CITY FROM P
             EXCEPT
             SELECT CITY FROM S )
```

("There's no city in S that's not in P, and there's no city in P that's not in S.")

> *Aside:* I've claimed that SQL has no direct support for table equality comparisons, and that's true. As a consequence, the following would-be SQL analog of the relational comparison S{CITY} = P{CITY}—
>
> ```
> ( SELECT DISTINCT CITY FROM S ) =
> ( SELECT DISTINCT CITY FROM P )
> ```

---

[51] Of course SQL does support a variety of generic table operations (UNION, NATURAL JOIN, etc.), but those operations were all defined independently—they were never associated with any TABLE type generator as such.

[52] The discussion that follows is based on material from my book *SQL and Relational Theory: How to Write Accurate SQL Code*, 3rd edition (O'Reilly, 2015).

—is illegal (it'll fail at compile time). But the odd thing is, SQL does have direct support for equality comparisons on *bags*,[53] including as a special case bags of rows in particular. Moreover, it also has an operator for converting a table to a bag of rows.[54] So we can do the desired equality comparison, in effect, by converting the tables to bags of rows and then comparing those bags. So far so good ... Believe it or not, however, the operator that converts a table to a bag of rows is called *TABLE* (!).[55] Thus, the desired comparison can legitimately be formulated in SQL as follows:

```
TABLE ( SELECT DISTINCT CITY FROM S ) =
TABLE ( SELECT DISTINCT CITY FROM P )
```

Note, however, that this trick only works for "equals" (and "not equals") comparisons; SQL has no direct support for "⊃", "⊂", etc.—certainly not for tables, and not for bags of rows either.

Incidentally, I observe in passing that the standard doesn't guarantee that the single result column, in each of the two bags of rows resulting from the two TABLE invocations in the foregoing example, has any prescribed column name. In particular, it doesn't guarantee that the column name in question is CITY. Of course, this fact is probably insignificant in the present context, but it could easily be very significant indeed in other contexts. *End of aside.*

Now, you might have been surprised to hear me claim that SQL has no TABLE type generator. Perhaps you're thinking: But what about CREATE TABLE? Doesn't CREATE TABLE generate a specific table type (as well as,

---

[53] A bag is like a set, except that it permits duplicates. Regarding bag equality, here's the pertinent text from the standard: "Two [bags] *A* and *B* are distinct if there exists a value *V* in the element type of *A* and *B*, including the null value, such that the number of elements in *A* that are not distinct from *V* does not equal the number of elements in *B* that are not distinct from *V*." I hope that's perfectly clear! Note in particular the reliance on what it means for one thing to be "distinct from" another in SQL, a topic discussed in detail earlier in this chapter. PS: For the record, the SQL term for "bag" is *multiset*. I prefer *bag*.

[54] Note carefully that a bag of rows in SQL is *not* the same thing as an SQL table—nor is there any way to convert it into one!—even though SQL tables do contain bags of rows. In particular, bags of rows can't be operated upon by means of SQL's regular table operators (UNION, NATURAL JOIN, etc.).

[55] What the SQL designers were thinking here is beyond me. Note that the one thing the TABLE operator most definitely doesn't do is return a table! Contrast, e.g., SQRT, which returns a square root; COUNT, which returns a count; AVG, which returns an average; and on and on. PS: The TABLE operator referred to here mustn't be confused with the other operator of the same name, which takes a named table (variable) as its operand and returns the current value of that table as a table (value), *not* as the corresponding bag of rows. For example, the expression TABLE S returns the current value of the suppliers base table.

perhaps, doing certain other things too)? Well, let's look at an example. Here's a CREATE TABLE statement for the suppliers table S:

```
CREATE TABLE S ( SNO    VARCHAR(5)  NOT NULL ,
                 SNAME  VARCHAR(25) NOT NULL ,
                 STATUS INTEGER     NOT NULL ,
                 CITY   VARCHAR(20) NOT NULL ,
                 UNIQUE ( SNO ) ) ;
```

What I'm claiming is that there's nothing—no sequence of linguistic tokens—in this example that can logically be labeled "an invocation of the TABLE type generator." This fact might become more apparent when you realize that the specification UNIQUE (SNO), which defines a certain integrity constraint on suppliers, doesn't have to come after the column definitions but can appear almost anywhere—e.g., between the definitions of columns SNO and SNAME. Not to mention the NOT NULL specifications on the individual column definitions, which also define certain integrity constraints. In fact, to the extent that table S can be regarded as having any type at all, that type is nothing more than *bag of rows*, where the rows in question are of the row type discussed earlier, viz.:

```
ROW ( SNO    VARCHAR(5)  ,
      SNAME  VARCHAR(25) ,
      STATUS INTEGER     ,
      CITY   VARCHAR(20) ) ;
```

All of that being said, I should perhaps add that SQL does support something it calls "typed tables." The term is hardly appropriate, however, because if *TT* is a "typed table" that's defined to be "of type *T*," then *TT* is *not* of type *T*, and neither are its rows![56] In any case, "typed tables" still don't provide any direct "=" support.[57]

---

[56] This strange but true state of affairs is explained in detail in my book *Type Inheritance and Relational Theory* (O'Reilly, 2016). PS: For the record, the "type *T*" that's allegedly (but not actually) the type of "typed table *TT*" is required to be a structured type specifically.

[57] What's more, I don't think you should use them anyway. Why not? Because they're inextricably intertwined with SQL's support for *pointers*, and pointers are, of course, just about as nonrelational as you can get.

CONCLUDING REMARKS

I began this chapter by saying "Everyone knows what equality means"—but now we've seen extensive evidence to demonstrate that, sadly, that's not true. As a matter of fact, I knew it wasn't true when I originally said it: not just because of SQL, but because of something else I happened to be aware of. That "something else" is an extensive set of lecture notes (effectively almost a book), by an old acquaintance of mine, the late Adrian Larner.[58]

In those notes, Adrian makes a very big deal of a concept he calls *criteria of identity*. Now, I find it hard to do justice to this concept—quite frankly (and with apologies to Adrian), I find the entire document extremely unclear—so perhaps the best thing I can do here is let Adrian speak for himself. Here's a quote from page 61 (but similar text, or text expressing a similar or related point of view) appears scattered throughout the subject document):

> [Relational theoreticians][59] think that there is an identity predicate, "is the same as," or "is the same thing as," or "=" (equals), and that this predicate holds between each thing and itself, but not between anything and anything else. Well, I'm not certain whether that formulation is correct—or even coherent—but, if it is coherent, I think it's wrong. And against me I have all mathematicians, and most logicians, and every data analyst and data base theorist I've ever met. I'll say that they believe in *absolute identity*: They think that "**x** is the same as **y**" makes sense, and I don't.

In other words, Adrian rejects the notion of "absolute identity"—i.e., equality, as I defined that concept earlier—utterly and entirely.[60] So what does he propose to put in its place? The answer seems to be what he calls *relative* identity (or *criteria of* identity—he uses both terms). Again, I have difficulty in understanding exactly what he means by these terms, but I *think* that what he's trying to get at is simply the well understood notion of an equivalence class. For example, I own two copies of *Pride and Prejudice*. Clearly, those copies are

---

[58] "Platoclast on Data – A New Approach to Relational Data Base Theory" (1992), privately distributed.

[59] Actually Adrian doesn't say "relational theoreticians" here, he identifies Codd and myself specifically.

[60] I have reason to believe that Adrian is following the logician P. T. Geach in this respect. (Also in others; for example, he also seems to reject the notion of sets, claiming that there are only individuals—a position that I find reminiscent of the belief, articulated by someone or other, "There's no such thing as society.") Well, I've tried several times to understand some of Geach's own writings on such matters but always failed, finding the writings in question to be almost impenetrably obscure. PS: I also have reason to believe that Geach was Adrian's mentor at university.

distinct books (otherwise I wouldn't know I had two!), so they're certainly not identical (or equal, as I've defined that term). At the same time, we might also say they're different copies of the same book—but if so, then we're using the terms "book" and "the same" in a slightly different sense. To make this latter statement more precise, we can say my two copies of *Pride and Prejudice*, though (to repeat) certainly not identical, are nevertheless *equivalent*, according to a certain well defined notion of equivalence[61]—in other words, they belong to the same *equivalence class*. Here are the pertinent definitions (taken from *The New Relational Dictionary* once again):

> **Definition (equivalence class):** A subset S' of some given set S with the property that the elements of S' are (a) all equivalent to one another, under some stated definition of equivalence, and (b) not equivalent to any other element of S, under that same definition of equivalence. Observe that (a) equivalence classes are pairwise disjoint, and (b) together, they partition the values in the given set S.

> **Definition (equivalent):** Let x and y be elements of some set, and let that set be partitioned into a set of equivalence classes. Then x and y are equivalent (in symbols, $x \equiv y$) if and only if they're members of the same equivalence class.

And here are a few simple examples:

1. Let Z be the set of all integers, and define integers x and y to be equivalent if and only if they have the same number of digits in conventional decimal notation (no leading zeros). Then the subset of Z containing all one-digit integers is an equivalence class under this definition of equivalence; so too are the subsets consisting of all two-digit integers, all three-digit integers, and so on.

---

[61] For example, the notion of equivalence being appealed to in this example might be "having the same title and the same author." What's more, I suppose that notion might be referred to as one possible *criterion of identity* for books, and I suppose we might then go further and say my two copies of *Pride and Prejudice* are "the same book" according to that criterion. But if so, then I'm tempted to add: So what? PS: But I suppose Adrian might reject the concept of "the same," as in "the same title" and "the same author." If so, however, I have no idea what he would put in its place! You have to start somewhere, and I think defining x to be the same as x for all x is a pretty good place to do so.

2. Consider the set of parts currently represented in the parts table P. Define two such parts to be equivalent if and only if they're of the same color. Then the set of all red parts currently represented in P is an equivalence class under this definition of equivalence; so too is the set of all blue parts, and so is the set of all yellow parts, and so on.

3. Consider the set of rows in the current value of the shipments table SP. Define two such rows to be equivalent if and only if they contain the same supplier number. Then the set of all such rows for supplier number S1 is an equivalence class under this definition of equivalence; so too is the set of all such rows for supplier S2, and so is the set of all such rows for supplier S3, and so on.

In all of these examples, we have "individuals"—the logicians' term—that are equivalent but not identical (or, as I would say, not equal).

In fact, let me now point out—and here perhaps I find myself in some slight sympathy with Adrian's position (?)—that we often use the term *equality* (and related terms) in informal discourse when what we should really be talking about, rather, is some form of equivalence. For example: "All persons are equal under the law." This statement obviously doesn't mean we're all the same person!—rather, it means we all have the same rights, and we're all entitled to equal treatment by the forces of law and order. But this chapter isn't concerned with informal discourse. Instead, it's concerned with various aspects of computing (and/or logic, and/or mathematics), where we necessarily have to be precise and somewhat formal. My definition of equality, and all of the arguments and discussions stemming from that definition, have of course assumed that more precise, more formal context.

APPENDIX A: THE MATCH OPERATOR

Note: This appendix is based on material from the book A Guide to the SQL Standard, by Hugh Darwen and myself (4th edition, Addison-Wesley, 1997).

MATCH is a boolean operator in SQL that always returns TRUE or FALSE, never UNKNOWN. The syntax is:

```
rx MATCH [ UNIQUE ]
         [ SIMPLE | PARTIAL | FULL ] ( tx )
```

Here *rx* and *tx* are expressions denoting a row *r* and a table *t*, respectively, such that for all *i* the types of the *i*th field of *r* and the *i*th column of *t* are comparable.[62] (Remember that rows and tables have a left to right ordering to their fields and columns, respectively, in SQL.) Thus, there are six cases to consider, depending on (a) whether the UNIQUE option is omitted or specified and (b) whether SIMPLE, PARTIAL, or FULL is specified (omitting this latter option entirely is equivalent to specifying SIMPLE). The following table summarizes the six cases:

	SIMPLE	PARTIAL	FULL
omitted	Case 1	Case 2	Case 3
UNIQUE	Case 4	Case 5	Case 6

Note first that PARTIAL and FULL effectively both degenerate to SIMPLE, and if specified can therefore effectively be ignored, if either (a) *r* and *t* are both of degree one or (b) every component of *r* has "nulls not allowed" (or both). More generally, however, the rules are as follows:

- *Case 1* (no UNIQUE, SIMPLE): The result is TRUE if either (a) any field of *r* is null[63] or (b) *t* contains at least one row, *r'* say, such that *r* = *r'* is TRUE; otherwise the result is FALSE.

- *Case 2* (no UNIQUE, PARTIAL): The result is TRUE if either (a) every field of *r* is null or (b) *t* contains at least one row, *r'* say, such that each nonnull field in *r* is equal to its counterpart in *r'*; otherwise the result is FALSE.

- *Case 3* (no UNIQUE, FULL): The result is TRUE if either (a) every field of *r* is null or (b) every field of *r* is nonnull and *t* contains at least one row, *r'* say, such that *r* = *r'* is TRUE; otherwise the result is FALSE.

---

[62] There's that notion of types being "comparable" again, by the way (see footnote 17).

[63] Note that here and throughout these rules, wherever condition (a) holds—i.e., whenever either "any field of *r* is null" (for Cases 1 and 4) or "every field of *r* is null" (for Cases 2, 3, 5, and 6)—we effectively have yet another situation in which *x* = *y* gives TRUE if *x* is null or *y* is null or both.

- *Case 4* (UNIQUE, SIMPLE): The result is TRUE if either (a) any field of *r* is null or (b) *t* contains exactly one row, *r'* say, such that *r = r'* is TRUE; otherwise the result is FALSE.

- *Case 5* (UNIQUE, PARTIAL): The result is TRUE if either (a) every field of *r* is null or (b) *t* contains exactly one row, *r'* say, such that each nonnull field in *r* is equal to its counterpart in *r'*; otherwise the result is FALSE.

- *Case 6* (UNIQUE, FULL): The result is TRUE if either (a) every field of *r* is null or (b) every component of *r* is nonnull and *t* contains exactly one row, *r'* say, such that *r = r'* is TRUE; otherwise the result is FALSE.

Foreign Keys

Foreign key or referential constraints in SQL are defined in terms of the MATCH operator. Ignoring aspects that are irrelevant for present purposes, the syntax of a foreign key definition is as follows:

```
FOREIGN KEY ( <column name commalist> )
        REFERENCES <table name> ( <column name commalist> )
                [ MATCH { SIMPLE | PARTIAL | FULL } ]
```

Explanation:

- The first <column name commalist> identifies the column(s) constituting the foreign key in the referencing table. Note that the syntax explicitly requires the columns in question to be denoted by their *unqualified* column names. (The same is true of the second <column name commalist> also.)

- The <table name> identifies the referenced or target base table.

- The second <column name commalist> must be the same (except possibly for the sequence in which the column names are listed) as the <column name commalist> in some key definition for the referenced table.

  > *Aside:* Actually there seems to be a mistake in the standard here. At first I thought that SQL was for once following the style of **Tutorial D** and matching up columns on the basis of their name, not their ordinal position (and I found it interesting to speculate on the reasons for this atypical

departure from SQL's usual bad practice). Here's a slightly paraphrased quote from Syntax Rule 3 of Subclause 11.8 ("<referential constraint definition>"):

> There shall be a one-to-one correspondence between [the two <column name commalist>s] such that corresponding column names are equivalent.[64]

In other words, there's no requirement that the sequence of names be the same in both commalists. But then Syntax Rule 9 of that same section says (again paraphrasing slightly):

> The ith column identified in the first <column name commalist> corresponds to the ith column identified in the second <column name commalist>.

Hence—given too that the MATCH operator certainly matches up fields and columns on the basis of ordinal position[65]—I conclude that Syntax Rule 3 of Subclause 11.8 is simply in error. *End of aside.*

■ The referential constraint is defined to be equivalent to the following CHECK constraint:

```
CHECK ( ( fk ) MATCH
            [ SIMPLE | PARTIAL | FULL ]
                       ( SELECT k FROM T ) )
```

Here:

a. *fk* is the first <column name commalist> from the foreign key definition.

b. *k* is the second <column name commalist> from the foreign key definition.

---

[64] What it means for two names to be "equivalent" doesn't seem to be explained anywhere, but I suppose it's a reasonable guess that at least two names are "equivalent" if (and only if?) they're in fact one and the same. Another kind of equality? We're talking about a *standard* here, recall.

[65] Note that "ordinal position" here refers to the position of the column name within some commalist of such names, not necessarily the position of the column as such within the pertinent table.

c. *T* is the name of the referenced base table from the foreign key definition.

d. SIMPLE, PARTIAL, or FULL is specified according as SIMPLE, PARTIAL, or FULL is specified in the foreign key definition.

Figuring out the detailed semantics is left as an exercise.[66]

APPENDIX B: KEY CONSTRAINTS IN SQL

I discussed the following example in the body of the chapter. We're given an SQL base table STN with current value as follows:

```
STN   |   X   |   Y
      |-------|-------
      |    7  | NULL
      | NULL  |    4
      | NULL  | NULL
```

Columns X and Y are defined to be of type INT, and the table is subject to the key constraint UNIQUE (X,Y). Given these definitions and the value shown, then, I claimed that the following INSERT statement—

```
INSERT INTO STN ( X , Y ) VALUES ( 7 , NULL ) ;
```

—would succeed, and the table would thereby now contain two (7,NULL) rows.

Now, Hugh Darwen was a reviewer of an early draft of this chapter, and he commented on this claim of mine as follows:

> I'm not sure this is true ... I'm not convinced [it's] possible [*i.e., for the table to contain two (7,NULL) rows*].

These comments bothered me considerably. Hugh isn't just a friend and colleague, he's my most trusted technical reviewer; what's more, he was an

---

[66] It might or might not interest you to know that Subclause 11.8 of the standard takes up 20 entire and highly detailed pages to perform this task—not to mention, of course, all of the references within those pages to other parts of the document, which also need to be understood in order to understand referential constraints fully.

active participant in the development of the SQL standard for some 16 years, from 1988 to 2004, and I regard him as my "go to" guy on all matters SQL. So I thought I'd better test my example on a real live SQL product. (And here let me acknowledge the assistance of my friend David McGoveran, who actually ran the test for me one of the best known mainstream products. I'll refer to that product here as System Q.)

Now, although as I say Hugh's comments did indeed bother me, I felt comparatively comfortable with my original claim. Imagine my dismay, then, when System Q rejected the INSERT with the following error message:

<violation of UNIQUE KEY CONSTRAINT 'XY'. Cannot insert duplicate key...>

Clearly I needed to take a more careful look at the SQL specification (I mean the standard)—and I did, and I'll describe my findings in that connection in just a moment. First, however, I'd like to offer a couple of general observations:

■ I was very struck by the fact that *people thoroughly familiar with SQL* didn't seem to be sure whether or not the INSERT should succeed. In this category I certainly include Hugh Darwen, of course, but he wasn't the only person I consulted that I'd regard as knowledgeable concerning SQL matters. Come to that, I think I'm fairly knowledgeable concerning SQL matters myself, and I wasn't sure about the issue either. (Originally I thought I was, but the comments of Hugh and others, and the System Q experience, rattled my confidence more than somewhat.)

■ What the issue boils down to, loosely speaking, is whether UNIQUE considers two nulls to be equal. Now, DISTINCT does (in, e.g., SELECT DISTINCT or IS DISTINCT FROM); so it seems to me that (a) if UNIQUE is supposed to do the same, then it would have been better to use the keyword DISTINCT instead of UNIQUE for an SQL key constraint; alternatively, (b) given that SQL *doesn't* use the keyword DISTINCT in a key constraint, then we're entitled to expect such a constraint to have semantics that differ in some way from the semantics of DISTINCT. (This is only a psychological argument, I know, but I think the point is at least worth mentioning.)

Anyway, let me now describe what I found in the standard.[67] First of all, that second (7,NULL) row certainly is inserted into the table, if only temporarily, before the UNIQUE constraint is checked. The following lightly edited quote from Subclause 4.18.2 ("Checking of constraints") of the standard explains the situation (note in particular the text from "at a certain point" to "effected," which I've set in boldface for emphasis)

> Whenever an SQL-statement is executed, every [nondeferred] constraint is checked, **at a certain point after any changes to SQL-data and schemas resulting from that execution have been effected,** to see if it is satisfied. A constraint is *satisfied* if and only if the applicable <search condition> ... evaluates to *True* or *Unknown*.[68] If any enforced constraint is not satisfied, then any changes to SQL-data or schemas resulting from executing that statement are canceled.

So in the example, the question becomes: After the second (7,NULL) row has been inserted, is the specified UNIQUE constraint satisfied? If it isn't, then the row will be removed again.

I now refer to Subclause 11.7 ("<unique constraint definition>"). The syntax rules and general rules of that subclause taken together say the following (in effect, interpreted in terms of the example in hand):

Let *SC* be the <search condition>

```
UNIQUE ( SELECT X , Y FROM STN )
```

... The unique constraint is not satisfied if and only if

```
EXISTS ( SELECT * FROM TNN WHERE NOT ( SC ) )
```

is *True*.

With respect to our example, *TNN* is STN and *SC* is as explained, and so the foregoing EXISTS invocation becomes

```
EXISTS ( SELECT * FROM STN
         WHERE NOT ( UNIQUE ( SELECT X , Y FROM STN ) ) )
```

---

[67] The version of the standard I consulted was SQL:2011, and all quotes from the standard in this appendix are taken from that version.

[68] Note that "or *Unknown*," by the way! See the discussion of such matters on page 26.

Well, the WHERE clause here includes an invocation of what SQL calls the <unique predicate>. So I turn to Subclause 8.11 ("<unique predicate>"), the Function subsubclause (?) of which states "Specify a test for the absence of duplicate rows" (!). General Rule 2 of that subclause reads as follows:

> If there are no two rows in *T* such that the value of each column in one row is nonnull and is not distinct from the value of the corresponding column in the other row, then the result of the <unique predicate> is *True*; otherwise, the result of the <unique predicate> is *False*.

(Actually I quoted this rule in the body of the chapter, on page 35.) In our example, *T* is the result of evaluating the expression

```
SELECT X , Y FROM STN
```

In other words, *T* is a table containing (a) the row (7,NULL), twice; (b) the rows (NULL,4) and (NULL,NULL), once each; and (c) nothing else. So:

a. There's no row at all in *T* such that "the value of each column [in that row] is nonnull," and so there are certainly "no two rows in *T* such that the value of each column in one [of those] row[s] is nonnull";

b. The <unique predicate> therefore evaluates to *True*;

c. The boolean expression in the WHERE clause therefore evaluates to *False*;

d. The argument to the EXISTS invocation is therefore empty;

e. That EXISTS invocation therefore returns *False*;

f. The <unique constraint> is therefore satisfied; and so

d. The second INSERT therefore succeeds, and the final value of STN does contains two copies of that (7,NULL) row.

So I conclude that I was right all along, and the second INSERT should be accepted. I conclude further that System Q has a bug in this area.

Chapter 2

Assignment

Seagoon: If you won't volunteer, we must draw lots. Eccles?
Eccles: Yeah?
Seagoon: Write your name on a piece of paper and put it in this hat.
Eccles: [Scribbles] There.
Seagoon: Now take it out and read it.
Eccles: Mrs – Phyllis – Quott.
Seagoon: You impostor, you're not Mrs Quott!

—Spike Milligan:
Tales of Men's Shirts: A Story of Down Under
(an episode of *The Goon Show*,
first broadcast by the BBC on December 31st, 1959)

In the previous chapter, I argued that it was worth giving an explicit definition for the concept of equality even though "everyone knows" what equality is. I also described, in somewhat excruciating detail, some of SQL's many failures in connection with that concept, suggesting that those failures might all stem from a more fundamental one: viz., the fact that SQL never bothered to spell out exactly what equality means in the first place. In this chapter, I turn my attention to something else that "everyone understands," namely assignment—and, in accordance with my stated position in connection with such matters, I'll begin with a definition:

Definition (assignment): An operator (":=") that assigns a value (the *source*, denoted by some expression) to a variable (the *target*, denoted by the name of that variable); also, the operation performed when that operator is invoked. The source and target must be of the same type,[1] and the operation overall is required to abide by (a) *The Assignment Principle*

---

[1] This sentence is 100 percent correct as stated, but it needs some elaboration in the context of type inheritance. As in the previous chapter, therefore, for reasons of simplicity I propose to ignore type inheritance in this chapter from this point forward, barring explicit statements to the contrary.

(always) as well as (b) **The Golden Rule** (if applicable). Every update operator, no matter how formulated in concrete syntax, is logically equivalent to an assignment in the first of the foregoing senses; hence, every invocation of such an operator is logically equivalent to an assignment in the second of the foregoing senses.

I'll define *The Assignment Principle* and **The Golden Rule** later in the chapter. Here just let me point out that it's a corollary of the foregoing definition that the would-be assignment

```
target := source ;
```

will or should fail, ideally at compile time, if *target* and *source* are of different types.

So how do assignments work in SQL? Well, one immediate oddity is that SQL does support an explicit assignment operator (for which it uses the keyword SET) for scalars, and rows, and even for bags and arrays—but not for tables![2] Of course, it does support table INSERT, DELETE, and UPDATE operators, and each of these can be regarded as shorthand for a certain special case of an explicit, albeit hypothetical, table assignment operator; unfortunately, however, that hypothetical operator is indeed hypothetical as far as SQL is concerned. Anyway, before we get to table assignment as such, let's take a look at the comparatively straightforward case of scalar assignment first.

SCALAR ASSIGNMENT IN SQL

To repeat, SQL's explicit assignment operator is called SET. SET as a standalone operator wasn't introduced into SQL until 1996, when SQL variables were added (as part of the Persistent Stored Modules feature, PSM); however, the SET keyword as such was available as part of the table UPDATE operator right from the very outset, of course. The syntax in the standalone case is:[3]

---

[2] The reason for this glaring omission is, I believe, the same as the one I gave in the previous chapter for the lack of table comparison operators: viz., the fact that SQL doesn't regard tables as "first class objects"—or, to put the point another way, the fact that it doesn't support a TABLE type generator.

[3] For definiteness I use a semicolon as the statement terminator throughout this chapter (in all cases, not just for SQL statements). *Note:* The full story regarding statement terminators in SQL in particular is actually a little complicated—but it's not very interesting, and I omit further discussion here.

```
SET <target> = <source> ;
```

To elaborate:

a. The <target> is the name of an SQL scalar variable.[4]

b. The <source> is an expression of the appropriate type (where exactly what *appropriate type* means is discussed further below).

And of course the semantics are that the value resulting from evaluation of the source expression is assigned to the target variable.

For the record, let me also give the syntax (deliberately somewhat simplified here) for what SQL calls its "searched UPDATE" operator:

```
UPDATE <target>
   SET <assign commalist>
     [ WHERE <boolean expression> ] ;
```

To elaborate again, albeit only very briefly:

a. The <target> is the name, *T* say, of an SQL table (meaning a table variable, of course—in other words, a base table or a view).

b. The <assign commalist> effectively constitutes a multiple assignment as described in various writings by myself (including Appendix A to the present chapter in particular). Each individual <assign> takes the form

```
<column> = <source>
```

Here <column> is the name of some column of *T*, and <source> is an expression of the corresponding type.

Aside: I must make it clear that everything I've said in this section to this point (with respect to the standalone SET statement in particular) represents my own

---

[4] There are other possibilities too, such as *host variable* and *parameter*, but there's no need to discuss those possibilities here. However, I should at least mention, for reasons of completeness if nothing else, that assignments to host variables also occur in connection with SQL's SELECT INTO and FETCH INTO operations. Neither of these operations involves an explicit SET operation as such, but they do follow the same general rules as SET assignments, except as otherwise noted.

attempt at explaining, or at any rate describing, assignment as supported by SQL. Here for the record is the SQL standard's own slightly bizarre explanation:

> **assignment:** The operation that causes the value at a site *T* (known as the *target*) to be a given value *S* (known as the *source*). Assignment is frequently indicated by the use of the phrase "*T* is set to *S*" or "the value of *T* is set to *S*".

And elsewhere:

> The instance [*sic*] at a site can be changed by the operation of *assignment*. Assignment replaces the instance at a site (known as the *target*) with a new instance of a (possibly different) value (known as the *source* value).

Note that the foregoing extracts make no mention of variables; instead, they use the term *site*.[5] What's a site? Here's the standard again:

> A *site* is a place that holds an instance of a value of a specified data type ... [The] principal kind of ... site is the base table. A base table is a special kind of site, in that constraints can be specified on its values ... Some sites may be referenced by their names — for example, base tables and SQL variables.

Well, it's a little strange to see the standard saying (a) that the target of assignment is a "site" and then (b) that the "principal kind of site is the base table," given that (as I've already said) tables are the one kind of "site" that SQL doesn't support explicit assignment for. It's also strange to see it saying, in connection with the same point, that sites in general hold "an instance of a value of a specified data type," given that the one obvious thing that tables in SQL (base or otherwise) don't have is a data type, specified or otherwise.

Note also that, according to the foregoing extracts taken together, a site apparently sometimes holds a value as such and sometimes an "instance" of a value. What's the difference? What exactly is an instance of a value? Here's the standard again:

> **instance (of a value):** A physical representation of a value. Each instance is at exactly one site. An instance has a data type that is the data type of its value.

---

[5] They also fail to make it clear whether the term *target* refers to a "site" as such or to the value (or "instance"?) at the pertinent "site." By contrast, the term *source* does apparently refer to a value (but then why the phrase "source value"?). And what exactly is a "new" instance?

And regarding "physical representation of a value," the standard offers no further explanation, except to say that such things are implementation dependent, or in other words undefined. But why is it talking about physical matters anyway? Surely physical matters are or should be beyond the purview of both SQL as such and the standard in particular?

Actually (and despite the terminology it uses), I don't think the standard *is* talking about physical matters here; I think rather that what it's attempting to get at in the extract quoted—but not really succeeding in that attempt!—is the logical difference between a value as such, on the one hand, and an appearance (or "instance," or "occurrence") of such a value in some particular context on the other. The following definitions are taken from my book *The **New** Relational Database Dictionary* (O'Reilly, 2016):

> **Definition (value):** An "individual constant" (for example, the individual constant denoted by the integer literal 3).[6] Values can be of arbitrary complexity; in particular, they can be either scalar or nonscalar (note in particular that tuples and relations are both [nonscalar] values). Values have no location in time or space; however, they can be represented in memory by means of some encoding, and those encodings or representations do have location in time and space—indeed, distinct occurrences of the same value can appear at any number of distinct locations in time and space, meaning, loosely, that the same value can occur as the current value of any number of distinct variables, and/or as any number of attribute values within the current value of any number of distinct tuple and/or relation variables (i.e., tuplevars and/or relvars), at the same time or different times.

> **Definition (appearance of a value):** An occurrence or "instance" of a value in some context. Observe that there's a logical difference between a value as such and an appearance of that value in some context—for example, as the current value of some variable or as an attribute value within the current value of some tuple variable (or "tuplevar") or relation variable (or "relvar"). Of course, every appearance of a value has an implementation that consists of some physical representation of the value in question (and distinct appearances of the same value might have distinct physical representations). Thus, there's also a logical difference between an appearance of a value, on the one hand, and the physical representation of

---

[6] "Individual constant" is a term sometimes used by logicians to mean what I mean by the term *value*.

that appearance, on the other; there might even be a logical difference between the physical representations used for distinct appearances of the same value. All of that being said, however, it's usual to abbreviate *physical representation of an appearance of a value* to just *appearance of a value*, or (more often) to just *value*, so long as there's no risk of ambiguity. Note, however, that *appearance of a value* is a model concept, whereas *physical representation of an appearance* is an implementation concept—users certainly might need to know whether (for example) two variables contain appearances of the same value, but they don't need to know whether those two appearances use the same physical representation.

End of aside.

Be all of that as it may, I'm now in a position to give the definition I promised for *The Assignment Principle*:

> **Definition (*The Assignment Principle*):** After assignment of value v to variable V, the equality comparison $V = v$ is required to evaluate to TRUE.

Aside: The Assignment Principle was first articulated in a paper ("Multiple Assignment") by Hugh Darwen and myself, which was originally published on the website *www.dbdebunk.com* in February 2004 and was then republished in my book *Date on Database: Writings 2000-2006* (Apress, 2006). As Hugh and I stated in that paper, the principle is so obvious—even trivial—that it might seem hardly worth stating, let alone dignifying with such a grand name. After all, it's more or less just the *definition* of assignment! But Hugh and I also observed in that same paper that it's violated ubiquitously in SQL in particular; and it's tempting to suggest that such violations occur, at least in part, precisely because the principle hadn't been properly spelled out previously. All of which constitutes the *raison d'être* (or a large part of the *raison d'être*, at any rate) for the present chapter, of course. *End of aside.*

Now—this shouldn't need saying, but in keeping with my belief that it's better to spell things out explicitly I'll say it anyway—the comparison $V = v$, in the definition of *The Assignment Principle*, is supposed to abide by the rules for such comparisons as spelled out in the previous chapter. In particular, therefore, the variable V and the value v are supposed to be of the same type. As you also know from that previous chapter, however, SQL *doesn't* require the variable V and the value v in such a comparison to be of the same type—and as I'm sure you've guessed, if you didn't know it already, it doesn't require the variable V and the value v in the assignment $V := v$ (or SET $V = v$, rather, in SQL) to be of the same type either. Instead, it makes liberal use of coercions once again. Let's take a closer look.

First of all, SQL supports a large number of what it calls "predefined" (i.e., system defined or built in) types: viz., NUMERIC, DECIMAL, SMALLINT, INT, BIGINT, FLOAT, REAL, DOUBLE PRECISION, CHAR, VARCHAR, CLOB, BINARY, VARBINARY, BLOB, BOOLEAN, DATE, TIME, TIMESTAMP, INTERVAL, and XML. All of these types are scalar, and they fall into a number of disjoint categories[7]—numeric, character string, bit string,[8] etc. So let variable V and value v be of predefined types TV and Tv, respectively. Then:

a. If TV and Tv belong to different categories, then the assignment SET $V = v$ is illegal (it'll fail at compile time).

b. If TV and Tv belong to the same category, then the assignment SET $V = v$ is at least syntactically legal, though some coercion might be required at run time. (Of course, that coercion might fail, in which case the assignment will fail at run time too.)

Aside: To repeat something I said in Chapter 1, it's in the nature of SQL that it's almost impossible to make a plain statement about any aspect of the language at all without immediately having to hedge that statement about with all kinds of ifs and buts. Well, I'm afraid what I've just been saying is a case in point ... Here are some of the ifs and buts that seem to be needed in connection with scalar types and related matters in SQL:

■ First of all, the question arises (as it did in Chapter 1) as to whether precisions, lengths, etc., are "part of the type." For example, are CHAR(5)

---

[7] Not to be confused with syntax categories in the usual BNF sense (see Chapter 3). In fact, the "disjoint categories" I'm talking about here can be regarded as equivalence classes, in the sense explained in Chapter 1. *Exercise:* What's the corresponding (and required) definition of equivalence?

[8] For the record, I note that the bit string types are BINARY, VARBINARY, and BLOB (which is short for BINARY LARGE OBJECT). In other words, the SQL keyword BINARY refers not to binary numbers but to bit strings. *Note:* As a matter of fact, SQL:1992 and SQL:1999 actually had BIT and BIT VARYING data types; however, SQL:1999 (though not SQL:1992) also had the BINARY LARGE OBJECT data type. In what was presumably some kind of rationalization, therefore, BIT and BIT VARYING were replaced by BINARY and VARBINARY, respectively, in SQL:2003.

and CHAR(6) one type or two, in SQL? I choose not to delve into the details of this question here.

- Second, DISTINCT types are scalar types too, but they're user defined, not predefined. Despite this latter, though, I do need to say something about them somewhere, and here's as good a place as any. So: Let *DT* be a DISTINCT type, let *PT* be the unique type—necessarily predefined, and therefore scalar—in terms of which *DT* is defined, and let *D* and *p* be a variable and a value of type *DT* and type *PT*, respectively. Then the assignment

      SET $D = p$;

  is legal (thanks once again to coercion). Believe it or not, however, the standard *doesn't seem to say* anywhere whether the comparison

      $D = p$

  is also legal (!). If it isn't, then I think it would be hard to find a more flagrant violation of *The Assignment Principle*.[9]

- And then there are structured types, which—at least according to the standard, though I'm not sure I believe it—also behave as if they're scalar, at least some of the time. Whether they do or not, however, we can ignore them for present purposes, because the rules that govern their behavior, regarding assignment in particular, all derive directly from the rules that apply to the types in terms of which the attributes of the structured type in question are defined.

- A similar remark applies to rows, bags, and arrays as well—that is, the rules that govern their behavior, regarding assignment in particular, all derive directly from the rules that apply to the types in terms of which the row, bag, or array in question is defined—and so I won't have much to say about these types in this chapter, either. (That said, however, Appendix C does consider the case of bags in particular in a little more detail.)

---

[9] "No more flagrant violation"—what am I saying? I'm forgetting nulls! Which I'll be discussing in a few moments.

■ Finally: As part of its temporal data support, SQL also supports something it calls *periods*, but—believe it or not—periods, like tables, aren't "first class objects" (there are no period types), and so there's no discussion of periods in the present chapter either.

End of aside.

For simplicity, I limit further consideration of scalar assignment in SQL to just the following two categories:

■ Numeric types—viz., NUMERIC, DECIMAL, SMALLINT, INT, BIGINT, FLOAT, REAL, and DOUBLE PRECISION

■ Character string types (string types for short)—viz., CHAR, VARCHAR, and CLOB (i.e., CHARACTER LARGE OBJECT)

Again consider the generic assignment SET $V = v$, where variable V and value v are of types TV and Tv, respectively. Then that assignment is syntactically legal—assuming as already stated that we're limiting our attention to numeric and string types only—if and only if one of the following is the case:

1. TV and Tv are both numeric types.

2. TV and Tv are both character string types ***and*** those types, and hence V and v, have the same associated character set.[10]

The actual assignment is performed in accordance with the following rules:

1. For a numeric assignment, v is coerced if necessary to the type TV of V (including precision and scale, as applicable) before the assignment is performed. *Note:* A run time exception is raised if the coercion causes one or more of the most significant digits to be lost. No exception is raised,

---

[10] Of course, SQL includes rules by which the character set associated with any given "instance" of any given character string can be determined. For example, if the instance in question appears as a value within some column of some base table or as the value of some SQL variable, the pertinent character set is the one specified when that column or variable is defined; if it's specified by means of a literal, the pertinent character set is specified as an (explicit or implicit) prefix to that literal, if it's the result of concatenating two strings $v1$ and $v2$, then $v1$ and $v2$ must have the same character set, and the result then has that same character set also; and so on. For further specifics, I refer you to the book *A Guide to the SQL Standard*, by Hugh Darwen and myself (4th edition, Addison-Wesley, 1997).

however, if that coercion causes one or more of the *least* significant digits to be lost (i.e., through rounding or truncation—see the text from Subclause 4.4.2 of the standard, "Characteristics of numbers," quoted in the discussion following Example 4 in the "Case 1" section in Chapter 1).

2. For a character string assignment:

■   If *TV* is fixed length, then:

a.   For a SELECT INTO or FETCH INTO operation, *v* is conceptually truncated on the right or padded on the right with space characters, as and when necessary, to make it the same length as *V* before the assignment is performed.[11]

b.   For other operations (SET operations in particular) the same rules apply, except that a run time exception is raised if truncation causes any nonspace characters to be lost.

■   If *TV* is varying length, then the current length of *V* is set to the lesser of its maximum length (whatever that might be) and the length of *v*, and the assignment is then performed as in the fixed length case.

So do these rules abide by *The Assignment Principle*? Not entirely. Let's consider numeric assignments first. At least it's true that if the coercion (if necessary) of value *v* to the type *TV* of variable *V* is successful, then the assignment will be successful too,[12] and moreover the comparison $V = v$ will give TRUE after the assignment is done[13]—but only because coercion will occur again in that comparison! (Thus the SQL comparison $V = v$ doesn't abide by the general rules for such expressions spelled out in the previous chapter, as indeed we already know from the discussions in that chapter.)

---

[11] Note that such padding with spaces *always* occurs if required—there's no question of the target having to have an associated PAD SPACE collation. (For SELECT INTO and FETCH INTO, in fact, the target is probably a host variable, in which case it probably doesn't even have an associated collation anyway.) PS: As explained in the previous chapter, such padding operations can be regarded as coercions, of a kind.

[12] I remind you that we're talking here about scalar assignment in particular. Assignment in general can fail if it violates an integrity constraint, but of course SQL doesn't support scalar integrity constraints.

[13] Well, maybe not, if any rounding or truncation has occurred.

Of course, there's a fly in the ointment: viz., *nulls* (and I'm tempted to add "as usual"). If *v* happens to be null—and by the way, the explicit assignment SET *V* = NULL is perfectly legitimate, in general—then the comparison *V* = *v* will *not* give TRUE after the assignment, it'll give UNKNOWN. Thus, for example, given the code fragment—

```
SET X = Y ;
IF  X = Y THEN CALL Q ;
```

—there can be no guarantee that Q will actually be called, if X and Y both have "nulls allowed." *Note:* So here incidentally we have another situation in which UNKNOWN is effectively coerced to FALSE (see Chapter 1). To elaborate, suppose the foregoing IF statement has an ELSE clause, as here:

```
IF X = Y THEN CALL Q ELSE CALL Q' ;
```

Then if the boolean expression ("X = Y") immediately following the IF evaluates to UNKNOWN, the action specified in the ELSE clause will be executed (in the example, Q' will be invoked).

A similar remark regarding the foregoing unfortunate effect of null on *The Assignment Principle* applies to every possible SQL assignment, of course.[14]

Turning now to character string assignments: Let *Tv* and *TV* be CHAR(3) and CHAR(5), respectively; let *Tv* and *TV*, and hence *v* and *V*, have the same associated character set; and let *v* be 'ABC'. After the assignment SET *V* = *v*, then, the value of *V* will be 'ABC ' (note the trailing spaces); the comparison *V* = *v* will thus give FALSE if NO PAD applies to the pertinent collation, and *The Assignment Principle* will thereby again be violated.

RELATIONAL ASSIGNMENT

Now I'd like to turn to tables and relations—meaning table and relation *variables*, of course, since by definition the target of an assignment operation always has to be a variable of some kind. What I plan to do is this: In this

---

[14] Including "table assignments" (i.e., INSERT, DELETE, and UPDATE operations) in particular—despite the fact that as we saw in the previous chapter there's no such thing as a null table, and there's no such thing as a table equality operator. (The point is, of course, that SQL tables can certainly *contain* a null, and the table equality workarounds discussed in that previous chapter will give UNKNOWN if either of the comparand tables contains any nulls. In the extreme case, a table could contain nothing but nulls—i.e., there could be a null at every row and column intersection. But it still wouldn't be a null table.)

section, I'll consider true relational assignment, in order to establish a basis for subsequent discussion. Then in the next section I'll consider to what extent (and, where applicable, how) the concepts described in this section are realized in SQL. As usual I'll begin with a definition:

> **Definition (relational assignment):** A special case of assignment in general, q.v.; more specifically, either (a) an operator (":=") that assigns a relation value (the source, denoted by some relational expression) to a relation variable or *relvar* (the target, denoted by the relvar name), or (b) the operation performed when that operator is invoked. The source and the target must be of the same type. The familiar operations INSERT, DELETE, and UPDATE are all special cases; in fact, every invocation of one of these operators is logically equivalent to some specific invocation of the explicit relational assignment operation as such. Fundamentally, therefore, relational assignment as such is the only relational update operator logically required.

To repeat, every INSERT or DELETE in particular is shorthand for a certain relational assignment as such. (The same is true for UPDATE too, of course, but for the moment I want to focus on INSERT and DELETE specifically.) But there's a kind of converse to the foregoing statement as well—viz., every explicit relational assignment is effectively equivalent to a certain DELETE / INSERT combination. To be specific, the explicit assignment

```
R := rx ;
```

(where *R* is a relvar name and *rx* is a relational expression of the same type as *R*) is logically equivalent to an explicit assignment of the form—

```
R := ( r MINUS ( d ) ) UNION ( i ) ;
```

—or equivalently (since, as explained below, (a) $d \subseteq r$ and (b) *i* and *r* are disjoint) to one of the form:

```
R := ( r UNION ( i ) ) MINUS ( d ) ;
```

Explanation:

■ *r* is the "old" value of *R*.

- *d* is the set of tuples to be deleted from *R* (the *delete set*).

- *i* is the set of tuples to be inserted into *R* (the *insert set*).

- *d* is a subset of *r* (i.e., $d \subseteq r$).

- *i* and *r* are disjoint.

- *d* and *i* are disjoint a fortiori.

- Given *r* and *rx*, *d* and *i* are uniquely determined; to be specific, *d* is *r* NOT MATCHING *rx* and *i* is *rx* NOT MATCHING *r*.

So the original assignment is logically equivalent to the following *multiple assignment*[15]—in fact, a multiple assignment in which the individual assignments both involve the same target:

```
DELETE R d , INSERT R i ;
```

Or equivalently (since, again, (a) $d \subseteq r$ and (b) *i* and *r* are disjoint):

```
INSERT R i , DELETE R d ;
```

Thus, any given relational assignment to relvar *R* can always be thought of as a combination of a delete operation on *R* and an insert operation on *R*. And if the delete set *d* is empty, the assignment is effectively a pure insert operation; if the insert set *i* is empty, it's effectively a pure delete operation.

For completeness, let me also give definitions—in effect, expansions—for the relational INSERT, DELETE, and UPDATE shorthands:

Definition (INSERT): An operator, shorthand for a certain relational assignment, that inserts specified tuples into a specified relvar. The syntax is:

---

[15] As indicated in an aside earlier in this chapter, multiple assignment is discussed in detail in Chapter 11 of my book *Date on Database: Writings 2000-2006* (Apress, 2006). See also Appendix A to the present chapter. *Note:* SQL doesn't support explicit table assignment, as we already know; as a consequence, it doesn't support explicit multiple table assignment either, a fortiori. Nor does it support an INSERT / DELETE equivalent.

```
INSERT R rx ;
```

Here *R* is a relvar name; *rx* is a relational expression, denoting some relation *r'* of the same type as *R*; and the effect is to insert the tuples of *r'* into *R*. In other words, the INSERT invocation just shown is shorthand for the following explicit assignment:

```
R := R UNION ( rx ) ;
```

Note: It follows from this definition in terms of UNION that an attempt via INSERT to insert a tuple that's already present is not considered an error. For that reason, it's desirable to support a variant form of INSERT called disjoint INSERT (D_INSERT), in which *r* (the old value of *R*) and *r'* (the value of *rx*) are required to be disjoint. The specifics of that operator are straightforward, however, and I omit them here.

Definition (DELETE): An operator, shorthand for a certain relational assignment, that deletes specified tuples from a specified relvar. The syntax is:

```
DELETE R rx ;
```

Here *R* is a relvar name; *rx* is a relational expression, denoting some relation *r'* of the same type as *R*; and the effect is to delete the tuples of *r'* from *R*. In other words, the DELETE invocation just shown is shorthand for the following explicit assignment:

```
R := R MINUS ( rx ) ;
```

Aside: In practice it'll often be the case with DELETE that the expression *rx* takes the form *R* WHERE *bx* (where *bx* is a boolean expression, default TRUE) and thereby denotes some restriction of the current value of relvar *R*. In such a case we permit the explicit reference to the target *R* to be elided. For example, the following DELETE—

```
DELETE P P WHERE COLOR = 'Red' ;
```

—can be abbreviated to just:

```
DELETE P WHERE COLOR = 'Red' ;
```

End of aside.

Note: It follows from the foregoing definition in terms of MINUS that an attempt via DELETE to delete a tuple that's not present in the first place is not considered an error. For that reason, it's desirable to support a variant form of DELETE called included DELETE (I_DELETE), in which r' (the value of rx) is required to be included in r (the old value of R)—i.e., r' is required to be a subset of r. The specifics of that operator are straightforward, however, and I omit them here.

Definition (UPDATE): Loosely, an operator that updates a given set of attributes in a given set of tuples in a given relvar; a little less loosely, an operator that replaces a given set of tuples in a given relvar by another such set. It's shorthand for a certain relational assignment. The syntax is:

```
UPDATE R [ WHERE bx ] :
        { attribute assignment commalist } ;
```

Here R is a relvar name; bx is a boolean expression (default TRUE); the targets for the attribute assignments are attributes of relvar R; and the invocation just shown is shorthand for the following explicit assignment:

```
R := ( R [ WHERE NOT ( bx ) ] )
        UNION
     ( EXTEND R [ WHERE bx ] :
                { attribute assignment commalist } ) ;
```

Of course, the optional WHERE clauses appear in the expansion if and only the optional WHERE clause was specified in the original UPDATE statement as such.

Note: If you're not familiar with the relational EXTEND operator, please see, e.g., my book *SQL and Relational Theory: How to Write Accurate SQL Code*, 3rd edition (O'Reilly, 2016).

TABLE ASSIGNMENT IN SQL

As I've said, SQL has no direct analog of relational assignment—that is, it has no explicit table assignment operator as such—but of course it does have its table INSERT, DELETE, and UPDATE operators, each of which can be regarded as shorthand for a special case of an explicit (though unfortunately hypothetical) table assignment operator. Before saying anything further regarding these operators, however, let me spell out another assumption: To be specific, I'm going to assume from this point forward that all of the table values and table variables involved in any of these operations are free of duplicates, always. Why? Because I simply don't want to waste time trying to wrap my brain around the unnecessary and irrelevant complications that arise if such is not the case. Of course, if you want to try adjusting everything that follows to allow for the possibility that duplicates might occur after all, then I certainly won't stop you.

All right ... A few words, then, regarding INSERT, DELETE, and UPDATE:

- Loosely speaking, INSERT can be thought of as inserting a table value *t1* into a target table variable *T*; DELETE can be thought of as deleting a table value *t2* from a target table variable *T*; and UPDATE can be thought of as, first, deleting a table value *t2* from, and then inserting a table value *t1* into, a target table variable *T*. What's more, the table variable *T* and the table values *t1* and *t2* here are all supposed to be of the same type. It's a little difficult even to talk about this requirement in SQL, however, because (as we saw in the previous chapter) SQL doesn't really have a notion of tables—be they table values or table variables—actually having a type in the first place. Not even if they're "typed tables"!

- It's a little difficult to talk about *The Assignment Principle* in connection with these operators, too. Why? Because (again as we saw in the previous chapter) SQL doesn't support an "=" operator for tables, and so we can't even do the comparison after the assignment that the principle calls for—at least, not directly, and not very easily. (It doesn't support any other comparison operators for tables either, but "=" is the important one here.)

- That said, these operators certainly do all suffer in spirit, as it were, from violations of *The Assignment Principle* in connection with updates to base tables. But the violations in question are all due in the final analysis to violations that occur in connection with scalar assignments as discussed earlier in this chapter; there's no need to discuss them any further, therefore, and I won't.

■   However, INSERT and UPDATE (though not DELETE, for reasons to be explained) also suffer from *Assignment Principle* violations in connection with *views*—and these latter violations I certainly do want to examine further.

VIEW ASSIGNMENT IN SQL

Unfortunately SQL often seems to forget that views are tables,[16] and more specifically that—just like base tables, in fact—they're actually table *variables*. But table variables is what they are. After all, their value certainly varies over time. What's more, they can be directly updated, though the amount of direct view updating SQL supports is somewhat limited (certainly it's less than what's logically possible). It follows that view assignment is a special case of table assignment in general, where of course "view assignment" must be understood to mean view INSERT and/or view DELETE and/or view UPDATE, in SQL.

Let's look at some examples. *Note:* The examples that follow and the associated discussion are based, mostly, on material from the book *A Guide to the SQL Standard*, by Hugh Darwen and myself (4th edition, Addison-Wesley,1997).

I'll start with our usual suppliers base table (S), with sample value as follows:

SNO	SNAME	STATUS	CITY
S1	Smith	20	London
S2	Jones	10	Paris
S3	Blake	30	Paris
S4	Clark	20	London
S5	Adams	30	Athens

---

[16] Indeed, the very keywords TABLE and VIEW, as used in CREATE TABLE and CREATE VIEW, respectively, suggest rather strongly that SQL regards tables and views as different things. *Note:* The standard also refers to views—fairly ubiquitously, in fact—as "viewed tables," a term the true significance of which I for one find a little hard to grasp. Are we to take it that base tables aren't "viewed"? If so, then what? What does it mean for a table to be "viewed" or "not viewed"?

Now let me define a view, GS ("good suppliers"), in terms of—or as some might say, "on top of"—this base table:

```
CREATE VIEW GS AS
        SELECT SNO , STATUS , CITY
        FROM   S
        WHERE  STATUS > 15 ;
```

Given the sample value shown for S, view GS looks like this:

SNO	STATUS	CITY
S1	20	London
S3	30	Paris
S4	20	London
S5	30	Athens

Two asides here: First, if I was doing this "for real," then as a matter of good programming practice I would spell out the names of the columns of view GS in the corresponding CREATE VIEW statement, thus—CREATE VIEW GS (SNO, STATUS, CITY) AS ... , etc.—even though those names are exactly the ones that are inherited from the view defining expression anyway, in this particular case. Similarly, I would spell out the target column names in all of my INSERT examples, and I would probably include the DISTINCT option in all of my SELECT clauses. I choose not to include all of these desirable specifications in my examples purely in order to avoid unnecessary distractions.

Second, please note that I limit my attention throughout this chapter to views defined in terms of restriction and/or projection only, and hence to views defined in terms of just one underlying table *T*—there's no need for present purposes (perhaps fortunately!) to worry about what happens if the view in question is defined in terms of, say, join or union or difference, and hence involves two or more probably (but not necessarily) distinct underlying tables *T*, *T'*, *T''*, etc.[17] Also, let me remind you that projection in general "eliminates duplicates," loosely speaking. SQL's analog of projection doesn't, of course (unless the DISTINCT option is specified explicitly). However, I've already stated as a ground rule that none of the tables I'm going to be talking about in this chapter permits duplicates; as a consequence, I'm going to have to assume—

---

[17] Perhaps I should add for the record that no view can be defined directly or indirectly in terms of itself.

actually, in most cases I'll show as much explicitly—that every view to be discussed in this section retains at least one key of the unique table in terms of which it's immediately defined. (By the way, note the recursive nature of the foregoing! Since views can be defined in terms of views, it's important to understand that views too have keys just like base tables do, even though SQL provides no easy way to declare such things.) *End of asides.*

Example 1: Suppose we try to insert a row into view GS as follows:

```
INSERT
INTO    GS
VALUES ( 'S6' , 30 , 'Madrid' ) ;
```

This INSERT will effectively cause the following INSERT to be executed against the underlying base table S:

```
INSERT
INTO    S
VALUES ( 'S6' , NULL , 30 , 'Madrid' ) ;
```

In other words, conceptually what happens in this example is that the row specified in the original INSERT—i.e., the row to be inserted into view GS, viz., (S6,30,Madrid)—is extended with a null in the SNAME position, and that extended row is then inserted into the underlying base table S. A row without that extension (which is to say, the row specified in the original INSERT) thus appears in GS as required, and *The Assignment Principle* is thereby satisfied, for both base table S and view GS. (Of course, the original INSERT will fail, and no update will occur, if column SNAME is declared to be NOT NULL.)

> *Aside:* Actually SQL supports a mechanism by which column SNAME could have a nonnull default value declared for it, in which case the expanded INSERT on table S would specify DEFAULT instead of NULL. NULL is the default default. For simplicity I'll ignore this DEFAULT possibility in what follows. *End of aside.*

Example 2: Suppose we try to update a row in GS as follows:

```
UPDATE GS
SET     STATUS = 10
WHERE   SNO = 'S1' ;
```

Should this UPDATE be accepted? If it is—as indeed it will be, barring any explicit specification to the contrary (see Example 3)—then it'll have the effect of (a) updating the status for supplier S1 in the underlying base table S, thereby (b) removing the row for supplier S1 from view GS (since that row will no longer satisfy the defining condition for that view, viz., STATUS > 15), and hence (c) causing *The Assignment Principle* to be violated for view GS (though not for base table S).

Similarly, the following INSERT

```
INSERT
INTO    GS
VALUES ( 'S8' , 7 , 'Stockholm' ) ;
```

(if it's accepted, which by default it will be) will insert a new row into S, but no counterpart to that new row will appear in GS. As far as GS is concerned, therefore, the INSERT will have no effect, and again *The Assignment Principle* will be violated.

> *Aside:* To repeat, what the foregoing example shows is that INSERT and UPDATE operations on a view both have the potential to violate *The Assignment Principle* for the view in question. As noted earlier, however, DELETE operations don't suffer from this problem. The reason is that if a DELETE operation is requested on view *V*, then *rows that don't satisfy the defining condition for V won't even be considered as candidates for deletion.* By way of example, consider the following DELETE on view GS:
>
> ```
> DELETE
> FROM    GS
> WHERE   CITY = 'Paris' ;
> ```
>
> Now, the corresponding implicit DELETE on base table S might reasonably have been expected to look like this:
>
> ```
> DELETE
> FROM    S
> WHERE   CITY = 'Paris' ;
> ```
>
> But it doesn't. Instead, it looks like this:

```
DELETE
FROM    S
WHERE   CITY = 'Paris'
AND     STATUS > 15 ;
```

Thus, rows that don't satisfy the defining condition STATUS > 15 certainly won't be deleted: not from base table S, and therefore not from view GS either. In other words, DELETE operations are handled in SQL differently from (in fact, more correctly than) INSERT and UPDATE operations, if the target is a view rather than a base table. Let me spell the situation out: If view *V* is the target of a DELETE operation, then every row that the DELETE in question causes to be deleted from *T*—where *T* is the unique table in terms of which *V* is immediately defined[18]—will satisfy the defining condition for *V*; that row of *T* will therefore have a counterpart row in *V*, and that counterpart row will be deleted from *V*. Thus, there's no possibility of a DELETE operation on *V* causing a violation of *The Assignment Principle* with respect to either *V* or *T*.

Let me return for a moment to the implicit DELETE that might have been expected, in the foregoing example, to be the one performed on base table S:

```
DELETE
FROM    S
WHERE   CITY = 'Paris' ;
```

Now, if this expected DELETE on S had in fact been performed, then the original DELETE on GS would have had the effect of deleting a row from S (viz., the row for supplier S2) that had no counterpart in GS. However, given that the original DELETE was requested against GS, that DELETE was, logically, a request to delete rows from S with city Paris *and status greater than 15*. So if the DELETE did cause the row for supplier S2 to be deleted from S—which it would have done, if the DELETE on S just shown had in fact been the one performed—then it would have violated *The Assignment Principle* with respect to S. To spell out the details:

a.   The DELETE originally requested is, logically, a table assignment.

b.   The table assignment in question specifies the deletion from S of rows with city Paris and status greater than 15. In pseudocode:

```
S := s MINUS x ;
```

---

[18] *T* is unique by virtue of our assumption that all views are defined in terms of just one underlying table.

Here *s* is the previous value of S and *x* is all rows of *s* with city Paris and status greater than 15.

c. In the example, *x* contains just the row for supplier S3. So *The Assignment Principle* requires that after the assignment, the comparison

```
S = s MINUS ( row for S3 )
```

(pseudocode) should yield TRUE. But it won't, if the assignment actually did cause the row for supplier S2 to be deleted from S as well.

Of course, the obvious question is: Given that DELETE operations are treated "properly" as explained above, why aren't UPDATE operations treated the same way? Unfortunately, a moment's thought shows that the simple approach used in connection with DELETE (viz., basically just apending the view defining condition) doesn't work for UPDATE. Here again is the UPDATE on view GS from Example 2:

```
UPDATE GS
SET    STATUS = 10
WHERE  SNO = 'S1' ;
```

The actual UPDATE performed on base table S is:

```
UPDATE S
SET    STATUS = 10
WHERE  SNO = 'S1' ;
```

But suppose instead it had been as follows:

```
UPDATE S
SET    STATUS = 10
WHERE  SNO = 'S1'
AND    STATUS > 15 ;
```

Well, I think you can see that this revision would have made no difference—the row for supplier S1 would still have been updated and would still disappear from the view, thereby violating *The Assignment Principle* for that view.

What about INSERT operations? Well, here again is the INSERT on view GS from Example 2:

```
INSERT
INTO    GS
VALUES ( 'S8' , 7 , 'Stockholm' ) ;
```

As you can see, in this case there isn't even any syntactic slot, as it were, for appending the view defining condition; so here the approach used with DELETE isn't even available for use. *End of aside.*

Example 3: The CHECK option is provided to help avoid the kind of counterintuitive behavior illustrated by Example 2. If a given view definition includes the clause WITH CHECK OPTION, then UPDATEs and INSERTs on that view will be monitored to ensure that the updated or newly inserted rows satisfy the view defining condition (and if they don't, the UPDATE or INSERT in question will be rejected). Thus, if the definition of view GS is extended as follows—

```
CREATE VIEW GS AS
       SELECT SNO , STATUS , CITY
       FROM   S
       WHERE  STATUS > 15
       WITH CHECK OPTION ;
```

—then the UPDATE and INSERT shown in Example 2 will both fail, and there won't be any *Assignment Principle* violations.

Three asides: First, the defining condition for a given view is actually an integrity constraint on that view, logically speaking (though SQL never refers to it as such). It follows that, again logically speaking, the CHECK option should *always* be specified, at least if the view in question is ever to be updated (see the discussion of **The Golden Rule** in the next section). Unfortunately, however, SQL has no such requirement, as the very fact that the CHECK option is indeed an option makes all too clear.

Second, to repeat, the CHECK option is indeed optional. But there's no explicit syntax for the case where that option isn't exercised—I mean, SQL provides no explicit WITHOUT CHECK OPTION option, as it were. Quite apart from anything else, it's difficult even to talk about something that can be specified only by saying nothing! For such reasons I'd like to propose the following as a general rule regarding language design:

Every possible alternative that can be specified for a given feature should be specifiable in terms of explicit, concrete syntax.

In other words, there should be no alternatives that are specifiable only by saying nothing. I'll have more to say about this proposed rule in the next chapter.

Third, Syntax Rule 16 of Subclause 11.22 ("<view definition>") of the standard unfortunately states that the CHECK option can be specified only for views that the standard considers to be updatable. But the problem here is, a given view might be considered not updatable in one version of the standard but updatable in the next (indeed, exactly this change has already occurred in the standard in connection with certain kinds of views). Each new version of the standard thus has the potential to require all existing view definitions to be reexamined, with a view (pun intended) to seeing whether they now need the CHECK option to be added. *End of asides.*

Example 4: Now I want to modify the "good suppliers" example, as follows. First, I'll define another view MS ("medium suppliers") of base table S, thus:[19]

```
CREATE VIEW MS AS
       SELECT SNO , STATUS , CITY
       FROM    S
       WHERE   STATUS < 25 ;
```

Given our usual sample data, view MS will contain rows for suppliers S1, S2, and S4 (with status values 20, 10, and 20, respectively), and no other rows.

Next, I (re)define view GS ("good suppliers") in terms of MS instead of directly in terms of base table S, again deliberately omitting the CHECK option:

```
CREATE VIEW GS AS
       SELECT SNO , STATUS , CITY
       FROM    MS
       WHERE   STATUS > 15 ;
```

This view will contain rows for suppliers S1 and S4 only, both with status value 20. The following picture summarizes the situation at this point:

---

[19] Don't pay too much attention to the labels "good" and "medium" that I'm using in connection with these views. They're introduced merely as a kind of vague mnemonic device, that's all.

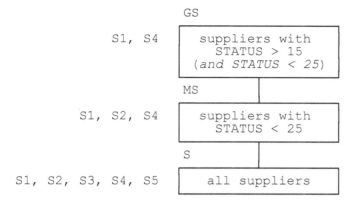

In other words, given our usual sample value for the supplier base table S, views MS and GS look like this:

MS

SNO	STATUS	CITY
S1	20	London
S2	10	Paris
S4	20	London

GS

SNO	STATUS	CITY
S1	20	London
S4	20	London

Now consider the following UPDATE on view GS:

```
UPDATE GS
SET    STATUS = STATUS + 20 ;
```

You should take a moment to figure out for yourself what happens here before reading any further. (Note carefully that, at least for the time being, neither view has the CHECK option specified.)

Well, I hope you can see that one surely rather surprising effect of this UPDATE is that view GS becomes empty!—suppliers S1 and S4 will each be updated in base table S to have status 40, and will thus no longer appear in view MS, and will thus no longer appear in view GS either, a fortiori.

Note very carefully the surprising and counterintuitive nature of the foregoing result: The user of view GS believes, quite rightly, that all suppliers visible in that view satisfy the condition STATUS > 15, and thus surely has a right to expect that *increasing* status values can't possibly violate that condition—yet the rows disappear, and *The Assignment Principle* is thereby violated, at least for view GS. (What about view MS?)

Example 5: With S, MS, and GS exactly as they were in Example 4—i.e., still no CHECK options—consider the following UPDATE on view GS:

```
UPDATE GS
SET    STATUS = STATUS - 20 ;
```

Again, one effect of this UPDATE is that GS becomes empty (though the result is arguably a little less surprising in this case, since at least this time status values are being *de*creased)—suppliers S1 and S4 will each be updated to have status 0, and will thus no longer satisfy the defining condition for view GS (though they'll still appear in view MS).[20] As in Example 2, however, the question is: Should a view UPDATE, or view INSERT, that obviously has the potential to violate the defining condition of the target view even be allowed to "succeed" in the first place?

LOCAL vs. CASCADED

In an attempt to avoid such surprises—be they truly unpleasant ones, as in Example 4, or merely annoying ones (?) as in Example 5—SQL:1992 added a LOCAL vs. CASCADED option to the CHECK option.[21] The new keyword, LOCAL or CASCADED, is specified between the WITH and CHECK keywords, and CASCADED is the default (the default, that is, if the CHECK option is specified at all; it's still possible to define views without it). The basic idea is as follows. Let view *V2* be defined in terms of view *V1*, thus:

```
CREATE VIEW V2 AS
       SELECT ...
       FROM   V1
       WHERE  ... ;
```

---

[20] As a thought experiment, suppose base table S is subject to the constraint that status values are supposed to be greater than zero. Then the UPDATE of Example 5 will fail—but will the constraint that makes it fail be visible to the user of view GS? Note that the user in question might well not be aware that view GS *is* a view, or that base table S even exists.

[21] I had some personal, albeit peripheral and somewhat inadvertent, involvement in the murky history of the LOCAL vs. CASCADED option. I won't tell the story here, however, since I've told it elsewhere. If you're interested, you can find it in Chapter 8 of my book *Fifty Years of Relational, and Other Database Writings: More Thoughts and Essays on Database Matters* (Technics Publications, 2020).

Further, let *T* be the unique base table ultimately underlying *V1*[22] (and therefore *V2* as well), where by "ultimately" I mean there might be any number *n* ($n \geq 0$) of intermediate views *V, V', V''*, etc., between *V1* and *T*. Then the question is: What checking is done in connection with updates on view *V2*? SQL's answer to this question is complicated. However, at least the following are both always true:

- Updates on *V2* are checked against all of the constraints that are checked for updates on *V1* (i.e., the unique view in terms of which *V2* is immediately defined). *Note:* Please pay careful attention to the wording here—"all of the constraints that are checked for updates on *V1*" does *not* necessarily include the defining condition for *V1*. (It should, of course, but it doesn't, not necessarily.)

- Updates on *V2* are checked against all of the constraints that are checked for updates on *T* (i.e., the unique base table in terms of which *V2* is ultimately defined).

So what we're left with is this two-part question: What about the constraints that apply to *V, V', V''*, etc. (i.e., the ones between *V1* and *T*)? And what about the constraints that apply to *V2* itself?

Before going any further, let me point out that checking against the constraints that apply to the underlying base table *T* must *obviously* be done—for otherwise an update on *V2* might cause *T* to violate its own constraints, a situation that clearly can't be tolerated (see **The Golden Rule**, discussed in detail in the next section). Moreover, there's another principle involved here, *The Principle of Interchangeability*, which in SQL terms can be stated as follows:

> **Definition (*The Principle of Interchangeability of Base Tables and Views*):** There should be no arbitrary and unnecessary distinctions between base tables and views; i.e., views should "look and feel" just like base tables so far as users are concerned.

And if this principle is to be taken seriously, the only possible answer—i.e., the only logically correct answer—to our two-part question is that *updates on V2 must be checked against all of the constraints that apply to V, V', V'', etc., as well*

---

[22] Footnote 18 applies here also.

as the ones that apply to V2 itself (plus the ones that apply to *V1* and *T*, of course, as previously discussed). SQL's answer to the question, however, is more "nuanced"—which is just a polite way of saying that (a) it's much more complicated, (b) it's at least partly illogical, and (c) to the extent that it's illogical, it's also incorrect. To spell the matter out, SQL's answer depends on what's specified in the definition of view *V2* (and please note the recursive aspects of the following rules):

- *Rule 1:* If *V2* has no CHECK option at all, then updates on *V2* are checked (a) against all of the constraints that are checked for updates on *V1* and *T* (as already stated), but (b) *not* against the defining condition for *V2*, and (c) *not* against the defining conditions for *V*, *V'*, *V''*, etc.

- *Rule 2:* If *V2* has LOCAL specified, then updates on *V2* are checked (a) against all of the constraints that are checked for updates on *V1* and *T* (as already stated), *and* (b) against the defining condition for *V2*, but (c) *not* against the defining conditions for *V*, *V'*, *V''*, etc.

- *Rule 3:* If *V2* has CASCADED specified, then updates on *V2* are checked (a) against all of the constraints that are checked for updates on *V1* and *T* (as already stated), *and* (b) against the defining condition for *V2*, *and* (c) against the defining conditions for *V*, *V'*, *V''*, etc.

The following picture summarizes the foregoing possibilities:[23]

	Rule 1 V2 nil	Rule 2 V2 LOCAL	Rule 3 V2 CASCADED
check T, V1	yes	yes	yes
check V2	no	yes	yes
check V, V', V''	no	no	yes

---

[23] I must make it clear, however, that the phrase—the abbreviation, really—"check *V2*" in the picture means checking the constraints that are checked for updates on *V2*, and those constraints do *not* necessarily include the defining condition for *V2*. A similar remark applies to "check *V*" and all of the other "check" phrases in the picture (except of course for "check *T*"—*T*, being a base table, doesn't have a defining condition).

Now, with respect to the example of good vs. medium suppliers, there are clearly nine possible combinations—each of GS and MS can have no CHECK option at all, or can have LOCAL specified, or (perhaps implicitly) can have CASCADED specified. The following picture summarizes the nine cases:

	none	LOCAL	CASCADED
none	Case 1	Case 2	Case 3
LOCAL	Case 4	Case 5	Case 6
CASCADED	Case 7	Case 8	Case 9

The possible specifications for GS are shown in the column at the left of the table, the possible specifications for MS are shown in the row along the top.

I now proceed to consider each of the nine cases in turn (not, I hasten to add, because I think you really need to understand all of those cases in detail, but merely to give some idea of the messes that can be caused by a failure to spell things out properly ahead of time—in this case, a failure to define properly ahead of time how assignment is supposed to work, and in particular a failure to realize the full significance of *The Assignment Principle*).

To fix our ideas, I'll consider what happens in each case with respect to the UPDATEs illustrated in Examples 4 and 5 specifically.[24] Here again are the UPDATEs in question (as you can see, I've labeled them "Update 1" and "Update 2" for purposes of future reference):

```
UPDATE GS
SET    STATUS = STATUS + 20 ;   /* "Update 1" */

UPDATE GS
SET    STATUS = STATUS - 20 ;   /* "Update 2" */
```

■ *Case 1:* GS none / MS none

I've already described this case—see Example 4 for Update 1 and Example 5 for Update 2.

---

[24] Naturally I've done my best to make those descriptions as accurate as I can, but I won't claim I haven't made any mistakes. In fact, if I have, then I think it just goes to prove my point.

■ *Case 2:* GS none / MS LOCAL

Clearly, the way to avoid the anomalous Case 1 behavior in connection with Update 1 is to have the system check updates on GS against the defining condition for MS. Suppose, therefore, that we specify LOCAL for MS (but not for GS, since the defining condition for GS is not an issue for Update 1). The question now is: Will that LOCAL specification be "inherited," as it were, by GS?—i.e., will it apply to updates on GS, as well as to updates on MS directly? By virtue of *Rules 1 and 2* taken together (see above), we see that the answer to this question is *yes*, and so Update 1 is rejected, as desired.

Note, however, that from the perspective of the GS user, Update 1 certainly *looks* reasonable; there's no way it can violate the GS defining condition (STATUS > 15). Yet it fails. Moreover, the user will presumably receive diagnostic information from the system to the effect that there's been a CHECK option violation—even though, so far as the user is concerned, there *is* no CHECK option. Thus, it could be argued that "encapsulation" (of a kind) has been violated: The user can't think in terms of view GS in isolation, but has to have some awareness of the definition of that view in terms of its underlying table (and similarly for that table in turn, if that table in turn is another view, and so on, recursively—assuming, of course, that all of those views also have a CHECK option).

Anyway, to repeat: Specifying LOCAL for MS does seem to solve the Update 1 problem. But does it really? Suppose MS were defined in terms of another view, *V* say (instead of directly in terms of base table S); suppose further that view *V* had no CHECK option. Then updates on GS would *not* be checked against the defining condition for view *V*. In particular, if MS were defined simply as SELECT * FROM *V* and *V* were defined like this:

```
CREATE VIEW V AS
      SELECT SNO , STATUS , CITY
      FROM   S
      WHERE  STATUS < 25 ;
```

(without a CHECK option, in other words, but otherwise just like our original MS), then specifying LOCAL for MS would be useless; Update 1 on GS would *not* be checked against the condition STATUS < 25, and the surprising result would still occur.

Note finally that Update 2 is certainly *not* rejected under Case 2. So Case 2 is far from being a perfect solution to our overall problem (namely, the problem of ensuring that all updates are treated correctly in all circumstances).

■ *Case 3:* GS none / MS CASCADED

Here again updates on GS will be checked against the defining condition for MS. They'll *also* be checked against the defining condition for the table underlying MS, if that table in turn is another view (and so on, recursively, regardless of whether those views have a CHECK option in turn), by virtue of *Rules 1 and 3* taken together. *Net effect:* Update 1 is treated correctly. However, Update 2 is not (the defining condition for GS is still violated).

■ *Case 4:* GS LOCAL / MS none

Now Update 2 is dealt with correctly but Update 1 isn't. Further, if MS were defined on top of another view *V* (instead of base table S), we would be in a Case 1, 2, or 3 situation, q.v., with *V* playing the role of MS and MS playing the role of GS.

The remaining five cases do all deal correctly with both Update 1 and Update 2. However, they're not all equally acceptable as solutions to the overall problem—viz., the problem of ensuring that all updates are treated correctly in all circumstances.

■ *Case 5:* GS LOCAL / MS LOCAL

Here, if another view *V* were to be defined on top of GS, we could be in a Case 2 or 8 situation, q.v., with *V* playing the role of GS and GS playing the role of MS.

- *Case 6:* GS LOCAL / MS CASCADED

  Here, if another view *V* were to be defined on top of GS, we would be in a Case 2, 5, or 8 situation, q.v., with *V* playing the role of GS and GS playing the role of MS.

- *Case 7:* GS CASCADED / MS none

  Here, if MS were defined on top of another view *V*, we could be in a Case 1 or 4 situation, q.v., with *V* playing the role of MS and MS playing the role of GS.

- *Case 8:* GS CASCADED / MS LOCAL

  Here, if MS were defined on top of another view *V*, we would be back in a Case 4, 5, or 6 situation, q.v., with *V* playing the role of MS and MS playing the role of GS.

- *Case 9:* GS CASCADED / MS CASCADED

  This case deals correctly with all updates, and continues to do so if additional views are introduced on top of GS or between GS and MS, provided those additional views also have the CASCADED check option.

  To summarize:

- If every view always has a CHECK option—which is the only safe case (and should have been the only case allowed from Day One, when SQL's view mechanism was first defined, but wasn't)—then all updates will be handled correctly, and it makes no difference whether those CHECK options are specified as LOCAL or CASCADED or any mixture.

- But if some views have no CHECK option, then in general some updates will be treated incorrectly and some *Assignment Principle* violations will occur.

■ And the same is true but possibly even more so (as it were) if some of the views that do have a CHECK option specify LOCAL instead of CASCADED.

How on earth was all of this complexity allowed to happen?[25]

THE GOLDEN RULE

The Golden Rule is another example of something that should have been clearly spelled out in the early days of "the database era" but wasn't. It's closely connected with assignment—specifically, relational (or table, in SQL) assignment—because it has to do with integrity constraints, and relational (or table, in SQL) assignment is the only way such constraints can possibly be violated. That's why I said near the beginning of this chapter, in the definition I gave for assignment in general, that "the operation overall is required to abide by **The Golden Rule** (if applicable)." To be specific, it's applicable, at least as far as we're concerned here, if and only if the assignment target is, specifically, a relvar in the database (or a table in the database, in SQL). Here are the pertinent definitions:

> **Definition (total relvar constraint):** The total relvar constraint for a given relvar is the logical AND of all of the constraints that mention (i.e., apply to) the relvar in question.[26]

---

[25] The question is rhetorical. In fact I know the answer (see footnote 21), but it's lengthy and tedious and would be out of place here. Suffice it to say that it has everything to do with my major theme: viz, that no one bothered early on to spell out how assignment logically ought to behave. *Note:* Of course, the foregoing represents my own opinion. For a contrary opinion—specifically, for an opinion of someone who, unlike me, is definitely an SQL apologist—I refer you to Chapter 6 ("*SQL and Relational Theory: A Response to Criticism*") of my book *Fifty Years of Relational, and Other Database Writings: More Thoughts and Essays on Database Matters* (Technics Publications, 2020).

[26] The phrase "all of the constraints" in this definition should really be "all of the constraints apart from type constraints." The type constraint for a given type is simply a definition of the set of values that go to make up the type in question. Such constraints, though important, have nothing to do with the present discussion, and apart from the present footnote I ignore them throughout this chapter. Just for the record, though: Type constraints are checked not on assignment but on invocation of the pertinent *selector* operation. For further details, see Chapter 4 ("Constraints and Predicates") of my book *Logic and Relational Theory: Thoughts and Essays on Database Matters* (Technics Publications, 2020).

Definition (total database constraint): The total database constraint for a given database is the logical AND of all of the constraints that mention (i.e., apply to) any relvar in the database in question.[27]

Definition (The Golden Rule): The rule—its name is set in boldface because of its fundamental importance—that no database is ever allowed to violate its own total database constraint. It follows that no relvar is ever allowed to violate its own total relvar constraint either, a fortiori.

Note: This latter, weaker requirement is often referred to as **The Golden Rule** as well, though strictly speaking it's merely a logical consequence of **The Golden Rule** proper.

Now, **The Golden Rule** is obviously tantamount to saying the following (in fact, it could be stated in this form):

No update operation must ever cause any database to acquire a value that makes its total database constraint evaluate to FALSE.

And this latter statement in turn, which as I've indicated is really just a slightly different formulation of **The Golden Rule** itself, implies that *all constraint checking must be immediate.* Why? Because it talks in terms of *update operations* (i.e., INSERT, DELETE, and UPDATE operations, loosely speaking), not in terms of transactions. It follows that **The Golden Rule** requires integrity constraints to be checked "immediately"—i.e., to be satisfied at statement boundaries[28]—and there's no notion of "deferred" or COMMIT-time integrity checking at all.

Detailed arguments in support of the foregoing position can be found in many places;[29] here I simply want to say something about SQL's violations of it. First, here in outline is how integrity checking works in SQL:

---

[27] The previous footnote applies here also.

[28] I realize I need to be more precise here, but making matters more precise depends to some extent on the particular language we're dealing with. For present purposes, suffice it to say that constraints must be satisfied at the end of each and every statement that contains no other statement nested syntactically inside itself. Or somewhat loosely: *Constraints must be satisfied at semicolons.* PS: Of course, the only statements for which constraints actually need to be checked are, specifically, ones that cause the database to be updated.

[29] See, e.g., the book and chapter mentioned in footnote 26.

■ At any given time, with respect to any given transaction, any given constraint is in either *immediate* mode or *deferred* mode.[30] *Immediate* mode means the constraint is checked immediately (i.e., on a statement by statement basis), *deferred* mode means it's checked at commit time.

■ Any given constraint definition can optionally include either or both of the following:

```
INITIALLY { IMMEDIATE | DEFERRED }
[ NOT ] DEFERRABLE
```

Explanation:

a. INITIALLY DEFERRED and NOT DEFERRABLE are mutually exclusive.

b. If the INITIALLY clause is omitted, INITIALLY IMMEDIATE is implied.

c. If INITIALLY IMMEDIATE is specified or implied, then if the DEFERRABLE clause is omitted, NOT DEFERRABLE is implied.

d. If INITIALLY DEFERRED is specified, then (to repeat) NOT DEFERRABLE mustn't be specified. DEFERRABLE can be specified, but is implied anyway.

e. INITIALLY IMMEDIATE and INITIALLY DEFERRED specify the initial mode of the constraint—i.e., its mode (a) immediately after it's defined and also (b) at the start of every transaction—as either *immediate* or *deferred*, respectively.

---

[30] That's what the standard says, but there are some cases (e.g., NOT NULL constraints, uniqueness constraints) where deferred mode seems to make no sense. Indeed, if table *T* has key *K* and key *K* is referenced by some foreign key *FK* somewhere, then the standard explicitly requires the key constraint for *K* to be NOT DEFERRABLE. In any case, it seems odd to me that the very same constraint should be allowed to have different modes in different transactions, or even—see later—different modes at different times in the same transaction. I would have thought rather that the mode that applies to a given constraint would be a property of the constraint in question, independent of any transaction. But then, of course, I disagree with the whole business of modes anyway.

      f. DEFERRABLE and NOT DEFERRABLE specify whether or not this constraint can ever be in *deferred* mode; DEFERRABLE means it can, NOT DEFERRABLE means it can't.

■ The SET CONSTRAINTS statement is used to change the mode for specified constraints with respect to the current transaction. The syntax is:

```
SET CONSTRAINTS { constraint name commalist | ALL }
                        { IMMEDIATE } DEFERRED } ;
```

Each constraint named must be DEFERRABLE; ALL is shorthand for "all deferrable constraints."

      a. If DEFERRED is specified, the mode of all indicated constraints is set to *deferred*.

      b. If IMMEDIATE is specified, the mode of all indicated constraints is set to *immediate*, and those constraints are then checked. If any such check fails, the SET CONSTRAINTS fails, and the mode of all indicated constraints remains unchanged.

■ COMMIT implies SET CONSTRAINTS ALL IMMEDIATE. If some implied integrity check then fails, the COMMIT fails, and the transaction is rolled back.

Well, what a very great deal of complexity could have been avoided if SQL had simply paid attention to **The Golden Rule**. Especially when you realize that, logically, none of these complicated features should ever be used.[31]

APPENDIX A: MULTIPLE ASSIGNMENT

Note: The following discussion is based on one in my book SQL and Relational Theory: How to Write Accurate SQL Code, 3rd edition (O'Reilly, 2015), where more details can be found. Also, for the purposes of the discussion I'll stick with

---

[31] Note that (to spell the point out) if the optional INITIALLY [IMMEDIATE | DEFERRED] and [NOT] DEFERRABLE specifications are both omitted, then INITIALLY IMMEDIATE and NOT DEFERRABLE are assumed, and all checking is thus immediate as it should be.

the SQL terminology of tables, rows, and columns, purely in order to avoid having to keep saying things like "relvars (or tables)."

The obvious question is: Why does SQL support deferred integrity checking in the first place? Presumably it does so because certain constraints—specifically, ones that interrelate two or more distinct base tables—suggest rather strongly that two or more distinct assignments are sometimes needed to keep the database in a state of integrity. For example, suppose the suppliers-and-parts database is subject to the following constraint:

```
CREATE ASSERTION SAME_CITY CHECK
  ( ( SELECT COUNT(*)
      FROM
      ( SELECT CITY FROM S WHERE SNO = 'S1'
        UNION
        SELECT CITY FROM P WHERE PNO = 'P1' )
                              AS POINTLESS ) < 2 ) ;
```

Well, this constraint looks a little complicated, but I hope you can see that what it says is merely that it must never be the case that supplier S1 and part P1 are in different cities.[32] Given our usual sample data values (in which supplier S1 and part P1 both currently have city London), then, each of the following SQL UPDATEs will fail under immediate checking:

```
UPDATE S
SET    CITY = 'Paris'
WHERE  SNO = 'S1' ;

UPDATE P
SET    CITY = 'Paris'
WHERE  PNO = 'P1' ;
```

In SQL, therefore, what we have to do is (a) make sure the SAME_CITY constraint is DEFERRABLE, (b) make sure the two UPDATEs are part of the same transaction, and (c) make sure also that the mode of the SAME_CITY constraint with respect to that transaction is *deferred*. Do note, however, that if we assume our usual sample values, then if the transaction asks the question "Are supplier S1 and part P1 in different cities?" between the two UPDATEs, it'll get the answer *yes*; in other words, it'll see the constraint being violated.

---

[32] As the example indicates, constraints are called *assertions* in SQL (at least some of the time, though not always); it is not known why this is. Also, the specification *AS POINTLESS* in the example is pointless but is required by the standard's syntax rules.

The relational (as opposed to SQL) solution to this problem is to make the two UPDATEs part of the same *multiple assignment*, thus:

```
UPDATE S
SET    CITY = 'Paris'
WHERE  SNO = 'S1' ,

UPDATE P
SET    CITY = 'Paris'
WHERE  PNO = 'P1' ;
```

Note the comma separator (hypothetical syntax as far as SQL is concerned, of course), which indicates that the end of the overall statement hasn't yet been reached. Multiple assignment thus effectively allows any number of individual assignments to be combined into one statement and performed "simultaneously," as it were, without any constraint checking being done until the end of the overall statement—in other words, until the semicolon is reached, loosely speaking. Observe in particular that now we can't even ask the question "Are supplier S1 and part P1 in different cities?" between the two UPDATEs, because now there's no concept of "between the two UPDATEs"—multiple assignment is a semantically atomic operation. Observe further that, given support for multiple assignment, there's no need for deferred integrity checking at all.

As noted earlier in this chapter, a much more extensive discussion of multiple assignment in general can be found in Chapter 11 of my book *Date on Database: Writings 2000-2006* (Apress, 2006). Here I just want to add one point, regarding SQL. The odd thing is, SQL has had support for a limited form of multiple assignment right from its very inception! By way of example, suppose table T has columns X and Y, both of type INT (integers), and consider the following UPDATE statement:

```
UPDATE T
SET    X = Y + 1 , Y = X + 1 ;
```

As noted earlier in this chapter, the SET clause in this UPDATE is clearly a multiple assignment, of a kind. (Note in particular that the source expressions Y+1 and X+1 are both evaluated before any assignments are done.) Likewise, if X and Y are SQL variables, the following SET statement—

```
SET ( X , Y ) = ( Y + 1 , X + 1 ) ;
```

—is also a multiple assignment. (Technically, in fact, it's a *row* assignment.) However, the specific kind of multiple assignment we need in order to deal with issues like the one described at the beginning of this appendix—i.e., the issue that certain integrity constraints interrelate distinct base tables, and hence that we sometimes need to be able to update the base tables in question without checking the constraints until all of those updates have been done—is, of course, multiple *table* assignment, and that's one kind that SQL doesn't support.

APPENDIX B: VALUES vs. VARIABLES

Here again is the definition—or the salient aspects of that definition, at any rate— that I gave for assignment at the beginning of the chapter:

> **Definition (assignment, abbreviated definition):** An operator (":=") that assigns a value (the *source*, denoted by some expression) to a variable (the *target*, denoted by the name of that variable). The source and target must be of the same type, and the operation overall is required to abide by (a) *The Assignment Principle* (always) as well as (b) **The Golden Rule** (if applicable).

As should be clear from this definition, any attempt to discuss assignment in general immediately has to face up to the fact that there's a logical difference between values and variables. In other words, given the generic assignment of v to V, we all understand that (a) the target V is a variable and (b) the source v is a value.[33] Indeed, the logical difference between values and variables is yet another of those notions that are so "obvious" and "universally understood" that we almost never bother to spell them out in practice.

To say it again, then, we all understand the difference between values and variables. Or do we? Note that the difference in question applies in particular to—among other things—relation values vs. relation variables (or table values vs. table variables, in SQL). And yet:

■ Sadly, Codd never, in all of his writings on the relational model, made this difference explicit. As a consequence, he repeatedly talked about "updating relations," a phrase that—if the unqualified term *relation* refers

---

[33] Of course, something else we all understand is that the target variable V is specified by means of its name, and the source value v is specified by means of some expression.

specifically to a relation value, which it certainly does elsewhere in Codd's own writings—doesn't make much sense.

■ By the same token, SQL never makes the difference between table values and variables explicit either. As a consequence, it commits the same kinds of mistakes as Codd did (mutatis mutandis), mistakes that have undeniably led to confusion in the past, and moreover can be observed in the SQL literature to this very day.

It might have been appropriate, therefore, to include another chapter in this "Stating the Obvious" series on values vs. variables—and I would do so, too, except that I've already written extensively about the issue elsewhere. To be specific:

■ Chapter 6 ("On the Logical Differences Between Types, Values, and Variables") of my book *Date on Database: Writings 2000-2006* (Apress, 2006) discusses the general case.

■ Chapter 4 ("To Be Is to Be a Value of a Variable") of my book *Fifty Years of Relational: More Thoughts and Essays on Database Matters* (Technics Publications, 2020) discusses the case of relation values and variables specifically.

Thus, I refer you to these two books for further discussion.

APPENDIX C: SQL ROW BAGS

As noted in Chapter 1, SQL supports a type generator it calls MULTISET, which allows the user to specify various specific multiset types (*multiset* being SQL's term for what I would much prefer, for a variety of reasons, to call a *bag*). Loosely speaking, a multiset or bag is like a set except that it permits duplicates (hence all sets are bags, but "most" bags aren't sets). The syntax for an invocation of SQL's MULTISET type generator is as follows:

```
<data type> MULTISET
```

For example, the invocation

```
INTEGER MULTISET
```

denotes the type "bag whose element type is INTEGER," or in other words just "bag of integers." Now, the specified <data type> can be any type supported by SQL;[34] in particular, it can be a *row* type (i.e., it can consist of an invocation of the SQL ROW type generator), thereby allowing the specification of "bag of rows of a given row type" as a legitimate bag type. The following example shows the declaration of an SQL variable of such a type:

```
DECLARE SRBV ROW ( SNO     VARCHAR(5)   ,
                   SNAME   VARCHAR(25)  ,
                   STATUS  INTEGER      ,
                   CITY    VARCHAR(20)  ) MULTISET ;
```

In this example, the text from the keyword ROW to the final closing parenthesis, inclusive, constitutes an invocation of the ROW type generator; that same text plus the additional keyword MULTISET constitutes an invocation of the MULTISET type generator; and SRBV ("suppliers row bag variable") is thereby declared to be an SQL variable of a certain "row bag" type.

Given the foregoing definition, the following is an example of a legitimate bag assignment:

```
SET SRBV = MULTISET ( SELECT SNO , SNAME , STATUS , CITY
                      FROM   S
                      WHERE  CITY = 'London' ) ;
```

(The expression on the right side here is an example of what the standard calls a *multiset value constructor*.)

Now, a row bag variable like SRBV does look something like a table variable (note that SQL tables do indeed contain bags of rows). However, an SQL row bag and an SQL table are *not* the same thing, because the operators that apply to the one aren't the same as the operators that apply to the other. In particular:

■ Explicit SET assignment is supported for bags but not for tables. Thus, for example, if we were to replace the name SRBV on the left side of the assignment shown above by the name S (denoting the suppliers base table), what would result wouldn't be a legitimate SQL statement.

---

[34] It can even be another multiset type.

■ At the same time, the INSERT, DELETE, and UPDATE "shorthands" are supported for tables but not for bags.

There are other differences too. For example, UNION applies to tables but not bags, while MULTISET UNION applies to bags but not tables.

Let's take a closer look at what's allowed to appear on the right side of a bag assignment in SQL. Basically, of course, it's a bag expression, or what SQL calls a *multiset value expression*, of the the same type as the bag variable whose name appears on the left side—or, at least, of a type that can be coerced to that type, but for simplicity let's agree to ignore the possibility of coercion. Also, bag expressions in general can involve any or all of the operators MULTISET UNION, MULTISET INTERSECT, and MULTISET EXCEPT (with an optional ALL or DISTINCT specification in each case),[35] but for simplicity again let's agree to ignore these possibilities as well.

Here then is the syntax—based on the BNF production rules for the standard's <multiset value expression> construct but simplified very drastically here—for what I'm calling a bag expression:

```
<bag expression>
    ::=   MULTISET ( <bag element commalist> )
        | MULTISET <subquery>
        | TABLE <subquery>
```

The first format effectively allows a bag to be specified by enumerating its elements (which will be rows, of course, if the bag in question is a row bag specifically). Here's an example:

```
MULTISET ( ROW ( 'S1' , 'Smith' , 20 , 'London' ) ,
           ROW ( 'S4' , 'Clark' , 20 , 'London' ) ,
           ROW ( 'S4' , 'Clark' , 20 , 'London' ) )
```

(This example is effectively a bag literal. Note, incidentally, that the specified bag does indeed contain rows, but those rows don't have any corresponding column names. Note too in the example that two of the rows are specified are duplicates of each other.)

The other two formats appear to be logically interchangeable, and we've already seen an example of one of them in the SET statement example above.

---

[35] The default if neither ALL nor DISTINCT is specified is ALL. Believe it or not! (I remind you that for regular UNION, INTERSECT, and EXCEPT, the default is DISTINCT.)

Other examples were given in Chapter 1. The following point was made in Chapter 1 as well: namely, that an expression of the form TABLE <subquery> returns a row bag, not a table, and there doesn't seem to be any way of "going the other way," as it were (i.e., converting a row bag into a table).

Finally, I can't resist mentioning the following. Let *mvx* be an SQL "multiset value expression." Then the following is a "multiset value function":

```
SET ( mvx )
```

This expression returns a result that's derived from *mvx* by eliminating redundant duplicates. Believe it or not, however (and despite that keyword SET), that result is still considered to be a bag, not a set. SQL doesn't have any set types.

Chapter 3

Naming

What's in a name? that which we call a rose
By any other name would smell as sweet.
　　　　　　　　　　　　　　　　—William Shakespeare:
　　　　　　　　　　　　　　　　Rome and Juliet (1595)

The Naming of Cats is a difficult matter.
　　　　　　　　　　　　　　　　　　—T. S. Eliot:
　　　　　　　　　　Old Possum's Book of Practical Cats (1939)

Today we have naming of parts.
　　　　　　　　　　　　　　　　　—Henry Reed:
　　　　　　　　　　　　　Lessons of the War (1946)

I've now discussed several concepts whose definitions are, or should be, so obvious that it hardly seems worth spelling them out explicitly. And yet, precisely because we don't usually bother to do so (spell out those definitions, I mean)—nor, perhaps I should add, do we bother to emphasize the fundamental importance of the concepts in question—SQL in particular manages to make serious mistakes in connection with all of them, as we've seen. Here are the issues I've discussed so far: equality; assignment; and, in connection with assignment, *The Assignment Principle*, **The Golden Rule**, and the logical difference between values and variables. Now we come to another big issue that you'd hardly think would need spelling out and whose significance you'd surely think would be obvious. Here it is. I call it *The Naming Principle*:

Definition (*The Naming Principle*): Everything we need to talk about should have a name.

In particular, of course, we need to talk about this principle itself, and thus it too should have a name—and so it does: viz., *The Naming Principle*. Indeed, it's very hard to talk about things that have no name! And yet examples of where the principle is violated abound. For instance, SQL includes a construct it calls an exception handler. But such handlers have no name, and so the SQL standard's explanation of them begins by saying, in effect, "Let *H* be a handler"[1] ... In other words, it finds, not very surprisingly, that it needs to introduce a name for the otherwise unnamed construct.

In this chapter I'll discuss a number of situations in which *The Naming Principle* is relevant but seems to have been ignored, or overlooked. The first has to do with language design.

LANGUAGE DESIGN

In the previous chapter I proposed the following as a rule that might profitably be adhered to in the design of any programming language:

> *Every possible alternative that can be specified for a given language feature should be specifiable in terms of explicit, concrete syntax.*

It seems to me that to adopt such a rule—which, in accordance with *The Naming Principle*, I hereby name *the explicitness rule*—would be a clear example of *The Naming Principle* in action, as it were. Not only that, but I think the rule is a strong candidate for inclusion in any list of principles for good language design. In fact, let me digress for a moment in connection with this latter point. Relational Model Prescription 26 of *The Third Manifesto*[2] ("RM Prescription 26" for short) reads as follows:

> ***D** shall be constructed according to well-established principles of **good language design**.*

To elaborate briefly: First of all, the name **D** is a generic name, standing for any database language that abides by, or conforms to, the prescriptions of the

---

[1] The standard's actual wording is "When the handler *H* ... is created"—wording that suggests rather strongly, at least to me, that the name *H* has already been defined (note the definite article in particular), which it hasn't.

[2] *The Third Manifesto*—"the *Manifesto*" for short—is described in detail in the book *Databases, Types, and the Relational Model: The Third Manifesto*, 3rd edition (Addison-Wesley, 2007)—"the *Manifesto* book" for short—by Hugh Darwen and myself. See also the website *www.thethirdmanifesto.com*.

Manifesto.[3] And in the *Manifesto* book Hugh Darwen and I go on to say the following—though the text is lightly edited here—regarding the foregoing RM Prescription 26:

> We recognize that this prescription isn't very precise as it stands, but it's difficult to make it more so. However, the general intent is just that **D** should avoid the many design errors we observe in SQL in particular [*and here we give a list of references to other writings by ourselves documenting some of those errors, and then go on to quote from one of those references as follows*]:
>
>> There are well established principles for the design of languages, but little evidence that SQL has been designed in accordance with any of them.
>>
>> Examples of such principles include *generality, parsimony, completeness, similarity, extensibility, openness*, and especially *orthogonality* [4]... In connection with orthogonality in particular, we'd like to say that we agree strongly with the following (italics as in the original):
>>
>>> Most languages are too big and intellectually unmanageable. The problems arise in part because the language is too restrictive; the number of rules needed to define a language increases when a general rule has additional rules attached to constrain its use in certain cases. (Ironically, these additional rules usually make the language *less* powerful.) ... *Power through simplicity, simplicity through generality, should be the guiding principle.*[5]

What I'm proposing, then, is that the foregoing list of language design principles, or rules—generality, parsimony, etc.—should be extended to include *explicitness* (by which I mean the explicitness rule, of course). Now, in the previous chapter I briefly discussed one aspect of SQL where the explicitness rule isn't followed: viz., views and the optional associated specification WITH

---

[3] In fact, we have right here, in that name **D**, another example of *The Naming Principle* in action (though this particular example doesn't have much to do with the subject of the present section, viz., the explicitness rule, as such). The point is, we clearly needed to introduce such a name in order to avoid, both in the *Manifesto* as such and in writings about it, clumsy, tedious, and repeated circumlocutions along the lines of "any language that abides by the prescriptions of this *Manifesto*" (etc., etc.).

[4] This list is taken from "Little Languages," which is a chapter in Jon Bentley's book *More Programming Pearls* (Addison-Wesley, 1988). *Note:* Orthogonality here refers to a language design principle, not to the database design principle of the same name. Regarding the former, see Chapter 18 ("A Note on Orthogonality") in my book *Relational Database Writings 1994-1997* (Addison-Wesley, 1998). Regarding the latter, see the introduction to this part of the present book.

[5] These splendid remarks are taken from the S-Algol Reference Manual, by R. Morrison (Internal Report CSR-80-81, Department of Computer Science, University of Edinburgh, February 1981).

CHECK OPTION. To be specific, SQL provides no explicit syntax for saying a given view *doesn't* have an associated CHECK option (there's no explicit WITHOUT CHECK OPTION or NO CHECK OPTION option, as it were). As a consequence, it's easy to find yourself, if you're not careful, saying clunky, convoluted things like "Suppose view *V* is defined without the WITH CHECK OPTION option."

Of course, supporting explicit syntax for every possible alternative doesn't mean that such explicit specifications always have to be used—i.e., it doesn't mean there can't be defaults. For example, suppose SQL were to introduce NO CHECK OPTION as a concrete alternative to WITH CHECK OPTION on a view definition. Then it would be perfectly possible—i.e., no harm would be done, and as a matter of fact it would be necessary anyway for reasons of backward compatibility—to include a syntax rule to the effect that if neither option is specified explicitly, then NO CHECK OPTION is assumed by default. Thus, another way of stating the explicitness rule is:

Syntax defaults should always be explicitly specifiable.[6]

Here are a few more examples of SQL violations of this rule:

- *NOT NULL:* The specification NOT NULL as part of the definition of column *C*—necessarily a column in a base table, incidentally—means that column *C* doesn't permit nulls.[7] But there's no way to state explicitly that a given column does permit nulls.

  > Aside: Of course, it's my position that nulls should never be permitted anyway; so it's rather unfortunate that the default, if NOT NULL isn't explicitly specified for a given column, is that the column in question does permit nulls. *End of aside.*

- *GRANT option:* In essence, GRANT in SQL is a statement that allows one user *U1* to grant certain access privileges to another user *U2*: for example, the privilege to perform INSERT operations (say) on the suppliers base

---

[6] I first proposed the explicitness rule in more or less this form in a paper I wrote way back in the early 1980s—"Some Principles of Good Language Design," originally published in ACM *SIGMOD Record 14*, No. 3 (November 1984) and then republished in my book *Relational Database: Selected Writings* (Addison-Wesley, 1986). Good grief—was it really that long ago?

[7] Note the appeal to *The Naming Principle* in this sentence!

table S (say). It also allows *U1* to grant to *U2* the right of granting that same privilege to a third user *U3*—please understand that I'm speaking rather loosely here!—by specifying WITH GRANT OPTION on the original GRANT statement. But there's no explicit syntax along the lines of WITHOUT GRANT OPTION or NO GRANT OPTION, and comments analogous to those made above in connection with the CHECK option apply here also, mutatis mutandis.

■ *Temporary tables:* When SQL was first defined, CREATE TABLE always created a "persistent" base table, or in other words one that remained in existence until it was explicitly destroyed by means a corresponding DROP TABLE. In 1992, however, CREATE TABLE was extended to support various kinds of "temporary" base tables as well, basically by specifying the keyword TEMPORARY between the CREATE and TABLE keywords. (I'm deliberately simplifying somewhat here. What I've just said is true enough—true to a first approximation, at any rate.) However, there's no corresponding PERSISTENT keyword; thus, the only way to specify that the base table being created is persistent is *not* to say it's temporary.

Adding Explicit Syntax Later

To continue with SQL for a moment, there are several SQL language features for which the default could originally be specified only by saying nothing, but explicit syntax corresponding to that default was added later. However, there can be traps in such an approach (adding explicit syntax later, I mean) ... Here are a few examples, some but not all of which involve such traps.

■ *WHERE:* The default WHERE clause is WHERE TRUE. However, a WHERE clause of that form couldn't be stated explicitly until SQL:1992, when type BOOLEAN, and in particular the boolean literal TRUE, were added to the language. No trap.

> *Aside:* In the interest of accuracy, I should explain that the SQL standard doesn't actually say the default WHERE clause is WHERE TRUE, even today. What it does say is as follows. First, it gives this "syntax rule" (paraphrased somewhat here):

The result if the optional <where clause> is omitted is a derived table whose row type *RT* is the row type of the result of the application of the immediately preceding <from clause>.[8]

(This rule is part of the definition of what the standard calls a <table expression>, a construct I'll have more to say about later.) Then it goes on to give the following "general rule" (again paraphrased slightly):

If the optional <where clause> is omitted, then the result is the same as the result of the immediately preceding <from clause>.

Now, it's not entirely clear to me why the first of these should be a "syntax rule" and the other a "general rule." I suppose the first one merely says the result is *some* derived table, while the second says *which particular* derived table that result table actually is; but saying the result is a derived table at all is surely a semantic issue, not a syntactic one. Of course, that first rule also specifies "the row type" of that result, but that too (a) is surely not a syntactic issue but a semantic one, and in any case (b) is surely implied by the second rule anyway. On reflection, in fact, I can't see what purpose is served by the first rule at all; the second seems to me to be saying all that needs to be said. But then I suppose "omitting the optional <where clause>" is a syntax issue, so maybe *some* syntax rule has to be included ... Well, personally, if I were responsible for the standard (which thankfully I'm not), I would rewrite the rules along the following lines:

(*Syntax rule*) Omitting the optional <where clause> is equivalent to specifying WHERE TRUE.

(*General rule*) If WHERE TRUE is specified or implied, the result is the same as the result of the immediately preceding <from clause>.

And then we could add the row type stuff to the general rule—not the syntax rule—if it really turned out to be needed for some reason, though I must say I don't know what such a reason might look like. (I mean, surely

---

[8] This rule is simplified slightly in SQL:2011. Now it just says: "The result is a derived table whose row type is the row type of the result of the immediately contained <from clause>." No use of the name *RT* to refer to the row type in question, as you can see, and (more important) no mention of the <where clause> at all—which is a reasonable simplification (and indeed an improvement), since whether a <where clause> is specified explicitly or not makes no difference to the fact that the result of the pertinent <table expression> is a derived table with the same row type as the result of the <from clause>.

that row type stuff should already have been included as part of the definition of the <from clause>. Why does it have to be repeated here?)

Be all that as it may, the standard's own syntax rule and the general rule, taken either together or separately, do boil down to saying what I've claimed: viz., that the default WHERE clause is WHERE TRUE.

As a kind of postscript to all of the above, let me now add that the syntax rule and general rule quoted above are taken from the standard's Subclause 7.4 ("<table expression>") and thus apply to WHERE clauses in the context of such expressions (which is to say, in the context of a SELECT – FROM – WHERE expression, loosely speaking). So my criticism, to the effect that the standard doesn't explicitly state that the default WHERE clause is WHERE TRUE, applies to that context specifically. By contrast (and rather oddly, I can't help thinking), the standard *does* state explicitly that the default WHERE clause is WHERE TRUE in the context of a DELETE statement! Here's the pertinent syntax rule from Subclause 14.7 ("<delete statement: searched>"):

> If WHERE <search condition> is not specified, then WHERE TRUE is implicit.

What makes this state of affairs odder still is that no exact analog of this rule is stated for UPDATE in Subclause 14.11 ("<update statement: searched>"). For the record, what this latter section does say is something like this: "If a <search condition> is not specified, then all rows of [the target named table] are the subject rows"—where "the subject rows" are the rows to which the UPDATE applies, of course.[9] *End of aside.*[10]

■ *HAVING:* The default HAVING clause is HAVING TRUE, as you'd probably expect. But it shouldn't be!—there's a logical glitch in SQL's definition of HAVING, and it shows up in this connection. Well, let me be a little bit more specific. The fact is, there are really two separate cases to

---

[9] This inconsistency of treatment between UPDATE vs. DELETE is remedied in SQL:2011.

[10] I've since been informed that "syntax rules" in the SQL standard don't really have to do with syntax, or at least not with syntax alone—rather, they have to do with everything that can be determined at compile time (assuming the compiler has access to the database catalog), which includes, in the case at hand, the type of the result. All right; but in that case they shouldn't be called syntax rules! As I'll be arguing at greater length later in this chapter, not only should everything we need to talk about have a name, but the names in question should be *appropriate*. PS: With respect to the specific issue at hand, viz., result types, I note that there could be situations (not in SQL, perhaps) where the precise type of the result isn't known until run time anyway. For example, such can sometimes be the case in the model of type inheritance developed by Hugh Darwen and myself in connection with *The Third Manifesto*. For further specifics, I refer you to my book *Type Inheritance and Relational Theory: Subtypes, Supertypes, and Substitutability* (O'Reilly, 2016).

consider. The first is as follows. Let *SFWG* be an SQL <table expression>—<table expression> being the term the standard uses in this context[11]—of the following generic form:

```
SELECT  items
FROM    tables
WHERE   boolean expression
GROUP   BY grouping columns
```

Observe that *SFWG* includes an explicit GROUP BY clause but no explicit HAVING clause. Then adding a HAVING clause of the form HAVING TRUE has no effect on the overall semantics; that is, the expression

```
SELECT  items
FROM    tables
WHERE   boolean expression
GROUP   BY grouping columns
HAVING  TRUE
```

is guaranteed to evaluate to the same result as *SFWG* does.

The second case, of course, is the case in which the original expression doesn't include a GROUP BY clause.[12] Thus, let *SFW* be an SQL <table expression> of the following generic form:

```
SELECT  items
FROM    tables
WHERE   boolean expression
```

Then adding a HAVING clause of the form HAVING TRUE does have an effect on the overall semantics; that is, the expression

```
SELECT  items
FROM    tables
WHERE   boolean expression
HAVING  TRUE
```

is *not* logically equivalent to the original expression *SFW*, in general.

---

[11] As noted previously, I'll have more to say regarding the SQL notion of table expressions in general later in this chapter (see the final section, "Syntax Categories").

[12] In passing, let me ask you a question: What explicit syntax do you think is equivalent to "no GROUP BY clause"? In other words, how can we state explicitly "don't do any grouping"?

So now let me focus on this second case. In fact this second case divides further into two subcases—one in which the result of the FROM and WHERE clauses taken together is empty, and one in which it's not. If it's not, there's no problem. For example, let table *T* be nonempty, and consider the following expression:

```
SELECT  COUNT(*)
FROM    T
```

(For simplicity I include no explicit WHERE clause.) This expression returns a table of one column and one row, containing the value *N*, where *N* is the cardinality of *T*. And the expression

```
SELECT  COUNT(*)
FROM    T
HAVING  TRUE
```

does exactly the same thing. *Explanation:* Specifying a HAVING clause without a GROUP BY clause against any table *T* causes *T* to be treated as a grouped table *GT*, where *GT* contains exactly one group. In the example, therefore, that single group contains all and only the rows of table *T*. The SELECT clause then does two things: First, it replaces the grouped table *GT* by another grouped table that also contains exactly one group (containing exactly one row, which contains in turn the cardinality *N*); second, it "ungroups" this latter grouped table, thereby producing the overall result already explained.[13]

So far so good, then; that is, if there's neither an explicit GROUP BY clause nor an explicit HAVING clause, assuming HAVING TRUE by default seems to be harmless—at least if the pertinent table *T* is nonempty. The problem comes in, of course, if table *T* is empty. Let me now explain this latter case (or try to; I deliberately present my argument one small step at a time). First, however, I apologize if you find my explanation hard to follow; it's always difficult to give a logical explanation of something if the something you're trying to explain isn't very logical in the first place. In fact there's another principle involved here, *The Principle of Incoherence*,

---

[13] In practice, of course, these two steps can be combined into one. But I think it helps the cause of understanding to realize that the SELECT clause does have to do two logically separate things—evaluate the various "SELECT items" (COUNT(*) in the example) *and* ungroup the grouped table that's its input.

defined in my book *The New Relational Database Dictionary* (O'Reilly, 2016) as follows:

> **Definition (*The Principle of Incoherence*):** A principle, sometimes invoked in defense of an attempt, successful or otherwise, at criticizing some technical proposal or position, to the effect that it's hard to criticize something coherently if what's being criticized is itself not very coherent in the first place—a state of affairs that goes some way toward explaining why such criticisms can often be longer (sometimes much longer) than what's being criticized. Occasionally referred to, a little unkindly, as *The Incoherent Principle*.

Anyway, here goes:

a. Let *GT* be a "grouped table" containing exactly *n* groups.

b. Then selecting *anything* from *GT* returns *n* rows.[14]

c. So if *GT* contains no groups, selecting anything from it returns no rows (i.e., the result is an empty table).

> *Aside:* Here's an example of this latter point. Let there be no shipments with a quantity greater than 1000 (as is indeed the case, given our usual sample value for the shipments table SP). Then the expression
>
> ```
> SELECT SNO , COUNT(*)
> FROM   SP
> WHERE  QTY > 1000
> GROUP  BY SNO
> ```
>
> returns an empty result. (The FROM and WHERE clauses together return a table with no rows; the GROUP BY clause applied to that intermediate result returns a grouped table with no groups; and the SELECT clause thus returns no rows.) *End of aside.*

---

[14] More precisely, it returns *at most n* rows. I'm tacitly assuming that either (a) those *n* rows are all distinct (which in practice they usually are, in this context) and/or (b) DISTINCT isn't specified (which in practice it usually isn't, in this context).

d. Specifying a HAVING clause without a GROUP BY clause against table *T* causes *T* to be treated as a grouped table *GT*.

e. If *T* is empty, it contains no rows, and *GT* should therefore contain no groups.

f. To repeat point d., HAVING without GROUP BY on table *T* causes *T* to be treated as a grouped table *GT*—but SQL says *GT* always contains exactly one group in this case, *even if T is empty*.[15] This behavior is logically incorrect; to repeat point e., if *T* contains no rows, then *GT* should contain no groups at all.

g. In accordance with point c., therefore, the overall result should be empty. But it isn't, in SQL.

h. As a concrete example of the point, therefore, the specific expression under discussion—

```
SELECT COUNT(*)
FROM    T
HAVING TRUE
```

—incorrectly returns a table of one column and one row, containing the value 0, if table *T* is empty.

Now, if we remove the HAVING clause from the SQL expression just shown, we're left with the following—

```
SELECT COUNT(*)
FROM    T
```

—and if *T* is empty, then of course this expression correctly returns a table of one column and one row, containing the value 0. Thus, omitting the HAVING clause and specifying HAVING TRUE *are* in fact equivalent after all, even in this arguably pathological case. But they shouldn't be!— at least, not in this (again) arguably pathological case. I'll leave it to you to

---

[15] Here's the actual wording from the standard: "If there are no grouping columns, then the result of the <group by clause> is the grouped table consisting of *T* as its only group." Note that there certainly aren't any grouping columns in the case at hand—i.e, SELECT COUNT(*) FROM *T* HAVING TRUE—because there's no GROUP BY clause.

decide whether there's a trap here or not (and if there is, then exactly what it is).

■ *MATCH:* I don't want to get into the semantics of this feature here (they're explained in Appendix A to Chapter 1)—I just want to say that the options originally available in connection with MATCH were FULL, PARTIAL, or neither, and of course the last of these was the default. Subsequently, however, the explicit keyword SIMPLE was introduced to mean neither FULL nor PARTIAL, and that made SIMPLE the default. No trap.

■ *DISTINCT vs. ALL:* Now this is an interesting one. As you surely know, SELECT DISTINCT eliminates duplicates and SELECT ALL doesn't, and ALL is the default. Similarly, UNION DISTINCT eliminates duplicates and UNION ALL doesn't—but here DISTINCT is the default! The reason for this anomaly goes all the way back to the original IBM dialect of SQL, which (a) didn't support the ALL keyword at all in these contexts and (b) did support the DISTINCT keyword for SELECT but not for UNION. The first version of the standard ("SQL/86") corrected these IBM SQL omissions, but—presumably for fear of causing existing implementations to become nonstandard—unfortunately didn't take the opportunity to tidy up the inconsistent default situation at the same time. Trap?[16]

■ *INSENSITIVE:* And this is a very strange one ... INSENSITIVE was introduced in SQL:1992 as an option that could be specified on a cursor declaration. In essence, what INSENSITIVE does is as follows. Let the cursor in question be C, and let the table being accessed via C be T. (Note the appeals here to *The Naming Principle* once again!) Then opening C effectively causes a separate copy of T to be created, and C then accesses that copy; thus, updates that affect T while C is open, either made via other cursors or not made via a cursor at all, won't be visible through this opening of C.[17]

---

[16] As noted in Chapter 2, I've recently learned that for MULTISET UNION (which wasn't added to the standard until SQL:2003) the default is ALL, not DISTINCT. Why?

[17] In other words, INSENSITIVE means the user wants not to "sense" such updates through cursor C. The keyword doesn't seem to capture this meaning very well, though; to me, at least, it suggests *indifference* ("go ahead, make your updates if you want to, see if I care—I'm a very insensitive person"). Something along the lines of NO INTERFERENCE or PROTECTED or PRIVATE might have been better (?).

Now, a cursor in SQL:1992 could be defined to be INSENSITIVE (explicitly) or "not INSENSITIVE" (implicitly, i.e., by saying nothing). Then in SQL:1999 the explicit keyword SENSITIVE was added—but SENSITIVE doesn't mean "not INSENSITIVE"![18] Loosely, (a) INSENSITIVE means independent updates mustn't be visible via this cursor, as already explained; (b) SENSITIVE means they must be; and (c) the default—for which the neologistic keyword ASENSITIVE is provided—means "don't care." Trap, I think.

UNNAMED OBJECTS

Direct and indeed more obvious violations of *The Naming Principle*—violations, I mean, that are more obvious than those caused by departures from the explicitness rule—are provided by objects that have no name at all. Objects with no name are a pain because, as I've more or less said already, there's no way—perhaps I should say no easy way, at any rate, and certainly no concise way—to refer to them.[19] Here are some SQL examples.

■ *Anonymous columns:* Let *TX* be an SQL expression denoting a table, and let *T* be the table that results from evaluating *TX*. Then *T* is allowed to have columns that have no name (thereby violating the prescriptions of the relational model, incidentally).[20] For example, given the familiar suppliers-and-parts database, the SQL expression

---

[18] Thereby violating another important principle, *The Principle of the Excluded Middle*—though such a violation is perhaps not all that surprising, coming as it does from a language that thinks nulls are a good idea. *Note: The Principle of the Excluded Middle* is one of the so called *Laws of Thought*. The other two are (a) *The Principle of Identity* (everything is equal to itself) and (b) *The Principle of Noncontradiction* (nothing possesses both a given property and the negation of that property). By the way, do you think SQL abides by these latter two principles? See Chapter 12 for further discussion!

[19] One example occurs in connection with the "Review" feature of Microsoft Word (at least the Office 2019 version of that product). That feature allows a reviewer to highlight and annotate a piece of text in a Microsoft Word document. It's very useful! What's truly annoying, though, is that those annotations have no identifying label or name by which they can be referenced elsewhere—in particular, in other annotations on the same document. What makes the situation even more annoying is that those annotations did have names in earlier versions of Word.

[20] They're also allowed to have two or more columns with the same name, but that particular failure on SQL's part is beyond the scope of this chapter. Well ... except, I suppose, inasmuch as *The Naming Principle* not only states that should everything have a name, but surely implies that such names should be unique as well, at least within some specific context. The relational model in particular certainly requires every attribute of every relation to have a name that's unique within the containing relation.

```
SELECT  SNO , SUM ( QTY )
FROM    SP
GROUP   BY SNO
```

returns a table of two columns, one named SNO and the other unnamed.

> *Aside:* SQL defenders might try to argue that the "anonymous" column here isn't really anonymous after all. For consider:
>
> 1. First of all, what the standard actually says in connection with such situations is that the column in question does have a name, a name that's required to be unique within its containing table but is otherwise "implementation dependent"—which, I would argue, effectively does mean it's unnamed for all practical purposes, since that implementation dependent name (a) isn't immediately visible to the user, (b) can only be discovered by the user with considerable difficulty, and (c) certainly can't be used elsewhere within the pertinent expression to refer to the column in question.[21]
>
> 2. Given that tables in SQL have a left to right ordering to their columns (another relational model violation, incidentally), the unnamed column in the example can certainly be identified *outside of the SQL context* as "the second column" of the table it appears in. But that qualifying phrase in italics is critical—the column in question obviously can't be referenced from inside some SQL expression by a name like "the second column." If you even think "the second column" is a name at all, that is, which I don't. (So what is it?)
>
> 3. In practice, commercial SQL products often invent names in such a situation. Oracle, for example, will invent the name "SUM(QTY)" for the otherwise unnamed column in the table resulting from the expression shown above. Note carefully, however, that such an invented name doesn't conform to the rules for what the standard calls a "regular identifier," and I very much doubt whether it can be used elsewhere in some SQL expression to reference the column in question without causing a syntax error.

---

[21] Exactly how such a name can be discovered is beyond the scope of this discussion. Suffice it to say that it involves access by means of special SQL statements such as GET DESCRIPTOR to the pertinent "SQL Descriptor Area" or SQLDA.

> All in all, I stand by my position that such columns are effectively unnamed. *End of aside*.

■ *Privileges:* As explained in the previous section, the GRANT statement is used to grant privileges in SQL. Here's an example:

```
GRANT INSERT ON S TO Monty_Python ;
```

What's happening here is that "the current user"—i.e., the user executing the GRANT statement—is granting the privilege of performing INSERT operations on the suppliers base table S to the user Monty_Python. Note, however, that the privilege in question has no explicit name of its own—it can be identified only by the combination of the grantor name (i.e., the name of the user who executed the GRANT statement), plus the grantee name (Monty_Python in the example), plus the name of the granted operation (INSERT in the example), plus the name of the object on which the privilege was granted (table S in the example).

In order to appreciate the significance of the foregoing point, consider the following scenario. Suppose users *U1* and *U2* both grant the same privilege *P* on the same object *O* to user *U3*, and user *U1* then revokes *P* on *O* from user *U3*.[22] In this example, *U3* is granted "the same privilege" twice, as it were; the REVOKE then drops one of them, but not the other, and so *U3* still holds *P* on *O*.

In fact, mention of REVOKE lends weight to my general point. If privileges were named, the privileges granted to *U3* by *U1* and *U2* in the foregoing example would have two different names—*P1* and *P2*, say—and the REVOKE could then take the following simple but hypothetical form:

```
REVOKE P1 ;
```

(say). As it is, however, the REVOKE actually has to take this rather more complicated form:

```
REVOKE INSERT ON S FROM Monty_Python ;
```

This REVOKE revokes, specifically, the INSERT privilege held on S by Monty_Python that was granted by "the current user"—in other words, the

---

[22] "The same privilege *P*"? What exactly do you think that symbol "*P*" is here?

specific privilege identified by the combination of "current user name" + Monty_Python + INSERT + S.

■   *Exception handlers:* I mentioned this one before—I repeat it here merely for ease of subsequent reference. Basically, an exception handler in SQL is a user supplied procedure that the system is supposed to invoke if a specified exception (such as "data not found" or an error of some kind) occurs at run time. But such handlers have no name, and so the explanation of them in the SQL standard begins by saying, in effect, "Let *H* be a handler" ... In other words, it introduces a name for the otherwise anonymous construct! So why not just give it a name in the first place?

Object Orientation

I've used the term *object* several times in this chapter already, but always in its normal, generic, natural language sense, not in the special sense in which it's used in the world of "object orientation" (OO for short). Now, however, I do want to say something about the OO world, and my use of the term *object* from this point forward should thus be understood in that special OO sense, barring explicit statements to the contrary.

OO in general is chockablock with violations of *The Naming Principle*. However, OO comes in numerous different varieties—there's no single, well defined, unanimously accepted "OO model." In fact, there isn't anything that even comes close, in my opinion.[23] Nor is there a single, unanimously accepted OO language. For example, Wikipedia lists all of the following as "significant OO languages": Java; C++; C#; Python; PHP; JavaScript; Ruby; Perl; Object Pascal; Objective-C; Dart; Swift; Scala; Common Lisp; MATLAB; and Smalltalk. Thus, the generic remarks regarding OO in the remainder of this chapter might or might not be applicable in any given case. But they're broadly correct.

First of all, then, I've said I'll be using the term *object* "in the special OO sense." But what is that special sense? Most writers in this field seem at least to agree that objects in general are of two kinds, mutable and immutable. All right, then; but as far as I can tell, a "mutable object" is just a variable; an "immutable object" is just a value; and "mutable" just means updatable. If these loose definitions are correct, then for immutable objects—in other words, values—it's

---

[23] For a detailed discussion and critique of one attempt at defining such a thing, see Chapter 9 ("An Overview and Analysis of ODMG") of the present book.

clearly sufficient that they be denotable by means of appropriate *literals*, or what some writers like to call self-defining symbols. For example, the literal or self-defining symbol 3 clearly and unambiguously denotes such an object, and no further name is needed.

Mutable objects are a different kettle of fish, though. As I've said, mutable objects are basically variables—by which I mean, specifically, variables in the usual programming language sense—and of course variables usually do have names. But mutable objects aren't *just* variables, they're variables of a certain special kind. To be specific, they're what some writers refer to as *explicit dynamic* variables (like "based variables" in PL/I, for example, if you happen to be familiar with that language). The storage for explicit dynamic variables, and hence for mutable objects, is allocated at run time by explicit program action. As a consequence:

a. There can be any number of "instances" of such objects in existence simultaneously at run time;

b. Those "instances" have, and can have, no distinguishing name of their own in the conventional sense;

and therefore

c. Those "instances" are, and can be, referenced only by their *address*, also known as their *object ID*.

So mutable objects are unnamed, and OO in general and OO programming in particular are therefore heavily reliant on object IDs, or in other words on *pointers*. (It's true that OO languages are often designed in such a way as to conceal that reliance from users, at least somewhat, but the fact remains that the reliance is there.[24]) And so the first violation of *The Naming Principle* in the OO world arises in connection with objects themselves.

---

[24] What I mean by this remark is the following. Let V be a conventional programming language variable, and let V contain as its current value the object ID o of some mutable object O. Then OO languages—not to mention OO writers and speakers—very typically describe variable V as having as its current value that object O as such, instead of that pointer o to O. Note, however, that this verbal sleight of hand breaks down if two distinct variables $V1$ and $V2$ both contain the same object ID o, and the corresponding object O is then updated via one of the two, say $V1$. Clearly, that update will be instantaneously visible via the other variable $V2$ as well, a state of affairs that certainly can't be, and mustn't be, "concealed from the user."

The second violation occurs in connection with *methods*. Methods—the term seems to me quite inappropriate, but let that pass[25]—are basically just operators; for example, there might be a method for retrieving the CITY value corresponding to a specified supplier object. But such methods are typically unnamed! In a conventional programming language, the operator just mentioned might reasonably be called CITY_OF, and a typical invocation might look as shown on the right side of this assignment statement:

```
CV := CITY_OF ( sx ) ;
```

Here *sx* is an expression that denotes the supplier we're interested in, and CV is a variable to which the pertinent CITY value is to be assigned.[26] But the analog of this statement in an OO language is likely to look more like this:

```
sid . GET_CITY : CV .
```

Here *sid* is an expression that returns a pointer to the supplier we're interested in; GET_CITY is the name of a parameter to the method we want to invoke; and CV is the corresponding argument. Thus, the method in question is applied to, or invoked on, the object whose object ID is given by the value of the expression *sid*, and the effect is to update—i.e., assign to—the object, or variable, CV accordingly.[27] But what's "the method in question"? What method is it that we're talking about here? The invocation doesn't mention that method explicitly, because it can't—the method has no name! Instead, it's identified by its "signature," which for present purposes we can assume (but please understand that this definition, such as it is, is wildly oversimplified) consists of the combination of:

a. The type, or "class," of the object the method will be applied to at run time (the supplier class, in the example), and

---

[25] It does have a certain pedigree, though, of a kind. To be specific, IBM introduced the term (also inappropriate, in my opinion) *access method* in connection with its System/360 computers to refer to those components of the operating system that had to do with data storage and retrieval.

[26] In a language based on the tuple relational calculus, dot qualification might be used instead—i.e., we might write *sx*.CITY instead of CITY_OF (*sx*). I'll have more to say regarding the tuple calculus in the next section. *Note:* OO languages sometimes use dot qualification too, as we'll see in just a moment, though the precise significance of those OO dots is arguably somewhat different from that of those tuple calculus ones.

[27] Or more likely to update the object whose object ID is contained in CV.

b. The name(s) of the parameter(s) to that method (GET_CITY, in the example).

> *Aside:* OO languages typically don't talk about "methods being applied to" or "invoked on" objects, they talk about *messages* being *sent* to objects. In the foregoing example, therefore, a message is being sent to the pertinent supplier object saying "execute the pertinent method on yourself, using the specified argument for the specified parameter." Observe how difficult—personally, I'd say how *unnecessarily* difficult—this idea is just to explain, given that we can't refer to either "the pertinent object" or "the pertinent method" by name. *End of aside.*

By the way, note that it follows from the foregoing notion of methods being identified by "signatures" that there mustn't be—in fact, there can't be—two distinct methods, each applying to suppliers and each having the same parameter names.

And yet ... As it turns out, it *is* possible to have two distinct methods, each applying to suppliers and each having *no parameters at all*—in which case the methods typically do have to be given distinguishing names of their own, after all. Thus, some methods do have names after all! Typical examples might be a NEW method (used to create "new instances" of the pertinent object class) and a DISPLAY method (used to display the pertinent object on the screen). Why?

So methods are typically unnamed (though not always). But that's not the end of the story. In the supplier city example, the specific object to which the method is applied—the specific object to which the message is sent, if you prefer—also constitutes an argument to the method invocation, and thus corresponds to a certain parameter. Unlike the other parameters, however, that particular parameter is typically unnamed. Instead, it's typically denoted, inside the code that implements the method in question, by the reserved keyword SELF.[28] Well ... I guess it does have a name, therefore, but that name is always SELF, in every method. Why?

---

[28] As Bruce Lindsay of IBM once remarked to me, object systems are obsessed with self.

REFERENTS

I'd like to close this chapter by briefly discussing a couple of further issues arising from (a) the concept of naming in general and (b) *The Naming Principle* in particular. The first, to be discussed in the present section, is the issue of *referents*.

The Naming Principle says that everything we need to talk about should have a name. But there's a converse, too: Every name should refer to something; that is, every name should have a *referent*, viz., the thing it refers to. Predictably, there's at least one situation in which SQL falls foul of this one, too. To be specific, SQL makes a great deal of use of something it calls a *correlation name*—but it isn't entirely clear, and frankly never was clear, exactly what it is that such names *name*. Certainly there's no such thing in SQL as a "correlation."

Let me state for the record what I think is going on here:

- In the tuple relational calculus (tuple calculus for short),[29] there are *range variables* (which are variables in the sense of logic, please note, not variables in the ordinary programming language sense). Here by way of example is a tuple calculus formulation of the query "Get supplier numbers for suppliers in Paris who supply part P2":

```
RANGEVAR SX   RANGES OVER S  ;
RANGEVAR SPX RANGES OVER SP ;

{ SX.SNO } WHERE SX.CITY = 'Paris' AND EXISTS SPX
              ( SPX.SNO = SX.SNO AND SPX.PNO = 'P2' )
```

In this example the first two lines are definitions, defining SX and SPX as range variables that range over S and SP, respectively. What those definitions mean is that, at any given time, the value of SX is some tuple in the relation that's the value of relvar S at that time; likewise, the value of SPX is some tuple in the relation that's the value of relvar SP at that time.

- Now, one possible SQL formulation of the foregoing query looks like this:

---

[29] On which SQL is at least partly based, despite documented claims to the contrary. See, e.g., the very first published paper on what ultimately became SQL—viz., "SEQUEL: A Structured English Query Language," by Donald D. Chamberlin and Raymond F. Boyce (Proc. 1974 ACM SIGMOD Workshop on Data Description, Access, and Control, May 1974)—where such contrary claims are stated explicitly.

```
SELECT  SX.SNO
FROM    S AS SX
WHERE   SX.CITY = 'Paris'
AND     EXISTS
      ( SELECT *
        FROM    SP AS SPX
        WHERE   SPX.SNO = SX.SNO
        AND     SPX.PNO = 'P2' ) )
```

And it's clear from comparing the two formulations that the symbols "SX" and "SPX" are serving the same purpose in both (in particular, the AS specifications in the SQL formulation correspond to the RANGEVAR definitions in the calculus version). So I would say it's obvious in the SQL version that those two symbols are range variable names, and they denote range variables. But SQL calls them correlation names, and it never says what they denote at all.

Well, actually, what I've just said isn't entirely true. In fact the standard does try to explain what a correlation name denotes, but it gets it wrong. (Or maybe I should say, a little more charitably perhaps, that it gets itself into a muddle.) In Subclause 5.4 ("Names and identifiers") we find this:

An <identifier> that is a <correlation name> is associated with a table ... [A] <correlation name> identifies a table.

And in Subclause 4.14.6 ("Operations involving tables") we find the following (which, I can't help noting, raises all kinds of further points that simply cry out for further clarification, but let that pass):

An operation involving a table *T* may define a *range variable RV* that ranges over rows of *T*, referencing each row in turn in an implementation dependent order. Thus, each reference to *RV* references exactly one row of *T*. *T* is said to be the *table associated with RV*.

And in Subclause 7.6 ("<table reference>") we find:

If a <table factor> *TF* simply contains a <correlation name>, then let *RV* be that <correlation name>; otherwise, let *RV* be the <table or query name> simply contained in *TF*. *RV* is a range variable.

According to these quotes, then, a correlation name *is associated with* a table (and vice versa), and/or it *identifies* a table, and/or it *is* a range variable. I don't think these statements can all be correct! Well, let's think about it:

- I suppose *is associated with a table* is correct, though it's pretty loose. But given that the term *table* in SQL is often taken to refer to a base table specifically, the fact that the table in question here *doesn't* have to be a base table specifically would probably have been worth calling out explicitly. And does that "table in question" have to be a table variable (which is what "table" in SQL often means, though not always), or can it be just a table value?[30] And does that "table in question" have to be unique, or can the same correlation name be "associated" with two or more different tables? At least at different times?

- *Identifies a table* is definitely wrong, except inasmuch as (to be charitable again) I suppose that if any given correlation name *CN* does happen to be associated with just one table *T*, then we might say that, given *CN*, the associated unique *T* is thereby implicitly "identified." But of course it's not correct to say that "any given correlation name *CN* is associated with just one table *T*," because the definitional phrase AS *CN* (which is SQL's analog of a range variable definition, recall) can appear repeatedly, with different connotations, in any number of different contexts—even, let me point out, different contexts within the same overall SQL expression.[31]

- *Is a range variable* is wrong, too—"is a range variable name" would be closer to the truth. But if a correlation name is indeed just a range variable name, then a "correlation" is presumably just a range variable; so why do we have to have all of this talk of "correlations" at all? And why does the standard have both "correlations" and range variables, anyway? Are there two concepts here or only one?

---

[30] Actually it *is* just a table value. For example, the specification FROM S AS SX within the SQL expression on page 119 means that, at any given time, the value of SX is some row in the table that's the value of S at that time.

[31] So now I've answered some of the questions I raised in the previous bullet item. But my point is, the *standard* doesn't answer them!—at least, not in those sections where we'd surely expect to find such answers, which is to say in the sections defining the terms in question.

SYNTAX CATEGORIES

To say it again, *The Naming Principle* says that everything we need to refer to should have a name—and now I'd like to add that, insofar as possible, those names should be appropriate ones, too. Hugh Darwen once complained to me, in a private communication, about what he described as "the outstanding and widespread inability of people in our business to come up with appropriate terminology." Sadly, I think this complaint is all too justified. And one place where *in*appropriate terminology seems to be all too prevalent is in the choice of names for syntax categories (categories for short) in the SQL standard.

Before getting into SQL specifics, though, let me give an example that's a little closer to home, in a sense. Here's a rather heavily edited extract from the BNF grammar that Hugh Darwen and I constructed for our relational language **Tutorial D**:[32]

```
<assignment>
   ::=   <assign commalist> ;

<assign>
   ::=   <name> := <expression>

<expression>
   ::=   <with expression>
       | <nonwith expression>

<with expression>
   ::=   <with clause> : <expression>

<with clause>
   ::=   WITH ( <name intro commalist> )

<name intro>
   ::=   <introduced name> := <expression>
```

And an *<introduced name>* is basically just a *<name>*. As I hope you can see, therefore, a *<name intro>* is syntactically indistinguishable from an *<assign>*, and what goes between the parentheses in a WITH clause is thus syntactically indistinguishable from a *<assign commalist>*. With hindsight, therefore, I think I'd like to revise the foregoing production rules accordingly. To be specific, I'd like to drop the one for *<name intro>*, and I'd like to revise the one for *<with clause>* to read as follows:

---

[32] A complete grammar can be found at the website *www.thethirdmanifesto.com*.

```
<with clause>
   ::=   WITH ( <assign commalist> )
```

Aside: Let me add two points here, the first of which might serve as some slight excuse for the poor taste in BNF design illustrated by the foregoing example, though I don't think the second does. First, then, there's an important logical difference between the *<assign commalist>* appearing in an *<assignment>* and the *<assign commalist>* (if you'll now let me refer to it as such) appearing in a WITH clause, which can be stated briefly, albeit not entirely accurately, as follows:

- In the former case the individual *<assign>*s are executed in parallel.

- In the latter case they're executed in sequence.[33]

Thus, an argument could be made—though not by me—that the two cases should "look different" in the BNF.

The second point is this: I invented the syntax categories *<name intro>* and *<introduced name>* because I intended, and assumed, that those "introduced names" would be just that, viz., names introduced on the fly (as it were) that were purely local to the expression of which the WITH clause was a part.[34] But it's a very bad idea to name syntax categories on the basis of such intentions and assumptions! In particular, suppose we found we sometimes needed to allow the target of an *<assign>* inside a *<with clause>* *not* to be local to the expression of which that *<with clause>* is a part; then the name used to refer to that target would quite clearly not be "introduced" in the foregoing sense. So "introduced name" was quite simply an inappropriate choice on my part, and I hereby apologize to anyone for whom that choice by me caused any kind of grief. *End of aside.*

Now I turn to SQL. (The remainder of this section is simplified in various ways in order to avoid distracting irrelevancies, but the text is accurate in all essential respects.) I'll begin with a trivial but to me glaring example. SQL

---

[33] Precisely for that reason, in fact, I'd really prefer to define what goes between the parentheses in a *<with clause>* as an *<assign semicolonlist>* instead of an *<assign commalist>*—but that's a separate issue, beyond the scope of the present discussion.

[34] I also used that same category *<introduced name>* in other contexts—e.g., within a RENAME or GROUP invocation—for similar though not identical reasons. That was probably a bad choice on my part too, again for similar though not identical reasons.

uses CREATE TABLE to create a base table and CREATE VIEW to create a view. But base tables and views are both tables—more precisely, they're both table variables—and to a very large extent, therefore, what's sauce for the goose really ought to be sauce for the gander as well.[35] But it often isn't, in SQL. Here's a hugely trimmed and otherwise edited excerpt from the standard's BNF grammar for CREATE TABLE:

```
<table definition>
   ::=    CREATE TABLE <table name>
                    ( <table element commalist> ) ;

<table element>
   ::=    <column definition>
        | <table constraint definition>

<column definition>
   ::=    <column name> <data type name>

<table constraint definition>
   ::=    [ CONSTRAINT <constraint name> ] <table constraint>

<table constraint>
   ::=    <unique constraint definition>
        | <referential constraint definition>
        | <check constraint definition>
```

Observe from the foregoing how various syntax categories—<table name>, <table element>, <table constraint>, and others not mentioned here—are given names that tacitly assume that the term "table" refers to a base table specifically and not a view.[36] Could that tacit assumption be what lies behind the fact that, in most cases, those categories—or the concepts denoted by those categories, rather—don't have any counterpart when it comes to views? Here's the syntax for CREATE VIEW:

---

[35] One reviewer objected at this point that a view can surely be regarded as a variable only if it's an "updatable view" specifically. Well, yes—but it's my position (explained in detail in my book *View Updating and Relational Theory: Solving the View Update Problem*, O'Reilly, 2013) that *all* views are updatable in principle, although it's true that certain updates on certain views will fail on integrity constraint violations. In other words, I reject the concept of an "updatable view" (at least if it's meant to imply that there's such a thing as a nonupdatable view). And in any case a view is certainly a variable in the sense that its value can change if the value of some underlying table changes.

[36] Not to mention the fact that the concrete syntax involved in these operators (CREATE TABLE vs. CREATE VIEW) sends very much the same message.

```
<view definition>
    ::=    CREATE VIEW <table name> [ <view column list> ]
              AS <query expression>
              [ WITH [ LOCAL | CASCADED ] CHECK OPTION ] ;

<view column>
    ::= <column name>
```

Well, it's interesting to see that view names are at least defined to be <table name>s, but that's where the parallel ends. In particular, view definitions don't have either <column definition>s or <table constraint>s. Now, it can be argued—and I'm sure SQL apologists would argue—that they don't need these things, because the column definitions and table constraints that apply to a given view are all, in the final analysis, derived from those that apply to the base table(s) in terms of which the view in question is defined.[37] But remember *The Principle of Interchangeability*, which I discussed in Chapter 2:

> **Definition (*The Principle of Interchangeability of Base Tables and Views*):** There should be no arbitrary and unnecessary distinctions between base tables and views; i.e., views should "look and feel" just like base tables so far as users are concerned.

So if a view is supposed to look and feel just like a base table to the user, that user needs to see the column definitions and table constraints that apply to that view (and *not* to see the applicable view defining <query expression>, by the way). Thus, there really ought to be explicit syntax for specifying such things, even if all the DBMS does with such specifications is check to see that they're consistent with the ones derived from the underlying base table(s).[38] As a matter of fact, it could be argued that the explicitness rule, discussed earlier in this chapter, effectively mandates the provision of such explicit syntax.

---

[37] Indeed, that's exactly why the <view column list> is optional, because column names for the view can always be inherited from the <query expression> if that <query expression> is constructed in accordance with certain relational principles. See my book *SQL and Relational Theory: How to Write Accurate SQL Code*, 3rd edition (O'Reilly, 2015) for more specifics.

[38] Actually this whole business of making views look like base tables is intertangled with something else that today's DBMSs get wrong, having to do with how tables in the database (regardless of whether they're base tables or views) ought to be perceived by applications, but aren't. For further explanation, I refer you to the discussion of "public relvars" in Chapter 10 ("Relational Algebra") of my book *Fifty Years of Relational, and Other Database Writings: More Thoughts and Essays on Database Matters* (Technics Publications, 2020).

Aside: There are a couple more points I'd like to make in connection with the BNF production rules for CREATE TABLE. First let me repeat those rules for convenience:

```
<table definition>
    ::=   CREATE TABLE <table name>
                    ( <table element commalist> ) ;

<table element>
    ::=   <column definition>
        | <table constraint definition>

<column definition>
    ::=   <column name> <data type name>

<table constraint definition>
    ::=   [ CONSTRAINT <constraint name> ]
                        <table constraint>

<table constraint>
    ::=   <unique constraint definition>
        | <referential constraint definition>
        | <check constraint definition>
```

Note first the apparently arbitrary division of syntax category names into ones that include the word *definition* and ones that don't. For example, why "<table element>" and not "<table element definition>"? Alternatively, why "<unique constraint definition>" and not "<unique constraint>"?

Of course, I realize that such arbitrariness is a very minor point in the overall scheme of things; however, it does give rise to annoying distractions—distractions, moreover, that could so easily have been avoided. It also makes the rules harder to remember. And, of course, it does all have to do with the overarching idea that names should be *appropriate*.

As for my second point ... Well, actually, my second point is related to my first. Here again is the production rule as given above for <column definition>:

```
<column definition>
    ::=   <column name> <data type name>
```

But the actual rule as given by the standard looks more like this:

```
<column definition>
    ::=   <column name> <data type>
```

This time I think I'll leave any further comments to you. *End of aside.*

Here's what seems to me another "trivial but glaring" example of an inappropriate choice of syntax category names. SQL follows the tuple calculus in making heavy use of dot qualified names—i.e. names of the form $X.Y$, where X is a correlation name (or range variable name, in relational terms)[39] and Y is the name of a column of the table (or attribute of the relation, in relational terms) associated with X. Typical examples are SX.CITY and SPX.PNO (see the sample SQL expression on page 119). Now, such dot qualified names clearly denote *references* to *columns*. Thus, I would have expected the corresponding production rule in the BNF grammar for SQL to look something like this:

```
<column reference>
    ::=    <name> . <name>
```

(with, of course, additional rules, expressed probably in natural language prose, to say the first <name> identifies a range variable and the second a column).[40] Imagine my surprise, therefore, when I discovered that the production rule in question actually looks more like this:

```
<column reference>
    ::=    <name> . <qualified name>
```

In other words, the SQL category <qualified name> denotes, very specifically, an *un*qualified name!

Note: In case you were wondering, the grammar effectively continues thus:

---

[39] X can also be a table name in SQL (i.e., the name specified in some CREATE TABLE or CREATE VIEW statement)—but if it is, then in that context that table name doesn't denote that table as such, it denotes an implicitly defined range variable that (a) ranges over that table and (b) has the same name as that table. Thus, for example, the SQL expression SELECT * FROM T WHERE ... must be understood as shorthand for the expression SELECT * FROM T *AS T* WHERE ... (emphasis added), and references elsewhere in the overall expression of the form T.C must be understood as making use of a range variable called T that ranges over the table called T. (Though I must admit here to a sneaking sympathy with an old IBM colleague of mine, who once said to me, in connection with this very point: "You mathematicians are all the same. You spend hours agonizing over things that are perfectly obvious to everybody else.")

[40] Alternatively, I *might* have expected the production rule to look like this:

```
<column reference> ::= <range variable name>.<column name>
```

Even if it did, however, additional prose rules would still be needed (right?).

```
<qualified name>
   ::= <name>
```

As a matter of fact I think I know how the foregoing state of affairs arose, and I'll come back to it in a few moments. First, however, I'd like to consider another example, one that seems to me rather more serious, though possibly less glaring, than the one we've just looked at:

■ The SQL grammar includes a syntax category called <query expression>. Now, it's certainly true that such an expression can be used as the SQL formulation of some query. But it's also true—and, I would say, much more important—that such expressions can be used in other contexts as well: for example, in the formulation of certain integrity constraints. In fact, the real point about such an expression is that it denotes a *table value*, and it should therefore be allowed to appear wherever such a value is required. Or let me rephrase that slightly: If you'll allow me to abbreviate "table value" to simply *table* (just as we abbreviate "integer value" to simply *integer*, or "relation value" to simply *relation*), then I'll say such an expression denotes a *table*, and it should be allowed to appear wherever a table is required.

> *Aside:* Two points here: First, whether SQL does actually allow such an expression to appear in all contexts where a table is required is a separate question, of course. In fact it doesn't (were you surprised?); but that's not an issue I want to discuss further right now.
>
> Second, please note that I carefully distinguish here between tables—meaning, specifically, table values—and table *variables*, which is what CREATE TABLE and CREATE VIEW create. Thus, "all contexts where a table is required" certainly doesn't include the context "target of a table assignment," where a table variable is required, not a table. *End of aside.*

So if

a. A <query expression> is an expression that evaluates to a table, and

b. The *only* kind of SQL expression that evaluates to a table is, ultimately, some kind of <query expression>, then the most appropriate name for that syntax category would surely be not <query expression> but <table expression>.

> *Aside:* More ifs and buts coming up (see Chapter 1 if you need to refresh your memory regarding what I mean by this phrase in this context!): What I've said under a. above is true, of course; however, what I've said under b. above *ought* to be true, but it isn't, not quite. It's not worth going into full details here of why it isn't, but the basic point is that in SQL, if *tx* is an expression that evaluates to a table, that expression *tx* typically can't appear in isolation to denote the table in question—instead, it has to have the essentially meaningless incantation "SELECT * FROM" stuck on to it as a prefix (and that prefix turns it into a <query specification>, something I'll be discussing further in a few moments). *End of aside.*

As a general rule, in fact, I don't think syntax categories should be named for the context—or one of the contexts—in which they're expected to be used (especially since some of those contexts might not even have been foreseen when the language was first defined);[41] rather, I think they should be named for what they denote, or else perhaps named in a way that hints at their internal syntactic structure (see the next bullet item below). That's why I think <table expression> is superior to <query expression> as a name for the particular syntax category under consideration here.

> *Aside:* Now I can explain the reason (at least, what seems to me likely to be the reason) why SQL refers to the second component of a column reference as a qualified name and not just as a name. I think it's because, *in that context*, that second name is indeed qualified—it's qualified by the first name. But if you're going to pay attention to context in this way, which I've already said you shouldn't, then I suppose you might as well say the first component is a <qualifying name>.[42] Why not? What exactly are the rules here? *End of aside.*

Let's consider some more examples.

---

[41] I touched on this issue earlier, when I discussed "introduced names" in **Tutorial D**.

[42] Actually the standard does do something along such lines—in some contexts but not all, and not consistently, and in particular not in the case at hand.

■ One particular kind of <query expression> in SQL is what's called a <query specification>. Simplifying slightly once again, the pertinent production rule looks like this:

```
<query specification>
    ::=   SELECT [ DISTINCT | ALL ] <select list>
                                    <table expression>
```

And so we see that, unfortunately, SQL already has a syntax category it calls <table expression>—in fact, it usurps that rather general label and uses it for a very special case, namely, an expression that consists in sequence of a FROM clause, a GROUP BY clause, and a HAVING clause (the last two of which are optional, of course).[43] So of course it's true that a <table expression> in SQL does at least denote a table. But the point is, other expressions do so too, though as I've said already those other expressions all boil down—or at least, they *should* all boil down (as indicated earlier, there's a glitch, having to with "SELECT * FROM")—to <query expression>s, in some shape or form.

So my preference would be, first, to use a name such as <select expression> in place of <query specification>, and then—if it really is necessary to be able to consider (i.e., as a single, separate, syntax category of its own) that portion of a <select expression> that consists of just the applicable FROM, GROUP BY, and HAVING clauses in combination[44]—to use a name such as <fgh clauses> (say) for that category.

■ Here are the production rules for <table expression> and <from clause>:

```
<table expression>
    ::=   <from clause>
          [ <where clause> ]
          [ <group by clause> ]
          [ <having clause> ]

<from clause>
    ::=   FROM <table reference list>
```

---

[43] There's also an optional WINDOW clause, which I choose to ignore.

[44] Actually I don't think it *is* necessary. It's true that the *term* "<table expression>" appears all over the place in the prose part of the standard, but the only place the syntax category, as such, appears in the BNF grammar is in the context of a <query specification> (which as indicated above I'd prefer to call a <select expression> anyway).

And so we see that SQL has used yet another category name—this time, <table reference>—in a most inappropriate fashion. In the world of BNF grammars, the term *reference* is used almost universally to mean a reference to—very often, in fact, just the name of—a variable of some kind; thus, for example, the syntax category <relvar reference> would typically denote a reference to a relvar or relation variable, and the syntax category <tuplevar reference> would typically denote a reference to a tuplevar or tuple variable. By contrast, the term *expression* is invariably used to mean something that denotes a *value* of some kind; thus, for example, the syntax category <integer expression> would typically denote an integer value, or just an integer for short.

Now, it's true that SQL often muddies the distinction between values and variables, especially when it comes to tables; nevertheless, normal usage would surely dictate that "table reference" ought to mean a reference to a table variable. But what's allowed where SQL says a <table reference> is required—in a FROM clause in particular—is certainly not limited to just references to table variables.[45] In fact, what *ought* to be allowed to appear in that context, if the language had been properly and orthogonally designed, would be what SQL calls a <query expression>, but I personally would much prefer to call a <table expression>.

> *Aside:* It seems to me that *expression* is yet another of those concepts that "everyone understands" and whose meaning is therefore never spelled out explicitly. While working on this chapter, I took the trouble to examine (a) a variety of books on programming languages in general, (b) a number of user manuals on individual programming languages in particular, and (c) several books on mathematics—mathematics being where the expression concept had its origins, after all—and it's safe to say that *none* of those sources even came close to providing a good definition for expressions in general. So let me therefore offer my own definition here, for the record:

---

[45] Actually, in the first version of the standard ("SQL/86"), it *was* so limited; that is, the arguments to a FROM clause could only be (values of) named tables, and so <table reference> might not have been totally inappropriate at that time. (It would still have been misleading, though.) But in 1992 the language was extended considerably, and that limitation in particular was dropped; thus, the appropriate move at that time would have been to replace <table reference> by <table expression>. But it looks as if <table reference> was kept on, despite the fact that it was no longer very apt. *Note:* I have no idea if the foregoing explanation is historically accurate—I no longer have access to the SQL/86 and SQL:1992 definitions—but it looks plausible to me.

Definition (expression): In a programming language, a read-only operator invocation; a construct that denotes a value; in effect, a rule for computing, or determining, the value in question. Every expression is of some type—namely, the type of the value it denotes. Literals, constant references, and variable references are all considered to be read-only operator invocations and thus all constitute legal expressions.

Points arising from this definition:

1. Note the final sentence in particular, which states among other things that an expression might consist of nothing but a variable reference; in other words, it might consist of just a variable name, syntactically speaking. In such a case, however, the variable reference (or variable name) in question is taken to denote not the pertinent variable as such but, rather, the current value of that variable.

2. Any given expression is a read-only operator invocation, and in general such invocations require arguments. All such arguments are denoted by further expressions (subexpressions of the original expression)—though those subexpressions might consist of simple variable references, or even just literals.

End of aside.

■ After the <from clause>, the next component of an SQL-style <table reference> is the optional <where clause>. Here's the relevant production rule:

```
<where clause>
   ::=   WHERE <search condition>
```

And once again we run into a category name that seems to me highly inappropriate: viz., <search condition>. What's a <search condition>? *Answer:* It's an expression that denotes a boolean value. So call it a <boolean expression>! And indeed, if we look for the SQL production rule for <search condition>, this is what we find:

```
<search condition>
    ::=    <boolean value expression>
```

Well, some obvious questions arise:

1. Why does the category <search condition> even exist?[46] What purpose does it serve?

2. And second, why is the category <boolean *value* expression>— emphasis added—so called? Every expression denotes a value by definition; so every expression is a "value expression" by definition, and use of the qualifier *value* in such category names, which in the SQL grammar is ubiquitous, is simply redundant.[47]

■ Regarding that category <boolean value expression>, by the way, another small but strange point arises. The syntax of such expressions is defined in Subclause 6.34 of the standard, where we learn (after following several chains of references to other parts of the standard and other production rules) that one valid form of <boolean value expression> is—as would surely be expected—a <boolean literal>, defined in Subclause 5.3 ("<literal>") as follows:

```
<boolean literal>
    ::=    TRUE
        |  FALSE
        |  UNKNOWN
```

OK, fine. But to get back to Subclause 6.34 as such ("<boolean value expression>"), we also find that one form of <boolean value expression> is a <boolean test>:

```
<boolean test>
    ::=    <boolean primary> [ IS [ NOT ] <truth value> ]
```

---

[46] The answer is probably historical—SQL had "search conditions" long before it had a boolean data type. But that's a serious criticism right there, both of the language as such and of the way it was designed. And even without a boolean data type, I would still argue that (e.g.) <conditional expression> would be a much better name than <search condition> for the syntax category under discussion.

[47] For interest—and for the record—here's a list of all of the things that X can be in the generic SQL category <X value expression>. First of all, the X can be omitted entirely; I mean, <value expression> is a genuine (and generic) SQL category. Second, X can be any of the following: absolute; array; binary; blob; boolean; character; collection; common; datetime; interval; multiset; next; numeric; parenthesized; reference; row; string; user defined type. And do you see what's missing from this list? That's right: table.

```
<truth value>
    ::=    TRUE
         | FALSE
         | UNKNOWN
```

What's going on here? Why doesn't the production rule for <boolean test> refer to the <boolean literal> category? Exactly what purpose is being served by the category <truth value>? (I note for what it's worth that it isn't mentioned in any other production rule in the standard at all.)

And on and on ... In fact, I strongly suspect I could find something to criticize in just about every category name in the SQL standard. But I think I've said enough (more than enough, probably) to make my point, which is, to repeat: Names should be *appropriate*.

Part II

SAYING IT TWICE,

OR NOT CLEARLY

Natural languages typically display a high degree of redundancy—indeed, they typically display redundancies of several different kinds. And one particular kind that we're all familiar with resides in the fact that they typically provide many different ways of saying the exact same thing. Indeed, this state of affairs can be quite beneficial from the point of view of rhetoric; it's often an advantage if the same thing can be stated repeatedly in different ways, since such "repetition with variations" can help get the message across.

At the same time it has to be admitted that natural language can also be ambiguous or imprecise, or even misleading. Wittgenstein famously claimed that "What can be said at all can be said clearly";[1] but T. S. Eliot apparently disagreed when he wrote that "Words strain, crack and sometimes break, under the burden."[2] And I think Bertrand Russell was siding with T. S. Eliot when he wrote that "Writing can be either readable or precise, but not at the same time."

Be all that as it may, it seems to me undeniably true that statements in natural language aren't always as clear, or *determinate*, as they might be, and we simply have to live with this state of affairs somehow.[3]

So much for natural language; but what about formal languages—in particular, the languages we use to communicate with computers? Here we're dealing with *logic*, not rhetoric, and matters are rather different. Well, I suppose

---

[1] *Tractatus Logico-Philosophicus* (1922).

[2] "Burnt Norton" (*Four Quartets*, 1936).

[3] Of course, there are those—certain politicians come to mind—who actively try to take advantage of this situation. In my opinion, such people are beneath contempt.

redundancy in a formal language isn't *necessarily* bad; after all, even in logic there are usually (perhaps always) many different ways of saying the same thing. For example, NOT(*p* AND *q*) and (NOT *p*) OR (NOT *q*) certainly both say the same thing, as is well known. On the other hand, it's hard to see how such redundancy actually helps ... If there are many different ways of saying something in such a language, then there are at least two negative consequences—first, users have more to learn; second, they also have more decisions to make. Moreover, they have to make those decisions without necessarily being aware of all of the arguments, pro and con, that might be made in connection with them. And the situation is made still worse, in my opinion, by what might be called "pseudo redundancies": that is, by that phenomenon according to which two distinct constructs in the language have meanings that overlap—indeed, are *almost* identical—and yet aren't quite the same, in the sense that each has some nuance of meaning that the other doesn't.

Turning now to precision, or determinacy: Personally, I would have thought it a sine qua non that every legitimate, well formed construct in the formal language in question have a single, precise, determinate meaning.[4] The imprecision that seems to be inherent in so many natural language utterances surely has no place in the kind of formal language under consideration here.

Well, the foregoing remarks are all by way of background. The two chapters in this part of the book examine the language SQL in the light of those remarks and (I'm sorry to say) find it wanting in both cases. Chapter 4 considers the question of redundancy and Chapter 5 the question of determinacy.

---

[4] I exclude from consideration here language constructs explicitly designed to have some unpredictability to them, such as a function that's defined to return random (or pseudorandom) numbers.

Chapter 4

Redundancy in SQL

Le superflu, chose très nécessaire
—François-Marie Arouet Voltaire:
Le Mondain (1736)

*This chapter is based in part on a series of articles that originally
appeared in the magazine Data Base Programming & Design and/or on
the website www.dbpd.com in May, June, and July, 1998. The material,
though revised considerably here, is thus not entirely new. However, I
do think it's worth preserving—and since the original articles are no
longer available (the referenced magazine and its associated website
both appear to be defunct), I've decided to reproduce it, suitably
modified, in the form of what follows.*

What exactly does it mean to say something's redundant? A little surprisingly, it
turns out to be quite difficult to come up with a precise definition. The best
Chambers Twentieth Century Dictionary (usually so good and pithy in its
definitions) is able to come up with is the following:

redundant copious: over-copious: superfluous

However, *Chambers Twentieth Century Thesaurus* (a companion to the
Dictionary) gives the following splendid list of synonyms or near synonyms:

redundant *de trop*, diffuse, excessive, extra, inessential, inordinate, padded,
periphrastic, pleonastical, prolix, repetitious, supererogatory, superfluous,
supernumerary, surplus, tautological, unemployed, unnecessary, unneeded,
unwanted, verbose, wordy

Incidentally, that same source also gives the following nice list of antonyms:

concise, essential, necessary

Well, that's all as may be. But did you know that the GROUP BY and HAVING clauses—hereinafter referred to, separately and/or collectively, as GBH—are effectively redundant in SQL? That is, any sensible query that can be expressed in SQL using either or both of these clauses can also be expressed without them. (I'll explain later what I mean by "any sensible query"!) And did you know that range variables in SQL are also effectively redundant in that same sense? In this chapter I'll illustrate these points and discuss some of their implications.

Note: By *SQL* I mean (as always) the standard version of that language, barring explicit statements to the contrary. Your mileage may vary.

GROUP BY WITHOUT HAVING

I'll use the familiar suppliers-and-parts database as the basis for my examples. Fig. 4.1 below gives the usual sample value for this database:

S

SNO	SNAME	STATUS	CITY
S1	Smith	20	London
S2	Jones	10	Paris
S3	Blake	30	Paris
S4	Clark	20	London
S5	Adams	30	Athens

P

PNO	PNAME	COLOR	WEIGHT	CITY
P1	Nut	Red	12.0	London
P2	Bolt	Green	17.0	Paris
P3	Screw	Blue	17.0	Oslo
P4	Screw	Red	14.0	London
P5	Cam	Blue	12.0	Paris
P6	Cog	Red	19.0	London

SP

SNO	PNO	QTY
S1	P1	300
S1	P2	200
S1	P3	400
S1	P4	200
S1	P5	100
S1	P6	100
S2	P1	300
S2	P2	400
S3	P2	200
S4	P2	200
S4	P4	300
S4	P5	400

Fig. 4.1: The suppliers-and-parts database—sample value

And since this chapter is all about SQL, I'll give the pertinent data definitions in SQL:

```
CREATE TABLE S          /* suppliers */
     ( SNO    VARCHAR(5)   NOT NULL ,
       SNAME  VARCHAR(25)  NOT NULL ,
       STATUS INTEGER      NOT NULL ,
       CITY   VARCHAR(20)  NOT NULL ,
       UNIQUE ( SNO ) ) ;

CREATE TABLE P          /* parts */
     ( PNO    VARCHAR(6)   NOT NULL ,
       PNAME  VARCHAR(25)  NOT NULL ,
       COLOR  VARCHAR(10)  NOT NULL ,
       WEIGHT NUMERIC(5,1) NOT NULL ,
       CITY   VARCHAR(20)  NOT NULL ,
       UNIQUE ( PNO ) ) ;

CREATE TABLE SP         /* shipments */
     ( SNO    VARCHAR(5)   NOT NULL ,
       PNO    VARCHAR(6)   NOT NULL ,
       QTY    INTEGER      NOT NULL ,
       UNIQUE ( SNO , PNO ) ,
       FOREIGN KEY ( SNO ) REFERENCES S ( SNO ) ,
       FOREIGN KEY ( PNO ) REFERENCES P ( PNO ) ) ;
```

Here now is a query against this database ("Query Q1") for which most people would "naturally" use GROUP BY:

Q1:   For each part supplied, get the part number, maximum quantity, and minimum quantity supplied of that part.

A "natural" (i.e., GROUP BY) formulation of this query in SQL might look like this:[1]

```
SELECT SP.PNO ,
       MAX ( SP.QTY ) AS MXQ ,
       MIN ( SP.QTY ) AS MNQ
FROM   SP
GROUP  BY SP.PNO
```

The result, given the sample data of Fig. 4.1, is shown in Fig. 4.2:

---

[1] For reasons of clarity I'll use explicitly qualified names (such as SP.PNO, SP.QTY) in SQL expressions throughout this chapter, even when the qualifiers in question can safely be omitted.

PNO	MXQ	MNQ
P1	300	300
P2	400	200
P3	400	400
P4	300	200
P5	400	100
P6	100	100

Fig. 4.2: Result of Query Q1

Here by contrast is another SQL formulation of the same query that makes no use of GROUP BY:

```
SELECT DISTINCT SP.PNO ,
               ( SELECT MAX ( SPX.QTY )
                 FROM   SP AS SPX
                 WHERE  SPX.PNO = SP.PNO ) AS MXQ ,
               ( SELECT MIN ( SPY.QTY )
                 FROM   SP AS SPY
                 WHERE  SPY.PNO = SP.PNO ) AS MNQ
FROM    SP
```

Of course, it's true that this latter formulation is longer—i.e., requires more keystrokes—than the previous one, but logically the two are equivalent. And of course it's easy to generalize from this example, as follows: Given table T, with columns A, B, etc., let *agg* be an aggregate operator (such as SUM or MAX or MIN) that's applicable to column B. Then the expression

```
SELECT T.A ,
       agg ( [ DISTINCT ] T.B ) AS AGGB
FROM   T
GROUP  BY T.A
```

can be transformed into the longer, but logically equivalent, expression

```
SELECT DISTINCT T.A ,
               ( SELECT agg ( [ DISTINCT ] TX.B )
                 FROM   T AS TX
                 WHERE  TX.A = T.A ) AS AGGB
FROM    T
```

In what follows I'll refer to such a transformation as a *Type 1 transformation*, for brevity.

Next, we need to consider what happens if the GROUP BY formulation of some query also includes a WHERE clause. To illustrate, let me modify Query Q1 as follows:

Q2: For each part supplied, get the part number, maximum quantity, and minimum quantity supplied of that part; however, ignore shipments from supplier S1 throughout.

Here first is a GROUP BY formulation:

```
SELECT  SP.PNO ,
        MAX ( SP.QTY ) AS MXQ ,
        MIN ( SP.QTY ) AS MNQ
FROM    SP
WHERE   SP.SNO <> 'S1'
GROUP   BY SP.PNO
```

A formulation without GROUP BY—not the only one possible—is a little more tricky:

```
SELECT DISTINCT SP.PNO ,
              ( SELECT MAX ( SPX.QTY )
                FROM   SP AS SPX
                WHERE  SPX.PNO = SP.PNO
                AND    SPX.SNO <> 'S1' ) AS MXQ ,
              ( SELECT MIN ( SPY.QTY )
                FROM   SP AS SPY
                WHERE  SPY.PNO = SP.PNO
                AND    SPY.SNO <> 'S1' ) AS MNQ
FROM    SP
WHERE   SP.SNO <> 'S1'
```

As you can see, the WHERE clause from the GROUP BY formulation not only has to be retained in situ, as it were, but also has to be replicated, albeit in slightly modified form, inside the two inner SELECT expressions (i.e., the ones nested inside the outer SELECT clause). The reason is that the WHERE clause in the original formulation governs both the GROUP BY clause and the SELECT clause in that formulation. And the reason for *that* state of affairs is that SQL requires the clauses to be written in a slightly illogical sequence! In general, the clauses of a given SELECT – FROM – WHERE – GROUP BY expression in SQL are evaluated in the order FROM – WHERE – GROUP BY – SELECT; thus, it might have made more sense if SQL had required them to be written in that order. But it didn't.

Two asides here: First, there's another way to think about the repetition involved in the foregoing SQL formulation, one you might like better. To be specific, you can think of the transformed version of the query as involving three separate copies of the shipments table, one referred to by its actual name SP and the other two by the "correlation names" SPX and SPY.[2] And, per the conditions of Query Q2 (natural language version), we need rows for supplier S1 to be excluded from all three copies. So each of the three individual FROM clauses has to be followed by a WHERE clause to do the necessary.

Second, we can factor out part of the repetition anyway—though actually at the cost of *increasing* the number of keystrokes, slightly—by using SQL's WITH construct, as follows:

```
WITH SPZ AS ( SELECT SP.SNO , SP.PNO , SP.QTY
              FROM    SP
              WHERE   SP.SNO <> 'S1' )

SELECT DISTINCT SPZ.PNO ,
              ( SELECT MAX ( SPX.QTY )
                FROM    SPZ AS SPX
                WHERE   SPX.PNO = SPZ.PNO ) AS MXQ ,
              ( SELECT MIN ( SPY.QTY )
                FROM    SPZ AS SPY
                WHERE   SPY.PNO = SPZ.PNO ) AS MNQ
       FROM    SPZ
```

For simplicity, however, I'll ignore SQL's WITH construct in my query formulations from this point forward.[3] *End of asides.*

Anyway, the fact is that (as you can see) the Type 1 transformation rule needs to be extended slightly to take care of WHERE clauses. I'll skip the details here, since they're essentially straightforward.

---

[2] I'll have more to say about correlation names later in this chapter. At this point let me just note that when I say that one copy of the table is being referred to by its actual name SP, I'm really being a little bit sloppy; actually, the appearance of that name SP, like the two appearances of the name SPX, is serving in this context as a correlation name, not as a table name as such. In other words, the FROM clause FROM SP can be thought of as shorthand for one of the form FROM SP AS SP. See footnote 39 in Chapter 3 for further explanation.

[3] In any case, SQL's overall lack of orthogonality makes its WITH construct very much less useful than it might be, as I've explained elsewhere—see, e.g., Chapter 16, "SQL Criticisms," of my book *Fifty Years of Relational, and Other Database Writings: More Thoughts and Essays on Database Matters* (Technics Publications, 2020).

Now let me modify the example again. Suppose the original query had been as follows:

Q3:   For each part supplied, get the maximum quantity supplied of that part, but not the part number.

Here first is a GROUP BY formulation:

```
SELECT MAX ( SP.QTY ) AS MXQ
FROM   SP
GROUP  BY SP.PNO
```

Applying the Type 1 transformation rule, we obtain:

```
SELECT DISTINCT ( SELECT MAX ( SPX.QTY )
                  FROM   SP AS SPX
                  WHERE  SPX.PNO = SP.PNO ) AS MXQ
FROM   SP
```

The results of evaluating these two SQL expressions are shown in Fig. 4.3:

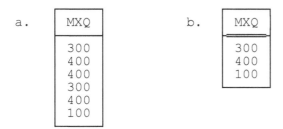

Fig. 4.3: Result of Query Q3 (a) using GROUP BY,
                              (b) avoiding GROUP BY

As you can see, the two expressions don't give quite the same result, and therefore they're not quite equivalent; in other words, the Type 1 transformation isn't valid in this case, not quite. But the real reason for this lack of equivalence is that the first expression, using GROUP BY, gives a result that's not a relation! Let's examine the situation a little more closely.

First of all, the result produced by the GROUP BY formulation is *obviously* not a relation, because it contains duplicate rows. Well, that's bad enough; but what at least arguably makes matters worse is that those duplicates are *essential*,

in the sense that, for example, the two "300" rows have different meanings[4]—
one means some part is supplied in a maximum quantity of 300, the other means
some *other* part is also supplied in that same maximum quantity. And "essential
duplicates" constitute a major departure from the precepts of the relational
model—in fact, they constitute a violation of Codd's *Information Principle*,[5]
which states that all information must be cast explicitly in terms of relations and
in no other way. Indeed, the fact that SQL includes the notion of "essential
duplicates" constitutes very strong evidence that SQL is not now, and never was,
truly relational.

> *Aside:* As a consequence of the foregoing (i.e., the fact that the result produced
> by the GROUP BY formulation contains duplicate rows), that result certainly
> doesn't satisfy any kind of key constraint, which is why there's no double
> underlining in part a. of Fig. 4.3. More important, note that precisely because it
> isn't a relation, it can't be used as input to any operator, such as join, that
> requires its input to be a relation! (Of course, it *can* be used as input to SQL's
> analog of such an operator—but that state of affairs simply demonstrates that
> SQL's operators aren't relational, and hence, once again, that SQL itself isn't
> relational either a fortiori.) *End of aside.*

Note: I should point out in passing that "essential duplicates" arise in SQL
in many other contexts in addition to the one under discussion. For example,
even such a simple expression as

```
SELECT CITY
FROM   S
```

gives a result containing "essential duplicates," in general.

But let's think a little more carefully about Query Q3. What does that
query really mean? I submit that what it's really asking for is simply *the set of
maximum shipment quantities in SP*. The formulation without GROUP BY
correctly produces this information. It's true that it doesn't show *which*

---

[4] See either Chapter 11, "Essentiality," in my book *Relational Database Writings 1991-1994* (Addison-Wesley, 1995), or Chapter 6, "The Essentiality Paper," in my book *E. F. Codd and Relational Theory: A Detailed Review and Analysis of Codd's Major Database Writings* (Lulu Press, 2019).

[5] At least, they do so if they appear in the database as such. In the case at hand, we're not talking about something that appears in the database, we're just talking about the result of a query. But of course the relational closure property dictates, in effect, that we should be able to keep the result of that query in the database if we wanted to, in which case those essential duplicates would appear in the database after all.

particular parts have *which* maximum quantities, but—as you can see from the original natural language wording—that information wasn't asked for.

Now, the GROUP BY formulation also produces the same information, of course (that is, the maximum shipment quantities, again without showing which parts correspond to which maximum quantities). To that extent, we might agree that the formulation is acceptable. However, some people—not me!—might go on to argue that it *also* produces the information that there are six different parts, and hence that it's preferable to the formulation without GROUP BY. *Note very carefully, however, that it provides that additional information **in a nonrelational form*** (it does so by means of "essential duplicates," as already explained). In my opinion, if we'd actually wanted to obtain that additional information, then we should have stated the original natural language query accordingly, and that different natural language statement would then have led to an SQL formulation that would have produced the desired information in proper relational form:

```
SELECT DISTINCT SP.PNO ,
             ( SELECT MAX ( SPX.QTY )
               FROM   SP AS SPX
               WHERE  SPX.PNO = SP.PNO ) AS MXQ
FROM    SP
```

This formulation corresponds, in effect, to a simplified version of Query Q1, and the result thus consists of the projection on PNO and MXQ of the result of Query Q1. (Just to remind you, the result of Query Q1, given our usual sample data, is shown in Fig. 4.2.)

> *Aside:* You might be thinking we could preserve the equivalence of the two formulations by dropping the DISTINCT from the second one (the one without the GROUP BY). But this ploy—fairly obviously—doesn't solve anything. First, the result will now contain twelve rows, not three and not six (so the revised formulation isn't logically equivalent to either of the other two). Second, those twelve rows will again include "essential duplicates," and the formulation (like the original GROUP BY formulation) will thus again not be truly relational. *End of aside.*

Finally, I feel bound to point out that (in my opinion) queries such as Query Q3, though legal, aren't very *sensible.* I say this because, almost by definition, such queries effectively ask for information to be thrown away that we probably don't *want* to be thrown away. (In the example, what's being thrown away is the information as to which parts have which maximum quantities.) In SQL terms, such queries typically lead to GROUP BY formulations in which some column is mentioned in the GROUP BY clause and not in the corresponding SELECT clause. And such formulations are precisely the ones for which our Type 1 transformation rule doesn't quite "work right." By contrast, the rule does always work right for "sensible" queries.

GROUP BY WITH HAVING

Now I turn to the HAVING clause. Here's a query for which most people would "naturally" use HAVING:

Q4:   For each part supplied by more than one supplier, get the part number.

A GBH formulation of this query might look like this (recall that I'm using "GBH" to stand for the GROUP BY and HAVING clauses considered either separately or together):

```
SELECT SP.PNO
FROM   SP
GROUP  BY SP.PNO
HAVING COUNT(*) > 1
```

The result of this query, given the sample data of Fig. 4.1, is shown in Fig. 4.4:

PNO
P1
P2
P4
P5

Fig. 4.4: Result of Query Q4

Here by contrast is a nonGBH formulation of the same query (that is, a formulation that makes no use of either GROUP BY or HAVING):

```
SELECT  DISTINCT SP.PNO
FROM    SP
WHERE ( SELECT  COUNT(*)
        FROM    SP AS SPX
        WHERE   SPX.PNO = SP.PNO ) > 1
```

Once again it's true that the alternative formulation is a little longer than the GBH version, but logically the two are equivalent. And once again it's easy to generalize from this example. Using the same notation as in the previous section, the expression

```
SELECT  T.A
FROM    T
GROUP   BY T.A
HAVING  agg ( [ DISTINCT ] T.B ) comp scalar
```

(where *comp* is some scalar comparison operator such as "=" or "<" and *scalar* is some scalar expression) can be logically transformed into the equivalent expression

```
SELECT  DISTINCT T.A
FROM    T
WHERE ( SELECT  agg ( [ DISTINCT ] TX.B )
        FROM    T AS TX
        WHERE   TX.A = T.A ) comp scalar
```

(where *comp* and *scalar* are as in the original GBH formulation). In what follows I'll refer to such a transformation as a *Type 2 transformation*.

Again, however, we need to consider what happens if the original GBH formulation includes a WHERE clause. Let's extend Query Q4 as follows:

Q5: For each part supplied by more than one supplier (not counting supplier S1), get the part number.

GBH formulation:

```
SELECT  SP.PNO
FROM    SP
WHERE   SP.SNO <> 'S1'
GROUP   BY SP.PNO
HAVING  COUNT(*) > 1
```

Again the nonGBH equivalent is a just a little tricky:

```
SELECT DISTINCT SP.PNO
FROM    SP
WHERE   SP.SNO <> 'S1'
AND   ( SELECT COUNT(*)
        FROM    SP AS SPX
        WHERE   SPX.PNO = SP.PNO
        AND     SPX.SNO <> 'S1' ) > 1
```

Note again that the WHERE clause from the original GBH formulation not only has to be retained in situ, as it were, but also has to be replicated (in slightly modified form) inside the inner SELECT expression (i.e., the one nested inside that outer WHERE clause).[6] And the reason is basically the same as before: viz., that the WHERE clause in the original GBH formulation governs both the GROUP BY clause and the HAVING clause (as well as the SELECT clause) in that formulation. Thus, the Type 2 transformation rule (like the Type 1 transformation rule discussed earlier) needs to be extended to take care of WHERE clauses. I'll skip the details, since again they're basically straightforward.

Here now is a slightly more complicated example, involving an aggregate operator invocation in both the SELECT clause and the HAVING clause:

Q6: For each part supplied by more than one supplier, get the part number and the total quantity supplied of that part.

GBH formulation:

```
SELECT SP.PNO , SUM ( SP.QTY ) AS TQY
FROM    SP
GROUP   BY SP.PNO
HAVING COUNT(*) > 1
```

Applying both the Type 1 *and* Type 2 transformation rules, we obtain:

```
SELECT DISTINCT SP.PNO , ( SELECT SUM ( SPX.QTY )
                           FROM    SP AS SPX
                           WHERE   SPX.PNO = SP.PNO ) AS TQY
FROM    SP
WHERE ( SELECT COUNT(*)
        FROM    SP AS SPX
        WHERE   SPX.PNO = SP.PNO ) > 1
```

---

[6] *Exercise:* Give a formulation of Query Q5 that uses WITH to avoid the repetition. Does your revised formulation save you any keystrokes?

And one more example:

Q7: For each part supplied by more than one supplier, get the total quantity supplied of that part, but not the part number.

GBH formulation:

```
SELECT SUM ( SP.QTY ) AS TQY
FROM   SP
GROUP  BY SP.PNO
HAVING COUNT(*) > 1
```

Applying the Type 1 and Type 2 transformation rules, we obtain:

```
SELECT DISTINCT ( SELECT SUM ( SPX.QTY )
                  FROM   SP AS SPX
                  WHERE  SPX.PNO = SP.PNO ) AS TQY
FROM   SP
WHERE  ( SELECT COUNT(*)
         FROM   SP AS SPX
         WHERE  SPX.PNO = SP.PNO ) > 1
```

The results of evaluating these two SQL expressions are shown in Fig. 4.5:

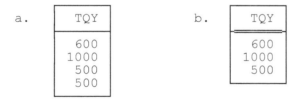

Fig. 4.5: Result of Query Q7 (a) using GBH, (b) avoiding GBH

Once again the two expressions don't give quite the same result, and therefore aren't quite equivalent. But—as I'm sure you realize—the situation here is precisely analogous to that already discussed under Query Q3. In other words, Query Q7 suffers from the same kinds of problems as Query Q3 does; the discussion of Query Q3 from the previous section is thus applicable here also, mutatis mutandis, and no further commentary seems necessary.

Aside: There's still another reason to avoid the use of GBH expressions, which is that they don't always mean what you might think they mean—i.e., they give what might loosely be called wrong answers (more precisely, they give the right answer to the wrong question). Consider this query: "For each supplier who supplies fewer than three parts, get the supplier number and city and the total quantity of parts supplied by that supplier." Consider also the following GBH expression:

```
SELECT  S.SNO , CITY , SUM ( QTY ) AS TPQ
FROM    S , SP
WHERE   S.SNO = SP.SNO
GROUP   BY S.SNO , CITY
HAVING  COUNT ( * ) < 3
```

Now, you might easily be led to think this GBH expression represents the specified query, but of course it doesn't—it misses suppliers such as supplier S5 in Fig. 4.1 who supply no parts at all.

I'll leave it as another exercise to fix up the GBH expression to avoid this problem (if you can). Note carefully, however, that the following nonGBH expression doesn't suffer from the same problem:

```
SELECT SNO , CITY , ( SELECT SUM ( QTY )
                      FROM   SP
                      WHERE  SP.SNO = S.SNO ) AS TPQ
FROM    S
WHERE   ( SELECT COUNT ( * )
          FROM   SP
          WHERE  SP.SNO = S.SNO ) < 3
```

End of aside.

HAVING WITHOUT GROUP BY

Thus far I've shown that any sensible SQL query involving a GROUP BY clause, either with or without an accompanying HAVING clause, can also be expressed without using those clauses. But what about queries that use a HAVING clause without an accompanying GROUP BY clause?

Now, you might be surprised to learn that it's legal for an SQL SELECT expression to include a HAVING clause without an associated GROUP BY clause, but in fact it is.[7] To spell out the semantics, the SQL expression

---

[7] The discussion that follows consists in part of a repetition and elaboration of material from Chapter 3.

```
SELECT  A ,  B ,  ...
FROM    T
HAVING  bx
```

(where *bx* is a boolean expression) is defined to be shorthand for

```
SELECT  A ,  B ,  ...
FROM    T
GROUP   BY  ( )
HAVING  bx
```

And grouping by no columns, as in this latter expression, is defined to mean that the entirety of table *T* is to be treated as a single group, containing (of course) just the rows of *T*.[8]

Let's consider an example:

Q8: Get the total shipment quantity for all parts, if and only if the smallest quantity in which any part is supplied (i.e., by any supplier) is greater than 50.

Before going any further, let me point out that this query as stated is in fact underspecified, because it doesn't say what should be returned if the smallest quantity in which any part is supplied is *not* greater than 50. However, I'm going to overlook this point for the moment. In fact, I think a helpful way to consider this example is to break it down into three separate scenarios, or cases, which I'll do in the three subsections immediately following.

Query Q8, Case 1

Assume first that, as with the sample data shown in Fig. 4.1, (a) there's at least one shipment and (b) every such shipment involves a quantity greater than 50 (and hence it's certainly the case that the smallest such quantity is greater than 50). Then the following SQL formulation will suffice:

---

[8] Two points here: First, you might be surprised to learn that the standard does permit the commalist of GROUP BY arguments to be enclosed in parentheses; moreover, such parentheses are required if that commalist happens to be empty, as in the example. Second, my text says that if the grouping is done on the basis of no columns at all—i.e., if that commalist is indeed empty—then the entire table is treated as a single group. This statement is true, but shouldn't be! Further explanation to come, in the subsection "Query Q8, Case 3."

```
SELECT SUM ( SP.QTY ) AS TQY
FROM   SP
HAVING MIN ( SP.QTY ) > 50
```

Given the sample data values shown in Fig. 4.1, this expression will produce a result consisting of one column (called TQY) and one row, containing the value 3100:

TQY
3100

Explanation: Since there's no GROUP BY clause, the HAVING clause is regarded (as previously explained) as applying to a "grouped" version of SP that contains exactly one group. If the expression in the HAVING clause evaluates to TRUE for that group—which, given the sample data values from Fig. 4.1, it does—then the SELECT clause returns the desired sum. *Note:* The fact that column TQY in the picture has no double underlining is *not* a mistake. See Chapter 8 ("Drawing Relations as Tables") of my book *Fifty Years of Relational, and Other Database Writings: More Thoughts and Essays on Database Matters* (Technics Publications, 2020) if you require further explanation.

Query Q8, Case 2

I turn now to a second possible scenario. Suppose we can't rely on that simplifying Case 1 assumption after all; more specifically, let's assume that (a) again there's at least one shipment but (b) at least one of those shipments involves a quantity of 50 or less. Nevertheless, let's assume also that we use the same SQL formulation as before:

```
SELECT SUM ( SP.QTY ) AS TQY
FROM   SP
HAVING MIN ( SP.QTY ) > 50
```

Again, then, because there's no GROUP BY clause, SQL says the HAVING clause is applied to a "grouped" version of SP that contains exactly one group. But under our new assumption (at least one shipment involving a quantity of 50 or less), the expression in the HAVING clause evaluates to FALSE for that group, so that group is discarded, leaving no groups at all. Thus, the SELECT clause—which in general, when applied to a "grouped table" of n groups, produces a result table of at most n rows[9]—produces a result table with no rows, because $n = 0$ in this case:

Now, a good question to ask at this juncture is: Is this result correct? My own opinion, for what it's worth, is as follows. Observe first that the logically correct interpretation of the result just shown is precisely the following:

No value TQY exists such that both the following are true:

    a. No part is supplied by any supplier in a quantity of 50 or less, and

    b. TQY is the total quantity of all parts supplied.

Thus, I think the result is indeed correct so long as the original query (i.e., Query Q8), in its underspecified form, is understood to be slightly sloppy shorthand for the following fully specified form:

If the minimum quantity in which any part is supplied is greater than 50, then get the total shipment quantity for all parts; otherwise don't get any value at all.

I'll stay with this understanding of the query for the remainder of this discussion.

Query Q8, Case 3

Suppose now that there aren't any shipments at all—i.e., table SP is currently empty (has no rows). Then it's certainly the case that no value TQY exists such that both the following are true: (a) no part is supplied by any supplier in a quantity of 50 or less, and (b) TQY is the total quantity of all parts supplied. Thus, the result should be empty again, as in Case 2. And indeed so it is—but

---

[9] It'll be fewer than n rows if any duplicate rows are eliminated. See footnote 14 in Chapter 3.

for the wrong reason! Let me elaborate. I'll begin by spelling out the sequence of steps as they logically *ought* to be:

1. The specified SQL formulation is defined to be shorthand for the following:

    ```
    SELECT SUM ( SP.QTY ) AS TQY
    FROM    SP
    GROUP  BY ( )
    HAVING MIN ( SP.QTY ) > 50
    ```

2. The FROM clause returns an empty table, so the implicit GROUP BY clause is applied to that empty table.

3. Since there are no rows in the GROUP BY input, there should be no groups in the GROUP BY output.

4. Therefore the HAVING clause should be applied to an empty set of groups.

5. If there are no groups in the HAVING input, there'll be no groups in the HAVING output.[10]

6. If there are no groups in the HAVING output, the SELECT clause will be applied to a "grouped table" consisting of an empty set of groups.

7. In general, if the SELECT clause is applied to a "grouped table" consisting of n groups, it produces a result consisting of at most n rows.

8. So if $n = 0$, the final result should be empty.

And as I've said, an empty result is indeed what SQL gives us in the case at hand. However, it does so not because it goes through the foregoing logically correct sequence of steps, but rather because it commits not one but two logical errors which have the effect of canceling each other out. In what follows, I'll repeat that sequence of steps, but indicate in italics how and where SQL departs from it. (The steps that SQL agrees with I'll flag as "OK," also in italics.)

---

[10] Note that this observation is valid regardless of the form the boolean expression *bx* in the HAVING clause actually takes. (By definition, if there are no groups in the HAVING input, then there are certainly no groups in the HAVING input for which *bx* evaluates to TRUE. Nor are there any for which it evaluates to FALSE, come to that.)

1. (*OK*) The specified SQL formulation is defined to be shorthand for the following:

```
SELECT SUM ( SP.QTY ) AS TQY
FROM   SP
GROUP  BY ( )
HAVING MIN ( SP.QTY ) > 50
```

2. (*OK*) The FROM clause returns an empty table, so the implicit GROUP BY clause is applied to that empty table.

3. Since there are no rows in the GROUP BY input, there should be no groups in the GROUP BY output. *But SQL says there's exactly one group in the output—a group that, of course, necessarily contains no rows.*[11] That's the first logical error.

4. Therefore the HAVING clause should be applied to an empty set of groups. *But (thanks to the first logical error) SQL says it's applied to a set containing exactly one group.*

5. If there are no groups in the HAVING input, there'll be no groups in the HAVING output. *But in SQL, the expression in the HAVING clause is evaluated against a single (empty) group. In the example, that expression is MIN(QTY) > 50. MIN in SQL on an empty argument is defined to return null,*[12] *so the expression reduces to NULL > 50, which returns UNKNOWN. That UNKNOWN is then effectively coerced to FALSE—that's the second logical error—and so the group is discarded, leaving no groups at all.*

---

[11] To quote the standard: "If there are no grouping columns, then the result of the <group by clause> is the grouped table consisting of *T* as its only group." Here *T* is the result of applying the preceding <where clause>—default WHERE TRUE—to the result of the preceding <from clause>. Note carefully, therefore, that "the result of the <group by> clause is "the grouped table consisting of *T* as its only group" *even in the special case when T is empty*—which is, of course, the case at hand.

   PS: It might help to point out that what we're talking about here is the logical difference between (a) the empty set { } and (b) the set {{ }}, which isn't empty but contains one element, viz., the empty set. Grouping an empty table by no columns ought logically to yield the first of these but (in SQL) yields the second instead.

[12] That's surely a logical error too. If the argument to either of the aggregate operators MAX and MIN is some set of values *S*, then the semantics should surely be that the result is some value from *S*. So if *S* happens to be empty, I think that rather than returning a null, an exception should be raised ("max or min not defined").

6. (*OK*) If there are no groups in the HAVING output, the SELECT clause will be applied to a "grouped table" consisting of an empty set of groups.

7. (*OK, but see the discussion in the subsection immediately following*) In general, if the SELECT clause is applied to a "grouped table" consisting of *n* groups, it produces a result consisting of at most *n* rows.

8. (*OK, but see the discussion in the subsection immediately following*) So if *n* = 0, the final result should be empty.

More Logical Errors

Several further points arise from the foregoing discussion, points that are somewhat tangential to my main argument but I don't want to lose. First of all, suppose until further notice that the shipments table SP is empty, and consider the following simple SQL expression:

```
SELECT  SP.QTY
FROM    SP
```

Clearly, the result of evaluating this expression is empty; more precisely, it's a table of one column and no rows. But suppose we modify the expression as follows:

```
SELECT  SUM ( SP.QTY ) AS TQY
FROM    SP
```

Now the result is a table of one column and *one* row (and that row contains a null)! Well, that certainly looks like a logical error—surely, selecting *anything* from a table of *n* rows should return a result of at most *n* rows. Personally, I would say it *is* a logical error, but SQL explains the error away, as it were, by special casing. Full details of how it achieves this effect are far too complicated to repeat here, but what they boil down to is as follows: Let *exp* be the expression SELECT <select item commalist> FROM *T*. Then if *T* is empty but every <select item> consists of an aggregate operator invocation, the result of evaluating *exp* isn't empty as might have been expected, but is instead a table containing exactly one row.

To repeat, then: The result in the example is a table of one column and one row, and that row contains a null. But therein lies yet another logical error!—the sum of an empty set, or more generally an empty bag, should be zero, not null, as I now explain.

Let X be a bag or set of cardinality n, where the elements of X are values (e.g., integers) for which the notion of summing makes sense—in other words, values for which the dyadic operator of addition ("+") is defined. Then the following pseudocode procedure will compute the corresponding sum:

```
SUM := 0 ;
for each x in X do
    SUM := SUM + x ;
```

Note the initialization step, which sets SUM to 0. In choosing this initial value, I'm tacitly making use of the fact that 0 is the *identity* with respect to addition; that is, 0 is that special number that has the property that for all numbers x, $x + 0 = 0 + x = x$. So what happens if n is 0 (i.e., if the bag X is empty)? The answer, of course, is that the final value of SUM is just the initial value, viz., 0. Thus we can say that the sum of no numbers at all is 0 (the identity with respect to "+").

Now, we can get around the problem—viz., the problem that SQL incorrectly defines the result of invoking SUM on an empty set to be null—by modifying the original formulation of the query as follows:

```
SELECT COALESCE ( SUM ( SP.QTY ) , 0 ) AS TQY
FROM   SP
```

The result now looks like this:

TQY
0

In case you're not familiar with SQL's COALESCE operator, let me elaborate briefly. Essentially, COALESCE is an operator that lets us replace a null by some value[13] "as soon as it appears" (i.e., before it has a chance to do any serious damage). Here's the definition: Let a, b, ... be scalar expressions. Then the expression COALESCE (a, b, ...) returns null if its arguments are all null, or

---

[13] That value will be nonnull by definition, because null isn't a value (despite the unfortunate and all too commonly encountered phrase "null value"). The fact is, *all* values are "nonnull"; "null value" is a contradiction in terms, and indeed a solecism.

the value of its first nonnull argument otherwise. (Of course, to use the operator sensibly, we do need to ensure that at least one of the expressions *a*, *b*, ... evaluates to something that's not null.)[14]

Here again is the GBH expression I showed when I first started discussing HAVING without GROUP BY:

```
SELECT SUM ( SP.QTY ) AS TQY
FROM   SP
HAVING MIN ( SP.QTY ) > 50
```

Now, if table SP does happen to be empty as I'm currently assuming, then (as noted in the previous subsection) the MIN invocation in the HAVING clause will also return a null. Strictly speaking, therefore, if we want to avoid nulls entirely (and frankly I think we should), then we should use COALESCE in connection with the MIN invocation in the HAVING clause as well, perhaps like this:

```
SELECT COALESCE ( SUM ( SP.QTY ) , 0 ) AS TQY
FROM   SP
HAVING COALESCE ( MIN ( SP.QTY ) , 0 ) > 50
```

If we don't, however, then no real harm is done—but only because of one or more of the logical errors previously discussed![15] In the interest of brevity, therefore (though it really goes against my own better judgment), I won't bother to use COALESCE in such contexts for the remainder of the present chapter.

Let me now get back to this simpler example:

```
SELECT SUM ( SP.QTY ) AS TQY
FROM   SP
```

Of course, even if this expression is modified as recommended to make use of COALESCE in the SELECT clause, it still suffers from the defect that it produces a result table containing one row instead of the logically correct response, viz., an empty table. To emphasize just how illogical that result really is, I want to rub salt in the wound a little. (I'm afraid that what follows amounts to a digression within a digression, pretty much, but I do think the point is worth

---

[14] *Exercise:* Do you think I ought to have used COALESCE in any of the SQL expressions I've shown in this chapter prior to this point? If so, which ones?

[15] Which ones?

making.) Still assuming that table SP is currently empty, then, consider these two SQL expressions, deliberately shown side by side:

```
SELECT  COUNT(*)  AS  CT ,  SNO ,  PNO    SELECT  COUNT(*)  AS  CT
FROM    SP                                 FROM    SP
```

(I deliberately switch from SUM to COUNT here in order to avoid the distractions caused by nulls. SQL does correctly define the count of an empty set to be zero, not null.) Here then are the results:

Well, how can these results possibly make sense? I mean, to spell the point out, how can *removing* items from the SELECT clause *increase* the cardinality of—i.e., increase the number of rows in—the result?

Note: If you're having difficulty with the foregoing rhetorical questions, compare the expressions SELECT SNO, PNO FROM SP and SELECT SNO FROM SP. The second of these can't possibly produce a result with more rows than the first does.

> *Aside:* Actually—SQL being SQL—those two expressions both produce the *same* number of rows! To make my point properly, I should really be inviting you to compare the expressions SELECT *DISTINCT* SNO, PNO FROM SP and SELECT *DISTINCT* SNO FROM SP. Given the sample database value shown in Fig. 4.1, the first of these latter expressions will produce a result of twelve rows and the second a result of four rows. *End of aside.*

A NonGBH Formulation for Query Q8

Note: You might find this subsection a bit of an anticlimax after the complexity of preceding subsections! If so, then I apologize.

Let me get back to the issue of finding a formulation of Query Q8 that avoids the use of HAVING. Now, by this time I wouldn't blame you at all if you've forgotten exactly what Query Q8 was, so let me state it again to remind you:

Q8:   If the minimum quantity in which any part is supplied is greater than 50, then get the total shipment quantity for all parts; otherwise don't get any value at all.

Here again is the GBH formulation (with COALESCE):

```
SELECT COALESCE ( SUM ( SP.QTY ) , 0 ) AS TQY
FROM   SP
HAVING MIN ( SP.QTY ) > 50
```

The obvious nonGBH formulation to try (using a simplified Type 2 transformation—see the section "Both GROUP BY and HAVING," earlier) looks like this:

```
SELECT DISTINCT COALESCE ( SUM ( SP.QTY ) , 0 ) AS TQY
FROM   SP
WHERE ( SELECT MIN ( SP.QTY ) FROM SP ) > 50
```

And in fact this formulation does the trick, though for Case 3 it "works"— that is, it produces the right answer, viz., an empty table—only because of behavior on SQL's part that I've already explained is logically incorrect.

Another NonGBH Formulation for Query Q8

Consider the following simple SQL expression once again:

```
SELECT SUM ( SP.QTY ) AS TQY
FROM   SP
```

As we've seen, if table SP is currently empty, then this expression incorrectly produces this result—

—instead of this one:

```
┌──────────┐
│   TQY    │
├──────────┤
│          │
└──────────┘
```

Here for interest is an SQL expression that does produce this latter (correct) result if SP is currently empty, as well as producing the correct sum otherwise:

```
SELECT DISTINCT ( SELECT SUM ( SP.QTY ) FROM SP ) AS TQY
FROM    SP
```

Explanation: First of all, note that the sole item mentioned in the outer SELECT clause, following the keyword DISTINCT, is *not* a reference to the aggregate operator SUM as such, but rather a scalar subquery that happens to contain such a reference. The cardinality of the result of the expression overall (that is, the number of rows in that result) is therefore no different from what it would be if we were to replace that scalar subquery by any other scalar expression, such as SP.PNO, or SP.QTY, or even just a literal such as 0. To spell it out in detail, therefore, what happens is this:

■ Let the cardinality of table SP be n, and assume for the moment that the DISTINCT in the outer SELECT clause is omitted. Then the expression overall clearly returns a result with n rows.

■ If $n > 0$, the scalar subquery in that outer SELECT clause clearly evaluates to the desired sum; for example, given the sample values shown in Fig. 4.1, it evaluates to 3100. If we're not careful, though, the expression overall will then return a table containing n copies of that sum (twelve copies of that 3100, given the sample database value shown in Fig. 4.1). That's why that DISTINCT is needed.

■ On the other hand, if $n = 0$, it doesn't matter what the scalar subquery in the outer SELECT clause evaluates to, because in that case the expression overall will clearly return a table containing no rows at all.

Observe, moreover, that (bonus!) there's now no need to use COALESCE.

So now we can formulate another transformation rule, as follows: Given table T, with columns A, B, etc., let *agg1* and *agg2* be aggregate operators that are applicable to column A and column B, respectively. Then the expression

```
SELECT  agg1 ( T.A ) AS AGGA
FROM    T
HAVING  agg2 ( T.B ) comp scalar
```

can be transformed into the logically equivalent expression

```
SELECT DISTINCT ( SELECT agg1 ( T.A ) FROM T ) AS AGGA
FROM    T
WHERE ( SELECT agg2 ( T.B ) FROM T ) comp scalar
```

I'll leave consideration of what happens if the HAVING formulation includes a WHERE clause as an exercise.

> *Aside:* It's not directly relevant to the overall theme of this chapter, but there's another point I'd like to make in connection with the SQL expression I gave above as a correct formulation of Query Q8, viz.:
>
> ```
> SELECT DISTINCT ( SELECT SUM ( SP.QTY ) FROM SP ) AS TQY
> FROM    SP
> ```
>
> As we've seen, this expression produces as its result a table of one column, and that column is called TQY. Now consider the following slightly revised form of the same expression:
>
> ```
> SELECT DISTINCT ( SELECT SUM ( SP.QTY ) AS TQY FROM SP )
> FROM    SP
> ```
>
> Now it's the subquery in the SELECT clause that produces as its result a table of one column, that column being called TQY. Believe it or not, however, the single column in the *overall* result—which is, of course, still a table of one column—is now not guaranteed to have any particular name at all! In particular, it isn't guaranteed to have the name TQY. *End of aside.*

RANGE VARIABLES

Now I want to turn my attention, albeit briefly, to a rather different topic. Consider the following query:

Q9: Get all pairs of supplier numbers such that the two suppliers concerned are located in the same city.

A possible SQL formulation for this query is as follows:

```
SELECT FIRST.SNO AS SX , SECOND.SNO AS SY
FROM   S AS FIRST , S AS SECOND
WHERE  FIRST.CITY = SECOND.CITY
```

FIRST and SECOND here are examples of what SQL calls *correlation names*. Note, however, that (as explained in Chapter 3) SQL never states just what it is that such names *name!*—certainly there's no such thing in SQL as a "correlation." In relational calculus, by contrast, there's something called a *range variable*, and range variables play a role in the calculus that's analogous to the role that's played in SQL by whatever it is that correlation names are supposed to name. So I'll use the relational calculus terminology in what follows, as much as I can.

A range variable, then, is a variable that ranges over some specified table—i.e., it's a variable whose permitted values are rows of the table in question. Thus, if range variable R ranges over table T,[16] then at any given time the expression "R" stands for some row currently appearing in table T (or, loosely, just "some row of T"). In SQL, range variables are introduced as shown in the foregoing example: namely, by means of AS specifications in the FROM clause.

> *Aside:* Don't confuse AS specifications in the FROM clause and AS specifications in the SELECT clause. An AS specification in the SELECT clause introduces a name for a *column*, as many of the SQL examples earlier in this chapter have already illustrated. By contrast, an AS specification in the FROM clause introduces a name for a *range variable*, as just explained. *End of aside.*

Anyway, the point I want to make now is that, just like the GROUP BY and HAVING clauses, range variables are logically redundant in SQL (the fact that I've been making heavy use of them in my examples prior to this point notwithstanding). For example, here's a formulation of Query Q9 that avoids them—or ought to, at any rate (see the note immediately following the example for further explanation):

```
SELECT SX , SY
FROM ( SELECT S.SNO AS SX , S.CITY FROM S ) AS POINTLESS1
       NATURAL JOIN
     ( SELECT S.SNO AS SY , S.CITY FROM S ) AS POINTLESS2
```

---

[16] "Table T" here really means table *variable T*, of course.

Note: It's true that this formulation does involve two range variables, *POINTLESS1* and *POINTLESS2*, but logically it ought not to. Certainly they're never referenced. In fact, the only reason they're there is because SQL has a syntax rule saying they must be.[17] (Don't ask me to justify that rule, because I don't think I can.)

By way of another example, I return to Query Q1 from the section "GROUP BY Without HAVING":

Q1: For each part supplied, get the part number, maximum quantity, and minimum quantity supplied of that part.

Here's a formulation that "avoids" both (a) range variables and (b) the GROUP BY and HAVING clauses:

```
SELECT DISTINCT PX AS PNO ,
      ( SELECT MAX ( SP.QTY ) FROM SP
        WHERE  SP.PNO = PX ) AS MXQ ,
      ( SELECT MIN ( SP.QTY ) FROM SP
        WHERE  SP.PNO = PX ) AS MNQ
FROM ( SELECT SP.PNO AS PX FROM SP ) AS POINTLESS
```

(As with the previous example, this formulation does in fact involve a range variable, *POINTLESS*, but logically it ought not to. At least that range variable is never referenced.)

To close this section, let me point out that range variables *must* be redundant—i.e., logically unnecessary—in SQL, because:

1. The relational algebra has no range variables.

2. Every relational algebra expression has an exact counterpart in SQL[18] that also involves no range variables (except for ones that are never referenced and are there just because of a weird SQL syntax rule).

---

[17] To be specific, a "table subquery" that's being used to denote the table argument, or one of the table arguments, within a FROM clause is required to be accompanied by an associated AS specification, even if the range variable name introduced by that AS specification is never referenced anywhere else in the overall expression. See my book *SQL and Relational Theory: How to Write Accurate SQL Code* (3rd edition, O'Reilly, 2015) for further discussion.

[18] Except for algebraic expressions that evaluate to a relation of degree zero. But this oversight—this extremely unfortunate omission, rather—on SQL's part doesn't materially affect the argument.

3. SQL includes no relational functionality that the relational algebra doesn't.

THE STORY SO FAR

I've tried to show so far that the GROUP BY and/or HAVING clauses and range variables are all essentially redundant in SQL. It's interesting to note, therefore, that these are aspects of the language that are among the hardest to teach, understand, learn, and apply properly!—as I know from direct experience. Be that as it may, I'd like to come back and focus on GBH expressions in particular; more specifically, I'd like to suggest that the alternative formulations—i.e., the ones that avoid GROUP BY and HAVING altogether—are often actually preferable (in fact, *logically* preferable) to their GBH counterparts. By way of illustration, let's consider Query Q4 again from the section "Both GROUP BY and HAVING":

Q4: For each part supplied by more than one supplier, get the part number.

Here repeated from that earlier section are the GBH and nonGBH formulations I gave for this query (but now shown side by side for ease of comparison):

```
SELECT  SP.PNO            SELECT  DISTINCT SP.PNO
FROM    SP                FROM    SP
GROUP   BY SP.PNO         WHERE ( SELECT  COUNT(*)
HAVING COUNT(*) > 1               FROM    SP AS SPX
                                  WHERE   SPX.PNO = SP.PNO ) > 1
```

Well, it seems to me that:

■ First, the nonGBH version is at least logically cleaner and simpler than the GBH version, in that it specifically doesn't need the additional language constructs under discussion (I mean the GROUP BY and HAVING clauses).

■ Second, it's certainly not clear from the original statement of the problem that grouping as such is what's needed to formulate the query in SQL (and of course it isn't).

■ Third, it's also far from obvious that a HAVING clause is needed rather than a WHERE clause (and of course it isn't).

Indeed, the GBH version begins to look more like (a) a prescription for *solving* the problem—that is, a series of steps that must be gone through in order to *construct* the answer to the problem—instead of (b) just a description of what the problem *is*. In a word, it looks more procedural than declarative. And, of course, a general objective for the relational model has always been to prefer declarative formulations over procedural ones, for a variety of well known reasons (the most important being that declarative means the system does the work, whereas procedural means the user does the work).

Of course, there's no denying that the GBH version is more succinct than the nonGBH version. But if the sole advantage of GBH formulations is succinctness, it would have been better if such formulations had been explicitly *defined* as shorthands, which to my knowledge they never were. That way, the anomalies I identified in discussing the transformation rules in earlier sections would never have occurred (probably!), and implementation would have been easier too (again, probably). *Note:* The principle underlying the idea of explicitly defining language constructs as shorthands is referred to as *syntactic substitution*. See my book *Fifty Years of Relational, and Other Database Writings: More Thoughts and Essays on Database Matters* (Technics Publications, 2020) for further discussion of such matters.

Aside: I note in passing that **Tutorial D** does make extensive use of that design principle (I mean syntactic substitution). In particular, it uses it in connection with its analog of SQL's GROUP BY and HAVING features; that is, the analog in question is explicitly defined as a shorthand. Here by way of illustration is a **Tutorial D** formulation of Query Q4:

```
SP { SNO } WHERE COUNT ( IMAGE_IN ( SP ) ) > 1
```

The subexpression IMAGE_IN (SP) here is explicitly defined to be shorthand for the following longer one:

```
( SP JOIN RELATION { TUPLE { SNO SNO } } )
                                    { ALL BUT SNO }
```

This latter expression denotes the set of SP tuples having the same SNO value as "the current one" (where by "the current one" I mean the tuple of SP currently being considered for contributing to the overall result), projected on {PNO,QTY}.[19] *End of aside*.

FIFTY WAYS TO QUOTE YOUR QUERY

SQL suffers from many more redundancies than just the ones I've discussed in this chapter so far; for example, the SQL EXISTS operator is also one hundred percent redundant. As a direct result of this state of affairs, all but the most trivial of queries can be expressed in SQL in a huge number of different ways. Even a query as simple as "Get names of suppliers who supply part P2" can easily be expressed in at least eight different ways, all of them at least superficially distinct—and that's if we limit ourselves to features included in SQL/86, the original 1986 version of the standard! The number increases dramatically when features introduced with SQL:1992 and later versions are taken into account (see further discussion below).

Why is this state of affairs undesirable? Well, first of all, of course, such redundancy makes the language much bigger than it needs to be, with obvious negative implications for documentation, implementation, teaching, learning, and so on. In particular, the fact that a given query can be formulated in so many different ways has the serious consequence that users will often have to spend time and effort trying to find the "best" formulation (by which I mean the one that performs best)—which is, of course, one of the things the relational model was expressly intended to avoid in the first place.

Of course, this latter criticism wouldn't be valid if all formulations performed equally well, but that seems unlikely (i.e., I doubt whether the optimizer will be that good).[20] Indeed, the point is worth stressing that all of these redundancies make SQL harder to *implement* (especially to optimize), as well as to teach, learn, remember, and use. And this state of affairs is really rather strange, given that the people responsible for the design of SQL—by

---

[19] By the way, do you think the IMAGE_IN construct might be useful in SQL too? Justify your answer!

[20] A colleague of mine actually once carried out an informal experiment in this connection. Now, this was several years ago, and I don't claim his results are necessarily valid today, but they're certainly suggestive. What he did was take my eight SQL/86 formulations of the query "Get names of suppliers who supply part P2" and run them on a specific DBMS against a specific database, and measure the response times to see if they varied. Well, they certainly did; in fact they were all over the map. (Actually he performed this experiment on several different DBMSs as well, and found, unsurprisingly, that (a) some optimizers were worse than others in this regard and (b) there wasn't even a consistent pattern—with some optimizers some formulations performed better, with other optimizers other formulations did.)

which I mean, primarily, the people on the SQL standardization committees—are first and foremost representatives of the SQL DBMS vendors, who are, of course, precisely the ones who have to do that implementing.

Now, the title of this section is "Fifty Ways to Quote Your Query." It's tongue in cheek, of course; but the reason I chose that title is because I wanted to show you fifty different ways of formulating that simple query "Get names of suppliers who supply part P2." Before I do so, however, I'd just like to take a moment to consider just why it is that SQL does display so much redundancy. Part of the reason is, I believe, historical. Let me elaborate.

As is well known, Codd defined two distinct though equivalent formalisms for interacting with data in relational form: viz., the relational calculus, based on predicate logic, and the relational algebra, based on set theory. Thus, a relational language can be based on either the calculus or the algebra. By way of illustration, QUEL and Query-By-Example (QBE) are both based on the calculus, and ISBL and **Tutorial D** are both based on the algebra. So which is SQL based on? The answer, regrettably, is partly both and partly neither ... When it was first designed, SQL was explicitly intended to be different from both the calculus and the algebra (the former explicitly, the latter perhaps a little less so); indeed, such a goal was the prime motivation for the introduction of the SQL "IN <subquery>" construct.[21] As time went on, however, it turned out that certain features of both the calculus (e.g., explicit quantification) and the algebra (e.g., explicit union and join support) were needed after all, and the language grew to accommodate them. The consequence is that today some aspects of SQL are "calculus like," others are "algebra like," and still others are neither. And a consequence of *that* fact is redundancy! That is, as I've been trying to demonstrate throughout this chapter prior to this point, most queries, constraints, and so on, if they can be expressed in SQL at all, can in fact be expressed in numerous different ways.

Of course, the obvious question is *why*? That is, why did the original designers want SQL to be different from both the calculus and the algebra? I

---

[21] See Donald D. Chamberlin and Raymond F. Boyce: "SEQUEL: A Structured English Query Language," Proc. 1974 ACM SIGMOD Workshop on Data Description, Access, and Control, Ann Arbor, Mich. (May 1974). The name SEQUEL ("Structured English Query Language") was subsequently changed to SQL ("Structured Query Language") for legal reasons; whatever the name, however, the idea was just that queries would typically be formulated as subqueries nested inside other such queries or subqueries (i.e., that was the "structure" being alluded to). More specifically, the language allowed such subqueries—i.e., SELECT – FROM – WHERE expressions, loosely speaking—to appear nested inside the WHERE clause of another such expression, recursively. But that was all! The ability to nest subqueries elsewhere (in particular, inside the SELECT and FROM clauses) wasn't part of the language as originally defined, nor was it added until nearly 20 years later, as part of SQL:1992.

think the answer stems from what I regard as a fundamental misconception: namely, the misconception that the calculus and the algebra were both what might be described as "user hostile." But that perception, I believe, reflects a confusion over syntax vs. semantics. Certainly the syntax in Codd's early papers was a little daunting, based as it was on formal logical and/or mathematical notation. But semantics is another matter! The calculus and the algebra both have, I would argue, very simple semantics, and it's fairly easy (as numerous writers and languages have demonstrated) to wrap that semantics up in syntax that's very user friendly indeed.

Thus, the situation today is that numerous constructs could be removed from the SQL language with absolutely no loss of function at all. And, ironically enough, the "IN <subquery>" construct—the very construct that was the justification for that "Structured" in the name "Structured Query Language"—is one of them.

Be that as it may, let me now move on to those fifty ways of formulating the query "Get names of suppliers who supply part P2." Here they are:[22]

```
1.  SELECT  DISTINCT S.SNAME
    FROM    S , SP
    WHERE   S.SNO = SP.SNO
    AND     SP.PNO = 'P2'

2.  SELECT  DISTINCT S.SNAME
    FROM    S
    WHERE   S.SNO IN
          ( SELECT SP.SNO
            FROM    SP
            WHERE   SP.PNO = 'P2' )

3.  SELECT  DISTINCT S.SNAME
    FROM    S
    WHERE   S.SNO =ANY
          ( SELECT SP.SNO
            FROM    SP
            WHERE   SP.PNO = 'P2' )

4.  SELECT  DISTINCT S.SNAME
    FROM    S
    WHERE   S.SNO MATCH
          ( SELECT SP.SNO
            FROM    SP
            WHERE   SP.PNO = 'P2' )
```

---

[22] If there any SQL constructs used in these formulations that you're unfamiliar with, you can find them all fully described in the book *A Guide to the SQL Standard* (4th edition, Addison-Wesley, 1997), by Hugh Darwen and myself.

```
 5.  SELECT DISTINCT S.SNAME
     FROM    S
     WHERE   S.SNO MATCH UNIQUE
           ( SELECT SP.SNO
             FROM    SP
             WHERE   SP.PNO = 'P2' )

 6.  SELECT DISTINCT S.SNAME
     FROM    S
     WHERE   S.SNO MATCH PARTIAL
           ( SELECT SP.SNO
             FROM    SP
             WHERE   SP.PNO = 'P2' )

 7.  SELECT DISTINCT S.SNAME
     FROM    S
     WHERE   S.SNO MATCH UNIQUE PARTIAL
           ( SELECT SP.SNO
             FROM    SP
             WHERE   SP.PNO = 'P2' )

 8.  SELECT DISTINCT S.SNAME
     FROM    S
     WHERE   S.SNO MATCH FULL
           ( SELECT SP.SNO
             FROM    SP
             WHERE   SP.PNO = 'P2' )

 9.  SELECT DISTINCT S.SNAME
     FROM    S
     WHERE   S.SNO MATCH UNIQUE FULL
           ( SELECT SP.SNO
             FROM    SP
             WHERE   SP.PNO = 'P2' )

10.  SELECT DISTINCT S.SNAME
     FROM    S
     WHERE   EXISTS
           ( SELECT *
             FROM    SP
             WHERE   SP.SNO = S.SNO
             AND     SP.PNO = 'P2' )

11.  SELECT DISTINCT S.SNAME
     FROM    S
     WHERE ( SELECT COUNT(*)
             FROM    SP
             WHERE   SP.SNO = S.SNO
             AND     SP.PNO = 'P2' ) > 0
```

```
12.   SELECT DISTINCT S.SNAME
      FROM    S
      WHERE ( SELECT  COUNT(*)
               FROM    SP
               WHERE   SP.SNO = S.SNO
               AND     SP.PNO = 'P2' ) = 1

13.   SELECT DISTINCT S.SNAME
      FROM    S
      WHERE   'P2' IN
             ( SELECT SP.PNO
               FROM    SP
               WHERE   SP.SNO = S.SNO )

14.   SELECT DISTINCT S.SNAME
      FROM    S
      WHERE   'P2' =ANY
             ( SELECT SP.PNO
               FROM    SP
               WHERE   SP.SNO = S.SNO )

15.   SELECT DISTINCT S.SNAME
      FROM    S
      WHERE   'P2' MATCH
             ( SELECT SP.PNO
               FROM    SP
               WHERE   SP.SNO = S.SNO )

16.   SELECT DISTINCT S.SNAME
      FROM    S
      WHERE   'P2' MATCH UNIQUE
             ( SELECT SP.PNO
               FROM    SP
               WHERE   SP.SNO = S.SNO )

17.   SELECT DISTINCT S.SNAME
      FROM    S
      WHERE   'P2' MATCH PARTIAL
             ( SELECT SP.PNO
               FROM    SP
               WHERE   SP.SNO = S.SNO )

18.   SELECT DISTINCT S.SNAME
      FROM    S
      WHERE   'P2' MATCH UNIQUE PARTIAL
             ( SELECT SP.PNO
               FROM    SP
               WHERE   SP.SNO = S.SNO )
```

```
19.  SELECT DISTINCT S.SNAME
     FROM    S
     WHERE   'P2' MATCH FULL
             ( SELECT SP.PNO
               FROM    SP
               WHERE   SP.SNO = S.SNO )

20.  SELECT DISTINCT S.SNAME
     FROM    S
     WHERE   'P2' MATCH UNIQUE FULL
             ( SELECT SP.PNO
               FROM    SP
               WHERE   SP.SNO = S.SNO )

21.  SELECT S.SNAME
     FROM    S , SP
     WHERE   S.SNO = SP.SNO
     AND     SP.PNO = 'P2'
     GROUP   BY S.SNAME

22.  SELECT DISTINCT S.SNAME
     FROM    S , SP
     WHERE   S.SNO = SP.SNO
     GROUP   BY S.SNAME, SP.PNO
     HAVING SP.PNO = 'P2'

23.  SELECT DISTINCT S.SNAME
     FROM    S , SP
     WHERE   SP.PNO = 'P2'
     GROUP   BY S.SNO , S.SNAME , SP.SNO
     HAVING SP.SNO = S.SNO

24.  SELECT DISTINCT S.SNAME
     FROM    S , SP
     GROUP   BY S.SNO , S.SNAME , SP.SNO , SP.PNO
     HAVING SP.SNO = S.SNO
     AND     SP.PNO = 'P2'

25.  SELECT DISTINCT S.SNAME
     FROM    S CROSS JOIN SP
     WHERE   S.SNO = SP.SNO
     AND     SP.PNO = 'P2'

26.  SELECT DISTINCT S.SNAME
     FROM    S NATURAL JOIN SP
     WHERE   SP.PNO = 'P2'

27.  SELECT DISTINCT S.SNAME
     FROM    S JOIN SP USING ( SNO )
     WHERE   SP.PNO = 'P2'
```

```
28.  SELECT DISTINCT S.SNAME
     FROM    S JOIN SP ON S.SNO = SP.SNO
     WHERE   SP.PNO = 'P2'

29.  SELECT DISTINCT S.SNAME
     FROM    S NATURAL LEFT JOIN SP
     WHERE   SP.PNO = 'P2'

30.  SELECT DISTINCT S.SNAME
     FROM    S LEFT JOIN SP USING ( SNO )
     WHERE   SP.PNO = 'P2'

31.  SELECT DISTINCT S.SNAME
     FROM    S LEFT JOIN SP ON S.SNO = SP.SNO
     WHERE   SP.PNO = 'P2'

32.  SELECT DISTINCT S.SNAME
     FROM    S NATURAL RIGHT JOIN SP
     WHERE   SP.PNO = 'P2'

33.  SELECT DISTINCT S.SNAME
     FROM    S RIGHT JOIN SP USING ( SNO )
     WHERE   SP.PNO = 'P2'

34.  SELECT DISTINCT S.SNAME
     FROM    S RIGHT JOIN SP ON S.SNO = SP.SNO
     WHERE   SP.PNO = 'P2'

35.  SELECT DISTINCT S.SNAME
     FROM    S NATURAL FULL JOIN SP
     WHERE   SP.PNO = 'P2'

36.  SELECT DISTINCT S.SNAME
     FROM    S FULL JOIN SP USING ( SNO )
     WHERE   SP.PNO = 'P2'

37.  SELECT DISTINCT S.SNAME
     FROM    S FULL JOIN SP ON S.SNO = SP.SNO
     WHERE   SP.PNO = 'P2'

38.  SELECT DISTINCT S.SNAME
     FROM    S
             NATURAL JOIN
           ( SELECT SP.SNO
             FROM    SP
             WHERE   SP.PNO = 'P2' ) AS POINTLESS
```

```
39.  SELECT  DISTINCT S.SNAME
     FROM    S
             JOIN
           ( SELECT SP.SNO
             FROM    SP
             WHERE   SP.PNO = 'P2' ) AS POINTLESS
             USING ( SNO )

40.  SELECT  DISTINCT S.SNAME
     FROM    S
             JOIN
           ( SELECT SP.SNO
             FROM    SP
             WHERE   SP.PNO = 'P2' ) AS POINTLESS
             ON S.SNO = SP.SNO

41.  SELECT  DISTINCT S.SNAME
     FROM    S
             NATURAL LEFT JOIN
           ( SELECT SP.SNO
             FROM    SP
             WHERE   SP.PNO = 'P2' ) AS POINTLESS

42.  SELECT  DISTINCT S.SNAME
     FROM    S
             LEFT JOIN
           ( SELECT SP.SNO
             FROM    SP
             WHERE   SP.PNO = 'P2' ) AS POINTLESS
             USING ( SNO )

43.  SELECT  DISTINCT S.SNAME
     FROM    S
             LEFT JOIN
           ( SELECT SP.SNO
             FROM    SP
             WHERE   SP.PNO = 'P2' ) AS POINTLESS
             ON S.SNO = SP.SNO

44.  SELECT  DISTINCT S.SNAME
     FROM    S
             NATURAL RIGHT JOIN
           ( SELECT SP.SNO
             FROM    SP
             WHERE   SP.PNO = 'P2' ) AS POINTLESS

45.  SELECT  DISTINCT S.SNAME
     FROM    S
             RIGHT JOIN
           ( SELECT SP.SNO
             FROM    SP
             WHERE   SP.PNO = 'P2' ) AS POINTLESS
             USING ( SNO )
```

```
46.   SELECT DISTINCT S.SNAME
      FROM    S
              RIGHT JOIN
          ( SELECT SP.SNO
            FROM    SP
            WHERE   SP.PNO = 'P2' ) AS POINTLESS
            ON S.SNO = SP.SNO

47.   SELECT DISTINCT S.SNAME
      FROM    S
              NATURAL FULL JOIN
          ( SELECT SP.SNO
            FROM    SP
            WHERE   SP.PNO = 'P2' ) AS POINTLESS

48.   SELECT DISTINCT S.SNAME
      FROM    S
              FULL JOIN
          ( SELECT SP.SNO
            FROM    SP
            WHERE   SP.PNO = 'P2' ) AS POINTLESS
            USING ( SNO )

49.   SELECT DISTINCT S.SNAME
      FROM    S
              FULL JOIN
          ( SELECT SP.SNO
            FROM    SP
            WHERE   SP.PNO = 'P2' ) AS POINTLESS
            ON S.SNO = SP.SNO

50.   SELECT DISTINCT S.SNAME
      FROM ( ( SELECT S.SNO FROM S )
               INTERSECT
             ( SELECT SP.SNO FROM SP
               WHERE SP.PNO = 'P2' ) ) AS POINTLESS
             NATURAL JOIN S

51.   SELECT DISTINCT S.SNAME
      FROM ( ( SELECT * FROM S )
               INTERSECT CORRESPONDING
             ( SELECT * FROM SP
               WHERE SP.PNO = 'P2' ) ) AS POINTLESS
             NATURAL JOIN S

52.   SELECT DISTINCT S.SNAME
      FROM ( ( SELECT * FROM S )
               INTERSECT CORRESPONDING BY ( SNO )
             ( SELECT * FROM SP
               WHERE SP.PNO = 'P2' ) ) AS POINTLESS
             NATURAL JOIN S
```

Discussion

OK, I lied—it wasn't 50, it was 52. But, of course, the stopping place was arbitrary! Consider the following:

- We can obtain numerous further, albeit rather frivolous, variants on the formulations already shown by making use of the fact that (e.g.) $a < b$ is logically equivalent to $b > a$, or the fact that A NATURAL JOIN B is logically equivalent to B NATURAL JOIN A, or the fact that A LEFT JOIN B is logically equivalent to B RIGHT JOIN A. *Note:* Actually these last two equivalences aren't quite valid in SQL, owing to the fact that tables in SQL have a left to right ordering to their columns, but this flaw doesn't invalidate my basic point.[23] It does, however, make life still more difficult for the optimizer.

- I didn't even attempt to show various possible "tricky" formulations that made use of comparison operators such as LIKE and BETWEEN, nor ones that made use of the "TABLE <table>" construct.

- The three INTERSECT formulations shown (Nos. 50-52) each make use of a join. In each case, the NATURAL JOIN shown could be replaced by a JOIN USING or a JOIN ON or a LEFT NATURAL JOIN or a LEFT JOIN USING or a LEFT JOIN ON to produce further valid formulations of the original query.

- Any or all of the many SELECT clauses that appear in the various formulations without a DISTINCT option can be extended to include one.

- Let *snp* be an SQL formulation of the query "Get suppliers who *don't* supply part P2"—for example:

```
SELECT  *
FROM    S
WHERE   NOT EXISTS
      ( SELECT  *
        FROM    SP
        WHERE   SP.SNO = S.SNO
        AND     SP.PNO = 'P2' )
```

---

[23] Here's a test of your SQL knowledge: What *are* the columns of the result of A NATURAL JOIN B, in their left to right order? What about A LEFT JOIN B and B RIGHT JOIN A?

(Of course, there are any number of SQL expressions that can serve as a valid *snp*—i.e., any number of possible formulations of this query, all of them logically equivalent to the formulation just shown.) Then the expression

```
SELECT DISTINCT S.SNAME
FROM ( S EXCEPT ( snp ) )
```

is yet another valid SQL formulation of the original query ("Get names of suppliers who supply part P2"). Furthermore, this EXCEPT formulation itself has several variants (analogous to the variants already discussed in connection with the INTERSECT formulations).

■ Finally, let *exp* be any valid SQL formulation of the original query. Then the expression

```
SELECT DISTINCT SNAME
FROM ( exp ) AS POINTLESS
```

is yet another valid formulation! In other words, the number of valid formulations is quite literally infinite (in theory at least, though of course any real SQL implementation will have limits on such things as the maximum length of an SQL expression).

One further remark: It's true, of course, that many of the formulations I've shown—perhaps most of them—would never be directly produced by a human user as a "natural" formulation of what is, after all, an almost trivial query. But this observation misses the point (or two points, rather, and actually more[24]). First, if there are so many ways to formulate such a simple query, how many ways are there going to be for a more complicated one? Second, even in the simple case, the user might be querying a view rather than a base table, and the "query merge" process (that is, the process of combining the user's query and the view definition) might easily yield a fairly complex expression.

Let me close this section by noting that these redundancy problems—both the ones I've identified in this chapter, and others I haven't discussed here—are *not* easy to fix. What Hugh Darwen has called *The Shackle of Compatibility*

---

[24] Finding such a point that isn't one of the two mentioned is left as an exercise.

means that once a feature has been incorporated into a language, it can never be taken out again—because, of course, existing programs will fail if it is. That's why it's so important to get languages right first time. It's also one reason why language design is hard.

CONCLUDING REMARKS

I set out in writing this chapter to show that SQL is highly redundant, and I think I've succeeded in that aim. What I think the chapter also shows, however (though this wasn't my original intention), that SQL is extremely complicated as well—much more complicated, I venture to suggest, than its advocates would have you believe. How on earth did we let this happen? And why? Time to quote David Hilbert again, I think:

> *For what is clear and easily comprehended attracts; the complicated repels.*

Chapter 5

Indeterminacy in SQL

The assumption of an absolute determinism
is the essential foundation of every scientific enquiry.
—Max Planck (1858-1947)

I got determination ... C'mon, give me a break!
—The Ritchie Family

My bonds in thee are all determinate
—William Shakespeare:
Sonnet 73 (1609)

The SQL standard explicitly defines certain SQL expressions to be *indeterminate* (the SQL term is "possibly nondeterministic"), meaning the expression in question is allowed to produce different results on different evaluations even if the database hasn't changed in the interim. As the 1992 version of the standard ("SQL:1992") puts it:[1]

> A <query expression> or <query specification> is *possibly nondeterministic* if an implementation might, at two different times where the state of the SQL-data is the same, produce results that differ by more than the order of the rows due to General Rules that specify implementation dependent behavior.

Note: Implementation dependent is a term used throughout the SQL standard to refer to a feature whose specifics can vary from one implementation to another and don't even have to be defined for any individual implementation.

---

[1] The "possibly nondeterministic" concept was first defined in SQL:1992. For simplicity, throughout this chapter I take the terms *SQL* and *the SQL standard* to refer to that 1992 version and all subsequent versions considered generically (barring explicit statements to the contrary, of course). *Note:* I would rather have used a more recent version of the standard as my source document, but for reasons that should become apparent in Appendix A it turned out to be much too difficult to do so. As for that term *nondeterministic*, the standard usually hyphenates it ("non-deterministic"), but I prefer not to.

In other words, it effectively means "undefined"—the implementation is free to decide how it will implement the feature in question, and the result of that decision doesn't even have to be documented (it could change without warning from release to release, or perhaps even more frequently). A familiar example of an implementation dependent feature is ORDER BY: If what SQL calls the *sort keys* in some particular ORDER BY clause are such that n individual rows all "compare equal" with respect to them, then those n rows will certainly all appear together in the final result, but their relative ordering within that result can be any of $n!$ (i.e., n factorial) possibilities. Note, however, that even though the result in such a situation is certainly "implementation dependent" as just explained, this particular language feature—viz., an ORDER BY specification that produces an indeterminate result—is *not* considered to be "possibly nondeterministic," as the foregoing extract from the standard states quite explicitly.[2] The reason, presumably, is that the lack of determinacy involved in this particular case has no "knock on" effects, whereas the same can't be said for those cases considered to be truly indeterminate.[3] Examples to follow!

To illustrate the concept of indeterminacy in SQL expressions, consider the SQL data type VARCHAR(3). By definition, values of this type are character strings of maximum length three. So let X and Y be variables of this type, and let them have values 'AB' and 'AB ' (note the trailing space in the second of these), respectively. Further, let PAD SPACE apply to the pertinent "collation" (see the section immediately following if you're unfamiliar with this latter concept). Then the values of X and Y are definitely distinct—in particular, they're of different lengths—and yet they're considered to "compare equal" under that collation. As a direct consequence, if (a) SQL table T has just one column—call it Z—of type VARCHAR(3), and just two rows, and (b) those rows contain the values 'AB' and 'AB ', respectively, then (c) the SQL expression

---

[2] As a matter of fact the extract quoted is a little odd, inasmuch as <query expression>s and <query specification>s aren't supposed to produce results with row ordering anyway. Row ordering is produced by applying an ORDER BY clause to a table that, by definition, has no such ordering, and such a clause is part of either a <declare cursor> or what the standard calls a <direct select statement: multiple rows>. It isn't part of a <query expression> or <query specification> at all (at least, not as those constructs were originally defined, but see the next footnote). Also, the result of ORDER BY isn't a table anyway—at least, not as the term *table* is understood in SQL in general.

[3] Actually, the ability to specify ORDER BY was—very unfortunately, in my opinion—added to <query expression>s (though not <query specification>s) in SQL:2011. This change was made primarily, I think, in order to provide some support for quota queries (see my book *Logic and Relational Theory: Thoughts and Essays on Database Matters*, Technics Publications, 2020). But it presumably means that additional kinds of indeterminacy, and hence additional "knock on" effects, are now possible.

```
SELECT DISTINCT Z
FROM    T
```

can quite legitimately return either of the following results (I show the enclosing quotes for clarity):

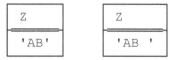

In other words, the specified SELECT expression is indeterminate ("possibly nondeterministic").

As the foregoing example might serve to suggest, character string comparisons are a major cause of indeterminacy in SQL;[4] so one thing we clearly need to do is take a more detailed look at such comparisons.

CHARACTER STRING COMPARISONS

Note: The matters discussed in this section are all rather more complicated than I'm pretending here. Of course I'm deliberately avoiding those complications!— but if you want to know more, you might want to take a look at the discussion of Example 3 in the section "Case 1 (equality true with distinct comparands)" in Chapter 1. I'd like to draw your attention to footnote 15 in that chapter in particular.

In SQL, any given character string contains characters from just one *character set* and is subject to just one *collation*. I assume you're familiar with the basic idea of a character set, although as a matter of fact even that apparently simple concept is surrounded by a certain amount of confusion in the SQL standard.[5] As for collations—the term is short for *collating sequence*—a collation is a rule that's (a) associated with a specific character set and (b) governs comparisons of

---

[4] Originally (i.e., in SQL:1992) they were the *only* cause, but later versions of the standard have unfortunately added many others. See the section "Possibly Nondeterministic Expressions," later; see also Appendix A.

[5] For examples in support of this claim, as well as much further discussion and explanation, see Chapter 1 of the present book; see also Appendix D ("Some Outstanding Issues") of *A Guide to the SQL Standard*, 4th edition, by C. J. Date and Hugh Darwen (Addison-Wesley, 1997).

strings of characters from that character set. Moreover, if *C* is a collation for character set *S*, and *a* and *b* are any two characters from *S*, then *C* is required to be such that exactly one of the comparisons *a* < *b*, *a* = *b*, and *a* > *b* evaluates to TRUE and the other two to FALSE, under that collation *C*.

> *Aside:* In SQL as originally defined there was just one character set and one collation, and that collation was based on the numerical order of the internal binary codes used to represent the characters in that character set. But there's no intrinsic reason why collating sequences should have to depend on internal coding schemes, and there are good practical reasons why they shouldn't. *End of aside.*

For simplicity, let's agree for the remainder of this chapter that all SQL character strings are made up of characters from the same character set *S* and are subject to the same collation *C*, barring explicit statements to the contrary.

Now let *x* and *y* be two SQL character strings. Then the comparisons *x* < *y*, *x* = *y*, and *x* > *y* are all legal, *even if x and y aren't of the same type*. In case you find the qualification here—I mean the clause in italics—a trifle surprising, let me elaborate briefly. The basic point is that, in SQL, VARCHAR(3) and VARCHAR(5)—to pick examples more or less at random—are really different types; in other words, the length is part of the type, loosely speaking.[6] Similarly, CHAR(3) and VARCHAR(3) are also different types. Thus (and contrary to popular opinion, perhaps), CHAR and VARCHAR aren't types, as such, at all; rather, they're type *generators*. Here's a definition of this latter concept, taken from my book *The **New** Relational Database Dictionary* (O'Reilly, 2016):

> **Definition (type generator):** An operator that's invoked at compile time instead of run time and returns a type instead of a value. For example, conventional programming languages typically support an array type generator, which lets users define an unlimited number and variety of individual array types. In the relational model, the tuple and (especially) relation type generators are the important ones; they allow users to define an unlimited number and variety of individual tuple and relation types.

---

[6] This point is *not* widely understood—the standard itself is very confused, not to say self-contradictory, in this connection—but the sentence is nevertheless correct as stated. See my book *Fifty Years of Relational, and Other Database Writings: More Thoughts and Essays on Database Matters* (Technics Publications, 2020) for an extended discussion of such matters.

That same source goes on to give the following example (based as usual on the familiar suppliers-and-parts database and expressed as usual in the language **Tutorial D**):

Consider the suppliers base relvar definition:[7]

```
VAR S BASE
    RELATION { SNO SNO , SNAME NAME ,
                            STATUS INTEGER , CITY CHAR }
    KEY { SNO } ;
```

This definition includes an invocation of the RELATION type generator (syntactically, everything from the keyword RELATION to the closing brace following the keyword CHAR, inclusive). That invocation returns a specific relation type—namely, the type

```
RELATION { SNO SNO , SNAME NAME ,
                STATUS INTEGER , CITY CHAR }
```

So this type is in fact a generated type—as indeed are all relation types, and all tuple types also.

Back to SQL. As you can see from the foregoing, an SQL type specification such as VARCHAR(3) is really an invocation of the VARCHAR type generator with a particular argument (3, in the example), and it returns a specific type: namely, and precisely, the type we commonly refer to as "VARCHAR(3)."

To repeat, therefore, VARCHAR(3) and VARCHAR(5), for example, are different types. As I've more or less said already, however, SQL does allow comparisons between values of type VARCHAR(3) and values of type VARCHAR(5), or more generally between values of any two character string types. Here are the rules regarding such comparisons (*x* and *y* are the character strings being compared and *C* is the pertinent collation):

■ The comparison is done character by character, pairwise, from left to right.

■ Let *x* and *y* be of equal length. Then if every pairwise comparison is such that the characters involved "compare equal" under *C*, then *x* and *y* "compare equal" also; otherwise, the overall result is defined to be the same

---

[7] The term *relvar* is shorthand for relation variable, and the suppliers relvar is a base relvar specifically.

as the result of the first pairwise comparison for which the characters involved fail to "compare equal."

■ Alternatively, let x and y be of different lengths, and assume without loss of generality that x is shorter than y. Now the rules depend on whether PAD SPACE or NO PAD was specified for collation C when that collation was defined:

1. Under PAD SPACE, x is conceptually padded at the right with spaces to make it the same length as y, and the rules for comparing equal length character strings are then applied. *Note:* Padding x with spaces can be regarded as *coercing* x to the type of y (see Chapter 1).

2. Under NO PAD, $x = y$ evaluates to FALSE. Moreover, if z is the leading substring of y that is of the same length as x, then (using the rules for comparing equal length character strings):

    a. If $x = z$ evaluates to TRUE, then $x < y$ evaluates to TRUE, even if all remaining characters of y are spaces.

    b. If $x < z$ evaluates to TRUE, then $x < y$ evaluates to TRUE.

    c. If $x > z$ evaluates to TRUE, then $x > y$ evaluates to TRUE.

Aside: As noted in an earlier aside, in SQL as originally defined there was only one collating sequence; moreover, that collating sequence was based on the internal IBM coding scheme (EBCDIC) and implicitly supported PAD SPACE only (NO PAD wasn't an option, and PAD SPACE couldn't be stated explicitly). The reason for this state of affairs was a desire on the part of the SQL designers to conform to the corresponding rules for PL/I. *End of aside.*

By way of example, let character strings p, q, and r have values and types as shown here:

```
p :  'ijk'    : VARCHAR(3)
q :  'ijk  '  : VARCHAR(5)
r :  'ij'     : VARCHAR(2)
```

Also, let collation *C* be such that (a) the familiar alphabetic ordering is preserved and (b) the space character precedes all alphabetic characters. Then the following table shows the results of the indicated comparisons under collation *C* (a) if PAD SPACE applies, (b) if NO PAD applies:

comparison	PAD SPACE	NO PAD
p = q	TRUE	FALSE
p < q	FALSE	TRUE
p > r	TRUE	TRUE

There's one more important point to be made in connection with the SQL collation concept. I've said that if *C* is a collation for character set *S* and *a* and *b* are any two characters from *S*, then *C* must be such that exactly one of the comparisons $a < b$, $a = b$, and $a > b$ gives TRUE and the other two give FALSE. It's important to note, however, that there's no requirement that if *a* and *b* are distinct, then $a = b$ must give FALSE! For example, we might define a collation called CASE_INSENSITIVE in which each lowercase letter is considered to compare equal to its uppercase counterpart. As a consequence, again, character strings that are clearly distinct will sometimes compare equal.

SOME IMPLICATIONS

To summarize to this point: We've seen that certain comparisons of the form $x = y$ can give TRUE in SQL even if *x* and *y* are distinct, and possibly even if they're of different types. I'll refer to such pairs of values as "distinct but considered equal." Now, equality comparisons are performed, often implicitly, in numerous contexts (examples of such contexts include DISTINCT, GROUP BY, LIKE, UNION, and JOIN), and the kind of equality involved in all such cases is indeed "distinct but considered equal." Here's a self-explanatory example:

- Let {DNO} in table EMP be a foreign key referencing the key {DNO} in table DEPT.

- Let those DNO columns in tables EMP and DEPT be of some specific character string type, and let the associated collation be the one mentioned at the end of the previous section (viz., CASE_INSENSITIVE); further, let PAD SPACE apply to that collation.

■ Let 'D2' and 'd2 ' be DNO values in, respectively, some row of EMP and some row of DEPT.

■ Then those two rows will be regarded as satisfying the foreign key constraint from EMP to DEPT, despite the fact that there's a difference in case involved, and despite the fact also that the foreign key value involves a trailing space (so the DNO value is two characters long in the EMP row and three characters long in the DEPT row).

A further implication, as we saw in the introduction to this chapter, is that certain SQL expressions—more specifically, certain expressions involving character string comparisons—are *indeterminate*. I'll have more to say about this concept later, in the section "Possibly Nondeterministic Expressions"; for now, I just want to stress the important point that such expressions aren't allowed in integrity constraints, on the grounds that they could cause updates to succeed or fail unpredictably. To quote the standard again:

> No integrity constraint shall be defined using a <query specification> or a <query expression> that is possibly nondeterministic.

The point is repeated elsewhere in the standard, too:

> The <search condition> [*within an integrity constraint*] shall not generally contain a <query specification> or <query expression> that is possibly nondeterministic.[8]

But is this prohibition—i.e., the prohibition against such expressions appearing in integrity constraints—reasonable? I'll consider this question later too (again, in the section "Possibly Nondeterministic Expressions"). But to get

---

[8] In case you were wondering, the foreign key constraint discussed earlier, involving tables EMP and DEPT, doesn't "generally contain a <query specification> or <query expression> that is possibly nondeterministic," and the example is thus legitimate. By the way, note that the standard's wording, in the two extracts quoted here, is presumably meant to be construed as saying that neither a <query specification> nor a <query expression> is allowed to be possibly nondeterministic if it appears in a constraint. However, note also that it could be construed as saying that (a) <query expression>s aren't allowed if they're possibly nondeterministic and (b) <query specification>s aren't allowed at all. As I've indicated, the first interpretation is presumably the correct one, but you can't conclude as much from the quoted extracts considered in isolation. It's tempting to suggest that those two extracts from the standard should be labeled "possibly nondeterministic" themselves.

ahead of myself for just a moment, let me note for the record here that (as we'll see in that same section) the prohibition implies among other things that many quite simple expressions—even simple SELECT expressions, sometimes—won't be allowed in constraints, if they involve a column of some character string type!

IS INDETERMINACY ALWAYS BAD?

I'd like to get away from SQL for a few moments and consider the more wide ranging question of indeterminate expressions in general. By way of a simple example, consider random numbers. Many languages provide an operator of the form RANDOM () for generating random (or, rather, "pseudorandom") numbers. Clearly, any expression that denotes an invocation of such an operator is effectively indeterminate; indeed, that's the whole point, pretty much. Nobody would or should argue that such expressions are undesirable in general. But should such expressions be allowed in constraints?

Well, a constraint along the lines of (e.g.) "the cardinality of relvar *R* must always be less than RANDOM ()" clearly makes no sense—but then nobody in their right mind would specify such a constraint, anyway, and it hardly seems necessary to build a formal prohibition against doing so into the language. What's more, there might be cases where using RANDOM () within a constraint does make sense, though I admit I can't immediately think of a realistic example of such a situation.

By way of another example, consider ORDER BY in SQL. Now, ORDER BY isn't in fact a relational operator at all, because it produces a result that isn't a relation (it does take a relation as input, but it produces something else, viz., a sequence of tuples, as output). Thus, suppose the suppliers relvar S (sorry, the suppliers table S—we're back in the SQL context now) has the following as its current value:

S

SNO	SNAME	STATUS	CITY
S1	Smith	20	London
S2	Jones	10	Paris
S3	Blake	30	Paris
S4	Clark	20	London
S5	Adams	30	Athens

By definition, then, the following, though it's certainly a legitimate SQL expression, is certainly not a relational expression as such:

```
SELECT  SNO
FROM    S
ORDER   BY CITY
```

However, the point I want to focus on here isn't so much that ORDER BY isn't relational, but rather that it isn't a *function*. Now, all of the conventional relational operators—restriction, projection, join, etc.—*are* functions, meaning there's always just one possible output for any given input. By contrast, ORDER BY can legitimately produce several different outputs from the same input. For example, if table S has the value just shown, and if column CITY is of type CHAR(25),[9] say, then the foregoing SQL expression can clearly produce any of the following orderings:

```
S5 , S1 , S4 , S2 , S3

S5 , S4 , S1 , S2 , S3

S5 , S1 , S4 , S3 , S2

S5 , S4 , S1 , S3 , S2
```

Now, to say that ORDER BY isn't a function is equivalent to saying it's indeterminate (being a function and being indeterminate are opposites, in a sense). But of course ORDER BY is a highly useful operator in practice, for display purposes if nothing else. Once again, then, we see that lack of determinacy isn't necessarily a bad thing.

By way of a final example, consider the well known—some might say notorious—axiom in logic called the axiom of choice. Here's a definition:

Definition (axiom of choice): An axiom of set theory to the effect that, given a set S of nonempty, pairwise disjoint sets $s1$, $s2$, ..., sn, there exists a set of n elements $x1$, $x2$, ..., xn such that each xi is an element of si ($i = 1, 2,$ ..., n). The axiom implies among other things that, given some set s, it must be possible to choose an arbitrary element x from that set.

---

[9] The precise type is somewhat arbitrary; I choose CHAR(25) just to be definite. I remark in passing, though, that the assumption implies that, e.g., the CITY value for supplier S1 isn't really just the string 'London' as such but, rather, the string 'London' padded at the right with nineteen spaces.

Note: The axiom of choice is obviously and intuitively valid (and noncontroversial) so long as the sets *s1, s2, ..., sn*, and *S* are all finite, but can be (and has been) questioned otherwise.

In database terms, the second sentence of the foregoing definition ("The axiom implies ...") shows that it would be perfectly reasonable to define an operator—I'll call it ZO—as follows:[10]

Definition (ZO): Given a relation *r*, ZO (*r*) returns a relation with heading the same as that of *r* and body either empty (if *r* is empty) or consisting of precisely one tuple (otherwise), that tuple being some arbitrary tuple from the body of *r*. The name ZO is shorthand for "zero or one"; it derives from the fact that the cardinality of the result is either zero or one.

Now, an invocation of this operator is clearly indeterminate, in general—and yet the following is a perfectly realistic and well defined example of its use within an integrity constraint:

```
CONSTRAINT ZOR IS_EMPTY ( R MINUS ZO ( R ) ) ;
```

Explanation: The expression within the outer parentheses defines a relation that's equal to the current value of relvar R, except that (assuming R contains at least one tuple) some arbitrary tuple of R has been removed. The IS_EMPTY invocation then requires that relation to be empty. In other words, the constraint overall states that the cardinality of relvar R must never be greater than one. Observe that while the subexpressions ZO (R) and R MINUS ZO (R) are both indeterminate (in general), the IS_EMPTY invocation is not—it's guaranteed to evaluate to TRUE if the cardinality of R is either zero or one and FALSE otherwise.

Of course, the same constraint could be formulated more directly thus:

```
CONSTRAINT ZOR COUNT ( R ) ≤ 1 ;
```

---

[10] ZO—a word well known to Scrabble® enthusiasts—could be a useful addition to **Tutorial D**. Note incidentally, that an argument could be made that such an operator is already present anyway (in somewhat concealed form) in the tuple calculus, which supports the notion of variables that "range over" the tuples of some specified relation and thus take on as their value the tuples of the relation in question one by one, in some indeterminate order.

However, the point of showing the ZO formulation is simply to demonstrate that not only are indeterminate expressions sometimes acceptable, but sometimes, *pace* SQL, we might even want to be able to use such expressions in integrity constraints. (Also, of course, the foregoing "more direct" formulation does rely on support for the aggregate operator COUNT, which the ZO formulation obviously doesn't.)

POSSIBLY NONDETERMINISTIC EXPRESSIONS

Now let's get back to SQL. SQL:1992's rules for regarding a given expression as "possibly nondeterministic" are as follows. Let *exp* be an SQL expression. Then *exp* is considered to be possibly nondeterministic if at least one of the following is true:

1. *exp* is a union (without ALL), intersection, or difference, and the operand tables include a column of some character string type.

2. *exp* is a SELECT expression, the SELECT item commalist in that SELECT expression includes an item (X say) of some character string type, and at least one of the following is true:

   a. The SELECT item commalist is preceded by the keyword DISTINCT.

   b. X involves a MAX or MIN invocation.

   c. *exp* directly contains a GROUP BY clause and X is one of the grouping columns.

3. *exp* is a SELECT expression that directly contains a HAVING clause and the boolean expression in that HAVING clause contains either of the following:

   a. A reference to a grouping column of some character string type

   b. A MAX or MIN invocation in which the argument is of some character string type

Aside: The rules as stated above represent my own understanding and paraphrasing of the pertinent text from the 1992 version of the standard (for the actual text from that reference, see Appendix A in the present chapter). More important, the rules as I've given them follow that 1992 version of the standard in talking in terms of expressions involving character string types only. Later versions have (very unfortunately, in my opinion) extended the rules to define numerous additional expressions as indeterminate, including, e.g., (a) certain expressions involving datetime data types, (b) expressions involving data of certain user defined types, and (c) expressions involving invocations of certain user defined operators (or "routines," to use the standard's term). Thus, the situation now seems to be even more undesirable—*much* more so, in fact—than it was under the original rules (again, in my opinion). *End of aside.*

Here are examples of each of the foregoing possibilities, based again on the familiar suppliers-and-parts database. I assume for the sake of these examples that tables S and P have values as follows:

S

SNO	SNAME	STATUS	CITY
S1	Smith	20	London
S2	Jones	10	Paris
S3	Blake	30	Paris
S4	Clark	20	London
S5	Adams	30	Athens

P

PNO	PNAME	COLOR	WEIGHT	CITY
P1	Nut	Red	12.0	London
P2	Bolt	Green	17.0	Paris
P3	Screw	Blue	17.0	Oslo
P4	Screw	Red	14.0	London
P5	Cam	Blue	12.0	Paris
P6	Cog	Red	19.0	London

Assume for definiteness that the two CITY columns, also the SNAME column in table S, are all of type CHAR(25)—though I remind you that (as pointed out in a footnote earlier) this assumption means that e.g., the CITY value for supplier S1 isn't really just the string 'London' but, rather, the string 'London' padded at the right with nineteen spaces. Here then are some "possibly nondeterministic" SQL expressions, labeled in accordance with the various cases of such expressions identified above:

```
1.  SELECT  CITY
    FROM    S
    UNION
    SELECT  CITY
    FROM    P

2a. SELECT  DISTINCT CITY
    FROM    S

2b. SELECT  MAX ( CITY )
    FROM    S

2c. SELECT  CITY , SUM ( STATUS ) AS ZZ
    FROM    S
    GROUP   BY CITY

3a. SELECT  SUM ( STATUS ) AS ZZ
    FROM    S
    GROUP   BY CITY
    HAVING  CITY = 'London'

3b. SELECT  SUM ( STATUS ) AS ZZ
    FROM    S
    GROUP   BY CITY
    HAVING  MAX ( SNAME ) < 'Lewis'
```

I freely admit that the last of these, at least, is highly contrived! Be that as it may, what I find most interesting about these examples is that SQL apparently *thinks* they're indeterminate, but they're clearly not (at least, not in any normal sense of the term). To elaborate:

- Let's assume that the pertinent collation is the conventional one, at least inasmuch as it abides by conventional alphabetic ordering.

- Let's also assume that NO PAD applies to that collation.

Then, given the sample values shown earlier, the first of those six SQL expressions (the one asking for the union of the set of supplier cities and the set of part cities) clearly yields the following result:

1.
```
CITY

London...................
Paris....................
Oslo.....................
Athens...................
```

Note: I deliberately show these CITY values "complete," with trailing spaces shown explicitly as dots, simply to emphasize the fact that there's no need in this example to worry over whether the values 'London' and 'London ' and 'London ' and 'London   ' (etc., etc.) are equal or not. Nor is there any need to worry over which particular values are supposed to appear in the result. In other words, there's absolutely no indeterminacy here whatsoever, except in SQL's mind.

Here then, under the same assumptions as before, are the results of the other five expressions (but I won't bother from now on to show all of those trailing spaces):[11]

2a.
```
CITY

London
Paris
Athens
```

2b.
```
CITY

Paris
```

2c.
```
CITY     ZZ

London   40
Paris    40
Athens   30
```

---

[11] The lack of double underlining in result 3a is *not* a mistake—see my book *Fifty Years of Relational, and Other Database Writings: More Thoughts and Essays on Database Matters* (Technics Publications, 2020).

3a.

```
ZZ
```
```
40
```

3b.

```
ZZ
```
```
40
30
```

To say it again, the only thing that's indeterminate about these examples is why on earth SQL should think they are (indeterminate, that is). So it does seem very hard—I'm tempted to say it's overkill on SQL's part—not to be allowed to use them in constraints. Certainly I can imagine situations in which I might want to use them (well, maybe not the last one) in a realistic constraint. For example:

```
CREATE ASSERTION XYZ CHECK
       ( 'Stuttgart...............'
         NOT IN
       ( SELECT CITY FROM S UNION SELECT CITY FROM P ) ) ;
```

("no supplier is in Stuttgart and no part is in Stuttgart").

In fact—to pursue the point a little further—it's quite hard to think of situations where allowing SQL's possibly nondeterministic expressions in constraints would lead to any problem at all. Certainly no harm seems to be done in the foregoing example. In fact, the only situation that comes to mind in which indeterminacy might be a problem in constraints is when the constraint in question involves an invocation of some operator such as CHAR_LENGTH that can produce different results on "distinct but considered equal" operands. For example, the strings 'London' and 'London ' might "compare equal," but their lengths (6 and 9, respectively) most certainly don't.

Another oddity is that SQL prohibits possibly nondeterministic expressions in constraints but not in queries or updates, and yet the potential for harm is surely at least as great (possibly even greater) in these latter two cases. For example, the following INSERT—

```
INSERT INTO T ( CITY )
       SELECT DISTINCT CITY FROM S ;
```

—could easily have an indeterminate effect on table T (especially if, e.g., the pertinent collation is CASE_INSENSITIVE as defined earlier in this chapter).

Yet another oddity is that SQL's rules for when an expression is possibly nondeterministic seem to be neither accurate nor complete.[12] For example:

- Surely a union *with* ALL is possibly nondeterministic if one of its operand expressions is possibly nondeterministic.

- An explicit NATURAL JOIN has exactly the same potential for indeterminacy as (e.g.) an intersection.

- The same goes for JOIN ON or JOIN USING, though presumably not for CROSS JOIN.

CONCLUDING REMARKS

In this chapter, I've tried to show among other things that:

- Indeterminism isn't necessarily a bad thing in general.

- But the SQL:1992 definition of when an expression is indeterminate ("possibly nondeterministic") both:

    a. Classifies as indeterminate some expressions that clearly aren't, and

    b. Fails to classify as indeterminate some expressions that clearly are.

- Moreover, SQL's rule prohibiting indeterminate expressions from appearing in constraints is unnecessarily restrictive, even when the allegedly indeterminate expression is in fact so.

- At the same time, there surely ought to be rules regarding the appearance of indeterminate expressions in queries and updates, but in SQL there aren't.

---

[12] Well, I think I've already shown they're not accurate. (At least—to put it more politely, perhaps—I've shown they're stronger than necessary in certain cases.) As for their being incomplete, I suppose some of the missing cases might be considered as being taken care of, at least in part, by the fact that the standard says (paraphrasing) that constraints mustn't "generally contain" possibly nondeterministic expressions—i.e., such expressions mustn't appear within constraints *at any level of nesting*. PS: I note too that some but not all of the objections I raise in the subsequent bullet list have been addressed in later versions of the standard.

So how did this (to me, rather weird) state of affairs come about? Well, I'm only speculating here, but the following scenario seems likely enough to me:

■   The introduction into the SQL standard of the concept of "possibly nondeterministic expressions" (which as already noted happened with the 1992 version of the standard—the concept was absent from earlier versions) represented a belated recognition of an existing and much more fundamental mistake: namely, the lack of proper, logically correct support for equality comparisons, as described in Chapter 1.

   Note: It might be argued that indeterminacy wasn't a problem—at least in constraints (?)—prior to the introduction of SQL's extended character string support, which also happened with the 1992 version of the standard.[13] Against this argument must be set the counterargument that the character string support in question is excessively complicated, quite muddled, and in fact seems to me to be a textbook example of misplaced ingenuity.[14] I mean, I venture to suggest that indeterminacy wouldn't have been a problem with character strings either, if only that character string support had been more carefully thought out and defined.

■   To put the point another way: The expressions in question (specifically, certain character string expressions) weren't explicitly designed to be indeterminate, and the fact that they were so was recognized only when it was too late to fix the problem. In other words, the standardizers were already committed to supporting the expressions in question before somebody pointed out the implications (for constraints in particular).

   Note: If my speculations are correct here, it seems to me to be another textbook example, this time of *The Law of Unintended Consequences* in action.

■   Users would be quite unlikely to realize those consequences for themselves (especially if I'm right in thinking it took a while before the standardizers themselves did so, and even more especially since the expressions in

---

[13] Actually, versions of the standard prior to 1992 didn't support much in the way of constraints anyway.

[14] Again see Chapter 1 of the present book, and/or Appendix D ("Some Outstanding Issues") of *A Guide to the SQL Standard*, 4th edition, by C. J. Date and Hugh Darwen (Addison-Wesley, 1997). Quite frankly, I wonder whether anyone has ever bothered to implement that extended character string support in full detail, anyway. (Evidence suggesting rather strongly that no one has is provided by the fact that, as noted in Chapter 1 of this book, the support in question has undergone major revisions—not to say gyrations—since it was first defined.)

question are only *implicitly* indeterminate, as well as often being only *possibly* so).

■ The standardizers therefore attempted to fix the problem by introducing the notion of "possible nondeterminism" and prohibiting "possibly nondeterministic" expressions from appearing in constraints. As I've pointed out, however, such expressions are still allowed to appear in queries and updates, where the implications are just as bad if not worse. (Of course, if those expressions were prohibited from queries and updates as well, then it wouldn't be possible to use them for any purpose at all!—an observation that I'd say raises certain obvious questions.)

The foregoing state of affairs contrasts strongly with a situation in which an operator is explicitly designed to be indeterminate (see the RANDOM, ORDER BY, and ZO examples discussed earlier). In such a situation, it seems to me, there's no need to attempt to "legislate morality" by introducing rules that (e.g.) prohibit such operators from constraints, because users *know* the operators are indeterminate—they know the relevant semantics—and they can surely be relied upon not to use those operators in ways that make no sense.

APPENDIX A: QUOTES FROM THE SQL STANDARD

SQL:1992

To say it one more time, the SQL "possibly nondeterministic" concept originated in the 1992 version of the standard. For purposes of reference, this subsection contains the entirety of what that version of the standard has to say on the topic.

From Chapter 4 ("Concepts"), Subclause 4.10 ("Integrity constraints"):

> A <query expression> or <query specification> is *possibly nondeterministic* if an implementation might, at two different times where the state of the SQL-data is the same, produce results that differ by more than the order of the rows due to General Rules that specify implementation dependent behavior ... No integrity constraint shall be defined using a <query specification> or a <query expression> that is possibly nondeterministic.

From Chapter 7 ("Query expressions"), Subclause 7.8 ("<having clause>"):

The <having clause> is *possibly nondeterministic* if it contains a reference to a column C of T that has a data type of character string[15] and:

a)   C is specified within a <set function specification> that specifies MIN or MAX, or

b)   C is a grouping column of T.

From Chapter 7 ("Query expressions"), Subclause 7.9 ("<query specification>"):

A <query specification> is *possibly nondeterministic* if any of the following conditions are true:

a)   The <set quantifier> DISTINCT is specified and one of the columns of T has a data type of character string; or

b)   The <query specification> directly contains a <having clause> that is possibly nondeterministic; or

c)   The <select list> contains a reference to a column C of T that has a data type of character string and either

    i)   C is specified within a <set function specification> that specifies MIN or MAX, or

    ii)   C is a grouping column of T.

From Chapter 7 ("Query expressions"), Subclause 7.10 ("<query expression>"):

A <query expression> is *possibly nondeterministic* if

a)   it contains a set operator UNION and ALL is not specified, or if it contains EXCEPT or INTERSECT; and

---

[15] *T* here is the intermediate result table produced by the immediately preceding FROM, WHERE, and GROUP BY clauses.

b) the first or second operand contains a column that has a data type of character string.

From Chapter 11 ("Schema definition and manipulation"), Subclause 11.9 ("<check constraint definition>"):

The <search condition> shall not generally contain a <query specification> or <query expression> that is possibly nondeterministic.

From Chapter 11 ("Schema definition and manipulation"), Subclause 11.34 ("<assertion definition>"):

The <search condition> shall not generally contain a <query specification> or <query expression> that is possibly nondeterministic.

SQL:2011

In an idle moment, I decided to take a look at what the 2011 version of the standard had to say about these matters ... Here's what I found. First, it turns out that the term "possibly non-deterministic" (note the hyphen) occurs in well over *60 different contexts* (!) in that version. Second, here in its entirety is the text of Subclause 4.17 ("Determinism"), quoted verbatim:

In general, an operation is *deterministic* if that operation assuredly computes identical results when repeated with identical input values. For an SQL-invoked routine, the values in the argument list are regarded as the input; otherwise, the SQL-data and the set of privileges by which they are accessed is regarded as the input. Differences in the ordering of rows, as permitted by General Rules that specify implementation-dependent behavior, are not regarded as significant to the question of determinism.

NOTE 47 — Transaction isolation levels have a significant impact on determinism, particularly transaction isolation levels other than SERIALIZABLE.[16] However, this International Standard does not address that impact, particularly because of the difficulty in clearly specifying that impact without appearing to mandate implementation techniques (such as row or page locking) and because different SQL-implementations almost certainly resolve the issue in significantly different ways.

---

[16] A major argument right here, one might think, for never using (and therefore, and preferably, not even supporting) any level of isolation other than SERIALIZABLE!

Recognizing that an operation is deterministic is a difficult task, it is in general not mandated by this International Standard. SQL-invoked routines are regarded as deterministic if the routine is declared to be DETERMINISTIC; that is, the SQL-implementation trusts the definer of the SQL-invoked routine to correctly declare that the routine is deterministic. For other operations, this International Standard does not label an operation as deterministic; instead it identifies certain operations as "possibly non-deterministic". Specific definitions can be found in other subclauses relative to <value expression>, <table reference>, <table primary>, <query specification>, <query expression>, and <SQL procedure statement>.

Certain <boolean value expression>s are identified as "retrospectively deterministic". A retrospectively deterministic <boolean value expression> has the property that if it is *True* at one point [in] time, then it is *True* for all later points in time if re-evaluated for the identical SQL-data by an arbitrary user with the identical set of privileges. The precise definition is found in Subclause 6.35, "<boolean value expression>".

Here's that "precise definition" from Subclause 6.35:

The notion of "retrospectively deterministic" is defined recursively as follows:

a) A <parenthesized boolean value expression> is retrospectively deterministic if the simply contained <boolean value expression> is retrospectively deterministic.

b) A <nonparenthesized value expression primary> is retrospectively deterministic if it is not possibly non-deterministic.

c) A <predicate> P is *retrospectively deterministic* if one of the following is true:

   i) P is not possibly non-deterministic.

   ii) P is a <comparison predicate> of the form "$X < Y$", "$X <= Y$", "$Y > X$", "$Y >= X$", "$X < Y + Z$", "$X <= Y + Z$", "$Y + Z > X$", "$Y + Z >= X$", "$X < Y - Z$", "$X <= Y - Z$", "$Y - Z > X$", or "$Y - Z >= X$", where Y is CURRENT_DATE, CURRENT_TIMESTAMP or LOCALTIMESTAMP, X and Z are not possibly non-deterministic <value expression>s, and the declared types of the left and right comparands are either both datetime with time zone or both datetime without time zone.

iii) *P* is a <quantified comparison predicate> of the form "*Y* > <quantifier> <table subquery>", "*Y* + *Z* > <quantifier> <table subquery>", "*Y* – *Z* > <quantifier> <table subquery>", "*Y* >=<quantifier> <table subquery>", "*Y* + *Z* >= <quantifier> <table subquery>", or "*Y* – *Z* >= <quantifier> <table subquery>", where *Y* is CURRENT_DATE, CURRENT_TIMESTAMP or LOCALTIMESTAMP, *Z* is a <value expression> that is not possibly non-deterministic, the<query expression> simply contained in the <table subquery> is not possibly non-deterministic, and the declared types of the left and right comparands are either both datetime with time zone or both datetime without time zone.

iv) *P* is a <between predicate> that is transformed into a retrospectively deterministic <boolean value expression>.

d) A <boolean primary> is retrospectively deterministic if the simply contained <predicate>, <parenthesized boolean value expression> or <nonparenthesized value expression primary> is retrospectively deterministic.

e) Let *BF* be a <boolean factor>. Let *BP* be the <boolean primary> simply contained in *BF*.

i) *BF* is called *negative* if *BF* is of any of the following forms:

```
NOT BP
BP IS FALSE
BP IS NOT TRUE
NOT BP IS NOT FALSE
NOT BP IS TRUE
```

ii) *BF* is retrospectively deterministic if one of the following is true:

1) *BF* is negative and *BF* does not generally contain a possibly non-deterministic <value expression>.

2) *BF* is not negative and *BP* is retrospectively deterministic.

f) A <boolean value expression> is retrospectively deterministic if every simply contained <boolean factor> is retrospectively deterministic.

And then in Subclause 4.18.1 ("Overview of integrity constraints") we find this:

No integrity constraint shall be defined using a <search condition> that is not retrospectively deterministic.

My understanding of this new "retrospectively deterministic" concept is basically this: If something isn't possibly nondeterministic, it's certainly retrospectively deterministic; however, something can be the latter without being the former. In other words, requiring something not to be possibly nondeterministic is more demanding than requiring it to be retrospectively deterministic. I hope you followed that.

Anyway, for the record, all of the following can be possibly nondeterministic in SQL:2011:

<contextually typed table value constructor>s
<data change delta table>s
<derived table>s
<joined table>s
<lateral derived table>s
methods
<nonparenthesized value expression primary>s
<query expression>s
<query name>s
<query specification>s
ROW_NUMBERs
<select statement: single row>s
SQL-invoked routines
<SQL procedure statement>s
<table name>s
<table primary>s
<table reference>s
<table value constructor>s
<value expression>s
<window function>s

I note, incidentally, that <having clause>s could be possibly nondeterministic in SQL:1992 but apparently not in SQL:2011 (?).

Part III

OBJECTS AND OBJECTIONS

There was a time, back in the 1990s or so, when it was believed—believed quite widely, in fact—that object technology was about to replace relational technology and take over the database world. Of course, that didn't happen; object DBMSs never did replace relational DBMSs, and we all know that now. But bad ideas do have a habit of resurfacing from time to time, and it can be useful to have a summary of the counterarguments available to rebut them, if and when they do. That's one of the purposes of this part of the book.

There are four chapters. The first three have to with *persistence*, *encapsulation*, and *decapsulation*, respectively. Persistence and encapsulation are widely perceived as key features of object databases in particular and object systems in general; my own perception of these concepts, however, is that they're muddled at best and wrongheaded at worst. As for decapsulation (more usually referred to as "breaking encapsulation"): Well, I think that's muddled and wrongheaded too, arising as it does from the original mistakes over encapsulation. All of which is fighting talk, I realize!—but that's why I wrote the chapters: namely, to try and persuade you that my perception of these notions is in fact the correct one.

Note: These three chapters are based in part on a series of articles that originally appeared in the magazine *Data Base Programming & Design* and/or on the website *www.dbpd.com* during the period September 1998 – January 1999. The material, though revised considerably here, is thus not entirely new. However, I do think it's worth preserving—and since the original articles are no longer available (the referenced magazine and its associated website both now appear to be defunct), I've decided to reproduce it, suitably modified, in the form of these chapters. (Portions of the material were also included, albeit in rather different form, in my book *Type Inheritance and Relational Theory: Subtypes, Supertypes, and Substitutability*, O'Reilly, 2016.) To repeat, therefore, the subject matter of those chapters isn't entirely new. I've simply looked around and realized that it needs to be said again.

Turning now to the fourth chapter: In 1791, when she was just 15, Jane Austen wrote a delightful little book she called *The History of England*, describing it as being by "a partial, prejudiced, and ignorant Historian." Following this splendid precedent, the last chapter in this part of the present book might not unreasonably be described as being by "a partial, prejudiced, and ignorant Database Professional" ... Be that as it may, an appendix to the second edition of the book by Hugh Darwen and myself on *The Third Manifesto* (*Foundation for Future Database Systems: The Third Manifesto*, Addison-Wesley, 2000) contained a detailed analysis of the proposals of the Object Data Management Group (ODMG), comparing them blow by blow with the various features of *The Third Manifesto* as defined at that time.[1] ODMG was a hot topic throughout the 1990s, but interest in it, and indeed in object databases in general, began to wane in the first decade of the new century,[2] and we decided to drop that appendix from the next edition of our *Manifesto* book (*Databases, Types, and the Relational Model: The Third Manifesto*, Addison-Wesley, 2007). However, ODMG as such isn't completely dead—at least, not according to Wikipedia—and in any case there's always a possibility that it or something like it might rear its head again at some future time; so I wanted to preserve our thoughts on the subject in case they ever become relevant again.

Note: I say "preserve our thoughts," but of course I've revised the original appendix—quite considerably, in fact—to bring it more into line with our most recent thinking on such matters. While the chapter resembles that original appendix in broad outline, therefore, it differs at a detailed level in many, many ways.

---

[1] That appendix as such was republished, largely unchanged, as Chapter 27 ("A Comparison Between ODMG and *The Third Manifesto*") in my book *Date on Database: Writings 2000-2006* (Apress, 2006). The current, most up to date version of *The Third Manifesto* itself can always be found at the website *www.thethirdmanifesto.com*. *Note:* I should state for the record that the "current version" of the *Manifesto* is fairly stable, and in fact has remained unchanged for several years at the time of writing.

[2] For very good reasons, in my opinion. See, for example, the papers "Why 'the Object Model' Is Not a Data Model" and "Object Identifiers vs. Relational Keys," both of which are included in my book *Relational Database Writings 1994-1997* (Addison-Wesley, 1998).

Chapter 6

Thinking Clearly about

Persistence

I don't mind your thinking slowly;
I mind your publishing faster than you think.
　　　　　　　　　　　　　—Wolfgang Pauli (attrib.)

The whole idea of object databases is founded on one basic principle, or dictum: namely, the dictum that *persistence* [should be] *orthogonal to type*, which I'll refer to as *POTT* for short. In this chapter, I want to offer arguments against that dictum—in other words, I want to show why I believe that persistence should *not* be orthogonal to type ("not POTT," if you like).

What POTT means, essentially, is that:

a. Any data structure that can be created in a conventional application program—for example, an array, a linked list, a stack—can be stored, "persistently," as an object in a database (an object database, of course), and moreover that

b. The structure of such database objects is visible to the user.[1]

For example, consider the object, EX say, that is—or rather denotes—the collection of all employees in a given department. Then EX might be implemented and stored in the database as either a linked list or an array (among other possibilities, of course, but let's agree to limit our attention for now to just

---

[1] I refer here and throughout this part of the book to "the user," but the point is worth making that users of an object database will almost certainly have to be application programmers specifically, not end users. How an end user can be supported is very unclear. Even the so called "Object Query Language" of ODMG—see footnote 2—is full of constructs that are likely to be beyond the abilities of the typical end user. (Of course, the same is true of SQL, too. Perhaps there's a lesson to be learned here.)

these two)—and users will have to know which it is, because the corresponding access operators will differ accordingly.

One of the earliest writings, if not *the* earliest, to articulate the POTT position was a paper by Atkinson and Buneman:

■ Malcolm P. Atkinson and O. Peter Buneman: "Types and Persistence in Database Programming Languages," *ACM Computing Surveys 19*, No. 2 (June 1987).

Atkinson in particular was also one of the authors of *The Object-Oriented Database System Manifesto*:

■ Malcolm Atkinson, François Bancilhon, David DeWitt, Klaus Dittrich, David Maier, and Stanley Zdonik: "The Object-Oriented Database System Manifesto," Proc. 1st International Conference on Deductive and Object-Oriented Databases, Kyoto, Japan (1989).

This document proposed a set of features that (in the opinion of its authors) a DBMS must support if it's to qualify for the label "object oriented"—and, of course, those features did include POTT. Subsequently, Stonebraker et al. produced the *Third Generation Database System Manifesto*:

■ Michael Stonebraker, Lawrence A. Rowe, Bruce G. Lindsay, James Gray, Michael Carey, Michael Brodie, Philip Bernstein, and David Beech: "Third Generation Database System Manifesto," *ACM SIGMOD Record 19*, No. 3 (September 1990).

While this latter manifesto can be seen in part as a refutation of the previous one, it did also endorse POTT as an objective for future database systems (to quote: "Persistent X for a variety of X's is a good idea"). And the authors of the following book ("the ODMG book" for short) agree also:

■ R. G. G. Cattell and Douglas K. Barry (eds.): *The Object Database Standard: ODMG 3.0* (Morgan Kaufmann, 2000).[2]

---

[2] "ODMG" stands for the Object Data Management Group, which is (or was) a consortium of participants from "member companies representing almost the entire [object database] industry." See Chapter 9 of the present book for an extended discussion of "the ODMG standard."

Here's a quote:

> [We] define an *object DBMS* to be a DBMS that integrates database capabilities with object-oriented programming language capabilities. An object DBMS makes database objects appear as programming language objects ... [it] extends the language with transparently persistent data ... and other database capabilities.

The position of *The Third Manifesto* is very different, however. First, here's the reference:

- C. J. Date and Hugh Darwen: *Databases, Types, and the Relational Model: The Third Manifesto*, 3rd edition (Addison-Wesley, 2007).[3]

And here's a quote:

> Databases (and nothing else) are defined to be persistent ... [Since] the only kind of variable we permit within a database is, very specifically, the [relation variable or] relvar, the only kind of variable that might possess the property of persistence is the relvar.

In this chapter, then, I want to try and explain why Hugh Darwen and I take the position we do in this regard.

POTT VIOLATES DATA INDEPENDENCE

One reason we reject POTT is that it can lead to a loss of data independence, as I now explain. As already noted, POTT means that any data structure that can be created in a conventional application program can be stored as a "persistent object" in an object database, and further that *the structure of such objects is visible to the user*. Now, this "anything goes" approach to what can be kept in the database is a major point of difference between the object and relational models, of course, so let's take a closer look at it.

Note: I assume for the sake of the discussion that the term *object model* is well defined and generally well understood, though in my opinion such an

---

[3] We chose the name *The Third Manifesto* precisely because of the two previous ones that had already been published, which we wanted it to be seen (at least in part) as a rebuttal to.

assumption is more than a little charitable to the object world. Be that as it may, one big difference between the two approaches can be characterized thus:

- The object model says we can put anything we like in the database (any structure we can create with the usual programming language mechanisms).

- The relational model effectively says the same thing, but then goes on to insist that whatever we do put there *be presented to the user in pure relational form.*

To put it another way, the relational model, quite rightly, says *nothing whatsoever* about what can be physically stored. It therefore imposes no limits on the structures that are allowed at the physical level; the only requirement is that whatever structures are in fact physically stored must be mapped to relations at the logical level, and hence be hidden from the user. Relational systems thus make a clear distinction between logical and physical (that is, between the model and its implementation), and object systems don't.

One consequence of this state of affairs is that as already claimed—but contrary to conventional wisdom!—object systems might very well provide less data independence than relational systems do. For example, suppose the implementation in some object database of the object EX mentioned near the beginning of the chapter, denoting the collection of all employees in a given department, is changed from an array to a linked list. What are the implications for existing code that accesses that object EX? *Answer:* It breaks.

I should perhaps ask the further question: Why would we *want* to change the implementation of EX in such a manner? The answer is surely *performance* ... Ideally, therefore, the change should not affect anything *except* performance; in practice, however, it does.

It seems to me, in fact, that the ability to have all of these different ways of representing data at the logical level is an example of what I've referred to elsewhere[4] as *spurious generality.* I would argue further that the whole idea stems from a failure to make a clean separation between model and implementation—we might need lots of different representations at the physical level, but we certainly don't need them all at the logical level. Indeed, I very well remember Codd, the inventor of the relational model, saying in response to a

---

[4] E.g., in my essay "Database Graffiti," in the book *Relational Database Writings 1994-1997* (Addison-Wesley, 1998).

question during a conference panel discussion: "If you tell me that you have 50 different ways of representing data in your system [*i.e., at the logical level*], then I'll tell you that you have 49 too many."

POTT CAUSES ADDITIONAL COMPLEXITY

I believe it should be obvious that POTT leads to additional complexity—and by "complexity" here I mean, primarily, complexity for the user, though life does get more complex for the system (i.e., the implementation) as well. For example, the relational model supports just one "collection type generator," viz., RELATION, together with a set of operators—join, project, and so forth—that apply to all "collections" of that type (in other words, to all relations). By contrast, the proposals of the ODMG book support *four* collection type generators: SET, BAG, LIST, and ARRAY, each with its own set of operators that apply to all collections of the type in question. And I would argue that the ODMG operators are simultaneously more complicated and less powerful than the analogous relational ones. By way of illustration, here are some of the ODMG operators that apply to lists (see Chapter 9 for further discussion):

```
IS_EMPTY
IS_ORDERED
ALLOWS_DUPLICATES
CONTAINS_ELEMENT
INSERT_ELEMENT
REMOVE_ELEMENT
CREATE_ITERATOR
CREATE_BIDIRECTIONAL_ITERATOR
REMOVE_ELEMENT_AT
RETRIEVE_ELEMENT_AT
REPLACE_ELEMENT_AT
INSERT_ELEMENT_AFTER
INSERT_ELEMENT_BEFORE
INSERT_ELEMENT_FIRST
INSERT_ELEMENT_LAST
REMOVE_FIRST_ELEMENT
REMOVE_LAST_ELEMENT
RETRIEVE_FIRST_ELEMENT
RETRIEVE_LAST_ELEMENT
CONCAT
APPEND
```

Incidentally, it's worth pointing out in passing that one "collection type generator" that ODMG *doesn't* support is RELATION! The ODMG book claims that "the ODMG data model encompasses the relational data model by defining a TABLE type," but that "TABLE type" (better: that TABLE type *generator*) is severely deficient in numerous respects. In particular, most of the crucial relational operators—join, for example—are missing. *Note:* In fact there are many further problems with claims to the effect that ODMG "encompasses" or "is more powerful than" the relational model, but space precludes detailed examination of those additional problems here. Some of them are discussed in Chapter 9, though.

Now, ODMG does also support what it calls a query language,[5] called OQL ("Object Query Language"). OQL is a read-only language (no update operators are included) that's loosely patterned after the retrieval aspects of SQL. To be more specific:

- OQL supports SQL-style SELECT – FROM – WHERE queries against sets, bags, lists, and arrays.

- It also includes analogs of the SQL GROUP BY, HAVING, and ORDER BY constructs.

- It also supports union, intersections, and differences, together with certain special operators for lists and arrays (for example, "get the first element").

- It also supports "path expressions" for traversing relationships between objects.

And the ODMG book makes a number of claims regarding OQL. Here are a couple of them (italics added in both cases):

We have used the relational standard SQL as the basis for OQL, where possible, *though OQL supports more powerful capabilities.*

[OQL] is *more powerful* [than a relational query language].

But it's my opinion—in sharp contrast to these claims—that OQL illustrates very well my point that POTT leads to additional complexity. That is, I would argue that OQL is certainly more *complicated*, but no more *powerful*

---

[5] Implying by that term, presumably, that the language is intended for end users—in which case, please see footnote 1.

(people in the computing community often seem to confuse these two notions), than a relational query language. And the extra complication derives from the fact that so many different data structures are exposed to the user. And *that* state of affairs is a direct consequence, it seems to me, of a failure to appreciate the advantages of keeping model and implementation rigidly apart.

Let me take a moment to examine this issue of increased complexity a little more closely. First of all, note that when we talk of lists in the database, arrays in the database, and so on, what we're really talking about is list *variables*, array *variables*, and so on—just as, when we talk of relations in the database, we really mean relation *variables* (relvars for short). Now, the only kinds of variables we find in the relational model are, of course, relation variables specifically (that is, variables whose values are relations); the relational model doesn't deal with list variables (variables whose values are lists), or array variables (variables whose values are arrays), or any other kinds of variables. It follows that to introduce (say) array variables would constitute a major departure from the classical relational model.

Why exactly would that departure be so major? Well, orthogonality would dictate, first of all, that we'd have to define a whole new query language for arrays—that is, a set of array operators (an "array algebra"?), analogous to the operators already defined for relations (the relational algebra). Of course, we'd certainly have to worry about *closure* in connection with that language. And we'd have to define a set of array update operators, analogous to the existing relational ones. We'd have to be able to define array integrity and security constraints, and array views. The catalog would have to describe array variables as well as relation variables. (And what would the catalog itself consist of?— array variables? or relation variables? or a mixture of both?) We'd need an array design theory, analogous to the existing body of relational design theory. We'd also need guidelines as to when to use array variables and when relation variables. And so on (I'm sure this list of issues isn't exhaustive).

The net of all this is:

- Assuming that such an "array algebra" can be defined, and that all of the other questions raised in the previous paragraph can be answered satisfactorily, now we'll have two ways of doing things where previously one sufficed. In other words (to say it again), adding a new kind of variable certainly adds complexity, but it doesn't add any power—there's nothing (at least, nothing useful) that can be done with a mixture of array and relation variables that can't be done with relation variables alone.

■ Thus, the user interface will now be more complex and involve more choices—most likely without good guidelines as to how to make such choices.

■ As a direct consequence of the foregoing, database applications—including in particular general purpose applications or "front ends"—will become harder to write, and harder to maintain.

■ Those applications will also become more vulnerable to changes in the database structure; that is (again as noted earlier), some degree of data independence will be lost. Consider what happens, for example, if the representation—the representation at the logical level, I mean—of some piece of information is changed from relation variables to array variables, or the other way around.

All of the foregoing is, of course, in direct conflict with Codd's *Information Principle*. Codd stated that principle in various forms and various writings over the years; indeed, I heard him refer to it more than once as "*the* fundamental principle of the relational model." It can be stated as follows:

At any given time, the entire information content of the database is represented (so far as the user is concerned) in one and only one way: namely, as relations.

Or equivalently, but a little more succinctly:

The only kind of variable permitted in a relational database (so far as the user is concerned) is the relation variable.

In his book,[6] Codd gives a number of arguments in support of this principle (arguments with which I concur, of course). In fact, the real point is this: As we've argued in *The Third Manifesto* and elsewhere, relations are both *necessary* and *sufficient* to represent any data we like (at the logical level, of course). In other words, we *must* have relations, and we don't need anything else.

---

[6] E. F. Codd: *The Relational Model for Database Management Version 2* (Addison-Wesley, 1990).

CONCLUDING REMARKS

So where did POTT come from? It seems to me that what we have here is (as so often) *a fundamental failure to understand—or at any rate appreciate—the crucial difference between model and implementation.* To be specific, it has been observed that certain SQL products don't perform very well on certain operations (especially joins); it has further been conjectured that performance would improve if we could use (say) lists or arrays instead of relations. But, of course, such thinking is seriously confused; in particular, it mixes logical and physical considerations. Nobody is arguing that (for example) lists might not be useful at the physical level; the question is whether lists and so forth should be exposed at the logical level. And it's the very strong position of relational advocates in general, and of the authors of *The Third Manifesto* in particular, that the answer to that question is an emphatic *no.*

Chapter 7

Thinking Clearly about

Encapsulation

Most people would sooner die than think—
in fact they do.

—Bertrand Russell (attrib.)

In the previous chapter I explained why I believe the object world dictum "persistence orthogonal to type" (POTT for short) is and always was a mistake. Now I want to turn my attention to another familiar object world concept, viz., *encapsulation*.

Encapsulation is widely perceived as a key feature, or advantage, of object technology in general. It seems to me, however, that the focus on encapsulation has always been a little bit off base; rather, what's important is just to make a clear distinction between types and representations. In fact, I feel encapsulation per se is something of a red herring, and in this chapter I'd like to try to explain just why I feel this way.

WHAT DOES ENCAPSULATION MEAN?

You probably have a pretty good idea already of what the term "encapsulation" means, but let me take a few moments to spell it out anyway. Basically, a data type is said to be *encapsulated* if and only if instances of the type in question have no user visible components. (I'm using "instances" here as a sloppy but convenient shorthand for *values and/or variables*.) For example, in their book on Smalltalk,[1] Goldberg and Robson say:

---

[1] Adele Goldberg and David Robson: *Smalltalk-80: The Language and its Implementation* (Addison-Wesley, 1983).

> An object consists of some private memory and a set of operators ... An object's *public* properties are the [operator specifications] that make up its interface ... An object's *private* properties are a set of [components] that make up its private memory ... . [*Italics added for emphasis.*]

As the passage just quoted indicates, objects in Smalltalk are certainly encapsulated, because users can operate on them only by means of the operators whose specifications make up that object's "interface." More precisely (though the passage quoted admittedly doesn't quite say as much in so many words), objects of a given type *T* can be operated upon *solely* by means of the operators that have been explicitly defined in connection with that type *T*. For example, we might have a type CIRCLE, and we might be able to invoke operators that return the area, or the circumference, or the radius (and so on) of any given circle. However, we can't say—at least, not legitimately—that circles have an area *component*, or a circumference *component*, or a radius *component* (and so on). One important consequence is that we don't know, nor do we need to know, how circles are represented inside the system; rather, that representation is visible only to the code that implements the operators. In other words, the *type* is of interest to users—it's part of the user interface—while the *representation* is of interest only to the implementation (it's under the covers).

Here's another quote that covers more or less the same ground as the previous one but goes into a little more detail. It comes from a tutorial on object databases by Zdonik and Maier:[2]

> Encapsulation [means each *type* has] a set of [operations and] a *representation* ... that is allocated for each of its instances. This representation is used to store the state of [objects of the type in question]. Only the methods implementing operations for the objects are allowed to access the representation, thereby making it possible to change the representation without disturbing the rest of the system. Only the methods would need to be recoded.[3] [*Italics added for emphasis.*]

---

[2] Stanley B. Zdonik and David Maier: "Fundamentals of Object-Oriented Databases," in Zdonik and Maier (eds.): *Readings in Object-Oriented Database Systems* (Morgan Kaufmann, 1990).

[3] As noted in Chapter 3 of this book, *method* is a term that appears ubiquitously in the object literature—and yet (like the term *object* itself, in fact) its meaning isn't always entirely clear. Sometimes, as here, it seems to mean the code that implements some operator, in which case it's hidden as far as the user is concerned. But sometimes it seems to mean some operator as such, in which case it's user visible. Chapter 9 has more to say regarding this confusion.

Observe now that, as indeed the foregoing quote effectively suggests, encapsulation is really just the familiar database notion of *data independence* in another guise. After all, if we do manage to distinguish type and representation properly, and if we also succeed in our goal of keeping the representation hidden, then we can change that representation as much as we like without having to change application programs (we only have to change the code that implements the operations)—and changing representations without changing applications is exactly what data independence is all about.[4]

Perhaps you can begin to see why I don't think the notion of encapsulation, as such, is all that significant. After all, it basically just means we don't need to worry about what we shouldn't *have* to worry about!—namely, physical representations (also known as actual or internal representations). In other words, encapsulation really is, as previously claimed, just a logical consequence of the crucial distinction we already draw, and indeed *must* draw, between types and representations. But of course there's quite a bit more that can usefully be said on the subject; hence the present chapter.

One last point on the definition of the term: While preparing this chapter, I took the trouble to look up "encapsulation" in a number of books (nearly 20 of them, in fact) on object technology and related matters. It was a pretty dispiriting exercise, I can tell you!—and I was very struck by the fact that I could nowhere find a really precise definition of the concept. (The best *explanations* were in the Smalltalk book already mentioned, and I think it's telling that that particular book doesn't appear to use the term "encapsulation," as such, at all. Certainly it's not in the index.) Anyway, one thing I did discover was that some writers seem to think the concept refers specifically to the *physical bundling*, or "packaging," of data representation definitions and operator definitions. For example (this quote is taken from a book on object databases):[5]

> Encapsulation refers to the concept of including processing or behavior with the object instances defined by the class. Encapsulation allows code and data to be packaged together.

---

[4] I use the term *data independence* here to mean what's sometimes called, a trifle more correctly, *physical* data independence. Though I feel obliged to add that, in my opinion, the term (with or without that "physical" qualifier) isn't particularly apt—I mean, it doesn't really capture the essence of what it's supposed to describe—but we've been using it for such a long time now that we're probably stuck with it.

[5] Douglas K. Barry: *The Object Database Handbook: How to Select, Implement, and Use Object-Oriented Databases* (John Wiley and Sons, 1996). By the way, the phrase "object instances defined by the class" in the quote should surely be just "object class." I mean, surely the code isn't repeated as part of every individual "object instance"? (Also, what exactly is the difference between an object, an instance, and an object instance?)

But it seems to me that to interpret the term in this way is to mix model and implementation considerations. The user shouldn't care, and shouldn't *have* to care, whether code and data are "packaged together"! Thus, it's my belief that—from the user's point of view, at least, which is to say from the point of view of the model and not the implementation—encapsulation simply means what I said before: namely, that the data in question has no user visible components and can be operated upon solely by means of the pertinent operators.

BUT WHAT ABOUT AD HOC QUERY?

However, there's a problem, as you might already have realized: namely, that the objective of encapsulation, as I've just loosely defined that term, is in conflict with the objective of being able to perform ad hoc queries. After all, encapsulation means data can be accessed only in predefined ways, while "ad hoc query" means, more or less by definition, that access is required in ways that aren't, and can't have been, predefined. By way of example, suppose we have a data type POINT, denoting points in two-dimensional euclidean space. Suppose we also have a predefined operator to "get"—that is, *read* or *retrieve*—the X coordinate of any given point, but no analogous operator to get the corresponding Y coordinate. Then even the following simple queries—

- Get the Y coordinate of point P

- Get all points on the X axis (i.e., all points with a zero Y coordinate)

- Get all points with Y coordinate less than five

- Is point P closer to the X axis than point Q?

(and many others like them)—obviously can't be handled; in fact, they can't even be formulated.[6]

---

[6] I'm deliberately ducking for now the question of what exactly it is that's being queried in queries like the second and third examples in this list might be. I'll come back to that question in the next section.

Now, *The Third Manifesto*[7] deals with the foregoing conflict by requiring that for any given scalar type—see the section "Scalar vs. Nonscalar Types," later—operators be defined that *expose some possible representation* for instances of that type. We call the operators in question "THE_ operators," for reasons that should quickly become obvious. In the case of type POINT, for example, we might define operators THE_X and THE_Y, thus allowing the user to perform "read" or "retrieval" operations such as the ones illustrated here on points:

```
Q := THE_Y ( P ) ;
/* get the Y coordinate of point P */
/* and assign it to variable Q      */

Z := SQRT ( THE_X ( P ) ^ 2 + THE_Y ( P ) ^ 2 ) ;
/* get the distance of point P from the origin */
/* and assign it to variable Z                 */
```

(The symbol "^" here denotes exponentiation.)

In other words, the operators THE_X and THE_Y effectively expose a possible representation—namely, cartesian coordinates X and Y—for points, thereby making it possible to perform ad hoc or arbitrary queries involving points. Note carefully, however, that this fact doesn't mean that points are *physically* represented by cartesian coordinates inside the system; it merely means, to repeat, that cartesian coordinates are a *possible* representation. The physical representation might be cartesian coordinates, or it might be polar coordinates RHO and THETA, or it might be something else entirely. In other words, THE_ operators don't violate encapsulation, and they don't undermine data independence.

I'll have quite a lot more to say about this notion of possible representations, and the thinking behind that notion, in the next chapter.

Aside: I remark in passing that DATE and TIME in SQL serve as examples of types (actually system defined types) for which certain possible representations are effectively exposed in something like the foregoing manner. Let me concentrate on type TIME, just to be definite. Values of that type—which is to say, individual times—have an exposed possible representation consisting of an HOUR component, a MINUTE component, and a SECOND component (each of which is defined in turn to be of a certain numeric type). But there's no requirement that

---

[7] See C. J. Date and Hugh Darwen: *Databases, Types, and the Relational Model: The Third Manifesto* (3rd edition, Addison-Wesley, 2007), also the website *www.thethirdmanifesto.com*.

the corresponding physical representation involve those same components;[8] it might, for example, consist simply of a count of the number of seconds—or microseconds, or some other suitable fractions of a second—that have elapsed since midnight. As for "THE_ operators": If *T* is an expression denoting some individual time, then the SQL analog of (e.g.) THE_MINUTE (*T*) is written thus: EXTRACT (MINUTE FROM *T*). *End of aside.*

WE DON'T ALWAYS WANT ENCAPSULATION

Another reason why I don't think encapsulation as such is all that important has to do with an issue over which there seems to be much confusion in the literature, and that's as follows: Some types are definitely *not* encapsulated anyway, nor do we want them to be! I refer in particular to certain "generated" type—types, that is, that have been defined by means of certain *type generators*, such as ARRAY, LIST, TUPLE, and RELATION. To fix our ideas, let's focus on RELATION as a familiar example (though remarks analogous to those that follow apply to ARRAY and the rest as well, of course). Suppose that, instead of the POINT type as discussed in the previous section, we had a POINT relvar (i.e., a relation variable called POINT) instead, defined as follows:

```
VAR POINT ... RELATION { X ... , Y ... } ... ;
```

Explanation: The keyword VAR means this is a variable definition; POINT is the name of the variable in question, and the text from the keyword RELATION to the closing brace, inclusive, specifies the type of that variable (see further discussion below). The various ellipses "..." stand for aspects of the definition—the types of attributes X and Y in particular—that aren't relevant to the present discussion and have therefore been omitted.

Now, this relvar definition makes use of the RELATION type generator to specify the (generated) type of the relvar, which is, of course, a relation type—namely, the relation type

```
RELATION { X ... , Y ... }
```

And this type is definitely not encapsulated—it has two user visible components, viz., the attributes X and Y. And, of course, it's precisely the fact that it does

---

[8] "No requirement" is correct here. I don't say there's no *suggestion.*

have those user visible components that makes it possible for us to perform ad hoc queries on relvar POINT. For example, we can project it over attribute X, or restrict it to just those tuples with Y value less than five:

```
POINT { X }
/* sample projection  */

POINT WHERE Y < 5.0
/* sample restriction */
```

Aside: I note in passing that Mike Stonebraker and his coauthors make some essentially similar observations in their book on object / relational DBMSs:[9]

> Base types are completely encapsulated. The only way to manipulate [an instance of] a base type is to retrieve it or execute a function that takes [an instance of that type] as an argument. In contrast, row types are completely transparent. You can see all the fields, and they are readily available in the query language. Of course, an intermediate position is to allow some fields of a row object to be public (visible) and the remainder to be private (encapsulated). This is the approach used by C++.

> I should add, however, that Stonebraker and his coauthors don't seem to agree with *The Third Manifesto* that what they call "base"—better: *scalar*—types should at least have (user visible) *possible* representations. Certainly they never discuss such a notion. *End of aside.*

Anyway, to get back to my main argument: Please observe very carefully that the fact that relation types aren't encapsulated doesn't mean we lose data independence! In the case of the POINT relvar, for instance, there's absolutely no reason why that relvar couldn't be represented physically in terms of polar coordinates RHO and THETA instead of cartesian coordinates X and Y.[10] Thus,

---

[9] Michael Stonebraker and Paul Brown (with Dorothy Moore): *Object-Relational DBMSs: Tracking the Next Great Wave* (2nd edition, Morgan Kaufmann, 1999). Note, however, that in the extract quoted the authors use "base type" to mean what I would call a scalar type, and "row type" to mean what I would call a tuple type. (To a first approximation, that is!—because rows, at least in SQL, have a left to right ordering to their components, which tuples don't.) At any rate, at least the authors agree that tuples (or rows) aren't encapsulated, and hence that relations (or tables) aren't encapsulated either.

[10] Yes, I know such a representation probably wouldn't be possible in today's SQL products, but that's a defect in those products, not a defect in what I'm suggesting should be possible. As I've had occasion to complain elsewhere—see, e.g., my book *SQL and Relational Theory: How to Write Accurate SQL Code* (3rd edition, O'Reilly, 2015)—today's SQL products provide very much less data independence than relational technology is theoretically capable of.

we do still have to make a clear distinction between types and representations, even with unencapsulated types like the relation type in the example, and "breaking encapsulation"—so long as that term is understood to mean exposing just some possible representation, not the physical representation—is *not* the same thing as undermining data independence. *Note:* I'll have a lot more to say about "breaking encapsulation" in the next chapter.

SCALAR vs. NONSCALAR TYPES

The Third Manifesto requires support for both a TUPLE and a RELATION type generator, thereby allowing users to specify their own tuple and relation types. It also requires users to be able to specify types that, unlike tuple and relation types, are just "simple" types—that is, types like POINT, and perhaps LENGTH, AREA, LINE, and so on—possibly even types like DATE and TIME, maybe even INTEGER and CHAR, if the system doesn't provide them as built in types. And we opted for the term *scalar* as a generic way of referring to such "simple" types (and then we naturally talked in terms of *scalar values* and *scalar variables* and *scalar operators* and *scalar expressions* as well).

Now, the reason we chose the term *scalar* was because:

a. It was already available (it had been used with the meaning we had in mind for many years in the world of programming languages).

b. What's more, it did seem to be the obviously correct term to contrast with nonscalar terms such as "tuple" and "relation" and "array" and "list" and all the rest. In fact, we would argue that it's obviously correct even though the physical representation of those "scalar" values and variables can be as complicated as you like. For example, a given scalar value might have a physical representation consisting of an array of stacks of lists of character strings, in appropriate circumstances. (Yet again I stress the importance of not confusing types and representations.)

And I now observe that our "scalar" means exactly the same thing as "encapsulated"!—that is, *a type is encapsulated if and only if it's scalar*, in the foregoing sense. I therefore feel that if the industry had opted, as we did in *The Third Manifesto*, for the already available term *scalar*, there would have been no need to invent the term *encapsulated* at all. And I further feel that we might thereby have avoided some of the many confusions I've been talking about in this chapter up to this point.

Note: Because they have no user visible components, scalar types (or encapsulated types, if you prefer) are sometimes described as *atomic.* I would rather not use such terminology, however, because it's led to too much misunderstanding in the past (on my own part as much as anyone else's, I hasten to add); instead, I prefer to concentrate on our "new, improved" understanding of the true nature of *first normal form.* But that's another matter I've discussed in detail elsewhere.[11]

CONCLUDING REMARKS

I've tried to show in this chapter why, in my opinion, the term "encapsulated" is more trouble than it's worth. To summarize:

- First of all, the term "scalar" seems (at least to me) to capture the essential idea better, and it has a longer and much more respectable pedigree than "encapsulated" does.

- Second, there seems to be a widespread misunderstanding to the effect that *all* data should be "encapsulated." I've tried to show that this idea is mistaken, and again I think that to talk in terms of scalar vs. nonscalar types makes the true state of affairs much clearer and reduces the risk of confusion.

- Third, some people seem to think of "encapsulation" as a physical rather than a logical concept anyway (see the remarks on this point at the end of the section "What Does Encapsulation Mean?").

I therefore think it's worth trying to avoid the term "encapsulation" altogether—in fact, as I claimed earlier, I think it's really nothing more than a red herring—and I propose to take my own advice in this regard in my writings from this point forward.

---

[11] See, e.g., Chapter 4, "FDs and BCNF (Informal)," in my book *Database Design and Relational Theory: Normal Forms and All That Jazz* (2nd edition, Apress, 2019), or Chapter 10, "Normal Forms from Last to First—BCNF to 1NF," in this book's predecessor *Logic and Relational Theory: Thoughts and Essays on Database Matters* (Technics Publications, 2020).

Chapter 8

Thinking Clearly about

Decapsulation

Curtsey while you're thinking what to say.
It saves time.

—Lewis Carroll:
Through the Looking Glass and What Alice Found There (1872)

In the previous chapter I explained why I feel that the focus on "encapsulation" in the object world is a little off base. Now I turn my attention to its inverse, which is usually referred to in the literature as "breaking encapsulation" but which, I suggest, might more conveniently be called *decapsulation.*

The apparent need for decapsulation—I stress that qualifier *apparent*—arises in object systems in connection with ad hoc query. Let me repeat something I said in the previous chapter in connection with encapsulation:

> However, there's a problem, as you might already have realized: namely, that the objective of encapsulation ... is in conflict with the objective of being able to perform ad hoc queries. After all, encapsulation means data can be accessed only in predefined ways, while "ad hoc query" means, more or less by definition, that access is required in ways that aren't, and can't have been, predefined.

And indeed object systems typically support ad hoc queries, etc., precisely by breaking encapsulation—i.e., by decapsulation—and thereby exposing physical representations! Here are a couple of quotes to illustrate the point:

1. From Mary E. S. Loomis: *Object Databases: The Essentials* (Addison-Wesley, 1995):

> All object DBMS products currently require that [all components of objects]
> referenced in ... queries be public [*i.e., visible to the user*].

2.   From Elisa Bertino and Lorenzo Martino: *Object-Oriented Database
     Systems: Concepts and Architectures* (Addison-Wesley, 1993):

> Query management ... is one situation where violating encapsulation is
> almost obligatory.

In sharp contrast to the foregoing, *The Third Manifesto* (the *Manifesto* for
short) addresses the problem by means of what it calls *possible representations*.
I introduced and briefly discussed this notion in the previous chapter. In a
nutshell, I explained how the *Manifesto* requires, for any given scalar type,
certain "THE_ operators" to be defined that expose some possible representation
for values and variables of the type in question. By way of illustration, I gave the
example of a type POINT, for which we might define operators THE_X and
THE_Y to expose a "cartesian coordinates" possible representation. However, I
also emphasized the fact that cartesian coordinates were only a *possible*
representation for such a type—the actual (i.e., physical) representation might be
cartesian coordinates, or polar coordinates, or something else entirely. Possible
representations are of interest to the user; physical representations, by contrast,
are of interest only to the implementation.

Now, the "possible representation" concept actually constitutes a very
fundamental part of the thinking underlying *The Third Manifesto*,[1] and there's a
lot more to be said about it than would have been appropriate in that previous
chapter. In this chapter, therefore, I'd like to examine and explain that concept in
a little more depth. I'll begin by discussing the associated notion of *selector
operators*.

SCALAR SELECTORS

For every data type—for every scalar type in particular—the *Manifesto* requires
among other things that an operator be defined whose purpose is simply to
"select," or in other words specify, an individual value of the type in question.
Such selector operators are in fact just a generalization of the familiar notion of a

---

[1] In particular, it's highly relevant to the (surprisingly complicated!) issue of type inheritance. See my book
Type Inheritance and Relational Theory: Subtypes, Supertypes, and Substitutability (O'Reilly, 2016).

literal (a literal is a special case of a selector invocation, but not all selector invocations are literals). For example, consider the following code fragment:[2]

```
VAR X RATIONAL ;
VAR Y RATIONAL ;
VAR P POINT ;

X := -4.0 ;
Y := +3.0 ;
P := POINT ( X , Y ) ;
```

The effect of this code fragment is, of course, to set the variable P to contain a particular POINT value: namely, the point whose cartesian coordinates are (−4.0, +3.0).[3] And the expression on the right side of the assignment in the last line is, precisely, an invocation of a selector for type POINT; its effect is, precisely, to select the point with the specified cartesian coordinates.

> *Aside:* In the example, if I'd written simply POINT (−4.0,+3.0) instead of POINT (X,Y)—which I could perfectly well have done, of course—then I would have been making use of a selector invocation that was actually a literal. A literal can be defined, recursively, as a selector invocation in which each argument is denoted by a literal in turn. *End of aside.*

Observe, therefore, that if *S* is a selector operator, then *the parameters to S together constitute—necessarily!—a possible representation PR for values of the pertinent type T.* In the example, cartesian coordinates X and Y constitute, necessarily, a possible representation for points (i.e., values of type POINT).

Now, object systems do have something analogous, somewhat, to selector operators (though the more usual object term is *constructor functions*), and users of those systems are thus necessarily aware of certain possible—maybe even physical?—representations.[4] As far as I know, however, object systems don't usually go on to insist that those representations be exposed for arbitrary

---

[2] Note that variables X and Y in this example are defined to be of type RATIONAL, not REAL. **Tutorial D** uses RATIONAL in place of the more usual REAL because, by definition, any number that's capable of representation in a computer must be a rational number specifically, not just some real number.

[3] If you happen to be familiar with object systems, I should emphasize that in our model the variable P really does now contain a point as such, not a "reference to" or "object ID of" or "pointer to" or "address of" such a point. In fact, *The Third Manifesto* explicitly proscribes all such "references," "object IDs," "pointers," and "addresses."

[4] Note, however, that constructor functions in object systems typically construct something that's best thought of as a *variable*, whereas our selector operators select a *value*.

purposes. For example, the user might know from the format of the points constructor function that points do have a "cartesian coordinates" possible representation—and yet, if the system doesn't provide operators to "get" both the X and Y coordinates of any given point, then there'll be all kinds of simple operations that the user won't be able to perform. Following on from the code fragment already shown, for example, if there's no "get Y" operation, then the user won't be able to ask what the Y coordinate of point P is, even though he or she *knows* it's 3.0! In other words, the object model seems to permit a design policy that isn't very sensible.

In view of the foregoing observations, we decided in *The Third Manifesto* to insist on some appropriate discipline. To be specific, we insist that:

- The definition of a scalar type must include the specification of at least one possible representation for values of that type.[5]

- Specifying a possible representation causes "automatic" definition of a corresponding selector operator. (I'll explain just what I mean by the term "automatic definition" in a later section.) Note, therefore, that every possible representation has a corresponding selector (and in **Tutorial D** we adopt the obvious convention that any given possible representation and the corresponding selector have the same name, to underscore their hand in glove relationship).

- Specifying a possible representation also causes "automatic" definition of a set of operators to expose that possible representation for arbitrary purposes (see the next section).

Here's an example (**Tutorial D** again):

```
TYPE POINT
    POSSREP POINT { X   RATIONAL , Y     RATIONAL }
    POSSREP POLAR { RHO RATIONAL , THETA RATIONAL } ... ;
```

This statement constitutes a definition for the type POINT already used in earlier examples. Type POINT has two possible representations ("possreps"), named POINT (cartesian coordinates) and POLAR (polar coordinates),

---

[5] Except possibly if the type in question is system defined (built in). I'll consider the case of system defined types in a few moments.

respectively, and two corresponding selectors with the same names. *Note:* We also adopt another convention in **Tutorial D** according to which a possible representation with no explicit name of its own inherits the name of the corresponding type by default; thus, the first of the two POSSREP specifications in the example could optionally have omitted the explicit possrep name POINT.

Of course, *The Third Manifesto* requires tuple and relation types to have selectors as well. For simplicity, I'm concentrating in the present discussion on scalar types specifically; however, let me at least close this section by giving a general definition for the record.

> **Definition (selector):** An operator for selecting, or specifying, an arbitrary value of a given type; not to be confused with either relational restriction (which is, perhaps rather unfortunately, sometimes called selection), or the SELECT operation of SQL. Every type *T* has at least one associated selector *S*.[6] Then (a) every value of type *T* is producible by means of some invocation of *S* in which the argument expressions are all literals, and (b) every successful invocation of *S* produces a value of type *T*. Note that, ultimately, the only way any expression can ever yield a value of type *T* is via invocation of some selector for type *T*.

To elaborate (but these details too are just for the record, and you can skip them if you like):

■ If *T* is a user defined scalar type, definition of a possrep *PR* for *T* causes automatic definition of a corresponding selector (with the same name as *PR*, in **Tutorial D**), which allows a value of type *T* to be selected by supplying a value for each component of *PR*.

■ If *T* is a system defined scalar type, one or more possreps might be defined for it. If one is defined (*PR*, say), then it behaves exactly as if *T* were user defined and *PR* were a corresponding possrep. If no possrep is defined, then at least one selector for type *T* must be provided by the system; in this case, however, invocations of any such selector might be limited to being simple literals.

---

[6] So long as *T* is nonempty, that is. An empty type can't have a selector, because there's no value that such a selector could possibly select! *Note:* Empty types have a crucial role to play if type inheritance is supported but probably aren't very important if it isn't. Again, see my book *Type Inheritance and Relational Theory: Subtypes, Supertypes, and Substitutability* (O'Reilly, 2016) for further discussion.

- If T is a tuple type, the unique corresponding selector allows a tuple of type T to be selected by supplying a value for each attribute of T.

- If T is a relation type, the unique corresponding selector allows a relation of type T to be selected by specifying a set of tuple expressions, each denoting one tuple of the relation in question.

THE_ OPERATORS

As noted in the previous section, *The Third Manifesto* also requires that, for each specified possible representation for a given scalar type, a set of operators be "automatically" defined whose purpose is to expose the possible representation in question. And as you know by now, in **Tutorial D** the operators that are used for this task are called *THE_ operators*. Here's a definition:

Definition (THE_ operator): Let PR be a possible representation for scalar type T; let PR have components $C1, C2, ..., Cn$; and let THE_$C1$, THE_$C2$, ..., THE_Cn be a family of operators such that, for each i ($i = 1, 2, ..., n$), the operator THE_Ci has the following properties:

- Its sole parameter is of type T.

- If an invocation of the operator appears in a "source" position (in particular, on the right side of an assignment), then it returns the Ci component of its argument. (More precisely, it returns the value of the Ci component of the possible representation $PR(v)$ of its argument value v.)

- If an invocation of the operator appears in a "target" position (in particular, on the left side of an assignment), then, first, its argument must be denoted by a scalar variable reference specifically, not by any other kind of scalar expression; second, the invocation acts as a *pseudovariable*, which means that it actually *designates*—rather than just returning the value of—the Ci component of its argument. (More precisely, it designates the Ci component of the possible representation *PR(V)* of its argument variable *V*. See further discussion below.)

Here's an example:

```
TYPE TEMPERATURE POSSREP CELSIUS { C RATIONAL } ;

VAR TMP TEMPERATURE ;
VAR CEL RATIONAL ;

CEL := THE_C ( TMP ) ;
THE_C ( TMP ) := CEL ;
```

Explanation:

- Suppose the current value of the variable TMP is CELSIUS (45.2), denoting a temperature of 45.2 degrees Celsius. (That expression CELSIUS (45.2) is a selector invocation corresponding to the CELSIUS possible representation for type TEMPERATURE; in fact, it's a CELSIUS literal.) Then the assignment in the last line but one of the foregoing code assigns the rational value 45.2 to the RATIONAL variable CEL.

- Suppose the current value of the variable CEL is 2.6. (That expression 2.6 is actually a RATIONAL selector invocation; in fact, it's a RATIONAL literal.) Then the assignment in the last line of the foregoing code assigns the temperature value CELSIUS (2.6) to the TEMPERATURE variable TMP. Moreover, in that assignment, the expression THE_C (TMP) on the left side is a *pseudovariable reference*—that is, it's an operational expression, syntactically speaking, but it's one that actually *designates* the C component of the variable TMP, thereby allowing that component to be directly updated.

The operator THE_C thus effectively exposes the "degrees Celsius" possible representation for temperatures (for both read-only and update purposes, please note—see the next section for further discussion of this point). However, that possible representation isn't necessarily a physical one; for example, temperatures might physically be represented in terms of degrees Fahrenheit, not degrees Celsius.

Note: The term *pseudovariable* is taken from PL/I. Be aware, however, that pseudovariables in PL/I can't be nested, but THE_ pseudovariables in

Tutorial D can. Loosely speaking, in other words, we do regard pseudovariable references as variable references, implying among other things that they can be used to denote the argument to other such references. To illustrate the point—pardon the pun—consider type POINT again, with its cartesian coordinate possible representation. First, let variables Z and P be of types RATIONAL and POINT, respectively. Then (as we know) the assignment

```
Z := THE_X ( P ) ;
```

assigns the X coordinate of the point denoted by the current value of P to Z, and the assignment

```
THE_X ( P ) := Z ;
```

uses the current value of Z to update the X coordinate of P (speaking a trifle loosely). But now suppose we have another type LINESEG (line segments), defined as follows:

```
TYPE LINESEG
     POSSREP { BEGIN POINT , END POINT }
             /* begin and end points -- corresp selector */
             /* is called LINESEG by default            */ ;

VAR LS LINESEG ;

Z := THE_X ( THE_BEGIN ( LS ) ) ;
THE_X ( THE_BEGIN ( LS ) ) := Z ;
```

The first of the two assignments here assigns the X coordinate of the begin point of the current value of LS to the RATIONAL variable Z, while the second uses the current value of that variable Z to update the X coordinate of the begin point of the variable LS—and of course it's that second assignment specifically that illustrates the idea of pseudovariable nesting. Note that the ability to nest THE_ pseudovariables in this fashion means, loosely speaking, that arbitrarily complex updates are possible (just as the ability to nest regular THE_ operator invocations means that arbitrarily complex retrievals are also possible).

By the way, I remind you from Chapter 2 that *The Third Manifesto* also supports a *multiple* form of assignment. For example, the statement

```
THE_BEGIN ( LS ) := P ,
THE_END   ( LS ) := Q ;
```

—note that the first line ends in a comma, not a semicolon—could be used to update the begin and end points of the line segment variable LS "at the same time" (i.e., in a single operation). For further explanation, I refer you to Chapter 4 ("Constraints and Predicates") in my book *Logic and Relational Theory: Thoughts and Essays on Database Matters* (Technics Publications, 2020).

> *Aside:* I mentioned in the previous chapter that in SQL, if *T* is an expression denoting some individual time, then the expression EXTRACT (MINUTE FROM *T*) can be used to retrieve the "minutes" component of the time denoted by *T*. EXTRACT in SQL thus behaves a little bit like a THE_ operator in **Tutorial D**. As the EXTRACT keyword might tend to suggest, however, EXTRACT in SQL, though it can obviously be used for retrieval purposes, *can't* be used for update purposes. In other words, there's no analog in SQL of **Tutorial D**'s THE_ pseudovariables. *End of aside.*

THE_ PSEUDOVARIABLES ARE JUST SHORTHAND

I now observe that THE_ pseudovariables, though highly desirable from an ergonomic point of view, are in fact logically unnecessary. Consider again the following example of an "updating" assignment from the previous section:

```
THE_C ( TMP ) := CEL ;
```

This assignment, which uses a pseudovariable, is logically equivalent to the following one which doesn't:

```
TMP := CELSIUS ( CEL ) ;
```

Similarly, the following assignment (which uses a pseudovariable)—

```
THE_X ( P ) := Z ;
```

—is logically equivalent to this one (which doesn't):

```
P := POINT ( Z , THE_Y ( P ) ) ;
```

One further example:

```
THE_X ( THE_BEGIN ( LS ) ) := Z ;
```

Here's a logical equivalent:

```
LS := LINESEG ( POINT ( Z , THE_Y ( THE_BEGIN ( LS ) ) ,
              THE_END ( LS ) ) ;
```

In other words, pseudovariables per se aren't strictly necessary in order to support the kind of component at a time updating I've been discussing in this chapter up to this point (where by "component" I mean a component of a possible representation, of course). However, the pseudovariable approach does seem intuitively more attractive than the alternative, for which it can be regarded as shorthand.[7] It also provides a higher degree of imperviousness to changes in the syntax of the corresponding selector. And (bonus!) it might possibly perform better—though matters of performance fall outside the purview of the model, of course, and I shouldn't really discuss or even mention them here; so I won't.

A REMARK ON TYPE CONSTRAINTS

Let T be a scalar type; then the definition of type T necessarily includes, at least implicitly, a corresponding *type constraint*. In general, the type constraint for any given type T is simply a definition of the set of values that constitute that type T. For example:

```
TYPE TEMPERATURE
     POSSREP CELSIUS { C RATIONAL }
     CONSTRAINT C ≥ -100 AND C ≤ +100 ;
```

By this definition, permitted TEMPERATURE values are all and only those values that can possibly be represented by a rational number C in the range from negative 100 to positive 100, inclusive.[8] (If a given scalar type definition contains no explicit CONSTRAINT specification, then CONSTRAINT TRUE is assumed by default. In the TEMPERATURE example, therefore, omitting the CONSTRAINT specification would simply mean that anything that can be

---

[7] For reasons beyond the scope of the present discussion, it turns out to be even more attractive (though still not *logically* necessary) if type inheritance is supported.

[8] I assume for simplicity throughout this section that comparisons and arithmetic operations involving a mixture of integers and rational numbers are legitimate.

represented by a rational number would be a valid temperature, and nothing else would be.)

Suppose now for the sake of the example that type TEMPERATURE has both a CELSIUS and a FAHRENHEIT possible representation. Then the pertinent type constraint will have to specify not just the permitted values as above, but also how those possible representations are interrelated:

```
TYPE TEMPERATURE
     POSSREP CELSIUS { C RATIONAL }
     POSSREP FAHRENHEIT { F RATIONAL }
     CONSTRAINT C ≥ -100 AND C ≤ +100
             AND F = ( 9 × C / 5 ) + 32   ;
```

Now:

- If *t* is an expression of type TEMPERATURE, then THE_C (*t*) will return a rational number *c* denoting the corresponding temperature in degrees Celsius, while THE_F (*t*) will return a rational number *f* denoting that same temperature in degrees Fahrenheit (and *f* will be equal to $(9 \times c / 5) + 32$).

- If *z* is an expression of type RATIONAL, then the expressions CELSIUS (*z*) and FAHRENHEIT ($(9 \times z / 5) + 32$) will both return the same TEMPERATURE value. (So long as the rational number denoted by *z* is in the right range, of course! If it isn't, those two selector invocations will both fail on a type constraint error.)

"AUTOMATIC DEFINITION"

I've shown that even in object systems—i.e., systems that support "encapsulated objects"—the user must necessarily be aware of certain possible representations for those objects. *The Third Manifesto* in effect takes advantage of, and formalizes, this state of affairs by insisting that every scalar type have at least one possible representation that's explicitly defined. So let *PR* be an explicitly defined possible representation for scalar type *T*. Then the definition of *PR* (part of the definition of *T*) causes "automatic" definition of the following more or less self-explanatory operators:

- Exactly one corresponding selector operator, which allows the user to specify or "select" any individual value of type *T* by supplying a value for each component of *PR*

- A set of THE_ operators (exactly one for each component of *PR*), which allow the user to access the corresponding *PR* components of (a) any specified value of type *T* (for retrieval purposes) and (b) any specified variable of type *T* (for update purposes)

And when I say the definition of *PR* causes "automatic definition" of these operators, what I mean is that whatever agency—possibly the system, possibly some human user—is responsible for defining type *T* is also responsible for providing the necessary implementation code for the operators in question. Further details are beyond the scope of this chapter.[9]

A CASE STUDY

Note: This section is based on Appendix B ("A Design Dilemma?") of Databases, Types, and the Relational Model: The Third Manifesto (3rd edition), by Hugh Darwen and myself (Addison-Wesley, 2007).

Given everything I've been saying about scalar types in this chapter so far (as well as in its two predecessors), you might be thinking that now we have some kind of design dilemma on our hands. For example, suppose we want to design a database containing information about employees, and suppose the information we want to record about a given employee consists of employee number, name, department number, and salary. Then it appears we have a choice: Apparently, we could represent employees either as a *type* (with a suitable set of "possrep" components) or as a *relvar* (with a suitable set of attributes).[10] Here are the two possibilities in **Tutorial D** (I'll call them Design T and Design R, respectively):

---

[9] But can be found in various other places—e.g., in the book mentioned in footnote 1, viz., *Type Inheritance and Relational Theory: Subtypes, Supertypes, and Substitutability* (O'Reilly, 2016).

[10] Actually I touched on this issue in an example earlier in this chapter, when I said "Suppose that, instead of the POINT type discussed in the previous section, we had a POINT relvar (relation variable) instead."

```
TYPE EMP POSSREP                          / * "Design T" */
  ( ENO CHAR , ENAME CHAR , DNO CHAR , SALARY MONEY ) ;

VAR  EMP BASE RELATION                    / * "Design R" */
   { ENO CHAR , ENAME CHAR , DNO CHAR , SALARY MONEY }
     KEY { ENO } ;
```

Note in particular that the EMP type is scalar or "encapsulated," while the EMP relvar isn't. Note also the KEY specification in Design R.

Now I want to argue that the apparent choice between these two designs is actually no choice at all. Observe first of all that Design T gives us no way to hire and fire!—and so that design is clearly inadequate as it stands. The reason is that, loosely speaking, type EMP is the set of *all possible* employees (i.e., it's not just the ones who currently work for the company), and there's simply no way to insert a new employee into that set or delete an existing one; in other words, types are *static*. To put it another way, the set in question contains all possible values of the form[11]

```
EMP ( eno , name , dno , sal )
```

(where *eno*, *name*, *dno*, and *sal* are values of types CHAR, CHAR, CHAR, and MONEY, respectively). Some of the values in that set will indeed correspond to employees who currently work for the company, but others (doubtless the vast majority) won't.

> *Aside:* If you're having difficulty with this idea, consider the simpler example of type INTEGER. That type just *is* the set of all integers, and it's clearly not possible to insert new integers or delete existing ones. (Just to beat the point to death: Suppose it were possible to "insert a new integer" after all. Where do you think that "new integer" would come from?) *End of aside.*

It follows from the above that Design T additionally requires an accompanying relvar, perhaps looking like this:

```
VAR EMPRV ... RELATION { EMP EMP } KEY { EMP } ;
```

Relvar EMPRV has a tuple for every employee currently of interest (meaning, presumably, every employee who currently works for the company), and of course we now do have a way to hire new employees and fire existing

---

[11] The "form" in question is actually that of an EMP selector invocation.

ones. Note carefully, however, that relvar EMPRV does indeed have just one attribute, not four, thanks to that "encapsulation"; that attribute is called EMP, and it's of type (i.e., "encapsulated" type) EMP. Note too that the KEY specification in the EMPRV definition is almost a "no op"; note in particular that what it *doesn't* say is that employee numbers are unique. If we did want to say such a thing—which in practice we presumably would want to do—we'd have to define a separate constraint, perhaps along the following lines:

```
CONSTRAINT ENO_UNIQUE
          COUNT ( EMPRV ) =
          COUNT ( ( EXTEND EMPRV :
                        { ENO := THE_ENO ( EMP ) } ) { ENO } ) ;
```

Explanation:

■ ENO_UNIQUE is just the constraint name.

■ Let *emps* be the relation that's the current value of relvar EMPRV. Then the expression COUNT (EMPRV) on the left side of the equality comparison returns a count of the number of tuples in *emps*. Let that count be *N1*.

■ The expression

```
EXTEND EMPRV : { ENO := THE_ENO ( EMP ) }
```

returns a relation identical to *emps* except that it has another attribute, called ENO, whose value in each tuple is equal to the ENO value from the sole defined possible representation for the EMP value in the corresponding tuple of *emps*. Let that returned relation be *emps*$^+$.

■ The expression on the right side of the equality comparison thus effectively reduces to the following:

```
COUNT ( emps+ { ENO } )
```

The expression in parentheses here denotes the projection of *emps*$^+$ on ENO, and the COUNT invocation thus returns a count of the number of tuples in that projection. Let that count be *N2*.

■ The constraint overall thus requires that *N1* and *N2* be equal. And if you think about it, what that constraint boils down to is indeed a constraint to the effect that employee numbers must be unique.

One implication of the Design T approach is thus that it tends to suggest that the database will wind up containing a large number of relvars with just one attribute each, and probably with a large number of constraints looking like the one just shown as well: a state of affairs that should give us some pause, you might think.

Anyway, now we can at least "hire and fire." We can also perform operations analogous—though *not* identical!—to the kinds of relational operations we would probably have performed on relvar EMP if we'd opted for Design R instead. Here are a couple of examples:

■ (*"Restriction"*) Get employees with salary greater than $50,000:

```
EMPRV WHERE THE_SALARY ( EMP ) > MONEY ( 50000 )
```

■ (*"Projection"*) Get all employee name / salary pairs:

```
( EXTEND EMPRV : { ENAME  := THE_ENAME  ( EMP ) ,
                   SALARY := THE_SALARY ( EMP ) } )
                                   { ENAME , SALARY }
```

Observe, however, that the result in this latter example has two attributes, not one. Indeed, it should be clear that (a) given the single-attribute relvar EMPRV required by Design T, we can create the four-attribute relvar required by Design R (as a view, perhaps); furthermore, (b) we'd probably want to do exactly that in practice, because that four-attribute relvar is considerably more convenient for a variety of reasons than the single-attribute one is. Here to spell it out is a definition for that four-attribute view (let's call it EMPV, for clarity):

```
VAR EMPV VIRTUAL
    /* views are called virtual relvars in Tutorial D */
    ( ( EXTEND EMPRV : { ENO    := THE_ENO    ( EMP ) ,
                         ENAME  := THE_ENAME  ( EMP ) ,
                         DNO    := THE_DNO    ( EMP ) ,
                         SALARY := THE_SALARY ( EMP ) } )
      { ENO , ENAME , DNO , SALARY } )
    KEY { ENO } ;
```

Note in particular that the KEY specification for this relvar EMPV does say that employee numbers are unique.

What the foregoing analysis demonstrates is that we can start off with Design T (the type design) if we like, which means we'll also need an associated single-attribute relvar—but we'll quickly find that, in effect, we'll have to create Design R (the relvar design) as well. So Design T implies that we wind up with everything in Design R, plus the type EMP, plus the single-attribute relvar EMPR and the constraint ENO_UNIQUE as well. So what was the point of opting for Design T in the first place? And what purpose is served, exactly, in Design T by that type EMP and that single-attribute relvar EMPRV and that constraint ENO_UNIQUE?

Given all of the above, what then is the criterion for making something a type and not a relvar? (We must have some types, of course, if only for the obvious reason that relvars can't be defined without them.) Well, here are some pertinent considerations:

■ In conventional design terms, types correspond, loosely, to *properties* and relvars to *entities* (or sets of properties and sets of entities, rather). Hence, if something is "only" a property, it should map to a type and not a relvar.

    The problem with this idea, of course, is that "one person's property is another person's entity." For example, consider colors. We'd normally tend to think of the color "red," say, as a property,[12] not an entity, and thus we'd normally represent colors as a type. But some users might be very interested in "red" as an entity, with further properties of its own (shade, for example, or intensity), in which case we might want to represent colors by a relvar. Perhaps this is an example of a situation where we need both a type and a relvar (the relvar representing just those colors that happen to be currently of interest for some reason).

■ Another important general point is that if the ability to "hire and fire"—or something analogous to that ability—is a requirement, then we're definitely talking about entities, not properties, and we should definitely be aiming for a relvar design.

Given such considerations, incidentally, it's odd that so many articles and presentations on object systems use employees, departments, and so forth as

---

[12] As a property of some entity, that is. The concept of a property in isolation makes no sense.

examples of object classes. Of course, an object class is basically just a type—at least, that's what it is as far as I'm concerned—and so those presentations are typically forced to go on to define some kind of "collection" for those employees, another such "collection" for those departments, and so on. What's more, those "collections" are collections of encapsulated objects, and they therefore effectively omit those all important, user visible attribute names. As a consequence, they don't lend themselves very well to the formulation of ad hoc queries, declarative integrity constraints, and so forth—a fact that advocates of the approach themselves often admit,[13] apparently without being aware that it's precisely the lack of user visible attribute names (in effect, the encapsulation) that causes the difficulties.

Thinking Clearly Again

Back to types vs. relvars. Overall, it's my belief that the most appropriate design approach will emerge if careful consideration is given to the distinction between (a) declarative sentences in natural language, on the one hand, and (b) the vocabulary used in the construction of such sentences, on the other. Basically, it's *unencapsulated tuples in relations* that stand for such sentences, and it's *encapsulated values in attributes in those tuples* that stand for particular elements—typically nouns—in those sentences. As I put it in my book *SQL and Relational Theory: How to Write Accurate SQL Code* (3rd edition, O'Reilly, 2015):

> Types give us our vocabulary—the things we can talk about—and relations give us the ability to say things about the things we can talk about.

Let me elaborate. First, consider the EMP relvar of Design R once again, and consider this tuple:[14]

```
TUPLE { ENO 'E7' ,    ENAME 'Amy' ,
                      DNO 'D5' , SALARY MONEY ( 60000 ) }
```

Inserting this tuple into the relvar means (let's agree) that the database now contains something asserting that the following declarative sentence is true:

---

[13] See the quotes near the beginning of the chapter (from the books by Loomis and by Bertino and Martino, respectively) for concrete examples of this phenomenon.

[14] This example illustrates, not incidentally, the **Tutorial D** syntax for a tuple selector invocation.

Employee E7, named Amy, is assigned to department D5 and earns a salary of $60,000.

By contrast, consider the EMP type of Design T. Where the relvar of Design R allowed us to insert the tuple just shown, with the interpretation just explained, the type of Design T merely allows us to write the following selector invocation:

```
EMP ( 'E7' , 'Amy' , 'D5' , MONEY ( 60000 ) )
```

This selector invocation doesn't in and of itself assert the truth of anything at all (nor does it deny it, of course). Rather, it constitutes nothing more than a certain rather heavy duty noun, something like "an E7-numbered, Amy-named, D5-assigned, $60,000-earning employee."

Now, we can if we like form a tuple containing just that "noun"—i.e., that EMP value—and then insert that tuple into the single-attribute relvar EMPRV that Design T additionally requires. Speaking a trifle loosely, however, to do what I've just described is simply (a) to place a "There exists" in front of that noun, thereby forming a certain declarative sentence, and then (b) to assert that the sentence in question is in fact true.

Of course, the "true fact" asserted by the four-attribute tuple in Design R is exactly the same as the "true fact" asserted in different words (as it were) by the one-attribute tuple in Design T. So which of the two ways of asserting that fact do you think is the more economical, the more communicative, and the more amenable to further reasoning?

Chapter 9

An Overview and Analysis

of ODMG

OMG: Net-centric abbreviation for the popular exclamation "Oh my God!"
(generally used in conversations to exclaim surprise or disgust)
—www.urbandictionary.com

The term *ODMG* is used in the database community at large, and in this chapter, as a convenient shorthand to refer to the proposals of the Object Data Management Group, a consortium of participants from "member companies representing almost the entire [object] DBMS industry."[1] The proposals in question consist of:

- An Object Model

- An Object Definition Language (ODL)

- An Object Query Language (OQL)

- An Object Interchange Format (OIF)

- Bindings of the Object Model, ODL, and OQL to the programming languages C++, Smalltalk, and Java

---

[1] All otherwise unattributed quotes in this chapter are taken from R. G. G. Cattell and Douglas K. Barry (eds.), *The Object Database Standard: ODMG 2.0* (Morgan Kaufmann, 1997), referred to hereinafter as "the ODMG book." This particular quote is from page 2. *Note:* Despite its "ODMG 2.0" title, the ODMG book actually describes the fourth version of the ODMG proposals (the first three were Versions 1.0, 1.1, and 1.2, respectively). A fifth version, Version 3.0, was described in yet another edition of the book—
R. G. G. Cattell and Douglas K. Barry (eds.), *The Object Database Standard: ODMG 3.0* (Morgan Kaufmann, 2000)—which appeared after the appendix to the *Manifesto* book, on which this chapter is based, was written.

Note: The first two of these components are based, respectively, on the Object Model and the Interface Definition Language (IDL) of the Object Management Group, OMG.[2] Observe that there's no "Object Manipulation Language" component; instead, object manipulation features are provided by whatever language ODMG happens to be bound to (C++, Smalltalk, Java, possibly others as well).

The following extract from page 3 of the ODMG book is worthy of note:

> [We] define an *object DBMS* to be a DBMS that integrates database capabilities with object-oriented programming language capabilities. An object DBMS makes database objects appear as programming language objects ... [It] extends the language with transparently persistent data, concurrency control, data recovery, associative queries, and other database capabilities.

We—i.e., Hugh Darwen and I, creators of *The Third Manifesto*—agree with the implication that "one language, not two" is a desirable goal. However, we most certainly don't agree with the further implication that "persistence orthogonal to type" is another; in fact, I wrote an entire paper some while ago debunking that idea.[3]

Incidentally, the ODMG book refers repeatedly, both in its title and throughout the text, to "the ODMG standard." While it's possible that ODMG might someday become a de facto standard[4]—to quote page 6, "ODMG ... member companies are committed to [supporting] this standard in the products by the end of 1998" [*sic*]—it's not a de jure one, since the ODMG committee has no official standardization authority. The bodies that do have such authority are (a) the International Organization for Standardization, ISO, for worldwide standards, and (b) various national bodies for individual countries (e.g., the American National Standards Institute, ANSI, for standards in the U.S.). However, it's at least true that the ODMG committee worked for a while with the ANSI SQL committee (X3H2) to try to achieve some degree of convergence between its proposals and the SQL standard as such.[5]

---

[2] See "The OMG Object Model," by Richard Mark Soley and William Kent (discussed in Appendix A to the present chapter), also the OMG website *www.omgwiki.org.*

[3] That paper is subsumed by Chapter 6 of the present book.

[4] Possible, yes, but highly unlikely, I'd say, writing now some 20 or so years later.

[5] I'm not aware that anything significant ever emerged from that activity.

The following quote from page 1 gives some idea of the committee's modus operandi and its own (rather self-congratulatory) assessment of the significance of its work:

> We have worked outside of traditional standards bodies for our efforts in order to make quick progress ... The intense ODMG effort has given the object database industry a "jump start" toward standards that would otherwise have taken many years ... It is to the personal credit of all participants that the ODMG standard has been produced and revised [so] expeditiously. All of the contributors put substantial time and personal investment into the meetings and this document. They showed remarkable dedication to our goals.

The following quote from page 2 is also noteworthy:

> [Object DBMSs] are *a revolutionary rather than an evolutionary development.* [*Italics added.*]

Note in particular the contrast here with *The Third Manifesto*, which is intended very explicitly to be evolutionary, not revolutionary, in nature.

I have to say too that the ODMG book includes many remarks that seem (a) to display a very poor understanding of the relational model, and/or (b) to mix matters that are genuinely relevant to the model as such (no matter whether it be relational or object oriented) with ones that should more properly be of concern to the implementation. Here are a few examples, some of which I choose to comment on though not all:

- (*From page 1*) The scope of object DBMSs is more far-reaching than that of relational DBMSs.

  Well, perhaps it depends on what you mean by "scope"—but in my opinion there's absolutely nothing useful that can be done with an object DBMS that couldn't be done with a true relational DBMS.

- (*From page 3*) The [ODMG] query language [OQL] is more powerful [than a relational query language].

  It's more complicated, certainly, but it's not more powerful. The added complication derives from the fact that ODMG in general, and OQL in particular, both expose many different data structures to the user ("persistence orthogonal to type")—a consequence, it seems to me, of a failure to appreciate the advantages of keeping model and implementation rigidly apart. (Similar remarks apply to most of the next few quotes also.)

■ (*From page 4*) We have used the relational standard SQL as the basis for OQL, where possible, though OQL supports more powerful capabilities.

■ (*From page 5*) We go further than relational systems, as we support a unified object model for sharing data across programming languages.

This claim in particular does seem a little strange! I mean, surely the *relational* model could reasonably be characterized as "a unified model for sharing data across programming languages"?—among many other things, of course.

■ (*From page 12*) Analogous to the ODMG Object Model for object databases is the relational model for relational databases, as embodied in SQL.

SQL and the relational model are *not* the same thing; the relational model as such is *not* "embodied in SQL"; and anyone who disagrees with either of these observations is merely demonstrating his or her lack of understanding of the relational model. The sad truth is, SQL is merely a deeply flawed attempt to realize in concrete syntactic form some (not all) of the components of the abstract relational model.

■ (*Also from page 12*) The ODMG Object Model ... includes significantly richer semantics than does the relational model, by declaring relationships and operations explicitly.

Apologies, but this is really such nonsense. First, the relational model quite deliberately doesn't "declare relationships explicitly"—instead, it represents both "entities" and "relationships" in the same uniform way.[6] Second, with respect to "declaring operations": While it's true that the relational model has nothing explicit to say regarding such a capability, it certainly implies it as a requirement as part of its support for types (*aka* domains).

---

[6] Some might argue that relational foreign key definitions constitute explicit relationship declarations. However, such definitions are really just shorthand for certain pragmatically important integrity constraint declarations.

■   (*From page 33*) The ODMG data model encompasses the relational data model by defining a TABLE type to express SQL tables. The ODMG TABLE type is semantically equivalent to a collection of structs.

One (huge!) problem with this particular claim is that it totally ignores the relational operators. For example, it's hard to see how the ODMG Object Model could be used to implement a generic join operation—i.e., one that would work on arbitrary "collections of structs."[7] (OQL does provide such an operation, but the Object Model per se doesn't.)

As for a "collection of structs" being "semantically equivalent" to an SQL table: First of all (and at the very least), *collection* should be replaced by *set* if we're truly talking about the relational model, or *bag* if we're talking about SQL; second, "structs" have object IDs, which relational tuples don't have; third, I believe "structs" have a left to right ordering to their components, which relational tuples also don't have. (The next section, "Objects and Operators," gives more details regarding ODMG's "structs.")

■   (*From page 36*) Relationships in the Object Model are similar to relationships in entity-relationship data modeling.

Well, "similar" is a pretty vague word, of course, but ODMG relationships do differ from "relationships in entity-relationship data modeling" in at least two major ways: First, they're binary only; second, they can't have properties. (The section mentioned in the previous bullet item, "Objects and Operators," gives more details regarding ODMG relationships also.)

Now I want to go on to give, in the next several sections, a general overview of the most important aspects of the ODMG proposals. For obvious reasons I'll concentrate on the ODMG Object Model specifically, for the most part. However, let me make it very clear that everything I have to say in what follows is, of course, based on my own reading and interpretation of the ODMG book. Naturally I believe my characterizations are accurate, but it's only fair to warn you that I might have misunderstood, and hence misrepresented, some

---

[7] Note carefully, moreover, that even if we did manage to implement such an operation, then we would merely have succeeded in writing a whole lot of code that in a relational DBMS would have been provided by the system itself.

points of detail; thus, this overview shouldn't be taken as definitive. The only definitive statement of the ODMG proposals is, of course, the ODMG book itself.

Note: The rest of this chapter does assume some familiarity on occasion with *The Third Manifesto* (referred to hereinafter, at least part of the time, as just the *Manifesto* for short), and sometimes with the associated inheritance model as well. However, I believe you should be able to gain some benefit from the discussions even if those assumptions happen not to be warranted in your own particular case.

OBJECTS AND OPERATORS

Every object in ODMG has its own unique object ID. There are three kinds of such objects: viz., *atomic*, *structured*, and *collection* objects. To elaborate:

- An ODMG atomic object corresponds roughly to a scalar variable, in *Manifesto* terms.

  Note: The ODMG book also occasionally talks about variables as such, but an ODMG variable and an ODMG object seem to be different things.[8] It also talks—fairly ubiquitously, in fact—about *instances*, which it seems to use as a synonym for *objects*. Following ODMG's lead, therefore, I'll do the same myself from time to time in what follows.

- An ODMG structured object corresponds roughly to a tuple variable, in *Manifesto* terms.

  Note: Tuples are called "structs" in ODMG; STRUCT is the ODMG counterpart to the *Manifesto*'s TUPLE type generator (see later)—except that, as noted earlier, "structs" have both object IDs and (I believe) a left to right ordering to their components, neither of which relational tuples have.

- An ODMG collection object is a set, bag, list, or array of other objects, all of which must be of the same type. Collections have no precise *Manifesto* counterpart. (It's true that relation variables—i.e., relvars—might be

---

[8] Actually the ODMG book never seems to come out and say exactly what it means by the term *variable*, unqualified. From what it does say, however, I strongly suspect the term refers specifically to an ordinary program variable (in the usual sense of this latter term) that's constrained to contain object IDs.

thought of as "collections," of a kind, but the kind in question is precisely one that the ODMG Object Model doesn't support.)

> *Aside:* More accurately, (a) a set collection object is a variable whose value at any given time is a set per se, and all of the sets that might ever be considered as values of the set collection object in question must be of the same type; (b) similarly for bag, list, and array collection objects, mutatis mutandis. ODMG tends to be quite sloppy over the distinction between values vs. variables. (More generally, in fact, it tends to be sloppy over the distinctions between values, variables, and types.) As for what it means to say that, e.g., a set is of a given set type, or (come to that) that the elements in a given set are of a given element type—well, these are questions I'm deliberately ducking at this point. I'll try to clear them up later. I might or might not succeed. *End of aside.*

Note: ODMG also supports another kind of collection called a *dictionary* (defined on page 25 of the ODMG book as "an unordered sequence [*sic!*] of key-value pairs with no duplicate keys"). I'll ignore dictionary collections in what follows, for simplicity.

Atomic Objects

The loose analogies above notwithstanding, there's at least one major difference between ODMG's atomic objects and the *Manifesto's* scalar variables: namely, that—to use object terminology—the former have user visible structure (the ODMG term is *properties*) as well as behavior, while the latter have behavior only. Just why "atomic" objects should have any structure at all—any user visible structure in particular—is never explained; it seems clear, however, that such a state of affairs violates encapsulation and undermines data independence. Let me elaborate briefly.

First of all, ODMG doesn't draw the clear distinction the *Manifesto* does between actual (i.e., physical) and possible representations. To quote from page 13: "[Each] property [maps to] an *instance variable* [in the representation]"—and the context makes it clear that *representation* here means the physical representation specifically. But that same page 13 also states that "separation between [object definition and object implementation] is the way that the Object Model reflects encapsulation"! (These two quotes—taken from the same page, let me stress, though they're paraphrased somewhat here—seem to contradict one another.) And then on page 36 we find: "While it is common for [properties] to be implemented as data structures, it is sometimes appropriate for [a property] to be implemented as a method" ... This quote seems to contradict the first of the previous two. Overall, the true situation is unclear.

> *Aside:* In case you're not familiar with the term *method* as used in the previous paragraph, here's a definition (it's taken from my book *The **New** Relational Database Dictionary*, O'Reilly, 2016):
>
> > Term used in [object] contexts to mean either an operator per se, which is a model concept, or [the] implementation ... of some operator, which is an implementation concept ... Unfortunately it's not uncommon to find the term used with both meanings in the same text, or even in the same sentence.
>
> By way of illustration of this latter point, here's a quote from R. G. G. Cattell, *Object Data Management: Object-Oriented and Extended Relational Database Systems* (revised edition, Addison-Wesley, 1994): "The [properties] associated with an object are private, and only an object's methods may examine or update these data; the methods are public." *End of aside.*

ODMG properties are of two kinds, relationships and attributes:

■ A *relationship* is, very specifically, a binary association—it involves exactly two objects, and it's realized in the Object Model by two "traversal paths" (one for each of the objects involved), each of which names the other as its inverse. For example, a given employee object *e* might have a traversal path to a certain department object *d*, and that department object *d* might have a traversal path to a certain set *se* of employee objects—a set that includes the original employee object *e*, of course. Note the redundancy here, incidentally; to be specific, the fact that employee *e* is in department *d* is represented twice, at least from the user's point of view. Note too that traversal paths aren't properties; to repeat, it's the relationship as such that's the property.

  Operators are provided to create, destroy, and traverse relationships (or relationship "members," rather—see the next paragraph). Moreover, those operators "vary according to the traversal path's cardinality" (page 38); that is, different operators are used depending on whether the relationship is one to one or otherwise (i.e., one to many, many to one, or many to many—though I'm tempted to add "whatever these various terms might mean").[9]

Caveat: Be aware that the ODMG book uses the term *relationship* in two different senses. Sometimes it uses it to mean an individual association between individual objects (e.g., the association between a specific employee and a specific department); sometimes it uses it to mean the set of all such individual associations considered generically (e.g., the set of all associations currently existing between any employee and any department).[10] The following quote illustrates both uses:

> (*From page 36*) Relationships are defined between types ... For example, *marriage* is a one to one relationship between two instances of type PERSON.

Note: It has to be said that ODMG's relationships look a lot like a throwback to the days of prerelational systems (and in any case, why the binary limitation?). The only justification for the idea to be found in the ODMG book—and it's a fairly weak one, in my opinion—seems to be this:

> (*From page 37*) The object DBMS is responsible for maintaining the referential integrity of relationships. This means that if an object that participates in a relationship is deleted, then any traversal path to that object must also be deleted.

Well, some might feel there's rather more to referential integrity than this brief characterization suggests. Note too that relationships aren't objects and have no properties (in particular, no user defined "behavior") of their own: a fact that in itself constitutes a major argument against the idea, one might have thought. (While it's true that distinguishing between "entities" and "relationships" can be useful informally in database design, the relational model, as pointed out earlier, deliberately makes no *formal* distinction between them, because—as is well known—the very same construct can quite legitimately be regarded as an entity by one person and as a relationship by another. Indeed, the ODMG book's own example of

---

[9] See Chapter 8 ("All for One, One for All") in my book *Logic and Relational Theory: Thoughts and Essays on Database Matters* (Technics Publications, 2020) for further discussion of this issue.

[10] In other words, it uses it to mean sometimes a relationship *type* and sometimes a relationship *instance*, or occurrence.

marriage is a perfect illustration of this point. While an individual marriage is obviously a relationship between two people—at least in a monogamous society—it also possesses certain related properties, such as wedding date and place.)

■ An attribute is any property that's not a relationship. There are two kinds: those whose legal values are *object IDs*, and those whose legal values are "*literals.*"

   1. An attribute whose legal values are object IDs "enables one object to reference another, without expectation of an inverse traversal path or referential integrity" (from page 37).
      Note: Attributes whose legal values are object IDs are often described—somewhat confusingly, I would have thought, though this manner of speaking seems to be common in the object world—as if their values were in fact those objects per se, instead of pointers to those objects (which is what those object IDs are).

   2. An attribute whose legal values are "literals" is simply an attribute that contains values that aren't pointers but are of some "literal" type (e.g., character strings).
      Note: See the section "Literals" below for a discussion of "literals"—in particular, for an explanation of why I often place the term in quotation marks in the ODMG context.

Structured Objects

Apart from differences already noted, a structured object is basically just a tuple variable; in particular, it's not encapsulated. The components of such an object—the ODMG term is *elements* or *members*—can be objects of any kind, "literals" of any kind, or a mixture of both. Operators are provided for accessing such components (typically using dot qualification syntax); however, ODMG seems not to provide analogs of all of the tuple operators required by *The Third Manifesto*. On the other hand, it does prescribe support for certain system defined structured object types: viz., DATE, TIME, TIMESTAMP, and INTERVAL, with semantics "as in the ANSI SQL specification."

Aside: This last claim is unfortunate if true, because the relevant features of "the ANSI SQL specification" are both inconsistent and incomplete (see C. J. Date and Hugh Darwen, *A Guide to the SQL Standard*, 4th edition, Addison-Wesley, 1997). And in any case—noting in particular that the comparison operators "<" and ">" make sense for dates and times but not for tuples—wouldn't the types mentioned be better regarded as scalar types, not "structured types"? (As in fact they are, in SQL. Well, kind of.) *End of aside.*

Collection Objects

Terminology in this area is used very inconsistently in the ODMG book.[11] I therefore choose not to follow the book's own terminology, although I recognize that my attempt to explain the concepts might therefore be a little incorrect. Anyway, it seems to me that ODMG supports certain *collection type generators*—SET, BAG, LIST, and so on—which can be used (of course) to define certain *generated collection types*. Let *T* be such a generated type; to fix our ideas, let's assume until further notice that *T* is defined using the type generator LIST. Then objects of type *T* are variables, and the value of such a variable at any given time is some specific list—either a list of object IDs or a list of "literals," depending on how *T* is defined (that is, either it's true for all time that every object of type *T* has a value that's a list of object IDs, or it's true for all time that every object of type *T* has a value that's a list of "literals").

■ In the former case, every object whose object ID can appear in any such list must be of the same type (a type specified in the definition of *T*), and the

---

[11] For example, consider the following text from page 20: "In the ODMG Object Model, instances of **collection** objects are composed of distinct elements, each of which can be an instance of an atomic type, another **collection**, or a literal type [*but not a structured object?—surely that's wrong?*] ... An important distinguishing characteristic of a **collection** is that *all* the elements of the **collection** must be of the *same* type. They are either all the same atomic type, or all the same type of **collection**, or all the same type of literal." The word *collection* occurs five times in this extract (I've set them in boldface in order to highlight them). The first occurrence is in the phrase "instances of collection objects," which seems to mean *all objects of some given collection type*. The second is in the phrase "another collection," which seems to mean *an object of some (arbitrary? and/or distinct?) collection type*. The third occurrence seems to mean *any given collection type*. The fourth seems to mean *any object of that particular collection type*. The fifth occurrence is in the phrase "the same type of collection," which might mean *of a collection type defined by means of the same type generator*, or it might mean *of the same generated collection type*. (Note that—as in fact my text above goes on to point out almost immediately—collection types are indeed generated types, though I don't think the ODMG book says as much anywhere.) And by the way: What exactly does it mean for two elements of a "collection object instance"—see the first sentence in the text quoted above from page 20—to be "distinct"? Especially when the elements in question are objects (i.e., "instances"), not "literals," and are therefore represented in the pertinent "collection object instance" by their object IDs?

objects whose object IDs appear in any given list are regarded as the elements of that list. (Note the level of indirection involved here.)

■ In the latter case, every "literal" that can appear in any such list must be of the same type (again, a type specified in the definition of *T*), and the actual "literals" themselves that appear in any given list are regarded as the elements of that list (no level of indirection).

As noted earlier, there's no ODMG "Object Manipulation Language" component as such. As explained in Chapter 6 of this book, however, the Object Model does require the pertinent programming language (i.e., the one ODMG happens to be bound to) to support all of the following operators for lists:

```
IS_EMPTY
IS_ORDERED
ALLOWS_DUPLICATES
CONTAINS_ELEMENT
INSERT_ELEMENT
REMOVE_ELEMENT
CREATE_ITERATOR
CREATE_BIDIRECTIONAL_ITERATOR
REMOVE_ELEMENT_AT
RETRIEVE_ELEMENT_AT
REPLACE_ELEMENT_AT
INSERT_ELEMENT_AFTER
INSERT_ELEMENT_BEFORE
INSERT_ELEMENT_FIRST
INSERT_ELEMENT_LAST
REMOVE_FIRST_ELEMENT
REMOVE_LAST_ELEMENT
RETRIEVE_FIRST_ELEMENT
RETRIEVE_LAST_ELEMENT
CONCAT
APPEND
```

Note, however, that the ODMG book has essentially nothing to say regarding the semantics of these operators, presumably on the assumption that they're largely self-explanatory (?).

Remarks analogous to the foregoing apply to all of the other ODMG collection type generators (SET, BAG, and so on). I feel bound to say, however, that the operators prescribed for sets in particular are strictly weaker—*much* weaker—than those defined for relations in the relational model. This fact very clearly gives the lie to claims to the effect that the Object Model "is more powerful than" or "encompasses" the relational model. Also, serious questions arise regarding the type of the object that results from (e.g.) ODMG set operators such as CREATE_UNION (page 23). I note too that ODMG's collection type generators have points in common with what our inheritance model would call *union types* (or, perhaps more accurately, *dummy types*, which are a special case of union types in general). As a consequence, if we define (say) two distinct specific list types, one in which the list elements are integers and one in which they're rectangles, we might well have to construct two distinct implementations of every single one of the operators prescribed for lists. Similarly for bags, sets, and so on, of course.

LITERALS

ODMG uses the term *literal* in what seems to me a very unconventional way. In conventional languages, if T is a type, then variables can be defined that are of that type T, and legal values of those variables are values of that type T; further, every such value can be denoted by some literal of that type T. Note, therefore, that it's normal to distinguish between:

a. Literals as such, which are symbols that denote values (in some more or less self-explanatory way), on the one hand, and

b. The values denoted by those symbols, on the other.

For example, the symbol 3.5 might be a literal denoting the value "three and a half." Note in particular that two or more quite different literals can all denote the same value (a fact that points up the distinction I'm trying to emphasize here). For example, the literals

```
TIME ( '10:00 am PST' )
```

and

```
TIME ( '6:00 pm GMT' )
```

(and many others of a similar nature) might all represent the same value of some TIME type.

The foregoing distinction, which might be called the symbol vs. denotation distinction (or, more simply, just the literal vs. value distinction) is certainly adhered to in *The Third Manifesto*. ODMG, however, doesn't seem to recognize that distinction; instead, it uses the term *literal* to include both the symbol as such and its denotation (which is why I often place the term in quotation marks in the ODMG context). To put it another way, ODMG sometimes seems to use the term to mean a literal as usually understood; but sometimes it seems to use it to mean the value represented by such a literal instead. And yet it also frequently talks about values as such; thus, it's really not clear whether an ODMG value and an ODMG "literal" are the same thing or not.

Be all that as it may, ODMG then goes on to distinguish between *literal types* and *object types* (implying among other things that a literal and an object can never be of the same type?). Apparently, instances of a literal type are literals (values?), while instances of an object type are objects (variables?). In fact, LITERAL_TYPE and OBJECT_TYPE are defined as the roots of two distinct *type hierarchies* [*sic*].[12] Moreover, there's no exact correspondence between the two; for example, there's a LONG (i.e., long integer) type in the "literal" hierarchy but no analogous type in the "object" hierarchy. Now, it's true that the user could presumably define an "atomic" object type with just one attribute, X say, of literal type LONG, and then it might be possible to perform, e.g., comparisons between values of that attribute X and LONG literals. However, on page 18 the ODMG book says that "literals ... are embedded in objects and cannot be individually referenced"—thereby implying, or at least strongly suggesting, that even a simple comparison such as $X = 3$ might not be legal (?). [13]

I note in passing that ODMG does at least agree with the *Manifesto* in not supporting implicit conversions between types (i.e., coercions).

Anyway, ODMG supports three kinds of literals, viz., *atomic*, *structured*, and *collection* literals:[14]

■ Atomic literals seem to be the ODMG analog of scalar values. To quote from page 32:

---

[12] I say "[*sic*]" here because the ODMG book does use the term—*type hierarchy*, that is—but what it refers to as *the* hierarchy (i.e., of system defined types) quite clearly consists of two separate hierarchies, not one.

[13] Though the OQL chapter later in the book includes plenty of examples of such comparisons.

[14] What the book actually says is: "The Object Model supports four literal types" (page 31). But "literal types" here doesn't literally mean "literal types," it means "kinds of literals."

Numbers and characters are examples of atomic literal types. Instances of these types are not explicitly created by applications, but rather implicitly exist.[15]

ODMG prescribes support for certain atomic literal types. Without going into details, I note that in addition to the types that one might expect (BOOLEAN, FLOAT, CHAR, etc.), the list includes ENUM ("enumeration"), which would surely be better regarded as a type generator.[16] (Specific enumerated types that are generated by means of that type generator, by contrast, might then perhaps be said to be "atomic," though I have to say they don't look very atomic to me.)

■　Next, structured literals: As noted earlier, ODMG supports a STRUCT type generator, analogous (somewhat) to the TUPLE type generator of *The Third Manifesto*; hence, "struct" types can be generated, and instances of such types then seem to be called structured literals, regardless of whether (in *Manifesto* terms) they're values or variables. To quote from page 33:

> A structured literal ... has a fixed number of elements, each of which has a ... name and can contain either a literal value [*sic!*] or an object [i.e., an object ID].

I remark that the idea of a *literal* (or value) including a component that's an *object* (i.e., a variable) seems to mix together some very basic notions that would surely be better kept separate. (Well ... to be a little less polite about the matter, I actually don't think the idea of a value containing a variable makes any sense at all. Exactly what *is* going on here?)

Note: ODMG requires support for certain system defined structured literal types, viz., DATE, TIME, TIMESTAMP, and INTERVAL (not to be confused with the structured object types of the same names).

---

[15] Like almost everything else in the ODMG book, this text raises more questions than it answers! Among other things, it says that numbers are a type; I would have thought they were *values* of a type. But it also says the type in question is a *literal* type, so those values are apparently literals. It also mentions "instances" of such a type; are "instances" the same as values and/or literals? (In other words, how many distinct concepts are we dealing with here?) It also says the type in question is an *atomic* literal type, and goes on to say that "instances" of that atomic literal type "implicitly exist." Does this latter statement imply that "instances" of nonatomic literal types don't "implicitly exist"? And on and on.

[16] It also includes STRING, to which a similar remark applies.

■ Finally, collection literals. Here once again the situation seems unnecessarily confusing. "Collection literals" are really collection type generators. To quote from pages 32-33:

> The ODMG Object Model supports collection literals of the following types:[17] SET, BAG, ... (etc.). These type generators [*sic!*] are analogous to those of collection objects ... Their elements ... can be of literal types or object types.

Apparently, then, we can have, e.g., a list object whose elements are literals, and a list literal whose elements are objects (?). Again, what exactly is going on here?

Note: The ODMG book also mentions a user defined UNION literal type, the semantics of which it doesn't explain. (I suspect it refers to heterogeneous collections, although collections are elsewhere stated to be homogeneous.) It doesn't say whether there's an analogous UNION object type.

In sum, I agree wholeheartedly that there's a vast and important logical difference between values and variables, but that particular difference doesn't seem to be the one that ODMG draws between literals and objects—nor is the precise nature of the difference that ODMG does draw in this connection particularly clear, at least to me. On the other hand, ODMG does make use of the value vs. variable terminology—but it doesn't *define* these concepts!

I conclude this section by noting that:

■ An ODMG literal (of any kind) isn't an object and doesn't have an object ID.

■ Although as noted earlier the Object Model prescribes certain operators for certain objects (especially collection objects), it doesn't appear to prescribe any operators for literals.

■ Indeed, if it's really true that object types and literal types are different kinds of things, it would seem that (e.g.) if operator *Op* is defined to work on, say, integer objects, it can't be invoked on integer literals (?).

---

[17] Footnote 14 applies here also, mutatis mutandis.

■ ODMG also supports a special "null literal." To quote from page 34:

> For every literal type ... there exists another literal type supporting a null value [*sic*] ... This nullable type is the same as the literal type augmented by the ... value [*sic*] *nil*. The semantics of null [*nil?*] are the same as those defined by [the SQL standard].[18]

However, this is certainly not the place to go into details of all of the problems with nulls.

TYPES, CLASSES, AND INTERFACES

Let me admit right away that it might have made more sense to discuss these concepts—types, classes, interfaces—before getting to this point in the chapter. I didn't do that, however, because (a) frankly, the concepts aren't as clear as they might be, and as a consequence (b) I felt you'd need some appreciation of the material discussed in previous sections in order to understand them. Consider the following quotes (both from page 12, boldface added for emphasis):

■ A **type** has an external *specification* and one or more *implementations*. The specification defines the external characteristics of the type. These are the aspects that are visible to users of the type: the *operations* that can be invoked on its instances [and] the *properties* ... whose values can be accessed ... By contrast, a type's implementation defines the internal aspects of the objects of the type [*or literals of the type, presumably, if the type in question is a literal type instead of an object type (?)*]: the implementation of the type's operations and other internal details.

■ An external specification of a type consists of an abstract, implementation-independent description of the operations ... and properties that are visible to users of the type. An *interface* definition is a specification that defines only the abstract behavior of an object type. A ***class*** definition is a specification that defines the abstract behavior and abstract state of an object type. A *literal* definition defines only the abstract state of a literal type.

Well, I for one find these extracts unclear in the extreme. Quite apart from anything else, it does seem as if the terms *type* and *class* are being used in a quite

---

[18] This claim is contradicted later, in the chapter on OQL.

unusual way: *Class* is being used to refer to what in more orthodox usage is usually called a *type*, and *type* is being used to refer to the combination of *class* in this unorthodox sense together with the *implementation* (possibly several implementations) of the class in question.[19] *Note:* I'll come back to "literal definitions" in a few moments and "interface definitions" in the next section.

But then what are we to make of the following, which appears just a couple of pages later, on page 15?

- Classes are types ... Interfaces are types ...

Most of the rest of the ODMG book then either ignores the distinction between types and classes or observes it in inconsistent ways. In what follows, I'll stay with the term *type* (mostly), which I'll use in the conventional sense; I mean, I'll use it to refer to "a specification of abstract state and behavior."

> *Aside:* Given my druthers, I'd prefer to abbreviate that loose definition to just "a specification of behavior" (assuming the type in question is scalar, that is).[20] Unfortunately, of course, scalar types in ODMG do have "state" as well as "behavior," and so I can't make that desired simplification : at least, not in the present context. *End of aside.*

As for the assertion that "a literal definition defines only the abstract state of a literal type": This statement, since it omits—apparently deliberately—all mention of "behavior," seems to suggest that no operations can be performed on literals, which can't possibly be correct. (Can it?) I suspect that what the ODMG book really means here is as follows:

---

[19] The ODMG terminology derives from that of OMG. Be aware, therefore, that other object texts and systems use the terms the other way around—i.e., they use *type* in the same way *The Third Manifesto* does, and *class* to mean the implementation of a type. See, for example, Michael Blaha and William Premerlani, *Object-Oriented Modeling and Design for Database Applications* (Prentice-Hall, 1998), or Ivar Jacobson (with Magnus Christerson, Patrik Jonsson, and Gunnar Övergaard), *Object-Oriented Software Engineering* (revised printing, Addison-Wesley, 1994). I wonder whether these latter authors and the OMG and ODMG people ever talk to each other?—and if they do, whether they actually manage to communicate?

PS: Another quote (from page 13): "A type can have more than one implementation, although only one implementation is usually used in any particular program." Any particular *program*? What *does* this mean? We're supposed to be talking about *data* here, data in *shared databases*.

[20] Well, given my *real* druthers, I'd prefer to define a type just as a set of values, and to specify the "behavior" of values and variables of the type in question separately. Which is basically what *The Third Manifesto* does, of course.

- First, the "literal definition" concept refers to nonscalar literals specifically (since scalar literals surely don't have "definitions," as such, at all, but just "implicitly exist").

- Second, a nonscalar "literal definition" is actually *an invocation of some type generator* (see the previous section), and therefore defines the unencapsulated logical structure of literals of the type in question, but doesn't define any operators that apply to such literals (the only operators that do apply being certain system defined ones, viz., those defined in connection with the pertinent type generator).

But I freely admit this is all pure guesswork on my part.

INHERITANCE

ODMG supports both multiple and (a fortiori) single inheritance, though the detailed semantics of that support aren't very clear. In fact, it supports both behavioral inheritance (which it calls *subtyping* or "the type-subtype relationship") and structural inheritance (which it calls *extension* or "the EXTENDS relationship").[21] I'll return to these two kinds of inheritance in a moment. First, however, I need to say something about the difference between interfaces and classes.

ODMG's "interfaces" correspond to our union types.[22] In other words, an ODMG interface is a type that isn't—in fact, isn't allowed to be—the most specific type of any value at all. (To quote from page 15: "Interfaces are types that cannot be directly instantiated.") Such a type must have proper subtypes, and every value of the type in question must be a value of one of those subtypes. For example, consider the types ELLIPSE, CIRCLE, and NONCIRCLE, where type CIRCLE and type NONCIRCLE are both proper subtypes of type ELLIPSE and the intuitively obvious semantics apply. Clearly, every instance of type

---

[21] These relationships aren't relationships as previously defined, however. In particular, they don't involve any traversal paths.

[22] Or, perhaps more accurately, *dummy* types, which as noted previously are a special case of union types in general. Now, I said earlier that ODMG's *collection type generators* "have points in common with" our union or dummy types; now I'm saying ODMG's *interfaces* "correspond to" our union or dummy types. So am I contradicting myself? No, I don't think so; rather, it seems to me that there's some overlap in functionality (or—perhaps a better way to say it—a certain lack of orthogonality) between these constructs, viz., ODMG-style collection type generators vs. ODMG-style interfaces. Of course, I could be wrong.

ELLIPSE is also an instance of one of the other two types, and so ELLIPSE isn't the most specific type of anything at all. In ODMG, then, a type like ELLIPSE in this example could be defined by means of an interface definition instead of a class definition. An interface definition defines behavior—i.e., what our own inheritance model would call "operator specification signatures"—but no structure.[23] Thus, it appears that as we travel down any given path in the type graph, operators must be explicitly specialized at the point where we first encounter a class instead of an interface.[24] Observe in passing, therefore, that ODMG unfortunately assigns a very special meaning to what is more usually a very general term (viz., interface).

The book then goes on to say (still on page 15):

> Subtyping pertains to the inheritance of behavior only; thus interfaces may inherit [behavior] from other interfaces and classes may also inherit [behavior] from interfaces ... [but] interfaces may not inherit [behavior] from classes, nor may classes inherit [behavior] from other classes ... [By contrast, the] EXTENDS relationship is a single inheritance relationship between two classes[25] whereby the subordinate class inherits all of the properties [i.e., structure] and all of the behavior of the class that it extends.

In other words, if *T* is a root type and *T′* is a leaf type (*Third Manifesto* terminology), then the path from *T* to *T′* consists of zero or more interfaces followed by one or more classes (i.e., once we meet the first class, the rest are all classes). Note too that if every such path contains just one class (i.e., all inheritance is via subtyping, not extension), then all instances are instances of leaf types. *Speculation:* It seems possible that what ODMG calls subtyping refers to "is a" relationships and thus does correspond, more or less, to type inheritance in the sense of our own inheritance model, while what it calls "the EXTENDS relationship" refers to "has a" relationships instead. More investigation is required to determine whether this speculation is anywhere close to being accurate—but if it is, then some of the **"conforms"** assessments later in this chapter (q.v.) might need to be changed to **"conforms (partly)"** or even to **"fails."**

---

[23] And yet later in the ODMG book we find numerous examples of interface definitions that do explicitly include "structure"—i.e., attribute and relationship definitions—as well as specification signatures (?).

[24] It also appears that once we encounter a class, any further subclasses of that class must then be defined using "the EXTENDS relationship" and not via subtyping.

[25] It could hardly be a *multiple* "inheritance relationship," of course, since it's "between two classes."

As already noted, ODMG does support multiple inheritance, but only for interfaces, not for classes (speaking a little loosely). More precisely, a type can have any number of proper supertypes, but at most one of them can be a class, not an interface. Also, note the following (from page 15 once again):

> The ODMG Object Model supports multiple inheritance of object behavior [only]. Therefore it is possible that a type could inherit operations that have the same name, but different parameters, from two different interfaces. The model precludes this possibility [*so in fact the "possibility" is not really a possibility after all*] by disallowing name overloading during [*what on earth does "during" mean in this context?*] inheritance.

While I'm on the subject of inheritance, incidentally, the ODMG book includes a nice example (page 14) of how difficult it can be to get the type hierarchy right:

> For example, ASSOCIATE_PROFESSOR is a subtype of PROFESSOR ... Where an object of type PROFESSOR can be used, an object of type ASSOCIATE_ PROFESSOR can be used instead, because ASSOCIATE_PROFESSOR inherits from PROFESSOR.

But surely professors have properties—perhaps tenure—that associate professors don't? In other words, isn't the hierarchy (at best) upside down?[26] ODMG doesn't distinguish between value and variable substitutability.

OBJECT DEFINITION LANGUAGE

So much for my overview of the major aspects of the Object Model (please note, however, that I've skipped over many features that, though obviously important, might be regarded as secondary; examples include details of the catalog or "metadata" and details of recovery and concurrency control). Now I turn to the Object Definition Language, ODL.

---

[26] On the other hand, if the hierarchy were the other way up—i.e., if PROFESSOR were defined to be a subtype of ASSOCIATE_PROFESSOR—then all professors would apparently be associate professors, and that can't be right either. What *is* the right design here, do you think?

ODL is "a specification language used to define the specifications of object types[27] that conform to the ODMG Object Model" (page 57). *Note:* As already mentioned in passing, ODL does support the definition of operator specification signatures (to use our own terminology)—including the names of any exceptions that might be raised by the operator in question—but doesn't provide a means of writing the code to implement such operators. Presumably that code must be written in the pertinent programming language (i.e., the one that ODMG happens to be bound to).

The chapter of the ODMG book that discusses ODL gives a number of examples, together with a complete definition of ODL syntax (a BNF grammar), but says almost nothing about semantics. Perhaps the reader is supposed to have read the OMG specifications (on which ODL is based) first. In any case, I omit the details of ODL here since matters of mere syntax aren't important for the purposes of this chapter.

OBJECT INTERCHANGE FORMAT

To quote the ODMG book, the Object Interchange Format (OIF) is "a specification language used to dump and load the current state of an object database to or from a file or set of files." As such, it's not very germane to my purposes in this chapter, and I omit the details here.

OBJECT QUERY LANGUAGE

The Object Query Language OQL can be characterized as a large superset of a small subset of SQL, with incompatibilities. It's not the ODMG "Object Manipulation Language" (as noted in the introduction to this chapter, no such language exists); rather, it's specifically a *query* language that supports nonprocedural retrieval (only) of data stored in an ODMG database. As such, it supports a variety of operators that aren't part of the Object Model per se. It's not computationally complete.

I don't intend to provide anything close to a complete description of OQL here. Suffice it to say that it supports:

---

[27] But what about "literal types"? And what exactly does it mean to "define specifications"?

- SQL-style SELECT – FROM – WHERE expressions on sets, bags, lists, and arrays

- Analogs of the SQL GROUP BY, HAVING, and ORDER BY constructs

- Union, intersection, and difference operations, together with certain special operations for lists and arrays (e.g., "get the first element")

- "Path expressions" for traversing relationships

There appear to be quite a few detail level incompatibilities, of both style and substance, between OQL and the Object Model. For example:

- (*From page 86*) [The] result of a query is an object with or without object identity.

  But surely objects always have identity in the Object Model? (In any case, I would have thought the result of a query was always a *value*.)

- (*From page 90*) OQL allows us to call a method ... anywhere the result type of the method matches the expected type in the query.

  But earlier in the book methods are defined to be part of the implementation, not part of the model.

- (*From page 90*) [OQL allows us to retrieve] the *i*th element of an indexed collection.

  The term *indexed* here doesn't mean what it means earlier in the book.

And so on. It should be noted too that the semantics of nulls and certain query constructs are—presumably unintentionally—rather different from those of their SQL counterparts.

RM PRESCRIPTIONS

I've now given as much of an overview of the ODMG proposals as I intend to; now I turn to my own brief analysis of those proposals. First, however, I'd like to repeat something Hugh Darwen and I said in this connection in the *Manifesto* book[28] (though I've abbreviated and edited this text somewhat for present purposes):

> Naturally we believe the ideas of *The Third Manifesto* are valuable in and of themselves. However, we also believe they can be useful as a yardstick or framework—i.e., as a basis against which alternative proposals, and indeed concrete implementations, can be carefully analyzed, criticized, evaluated, and perhaps judged. In what follows, we'll be using that framework to examine ODMG in particular. Please note immediately, however, that we expressly do not want our ideas to be used in connection with any kind of "checklist" evaluation, neither of ODMG as such, nor of anything else. We do think those ideas can serve as a convenient framework for structuring discussions, but they're not meant to serve as a basis for some kind of scoring scheme. We're not interested in scoring schemes.

Comparison format: The bulk of what follows consists of a series of point by point comparisons of pertinent features of ODMG with the various prescriptions, proscriptions, and "very strong suggestions" of *The Third Manifesto* and our inheritance model. *Note:* In case you're unfamiliar with the structure of *The Third Manifesto*, I should explain that it's divided into six sections, covering Relational Model Prescriptions ("RM Prescriptions"), RM Proscriptions, Other Orthogonal Prescriptions ("OO Prescriptions"), OO Proscriptions, RM Very Strong Suggestions, and OO Very Strong Suggestions, respectively. As for our inheritance model, it consists simply of a set of IM Prescriptions. The comparative analysis is thus divided into a total of seven sections accordingly, of which the present section is the first.

For the most part the comparisons are mostly presented just as bald statements of fact—I don't restate opinions, give value judgments, or comment on the relative severity of various points. Also, I use the terms **conforms** and **fails**, in boldface, to indicate my general finding in connection with each point. Very often these terms need some qualification, and sometimes I use both in connection with the same point. For example, ODMG sometimes conforms to (say) a certain prescription in some respects but fails in others, and sometimes it fails not because of specifics of the feature at hand, but rather because that

---

[28] The phrase "the *Manifesto* book" here refers to the second edition specifically, viz., *Foundation for Future Database Systems: The Third Manifesto*, by C. J. Date and Hugh Darwen (Addison-Wesley, 2000).

feature depends on some other feature on which it fails in turn. Such interdependencies are appropriately indicated.

I turn now to the point by point comparisons, beginning as advertised with the RM Prescriptions.

1. Scalar types

ODMG **conforms**, partly. However, (a) the distinction between literal and object "atomic" types seems unnecessary and confusing (at best it's unclear);[29] (b) there doesn't seem to be a way of destroying user defined scalar types; (c) ODMG objects ("atomic" ones in particular) have object IDs; (d) ODMG "atomic" objects have structure as well as behavior; (e) instead of supporting *Manifesto*-style selectors, ODMG requires "new object instances" (apparently uninitialized) to be "created" by means of a prescribed NEW operator. *Note:* However, OQL, as opposed to the ODMG Object Model as such, does include something it calls a "type name constructor" (?) that seems to be more akin to our selector.

2. Scalar values are typed

ODMG **conforms**, subject to the reservations indicated under RM Prescription 1.

3. Scalar operators

ODMG **conforms**, partly. However, (a) there doesn't appear to be a way of destroying user defined operators; (b) it's doubtful, or unspecified at best, as to whether ODMG conforms to the *Manifesto*'s many prescriptions regarding the distinction between read-only and update operators.

4. Actual vs. possible representations

ODMG **fails** (at the very least, it fails to distinguish clearly between these two kinds of representations; more likely, however, it has no notion of "possible representation" at all).

---

[29] In fact, it looks like a serious violation of orthogonality. At best, it requires many specifications—regarding legal operations, for example—to be duplicated; at worst, it introduces undesirable rules and distinctions.

5. Expose possible representations

ODMG **fails** a fortiori. However, it does expose *actual* representations. It's not clear whether it supports anything analogous to the *Manifesto*'s nestable THE_ pseudovariables.

6. TUPLE type generator

ODMG **conforms**, partly, through its support for "structs." However, (a) the distinction between literal and object struct types seems unnecessary, confusing, and unclear; (b) there doesn't appear to be a way of destroying user defined struct types; (c) ODMG's "struct objects" have object IDs; (d) instead of supporting struct selectors, ODMG requires "new object instances" (apparently uninitialized) to be "created" by means of a prescribed NEW operator; (e) ODMG does not support struct valued possible representation components (because it does not support the concept of possible representations at all); (f) ODMG struct types have explicit names; (g) it's not clear when two ODMG struct types are regarded as equal; (h) ODMG's struct types appear to have a left to right ordering to their components; (i) most of the *Manifesto*'s required tuple operators aren't supported for structs in the ODMG Object Model (though it might be possible to simulate them in OQL). *Note:* However, OQL, as opposed to the ODMG Object Model as such, does include a construct that seems to be somewhat more akin to our tuple selector.

7. RELATION type generator

ODMG **fails**. The comments under RM Prescription 6 apply here also, mutatis mutandis. Note in particular that most of the operators of the relational algebra aren't supported in the ODMG Object Model (though they can probably be simulated in OQL).

8. Equality

ODMG almost certainly **fails**. First, it distinguishes between *identity* and *equivalence* (sometimes called deep equality vs. shallow equality, though authorities disagree as to which is which); second, it distinguishes between literals and objects. Both of these facts muddy the picture considerably. In addition, there does not appear to be any way to prevent users from defining an

"=" operator with any semantics they please (note that no "=" operator, as such, is actually prescribed). However, it is least true that support for a SAME_AS operator, with prescribed semantics, is required for objects (though apparently not for literals); SAME_AS tests to see whether two objects are "identical" (i.e., have the same object ID).

9. Tuples

See RM Prescription 6.

10. Relations

See RM Prescription 7.

11. Scalar variables

ODMG **conforms**, partly. At least, it supports *objects* of (user defined) "atomic" type *T*, and ODMG objects seem to be something like variables and ODMG "atomic" types seem to be something like scalar types. But the values of those "scalar variables" aren't exactly values of type *T*, owing to the distinction ODMG draws between literal and object types (in fact, it's quite difficult to say *what* they are). Also, "defining"—i.e., creating, via NEW—a scalar variable (or atomic object) doesn't appear to initialize that variable (or atomic object).

12. Tuple variables

The comments under RM Prescription 11 apply here also, mutatis mutandis.

13. Relation variables (relvars)

ODMG **fails** in all respects.

14. Real vs. virtual relvars, public vs. private relvars

ODMG **fails** in all respects.

15. Candidate keys

ODMG **fails** a fortiori, because it doesn't support relvars (in the full sense of the relational model) at all. However, it does allow support—optional support—for something it *calls* keys.[30] Here's an extended quote from page 16:

> The *extent* of a type is the set of all instances of the type within a particular database. If an object is an instance of type *A*, then it will of necessity be a member of the extent of *A* ... A relational DBMS maintains an extent for every defined table. By contrast, the object database designer can decide whether the object DBMS should automatically maintain the extent of [any given] type. Extent maintenance includes inserting newly created instances in the set ... In some cases the individual instances of a type can be uniquely identified by the values they carry for some property or set of properties. These identifying properties are called *keys*. In the relational model, these properties ... are called *candidate keys*. A *simple key* consists of a single property. A *compound key* consists of a set of properties. The scope of uniqueness is the extent of the type; thus a type must have an extent to have a key.

Well, I'm sorry, but this extract seems even more muddled than usual, even by ODMG standards. At the very least it raises so many questions that it virtually demands a blow by blow commentary. So here goes:

1. "The *extent* of a type is the set of all instances of the type within a particular database."

   Nothing analogous to this notion exists in the relational model at all—certainly not explicitly, and not really implicitly either. The closest we might come to it would be something like the following: Let *T* be a type and let *R* be a database relvar with an attribute *A* defined on *T*; then the extent of *T* would be the union of all unary projections of all such relvars *R* on all such attributes *A*. Points arising:

   a. The foregoing "definition" is still pretty loose! For one thing, it makes use of the concept *projection of a relvar*, which I won't bother

---

[30] *Candidate key* is the older, clunkier name for what in the relational world nowadays is more usually referred to as just a key. Here and elsewhere, therefore, the unqualified term *key* should be understood to mean just some candidate key (unless the context demands otherwise, of course). In particular, it does *not* necessarily mean a primary key specifically (again, unless the context demands otherwise).

to define precisely here but will simply assume is well understood.[31] For another, it ignores the business of attribute renaming, which might be needed before the pertinent union could even be formed. For yet another, it ignores values of type T appearing as values of some possrep component for values appearing in some attribute of some database relvar.

b. Modulo all of the foregoing considerations, we might say "the extent of type T" is the set of all values of type T currently appearing anywhere in the database. But that statement is still loose! First of all, note that that "extent" is, by definition, a relvar (a virtual relvar, in fact). As a consequence, the "instances" that go to make up that "extent" at any given time aren't actually values of type T but, rather, unary tuples each of which contains a value of type T.

c. By virtue of the previous point, those "instances" are definitely values, a state of affairs that seems to contradict point 2 below.

d. In any case, what purpose is served by that "extent"? What's it for? No useful purpose comes to mind; nor is one described in the ODMG book.

2. "If an object is an instance of type A, then it will of necessity be a member of the extent of A."

    Since objects seem to be variables—remember the distinction ODMG draws between objects and "literals"!—this sentence implies that the ODMG "extent of a type" consists at any given time of all *variables* of that type extant at that time (?). Again, how is this concept useful? What purpose does it serve? In particular, how can the ODMG user reference it?

3. "A relational DBMS maintains an extent for every defined table."

    No, it most certainly doesn't. Assuming, not unreasonably, that *table* here means a relvar and not a relation, what "a relational DBMS maintains" for

---

[31] A more detailed explanation of such matters can be found in Chapter 3 ("Normalization: Some Generalities") of my book *Database Design and Relational Theory: Normal Forms and All That Jazz*, 2nd edition (Apress, 2019).

such a thing is the current body, or in other words the set of tuples—tuple *values*—that correspond to currently true instantiations of the pertinent predicate. That body is most certainly not an "extent" in the ODMG sense of that term (whatever that sense might be, I suppose I have to add); in particular, it's not the extent of a type as such. (If it were, incidentally, it would imply that no two "defined tables" extant at the same time could ever be of the same type, which isn't true at all.)

4. "By contrast, the object database designer can decide whether the object DBMS should automatically maintain the extent of [any given] type."

   If the designer decides that the object DBMS *shouldn't* "automatically maintain" the extent of some type *T*, does that mean the user has to do it, or does it mean it doesn't get done? If the former, how? If the latter, how does this sentence square with the claim made in point 2 above?

5. "Extent maintenance includes inserting newly created instances in the set."

   I assume "newly created instances" here refers to the result of invoking the prescribed NEW operator. If I'm right in this assumption—and I think I must be, because *values* aren't "created" at all, they just "implicitly exist"—it reinforces what I said earlier under point 2 regarding variables. Moreover, it also implies that "automatic maintenance" of an extent means that creating a new instance of the pertinent type, via NEW, has the side effect of updating the database (assuming the extent in question is kept in the database, that is—but I certainly don't know where else it could be).

6. "In some cases the individual instances of a type can be uniquely identified by the values they carry for some property or set of properties. These identifying properties are called *keys*. In the relational model, these properties ... are called *candidate keys*."

   It's not "instances of a type" that need to be identified by keys, it's "instances within an extent." The ODMG book does say that "a type must have an extent to have a key" (see point 8 below), but this statement is back to front at best; to say it again in different words, keys are nothing to do with types. By the way: "Instances of a type" here seems to refer to values, not variables (?). Certainly it's values—tuple values, to be precise—that are, and need to be, "identified by keys"; variables are identified by name, and/or (in the object world) by addresses.

7. "A *simple key* consists of a single property. A *compound key* consists of a set of properties."

   I wouldn't draw the distinction ODMG draws here between simple and compound keys (at least, not in the same way). Keys always consist of sets of "properties," by definition. Though I suppose if the set has cardinality one (or zero?), then perhaps we might say the key is "simple."

8. "The scope of uniqueness is the extent of the type; thus a type must have an extent to have a key."

   This sentence seems to suggest that extents are made up of values, not variables.

What sense can one possibly make of such a muddle?

16. Databases

ODMG **conforms**, partly. However, ODMG databases aren't "named containers for relvars," they're named containers for objects (of any type). *Note:* ODMG also fails to specify how databases are created and destroyed—but then so does *The Third Manifesto* (deliberately).

17. Transactions

ODMG **conforms**, more or less.

18. Relational algebra

The Object Model **fails** in almost all respects. However, OQL does support analogs of most of the operators of the relational algebra. Unfortunately, it supports many other things as well.

19. Variable references, constant references

ODMG presumably **conforms** (to the extent that it supports variables and constants at all).

20. Tuple operators, relational operators, recursion

ODMG **fails**.

21. Assignments

ODMG **fails**. It does require support on the part of the applicable programming language for a large number of update operators—for example, NEW, APPEND, INSERT_ELEMENT, INSERT_ELEMENT_FIRST, INSERT_ELEMENT_LAST, INSERT_ELEMENT_AFTER, INSERT_ELEMENT_BEFORE, DELETE, REMOVE_ELEMENT, REMOVE_FIRST_ELEMENT, REMOVE_LAST_ELEMENT, REMOVE_ELEMENT_AT, and REPLACE_ELEMENT_AT in the case of lists, and analogous operators in the case of sets, bags, arrays, relationships, and so on—but it doesn't seem to require support for assignment per se.[32] It also doesn't support multiple assignment, a fortiori.

22. Comparisons

ODMG **fails**, except as noted under RM Prescription 8.

23. Integrity constraints

ODMG **fails** in almost all respects.

24. Total database constraint

ODMG **fails** a fortiori.

---

[32] Actually, object languages in general seem not to support assignment—at least, not en bloc assignment of some "object value" (?) to some "object variable" (?). Which is ironic if true, given that assignment is the only update operator that's logically necessary. Further evidence, I think, that the object world in general fails to make a clear distinction between model and implementation.

25. Catalog

ODMG **conforms,** partly (it does define a catalog, but of course that catalog contains objects, not relvars).

26. Language design

Not directly applicable. The ODMG analog of the hypothetical language **D** of *The Third Manifesto* is a combination of ODL and whatever language ODMG is bound to, plus OQL (which is really rather separate). OQL in particular is hamstrung by its goal of being "SQL like"; by definition, therefore, it can't possibly "be constructed according to well established principles of good language design" as RM Prescription 26 requires. (To be fair, I should add that OQL nevertheless does seem to be a little better designed than SQL in certain respects.)

RM PROSCRIPTIONS

1. No attribute ordering

ODMG **fails**—its "tuples" (actually structs) apparently do have a left to right ordering to their components, and it doesn't support relations at all.

2. No tuple ordering

ODMG **conforms** for sets and bags (of structs), but **fails** for relations a fortiori.

3. No duplicate tuples

ODMG **conforms** for sets (of structs), but **fails** for relations a fortiori.

4. No nulls

ODMG **fails**. What's more, ODMG nulls and SQL nulls are different.

5. No nullological mistakes

The Object Model probably **fails** (it's hard to tell). OQL definitely **fails**.

6. No internal level constructs

ODMG **fails**.

7. No tuple level operations

ODMG **fails** (in particular, it explicitly prescribes "iterators" over collections).

8. No composite attributes

ODMG apparently **conforms**.

9. No domain check override

ODMG **conforms**.

10. Not SQL

The Object Model **conforms**. OQL **conforms** (just).

OO PRESCRIPTIONS

1. Compile time type checking

ODMG allows, e.g., a parameter type to be specified as ANY, a fact that might possibly undermine the system's ability to perform compile time type checking. Otherwise, it probably **conforms**.

2. Type inheritance (conditional)

ODMG **fails** by definition here, because it obviously doesn't support our inheritance model. (What's more, its own "inheritance model" is scarcely defined at all, in my opinion.) I can be more specific in this connection, however, and I'll do so under the various IM Prescriptions (see later).

3. Computational completeness

OQL **fails**. As for the Object Model, the concept of computational completeness doesn't really apply (because there's no "Object Manipulation Language"). I note, however, that ODMG does share our distaste for the "embedded data sublanguage" approach adopted in SQL:

> (*From page 5*) Note that unlike SQL in relational systems, object DBMS data manipulation languages are tailored to specific application programming languages, in order to provide a single, integrated environment for programming and data manipulation. [*But what does "programming and data manipulation" mean? I mean, what distinction is being drawn between the two?*]

Note: The following quote is only tangentially related to OO Prescription 3, but it's significant and I don't want to lose it:

> (*From page 4*) It is possible to read and write the same database from C++, Smalltalk, and Java, **as long as the programmer stays within the common subset of supported data types.** [*Boldface added.*]

By the way, the reference to "the programmer" here seems to suggest that ODMG is aimed specifically at application programmers.[33] So what about end user access via OQL?

4. Explicit transaction boundaries

ODMG **conforms**.

5. Nested transactions

ODMG **fails**.

---

[33] In this connection, see footnote 1 in Chapter 6.

6. Aggregation over empty sets

Not applicable to the Object Model. OQL **fails.**

OO PROSCRIPTIONS

1. Relvars are not domains

ODMG **conforms**, inasmuch as it does at least distinguish between types and collections (where I take "collections" to include both collection values and collection variables, in the *Manifesto* sense of both *value* and *variable*).

2. No pointers (object IDs)

ODMG **fails** (of course).

RM VERY STRONG SUGGESTIONS

1. System keys

ODMG **fails** on both parts of this suggestion. *Note:* An argument might be made that object IDs make system keys unnecessary. Even if this argument is accepted, however, object IDs are still not keys in the relational sense, because:

a. Unlike keys, object IDs are represented differently (at the *logical* level) from other data,

and as a consequence

b. Unlike access via keys, access to data via object ID is different from access via other "properties."

2. Candidate key inference

ODMG **fails**.

3. Transition constraints

ODMG **fails**.

4. Quota queries

ODMG **fails**.

5. Generalized transitive closure

ODMG **fails**.

6. User defined generic operators

Not clear.

7. SQL migration

ODMG **conforms**, partly (at least for query operations, via OQL).

OO VERY STRONG SUGGESTIONS

1. Type inheritance

ODMG **fails** a fortiori, because it fails on OO Prescription 2, q.v.

2. Types and operators unbundled

ODMG **fails**. To quote:

> (*From pages 39-40*) An operation is defined on [*i.e., is bundled with*] only a single type ... [We] had several reasons for choosing to adopt this single-dispatch model rather than a multiple-dispatch model. The major reason was for consistency with the C++ and Smalltalk programming languages ... Another reason to adopt the classical object model was to avoid incompatibilities with the OMG ... object model, which is classical rather than general [*sic*].

3. Single level store

ODMG **conforms** (?).

IM PRESCRIPTIONS

1. Types are sets

ODMG possibly **conforms**, subject to the reservations expressed in the section "Types, Classes, and Interfaces" earlier, and subject also to the reservation that *object* types seem to be sets of variables, not sets of values (?).

2. Subtypes are subsets

ODMG **conforms**, subject to the reservations indicated under IM Prescription 1.

3. "Subtype of" is reflexive

ODMG probably **conforms**, although the ODMG book never explicitly mentions the fact that every type is both a supertype and a subtype of itself.

4. "Subtype of" is transitive

ODMG **conforms**—but note the class vs. interface distinction, which isn't part of our inheritance model (it's *not* the same as our "regular type" vs. "dummy type" distinction).

5. Proper and immediate subtypes and supertypes

ODMG probably **conforms**, although the ODMG book never discusses these concepts.

6. Scalar root and leaf types

ODMG probably **conforms**, more or less, although the ODMG book never discusses these concepts, and it certainly never mentions types *alpha* and *omega*.

7. Disjoint and overlapping types

Not clear. The ODMG book never discusses these issues.

8. Common subtypes and supertypes

Not clear. The ODMG book never discusses these issues.

9. Model of a scalar variable

Not clear. The ODMG book never discusses this issue. But there doesn't seem to be an ODMG term corresponding to our "declared type."

10. Specialization by constraint

ODMG **fails** completely; in fact, as the comment under RM Prescription 23 (q.v.) might suggest, it doesn't support type constraints at all.

11. Assignment with inheritance

Not clear. First of all, the reservations under IM Prescription 9 apply here a fortiori. Second, the Object Model doesn't support assignment as such anyway. The ODMG book does say (in connection with the example mentioned earlier involving types PROFESSOR and ASSOCIATE_PROFESSOR) that "where an object of [most specific] type PROFESSOR can be used, an object of [most specific] type ASSOCIATE_PROFESSOR can be used instead"; however, the semantic implications of this state of affairs, for assignment in particular, are left seriously underspecified.

12. Equality with inheritance

Not clear. The comments under RM Prescription 8 and IM Prescription 11 apply here also, mutatis mutandis.

13. Join etc. with inheritance

Not clear. Again, the comments under RM Prescription 8 and IM Prescription 11 apply here also, mutatis mutandis. However, OQL provides some rules regarding joins and similar operations that do seem to **conform**, more or less, to IM Prescription 13.

14. TREAT

The Object Model **fails** (it never mentions the concept at all). OQL probably **fails** too; it does seem to have something analogous to TREAT, but it's not fully specified.

15. Type testing

ODMG **fails**.

16. Value substitutability

ODMG **conforms**.

17. Operator signatures

ODMG almost certainly **fails,** in several different ways.

18. Read-only parameters to update operators

ODMG **conforms**.

19. Variable substitutability

ODMG almost certainly **fails**. Although the ODMG book never discusses the issue, it can safely be assumed that unconditional inheritance of update operators is required. Moreover, as noted earlier, ODMG fails to distinguish between value substitutability and variable substitutability.

20. Union and dummy types etc.

ODMG **fails**, except insofar as its "interfaces" and/or its collection types are counterparts to our union types (?).

21. Empty types

ODMG **fails**.

22. Tuple / relation subtypes and supertypes

ODMG **fails**.

23. Proper and immediate tuple / relation subtypes and supertypes

ODMG **fails**.

24. Common tuple / relation subtypes and supertypes

ODMG **fails**.

25. Tuple / relation maximal and minimal types

ODMG **fails**.

26. Tuple / relation root and leaf types

ODMG **fails**.

27. Tuple / relation most specific types

ODMG **fails**.

28. Model of a tuple / relation variable

ODMG **fails**.

CONCLUDING REMARKS

This marks the end of the body of the chapter. In closing, I feel I should apologize if you've found it difficult to read, and possibly even hard to understand in places. But let me say it hasn't been easy to write either! Many

years ago I came up with something I called *The Principle of Incoherence* ...
Here's a definition:

> **Definition (*The Principle of Incoherence*):** A principle, sometimes
> invoked in defense of an attempt, successful or otherwise, at criticizing
> some technical proposal or position, to the effect that it's hard to criticize
> something coherently if what's being criticized is itself not very coherent in
> the first place—a state of affairs that goes some way toward explaining why
> such criticisms can often be longer (sometimes much longer) than what's
> being criticized. Occasionally referred to, a little unkindly, as *The
> Incoherent Principle*.

Well, I hereby invoke the foregoing principle in my defense in connection
with the present chapter. I'll leave it up to you to decide whether that defense is
justified.

APPENDIX A: EXTRACTS FROM THE LITERATURE

I'd like to close this chapter by repeating a few pertinent references, with
annotation, from the third edition of the *Manifesto* book, because I think they can
be of some help in trying to understand (a) the background behind the ODMG
effort as such and (b) why there seems to be such a huge gap between that effort
and what the *Manifesto* is trying to achieve.

- R. G. G. Cattell: *Object Data Management* (revised edition, Addison-
  Wesley, 1994)

  The first book-length tutorial on the application of object technology to
  database management. The following extract (lightly edited here) suggests
  rather strongly that, at least at the time the book was written, the field was a
  long way from any kind of consensus:

  > Programming languages may need new syntax ... swizzling [*sic*],
  > replication, and new access methods also need further study ... new end user
  > and application development tools [are] required ... more powerful query
  > language features [must be] developed ... new research in concurrency
  > control is needed ... timestamps and object based concurrency semantics
  > need more exploration ... performance models are needed ... new work in

knowledge management needs to be integrated with object and data management capabilities ... this [will lead to] a complex optimization problem [and] few researchers have [the necessary] expertise ... federated [object] databases require more study.

■ Elisa Bertino and Lorenzo Martino: *Object-Oriented Database Systems: Concepts and Architectures* (Addison-Wesley, 1993)

Many publications from the object world try to draw a distinction (as ODMG does, in fact, and as our inheritance model does not) between types and classes, and this reference is one such:

> Object-oriented systems can be classified into two main categories— systems supporting the notion of *class* and those supporting the notion of *type* ... [Although] there are no clear lines of demarcation between them, the two concepts are fundamentally different [*sic!*] ... Often the concepts type and class are used interchangeably. However, when both are present in the same language, the type is used to indicate the specification of the interface of a set of objects, while class is an implementational notion. [*So why is it "in the language" at all?*] Therefore ... a type is a set of objects which share the same behavior ... [and] a class is a set of objects which have exactly the same internal structure and therefore the same attributes and the same methods. [*But if all objects in a "class" have the same attributes and the same methods, isn't that class a type, by the authors' own definition?*] The class defines the implementation of a set of objects, while a type describes how such objects can be used.[34]

The authors then go on to say:

> With inheritance, a class called a *subclass* can be defined on the basis of the definition of another class called a *superclass*.

But surely—in accordance with their own earlier definitions—they should be talking in terms of types here, not classes? And then they add:

> The **specification hierarchy** (often called *subtype hierarchy*) expresses ... subtyping relationships which mean that an instance of the subtype can be

---

[34] I can't resist pointing out that ODMG uses the terms *type* and *class* in almost exactly the opposite way.

used in every context in which an instance of the supertype can correctly appear (*substitutability*).

Observe that they do now speak of types, not classes. Observe too the failure to distinguish properly between values and variables (note the reference to "instances"), and the consequent failure to distinguish between value substitutability and variable substitutability.

- Ian Graham, Julia Bischof, and Brian Henderson-Sellars: "Associations Considered a Bad Thing," *Journal of Object-Oriented Programming* (February 1997)

I include this reference because I find it a good illustration of the huge gulf that sometimes seems to exist between the object and database worlds. First, however, I should explain what the authors are trying to achieve. Their thesis is that treating "associations" (*aka* relationships) either (a) as "first class objects" in their own right, or (b) as some totally different kind of construct, compromises encapsulation and reusability. They therefore propose, in effect, that, e.g., the association between suppliers and parts should be represented not by means of "shipments" as such, but rather, redundantly, by a parts attribute within suppliers and a suppliers attribute within parts (the two attributes in question being explicitly declared to the system to be "inverses" of each other).[35] And they then go on to propose a set of rules for maintaining referential integrity given such a design and for keeping the inverse attributes in synch with each other.

I won't comment further on the foregoing proposal as such. But I do want to quote and offer a few comments on certain remarks from the paper that, I believe, illustrate very well the gulf mentioned above:

- A study of the literature of semantic data modeling ... reveals that there are two fundamental ways to connect data structures or entity types [*sic!*]: *constructors* and *pointers* ... [In] the first approach, emphasis is placed on building structures using constructors such as the tuple or the set. In the second, the stress is on linking types using attributes.

---

[35] Which is what ODMG does. But doesn't such an approach in itself constitute "treating associations as some different kind of construct," which I thought was exactly what the authors were trying to argue was a bad idea?

Comment: From the context, "building structures using constructors" seems to mean that connections between data structures—"or entity types" (?)—are represented by foreign keys (or something very like foreign keys), while "linking types using attributes" means those connections are represented by pointers instead. At the very least, therefore, there does seem to be a *terminological* gulf.

■ In the 1980s the former approach [*i.e., "building structures using constructors"*] was dominant, largely because of the popularity and widespread use of relational databases. In entity-relationship models there are two logical types: *entity-relationships* and *relationship-relationships*. Both are represented by sets of tuples and no links between them are stored; the run-time system of the DBMS must search for the linkages.

Comment: Quite apart from (a) the fact that "entity-relationship models" have very little to do with relational databases anyway, and (b) the fact that the phrase "two logical types" is a little mysterious, the final sentence here betrays a serious lack of understanding of the relational model and relational implementation technology (which was well over 20 years old, incidentally, when this paper was published).

■ Attempts to enrich [*sic!*] the relational model led quickly to systems with more than two relationship types. This unsatisfactory situation soon led to suggestions to replace these arbitrary type systems with a single notion of classes reminiscent of object oriented programming ... The pointer-based approach is far more natural to an object oriented thinker [*I fully agree!*], but one suspects that the popularity of methods such as OMT [is] because developers with a relational background find the approach familiar and anodyne.[36] **The danger here is that object-oriented principles will be ignored and highly relational models produced instead of true object-oriented ones.** [*Boldface added.*]

Comment: Words fail me.

---

[36] The OMT reference is to the book by Blaha and Premerlani, discussed next.

■   Michael Blaha and William Premerlani: *Object-Oriented Modeling and Design for Database Applications* (Prentice-Hall, 1998)

Blaha and Premerlani's book isn't really concerned with the kinds of issues that are the principal concern of *The Third Manifesto*; rather, it's concerned with a particular design methodology called "Object Modeling Technique" (OMT for short). Nevertheless, I do have my reasons for mentioning it here, which I'll get to in just a moment.

   OMT is a variant of the well known entity / relationship model; like most such, therefore, it relies extensively on the use of graphical symbols ("boxes and arrows" and the like). The book consists primarily of a detailed description of OMT, with emphasis on its relevance to the design of databases in particular. An OMT database design doesn't, or at least shouldn't, depend on the capabilities of any particular DBMS; the authors therefore also offer a detailed discussion of how to map such a design to a design that *is* specific to a particular object DBMS or particular SQL DBMS.

   One reason I wanted to mention OMT at all here is because it provides a good example of a point I've made in many places elsewhere: namely, that even the term *object* itself has a variety of different meanings in the object world. In the present context, it clearly means what the database community would more usually call an *entity*—implying among other things that it's not encapsulated—whereas in object programming languages it generally means something that definitely *is* encapsulated. *Note:* These remarks aren't intended as a disparagement of Blaha and Premerlani's book; I'm only using their book to illustrate a point.

   Following on from that point, though, I now observe that, presumably because OMT objects are really entities, OMT maps them to tuples in relvars instead of to values in domains, or values of types. (More precisely, it maps *classes* to *relvars* instead of to domains.) OMT isn't alone in this regard, of course: Many other design methodologies do exactly the same thing. However, I speculate—and this is the crux of the matter—that it's precisely this state of affairs (viz., that "object modeling" is really just "entity / relationship modeling" by another name) that's the source of the infamous, widespread, and disastrous mistake, discussed at length in the *Manifesto* book and elsewhere, of equating relvars and classes.

   I note in passing that the OMT book uses several other terms in addition to "object" and "class" in ways that are at odds with the way they're used in the *Manifesto*. For example, on page 46 we find: "Do not confuse a domain with a class." At this point the book is certainly using *class* to mean what we would call a domain, or preferably a type (though elsewhere it seems to use it to mean a collection instead), so its use of *domain* doesn't accord with ours. And it uses *inheritance* to mean not type inheritance as that term is used in our inheritance model, but instead something akin to the rather suspect "subtables and supertables" notion (see my book *Type Inheritance and Relational Theory: Subtypes, Supertypes, and Substitutability*, O'Reilly, 2016, for an explanation of this latter notion). Polymorphism is mentioned only in passing, and substitutability not at all.

Finally, the book also contains an interesting observation regarding code reuse, which is one of the objectives of type inheritance. Of course, code reuse doesn't imply inheritance, but the kinds of reuse that aren't related to inheritance aren't new. And in this connection, the book makes the following point regarding DBMS code specifically:

> DBMSs are intended to provide generic functionality for a wide variety of applications ... *You are achieving reuse when you can use generic DBMS code, rather than custom-written application code* [my italics].

I agree, and observe that such reuse is supported very well by relational DBMSs, less well by object DBMSs.

- Richard Mark Soley and William Kent: "The OMG Object Model," in Won Kim (ed.): *Modern Database Systems: The Object Model, Interoperability, and Beyond* (ACM Press / Addison-Wesley, 1995)

The ODMG Object Model as discussed in the present chapter is based on the "core object model" of the Object Management Group, OMG. Like ODMG, OMG isn't a formal standards body; however, it's "developing standards in the form of wholesale agreements among member companies" (of which there were "about 340" at the time this paper was written).

The OMG core object model is based on "a small number of basic concepts: objects, operations, types, and subtyping." Note that values and variables aren't included in this list; however, the paper does also recognize something it calls *nonobjects*, and gives as examples of "nonobject types" such things as CHAR and BOOLEAN, suggesting that "nonobjects" might perhaps be values (or perhaps a "nonobject type" is just a primitive, and system defined, type?). Moreover, objects are certainly variables, although the term *variable* isn't used. But then the paper goes on to say that objects and nonobjects together "represent the set of denotable *values* in the core object model" (my italics).

Objects have object IDs, nonobjects do not. Further, objects have behavior and no user visible structure: "In the core object model, operations are used to model the external interface to state" (*state* here meaning the object's current value). But the paper then adds, somewhat confusingly, that "*attributes* and *relationships* ... can be used to model the externally visible declarations of state more succinctly."

Another puzzle concerns the distinction between read-only vs. update operators (to use *Third Manifesto* terminology). OMG expressly does not make any such distinction; in fact, it "defines a pass-by-value argument passing semantics" [*sic*], implying that operators are always read-only. However, it clearly also allows operations that produce "side effects, manifested in changes of state." There seems to be some kind of contradiction here.

OMG also draws a distinction between subtyping and inheritance:

> *Subtyping* [can be intuitively defined thus:] ... one type is a subtype of another if the first is a specialization or refinement of the second ... if *S* is a subtype of *T*, an object of type *S* may be used wherever an object of type *T* may be used [*note that this definition seems (a) to propose variable substitutability, since it's clear that objects are variables, and (b) not to propose value substitutability, since values are apparently not objects*] ... *Inheritance* is a notational mechanism for defining a type *S* in terms of another type *T* ... Intuitively, *inherit* means that the operations defined for *T* are also defined for ... *S*.

So far, the distinction doesn't seem very clear! Be that as it may, the paper continues:

> Subtyping is a relationship between interfaces (types). Inheritance can apply to both interfaces and implementations; that is, both interfaces and implementations can be inherited. The core object model is concerned with ... interfaces, ... not ... implementations." [*So why is the distinction even mentioned?*]

The paper then goes on to say (on the face of it, rather startlingly):

> Whether [the set of operations defined for *S*] is a superset of [the set of operations defined for *T*] or the two are disjoint sets is an implementation issue and does not affect the core object model semantics.

In addition to the foregoing puzzles, it has to be said too that the OMG model of subtyping and/or inheritance (like that of ODMG, in fact) appears to be considerably underspecified. Many of the features of our own inheritance model—for example, TREAT, the semantics of assignment, the semantics of equality comparison, notions such as "most specific common supertype," and numerous other aspects—seem to have no counterpart at all.

Finally, objects in OMG, even though they're variables, can never change their type; in particular, they can't be further specialized, implying that (e.g.) an object of type *employee* can never subsequently acquire the more specific type *manager*. Such restrictions surely constitute grounds for rejecting the frequently heard claims to the effect that objects—at least, OMG-style objects—are "a good model of reality." After all, "objects" in the real world certainly can acquire and lose types dynamically (for example, an employee can certainly become or cease to be a manager).

By the way, the singular nature of the book in which Soley and Kent's paper appears shouldn't be allowed to go unremarked. Its overall title is *Modern Database Systems*—yet it contains almost nothing on relational theory, which (in my opinion) is certainly relevant to "modern database systems," and will remain so for future ones, too, for as far out as anyone can see. The book in fact consists of two parts: "Next-Generation Database Technology" (512 pages) and "Technology for Interoperating Legacy Databases" (188 pages). Part I in turn consists entirely of a single subpart, "Object-Oriented Database" (Part Ia; there's no Part Ib). In other words, the book subscribes to the position—a position in stark contrast to that of Hugh Darwen and myself as documented in *The Third Manifesto*—that object DBMSs are the "next generation." And it therefore also subscribes to the position that we need to deal with the problem of "legacy databases" (by which the book clearly means SQL databases specifically)—a position we might agree with, though we have a very different interpretation of what it really means.

Part IV

NOT SO OBVIOUS

AFTER ALL?

Over the years I've written and published a considerable number of papers under headings such as "Relational Misrepresentations," "Relational Misconceptions," "Relational Myths," and so on. To summarize:

1. The first paper, titled "Some Relational Myths Exploded" (subtitle "An Examination of Some Popular Misconceptions Concerning Relational Database Management Systems") was originally published in two parts in *InfoIMS* (2nd and 3rd quarter 1984, respectively), and was then republished with the two parts combined in my book *Relational Database: Selected Writings* (Addison-Wesley, 1986).

2. The next two ("Relational Database: Further Misconceptions Number One" and "Relational Database: Further Misconceptions Number Two") were originally published in the first two issues of *InfoDB* (Spring and Summer 1986, respectively), and were then republished in considerably revised form as a combined paper under the title "Further Relational Myths" in my book *Relational Database Writings 1985-1989* (Addison-Wesley, 1990).

3. The next one ("Relational Database: Further Misconceptions Number Three") was published in my book *Relational Database Writings 1989-1991* (Addison-Wesley, 1992).

The abstract for all of these papers was basically the same (this is a slightly revised version of the abstract from the first one):

Relational database management is one of the key technologies of our time, yet the field of relational technology still suffers from a great deal of misunderstanding and misrepresentation. Misconceptions abound. The purpose of this paper is to identify some of those misconceptions.

Well, it would be nice never to have to write anything ever again of this same general nature—but, unfortunately, the nonsense just keeps on coming.[1] Hence this part of the book.

---

[1] Though to be fair, these criticisms on my part apply more to Chapters 12 and 13 than they do to Chapters 10 and 12. To some extent.

Chapter 10

Types, Units, and Representations: A Dialog, of a Kind

In accordance with their textbooks, they are always in motion; but as for dwelling upon an argument or a question, and quietly asking and answering in turn, they can no more do so than they can fly ... If you ask any of them a question, he will produce, as from a quiver, sayings brief and dark, and shoot them at you; and if you enquire the reason of what he has said, you will be hit with some other newfangled word, and you will make no way with any of them. Their great care is, not to allow of any settled principle either in their arguments or in their minds ... for they are at war with the stationary, and do what they can to drive it out everywhere.

—Plato (the speaker, Theodorus, is talking about the Ephesians), quoted in the essay "Sayings Brief and Dark" by Richard Mitchell: *The Leaning Tower of Babel* (2000)

Note: You might recognize the epigraph to this chapter—it's the same as the one I used for Chapter 6 ("SQL and Relational Theory: A Response to Criticism") of this book's predecessor, viz., Fifty Years of Relational, and Other Database Writings: More Thoughts and Essays on Database Matters (Technics Publications, 2020). I repeat it here because it's directly applicable to the present chapter as well.

There are some people with whom it seems impossible, or at best extremely difficult, to engage in any kind of sensible or serious debate. In his regular column in *DBMS* magazine in June 1995 (*DBMS 8*, No. 7), Joe Celko had this to say about *The Third Manifesto*,[1] by Hugh Darwen and myself:

> The part I don't agree with in *The Third Manifesto* is that simply defining a domain as having a data type and rules is not enough.

Well, I'm glad to see from his use of the definite article ("*The* part") that there's only one part of our *Manifesto* that Mr Celko doesn't agree with! Still, you won't be surprised to learn that the publication of his critique of that one part sparked off a lengthy exchange between us, and the present chapter is based on that exchange.

My contribution to the exchange began with a letter I wrote to the editor of *DBMS* magazine responding to Celko's June 1985 column. That letter was published in the September 1995 issue (*DBMS 8*, No. 10). The section immediately following contains the substance of that letter, though I've edited it somewhat for present purposes.

MY ORIGINAL LETTER

Overall, Celko's objections aren't very clear, but one thing he does make clear is that he thinks domains should be more than just "data types and rules"—and I believe, though I could be wrong, that by "rules" here he means *operators* (since domains in *The Third Manifesto* certainly do have operators associated with them, and they don't have anything else that might merit the label "rules").[2] As I understand it, therefore, he wants domains to be more than just data types and operators. If this interpretation is correct, though, then I confess I'm puzzled right away, since domains don't "have" data types, they *are* data types; in fact, the two concepts are identical, and the terms *domain* and *data type* (*type* for

---

[1] The first widely available description of the *Manifesto*, "Introducing ... The Third Manifesto," which Celko probably based his critique on, appeared in the magazine *Data Base Programming &Design 8*, No. 1 (January 1995). That article wasn't the *Manifesto* per se, of course, it was just "the view from 20,000 feet." The first version of the *Manifesto* as such was published a couple of months later (*ACM SIGMOD Record 24*, No. 1, March 1995), but it has since been refined and tightened up in a variety of ways. The easiest way to see the current version is to go to the website *www.thethirdmanifesto.com*.

[2] Well, they do have an associated *constraint*, but that constraint—the term is perhaps not very apt—is just a definition of the set of values that constitute the domain in question, and I certainly don't think it deserves to be called a *rule*.

short) are, or should be, completely interchangeable. Moreover, the data type notion by definition *includes* the notion that values of the type in question can be operated upon solely by means of the operators defined for that type; so the concept of "data types" subsumes the concept of "associated operators," and the phrase "data types and operators" is at best repetitive, if not tautologous.[3]

Celko gives an example involving domains "length in feet" and "weight in pounds," and then goes on to say:

> You cannot multiply pounds by pounds and get a meaningful result—there are no such things as square pounds. However, you can multiply feet by feet and get a result in square feet. How does the database disallow the operation in the first case and create an entire new domain in the second case?

This passage displays several confusions at once (in fact, it's extraordinarily muddled). Let me elaborate:

1. First of all, Celko is confused over domains as such. A domain such as "length in feet" makes no sense! After all, what would the values in such a domain look like? Well, suppose X is something—a garden path, for example—for which the question "What's the length of X in feet?" makes sense. The answer to that question might be, say, 36, meaning the path is 36 feet long. So the domain of that answer isn't "length in feet," it's just *numbers*.

2. If you're having difficulty with this first point, consider the question "What's the length of X in yards?" In the garden path example, the answer is 12, of course. So do you think the garden path has two distinct properties, length in feet and length in yards, corresponding to two distinct columns in the table and defined on two distinct domains?[4] Of course not! Rather, it has *one* property, length, corresponding to *one* column (LENGTH, say) and with *one* underlying domain, therefore (LENGTH_D, say). And what that domain and that column both contain, conceptually, is

---

[3] This sentence is perhaps not very well put. It reads as if I believe "the operators are part of the type," but that's not quite what I meant. As far as I'm concerned, a type is basically just a set of values. However, it's axiomatic that a value of type T can be operated on only by means of operators that have a parameter of type T, and that's what I meant when I said (paraphrasing slightly) that "the type notion includes the notion that values of a given type can be operated on solely by means of the operators defined for that type."

[4] Of course, I'm assuming here for definiteness that the garden path is represented by a row in some table.

lengths—not "lengths in feet," or "lengths in yards," or indeed lengths in *any* particular units of measurement.

Of course, we do need a way, when we ask the DBMS what the length of *X* is, to tell the DBMS what units we want that length to be returned to us in—feet, yards, meters, whatever. I'll come back to this issue later, in the section "The Temperature Example."

3. Indeed, Celko is confused over types vs. units. The question isn't whether we can multiply feet by feet or pounds by pounds, but rather whether we can multiply lengths by lengths or weights by weights. Now, I'll agree for the sake of discussion that square weights don't make sense—but, as Celko says, square feet certainly do (they're a unit of area). In other words, it's reasonable to claim that multiplication makes sense for two lengths (domain LENGTH_D as discussed under the previous point) but not for two weights (domain WEIGHT_D, say). Very well, then: The domain definer, or some other suitably authorized person, will define an operator MULT (say) that takes two arguments of type LENGTH_D and returns a result of type AREA_D, say ("area"). By contrast, if no one defines an analogous operator for arguments of type WEIGHT_D, then multiplication of two weights won't be possible.

4. Given the foregoing, the DBMS (*not* "the database," please) can now certainly "disallow the operation" for weights but allow it for lengths. But there's no question of it having to "create an entire new domain in the second case"! On the contrary, the domain of the result, namely AREA_D, will already have been defined to the DBMS, just as domains LENGTH_D and WEIGHT_D were—necessarily so, in fact, because otherwise the operator MULT couldn't even be defined.

5. Finally, Celko's text regarding this example suggests that perhaps when he talks about "rules" in this context, what he means is the mechanism, whatever it is, that enables the DBMS to "allow the operation for lengths but disallow it for weights." If so, well, I've just explained that mechanism in outline—it's simply a matter of defining the operators we want and not defining the ones we don't want—and I have to say I really don't think "rules" is the mot juste for the mechanism in question.

At the risk of beating the point to death, let me add that the problem of how to allow the multiplication of two lengths but not of two weights is precisely analogous to the problem of how to allow the multiplication of two integers but not of two strings. How does Celko suppose today's DBMSs deal with this latter problem?

Be that as it may, Celko then goes on to say:

> These rules get more and more complex as you add domains to the database. When you multiply feet by pounds, you get work expressed in foot-pounds. But not always—a man's height multiplied by his weight is nonsense, not foot-pounds. The relation or entity where the attributes reside matters quite a bit.

This passage too is rife with confusions, the most significant of which is, of course, the one already mentioned regarding types vs. units.[5] *There's no such thing as a domain of feet or a domain of pounds* (after all, what could such domains possibly contain?); there are only domains whose elements are *measurements*.[6] In the example, those measurements denote lengths and weights, respectively. Thus, the question of multiplying feet by pounds doesn't arise; rather, what does arise is the question of multiplying lengths by weights. For example, we might define domains DISTANCE_D and FORCE_D, say, containing length measurements and weight measurements, respectively, and "allow multiplication"—i.e., define an appropriate operator—between DISTANCE_D and FORCE_D values (to produce WORK_D values). At the same time, we might also define domains HEIGHT_D and WEIGHT_D, say, again containing length measurements and weight measurements respectively, and "disallow multiplication" (by not defining any such operator) between HEIGHT_D and WEIGHT_D values. And that's all! Note in particular that "the relation or entity where the attributes reside" has absolutely nothing to do with the case.

---

[5] Another is: No one "adds domains to the database." Domains don't belong to databases. (Which database do you think the domain of integers belongs to?)

[6] And then, as I've already indicated, there has to be a way to tell the system what units we want those measurements to be expressed in when they're returned to us as the result, or part of the result, of some query. Again, see the section "The Temperature Example," later.

CELKO FIGHTS BACK

Celko responded with a letter of his own, which appeared in the October issue of the magazine (*DBMS 8*, No. 11), to which I replied. My reply appeared in the issue of the following January. I no longer have a copy of that letter of Celko's, however, so I can't show it here; I do still have my reply to it, but I'll omit that too (you might be glad of that). However, Celko then responded to my reply with a much longer piece, which appeared the following month (February 1996) under the heading "Celko Fights Back." That longer piece I do still have a copy of, and the remainder of this section consists of that piece of Celko's, quoted in its entirety and absolutely verbatim, except that (a) I've revised the punctuation just slightly and (b) I've injected a few comments of my own here and there in the form of asides, footnotes, and so on.

<Celko Fights Back>

I think that much (if not all) of our disagreements are in terminology. Chris Date's terms are based on dividing the problem in a model and its implementation. Here are my definitions.

> *Aside:* Celko might be right in attributing some of our disagreements—but only some, and in my opinion not the major ones—to differences in our use of terms. That being so, however, it would be helpful if he would define some of the terms he uses (*domain*, *type*, *primitive*, *rule*, and so on—not to mention the term *model* itself). Thus, "Here are my definitions" is encouraging. But where are they? I don't see *anything* that looks like a proper definition, as such, in the rest of his text. For example, consider his very next sentence:
>
>> A (abstract) data type is a basic set of abstract primitives with certain properties.
>
> This sentence is the only thing in Celko's text that even approaches a "definition" of the concept *abstract data type*. But if it's supposed to be a definition, then I think it can reasonably be criticized on several grounds. For example, what does "basic" mean? What does "abstract primitive" mean? What does "certain properties" mean? As far as I can see, Celko's text doesn't provide answers for *any* of these questions. *End of aside.*

A (abstract) data type is a basic set of abstract primitives with certain properties. These are very high level abstractions. The sets of all integers, all reals, all character strings, and so forth, are data types. Peano's Postulates would be the rules for the integers. Data types are what we are trying to build into our computer hardware but cannot because, by their nature, data types tend to be infinite sets.

> *Aside:* Celko's remark re Peano's postulates (also known as Peano's axioms) also raises a number of issues. First of all, someone of a more suspicious nature than me might be tempted to think it's merely an attempt to blind the reader with science—especially since the axioms in question don't even do what Celko says they do, not quite. (To be specific, they're not "the rules for the integers," they're the rules for the natural or "counting" numbers 1, 2, 3, etc.—so, no negative values and, according to most authorities if not all, no zero either.) For the record, Peano's axioms can be stated as follows:
>
> a. There exists a natural number 1.
>
> b. Every natural number n has a successor n'.
>
> c. No natural number has 1 as its successor.
>
> d. If $n' = m'$ then $n = m$.
>
> e. Every set of natural numbers that contains 1 and the successor of every member of the set contains all of the natural numbers.
>
> To repeat, these axioms taken together can be regarded as a formal definition of the natural numbers. Thus, what Celko calls the "rules" associated with a given type seem to be nothing more than the corresponding (and required) *type constraint*.[7] But then where are the definitions of the corresponding operators? Note that there must be some—types are meaningless and useless without associated operators. *End of aside.*

---

[7] Two points here. First, the type constraint for any given type T is the constraint mentioned in footnote 2—i.e., it's the definition of the set of values that make up that type T (and *every* type T has such a constraint). Second, what Celko seems to mean by "rules" here is quite different from what he seemed to mean by that same term in connection with his "lengths and weights" example (see the previous section). It's very difficult to respond coherently to arguments that rely on such shifts—unexplained shifts at that—in the use and meaning of terms. PS: Celko's "fighting back" piece, the subject of the present section, goes on to use the term *rule* in at least two further senses, and possibly others as well.

Defining data types as an abstract "Platonic ideal" has advantages. I simply design my programming language as if I had a true infinite integer data type on an abstract computer. I then trust the hardware to have an approximation that is good enough for my work.

The next step is to move from the abstract data type to a physical level where you have a (physical or user-defined or hardware—pick your qualifying term) data type. If I have a 16-bit computer and a 32-bit computer, the floating point numbers will be based on the same data type: reals. However, the laws of floating point math are not quite those of real numbers. But they are well defined and built into my hardware, so I will use them as primitives. [*By "them" here, Celko presumably means "the laws of floating point math"—or does he just mean floating point numbers as such, whatever those happen to be on his particular computer? Or does he mean the FLOAT data type? His next paragraph suggests it's the last of these—but then why the plural?*]

These primitive (physical) data types and their hardware operators are used to construct what I am calling domains and, yes, I mean this in the sense of SQL-92. A domain is a data type with constraints and associated operators. A domain is all syntax, with no semantics. [*The points in this paragraph are of two kinds. Some are incomprehensible. The others are comprehensible but wrong.*]

At the next level, I want to use domains to model the attributes of an entity in my database. Thus, I might model the attribute "weight" as a floating point number with the constraints that it is greater than zero and that I can add weights together. Notice that "height" can also be modeled as a floating point number with the constraint that it is greater than zero and has addition, but they are different domains. I attach domains to attributes, but this is purely syntax.

If a data type and a domain were the same, a constraint could have a self-reference. This leads to formal paradoxes and practical problems, which is why SQL-92 explicitly forbids a CREATE DOMAIN statement constraint to use its own domain directly or indirectly.

A scale is a semantic concept that tries to attach meaning to a domain. The purposes of a scale are: to attach meaning to the value of an attribute in a uniform manner, and to attach meaning to calculations performed with other attributes of this and other entities.

One of the basic properties of scales is that operations must be done on the same type of scale. Another property is that you can form only certain compound units. There is a joke about a teacher asking his class, "What is 12 times 78?"

The first kid raises his hand and says, "Green!"

The second kid shouts out, "No, it's Thursday!"

The third kid announces, "936, teacher."

"That's very good, Billy. How did you get your answer?"

"I divided green by Thursday!"

This is funny because the wrong answers are values on scales that are non-numeric domains, and Billy's division operation is illegal for either of the two domains.

This leads to a second level of rules among entities, attributes, and scales. This is semantics at the entity level. It is why I can multiply feet and pounds to get foot pounds of work when I move an object, but cannot multiply a man's height by his weight to figure out how much work he can do.

I separate these three concepts—data type, domain, and scale—because you can change any one without *necessarily* changing the other two. For example, assume I want to store temperatures in my database. I probably start with the scale ("we keep records in Celsius"), because it is the most abstract level. [*Doesn't he mean the least abstract level?—"temperature" surely being **more** abstract than "degrees Celsius"?*] I then move to the domain ("we need whole numbers between −100 and +200"), and finally pick an available data type ("let's declare that column as INTEGER NOT NULL"). Now I can make changes to my data design:

1) If I decide to use the Fahrenheit scale, I can still use whole numbers and an INTEGER data type.

2) If I decide to change the domain to four digits, I can still use the INTEGER data type and the Celsius scale—I just modify my CHECK() clause.

3) If I decide to change the data type to DECIMAL (5,2), I can still use the Celsius scale, and all of the old domain values are still represented. I gain more precision in my measurement, however, and can store values that the old data type could not.

In fairness, there are often relationships among the data type, domain, and scale of an attribute that require a change in one to trigger a change in the others. For example, if I were to change a DECIMAL (5,2) column to INTEGER, I would need to decide how to get rid of the decimal places (round or truncate).

If there were no difference, then this would be fine. Using Date's example [*see the aside following Celko's next paragraph*] of quantitative (numeric scaled) and fuzzy (ordinal scale) temperature, I can find two reasons why they cannot be compared, in spite of their being drawn from the same data type. First, fuzzy temperature is one domain and quantity is another. Second, quantity is an absolute scale and fuzzy temperature is an ordinal scale; no matter what domain or data type you pick for them, they would not be comparable.

Taking Date's point number one [*my apologies, but I have no idea what this refers to*], I would say that the data type of the fuzzy temperature scale is a character string. The domain is limited to the set of strings ('hot', 'warm', 'cool', 'cold') and it has a collation from 'hot' to 'cold'. Concatenation will not work because it is not in the same domain as a regular character string.

> *Aside:* I could be wrong, but I think it was Celko, not me, that introduced the temperature example. Evidence in support of this claim: My January 1996 letter quotes Celko's October 1995 letter as saying the following: "Degrees Kelvin is one possible scale for temperature. I could use Celsius or Fahrenheit scales instead ... I could use an ordinal scale ... ('hot', 'warm', 'cool', 'cold') ... The data type is character string and I can apply an ordering rule called 'hotter than'." Plenty of muddles here, by the way!—which is why I rather fervently hope and believe this was Celko's example, not mine. For example:
>
> - What exactly is an ordinal scale? "Ordinal" refers to regular numeric ordering (first, second, third, etc.). So isn't, e.g., the Celsius "scale" an ordinal scale? *Note:* I see that Celko says "quantity is an absolute scale"—presumably contrasting such a "scale" with an "ordinal" one—but I don't know what he means by that remark. I might perhaps be persuaded that, e.g., type POINT, denoting points in two-dimensional euclidean space, is "absolute," in the sense that there's no obvious ordering that applies to POINT values (though even there a total ordering could be defined if desired); but it seems to me that quantities are very far from being "absolute" in any similar sense.
>
> - "The data type [*i.e., for 'hot', 'warm', etc.*] is character string": No, it isn't! The *data type* is temperature; "character string" is the *representation*. For example, we're not going to concatenate two temperatures (as we would be able to, if the data type truly were character string). This remark on his part makes me suspect rather strongly that Celko is confused over types vs. representations.

- We don't "apply an ordering rule"—rather, we define an *operator,* called "greater than" (">"), that applies to pairs of temperature values, according to which 'hot' is greater than 'warm', 'warm' is greater than 'cool', etc. Of course, I won't argue with you if you want to pronounce this operator "is hotter than." How you pronounce it isn't the point; how you think about what you're doing is the point.

- Of course, the operands and result of that ">" operator are of different types (the operands are temperatures, the result is a truth value). Could this be why Celko thinks we're talking about a rule, not an operator? But if it is, then he'd have to argue that, e.g., even the familiar ">" that applies to integers is a rule and not an operator!

And so on. *End of aside.*

What seems to be lacking in Date's modeling system, in which everything is a "data type," is a concept of an entity made up of attributes.[8] I see entities that have attributes, which have values, which are drawn from domains, which are constructed from data types, which are based on abstract data types.

Another reader pointed out to me that although adding two temperatures together by themselves makes no sense, we can and do add temperatures by averaging them over mass. The particular material and other conditions determine the time required. In short, the behavior of temperature is linked to the entity to which it belongs because the entity will have other attributes. Semantics need entities.

The weakness of SQL is that the language is all syntax and no semantics.[9] A table can model an entity (Date's Parts table) or a relationship (Date's Parts-Supplier-Job table) or something else. You cannot tell what a table means by looking at it.

I will concede that an OO database can capture more of the semantics and behaviors of what we are trying to model than a relational model. But I don't

---

[8] This particular complaint of Celko's would be beyond outrageous if it weren't so patently absurd. Is he hoping his readers have never read *anything* I've ever written? What on earth does he think the classic employees relation is all about, if it's not about employee "entities" and their "attributes" (etc.)? See in particular the section titled "A Case Study" in Chapter 8 of the present book.

[9] According to Celko, then: 1. "A domain is all syntax, with no semantics" (this chapter, page 302). 2. He "attaches domains to attributes, but this is purely syntax" (also page 302). 3. SQL is "all syntax and no semantics" (this page). Taken all in all, these remarks will surely be regarded as quite strange by many people, SQL language designers not least.

mind this, because I don't think that computers are good at semantics. Artificial intelligence's slow progress is proof of this.

I would also like to point out that sets defined by enumeration are fundamentally different from those defined by a rule. An enumerated set can only be finite or of size Alph Null;[10] a set defined by a rule can be of any size. This means that two different floating point representations are also different data types because the two underlying sets of real numbers do not match.

I would say that both are based on the abstract data type, real numbers, and have different domains. I have a rule for determining that they are compatible. I might have some trouble working with them in the same database, but it is a domain problem, not a data type problem.

Furthermore, there are sets that can be defined by a rule, and that cannot be enumerated and do not behave nicely—the Cantor sets, Julia set, the $(3n+1)$ problem set, and so on. Many of these sets have the property with which you can find out whether any single element from the universal set from which it is drawn is either in the set or not, but you cannot find all of the elements in the set. [*I suspect an element of blinding with science again in this paragraph. Even if not, what on earth does the paragraph have to do with the matter at hand?*]

Irrational numbers are the most common example. They are defined by the rule that you cannot represent them as (p/q), where p and q are integers. If Date will please enumerate all the irrational [*sic*] between 0 and 1, he will have done better than any mathematician in all history. This should be easy [*what should?*], because there is proof that there are more irrational than rational numbers in that segment.

I agree that I would like to have a single temperature domain that I could convert to display in a scale of my choice. I know this is possible because I have several different interval or ratio scales for temperature, and I know what the conversions will be because of the kind of scales I have. I do not care if it is explicit or under the covers, the calculation will be the same. I would hide the scale conversion in VIEWs.[11]

</Celko Fights Back>

---

[10] He means aleph null ($\aleph_0$), of course—the first of Cantor's transfinite cardinals. That said, I'd love to see an attempt to enumerate the elements of a set of cardinality $\aleph_0$.

[11] For reasons unexplained Celko always sets the word *view* in all caps.

SOME REACTIONS TO THE FOREGOING

At this point I decided to terminate the correspondence—but not without a certain amount of chagrin and a great deal of frustration! You can't win; it's Plato's Ephesians problem, in spades. Here's how it works. Critic X criticizes something you've written; the criticism in question is rife with muddles, undefined terms, confusions, mistakes, contradictions, irrelevancies, blindings with science, and misrepresentations of your own position. You try to defend yourself. Critic X criticizes your defense; again, his criticism is rife with muddles, undefined terms, confusions, mistakes, contradictions, irrelevancies, blindings with science, and misrepresentations of your own position. (I'm assuming here that the critic is male, because in my experience such is usually the case.) If you now try to defend yourself again, then lo and behold!—suddenly you're engaged in a "debate" with the party in question.

This process is both frustrating in the extreme and completely unproductive. If you continue the "debate," you invest Critic X's ideas with a legitimacy they don't deserve. If you terminate it, you invest Critic X's ideas with a legitimacy they don't deserve. Of course, the latter alternative does have the advantage that the loop terminates, but it also has the disadvantage that it leaves onlookers with the impression that Critic X has "won."

All of that being said, there's one particular item in "Celko Strikes Back" that I do want to respond to in more detail, because I think by doing so I can shed light on quite a number of issues (actually nonissues, in many cases) raised in that piece.[12] The item in question is that temperature example once again See the section immediately following.

THE TEMPERATURE EXAMPLE

Note: Before getting into details here, let me repeat something I said earlier in the chapter:

---

[12] Though limiting myself to just the point in question does mean I won't be dealing adequately with all of the other "muddles, undefined terms, confusions, mistakes, contradictions, irrelevancies, blindings with science, and misrepresentations of my own position" that Celko's piece additionally contains. Actually, at one point I did start to write a response to all of these other issues—but any such response, if done as meticulously and thoroughly as it would need to be, would be many, many pages long, and I gave up. Life is too short.

Of course, we do need a way, when we ask the DBMS what the length of X is, to tell the DBMS what units we want that length to be returned to us in—feet, yards, meters, whatever.

In other words, we need a systematic means for dealing in our database systems with units of measure, and that's what this section—which can be seen in part as an elaboration of certain material from Chapter 8—is largely about. (As the title indicates, the section focuses on one particular example of the problem, but the points it makes can be made to apply, mutatis mutandis, to any situation where units of measure are relevant.)

I'll begin by repeating the pertinent portion of Celko's text:

> For example, assume I want to store temperatures in my database. I probably start with the scale ("we keep records in Celsius"), because it is the most abstract level. I then move to the domain ("we need whole numbers between −100 and +200"), and finally pick an available data type ("let's declare that column as INTEGER NOT NULL"). Now I can make changes to my data design:
>
> 1) If I decide to use the Fahrenheit scale, I can still use whole numbers and an INTEGER data type.
>
> 2) If I decide to change the domain to four digits, I can still use the INTEGER data type and the Celsius scale—I just modify my CHECK() clause.
>
> 3) If I decide to change the data type to DECIMAL (5,2), I can still use the Celsius scale, and all of the old domain values are still represented. I gain more precision in my measurement, however, and can store values that the old data type could not.
>
>   .....
>
> Another reader pointed out to me that although adding two temperatures together by themselves makes no sense, we can and do add temperatures by averaging them.

I'd now like to explain, in detail, how I would deal with this example in **Tutorial D**. To begin with, I note that:

■ What Celko calls the *scale*, I would call *units*, or *units of measure*.

■ What he calls a *domain*, I would call a *type*.

■ What he calls a *data type*, I would call a *representation.*[13]

So I would define Celko's example of a TEMPERATURE type as follows[14] (I've numbered the lines for purposes of subsequent reference):

```
1.  TYPE TEMPERATURE
2.      POSSREP C ( CD NUMERIC(5,2) )  /* degrees Celsius    */
3.      POSSREP F ( FD NUMERIC(5,2) )  /* degrees Fahrenheit */
4.      CONSTRAINT CD ≥ -100.00 AND
5.                 CD ≤ +200.00 AND
6.                 FD = ( 9 × CD ) / 5 + 32 ;
```

Explanation:

■ Line 1 simply says we have a type—a user defined type, in fact—called TEMPERATURE.

■ Line 2 defines a possible representation ("possrep") for temperatures. To be specific, it says that values of type TEMPERATURE can possibly be represented by decimal numbers CD with precision 5 and scale factor 2— informally, by degrees on the Celsius scale—though those numbers are subject to a certain constraint (see the discussion of Lines 4-6 below).
    Note: I use NUMERIC(5,2) in place of Celko's INTEGER type because I want to be able to handle values that aren't integers; after all, the temperature 72 degrees Fahrenheit (for example) is 22.22 degrees Celsius to two decimal places, which is obviously not an integer value.[15] Note too that "degrees Celsius" is only a *possible* representation!—it's not necessarily the pertinent *physical* representation, which is under the covers and concealed from the user. That physical representation *might* be in terms of degrees Celsius; or it might be in terms of degrees Kelvin, or degrees Fahrenheit, or degrees Réaumur; or it might be something else

---

[13] Though if *R* is a representation for type *T*, then of course *R* in turn is expressed in terms of other types, as we'll quickly see.

[14] As the previous footnote suggests, that type could then be used as the representation (or part of the representation) for other types as desired. However, I won't bother to illustrate that possibility here.

[15] In the interest of accuracy I should note that type specifications of the form NUMERIC(*p*,*q*) aren't supported in **Tutorial D** as currently defined (the only system defined numeric types currently supported are INTEGER and RATIONAL).

entirely. As far as the user is concerned, however, that physical representation, whatever it is, is (of course!) totally irrelevant.

- Line 3 defines another possible representation for temperatures. To be specific, it says that values of type TEMPERATURE can also possibly be represented by decimal numbers FD with precision 5 and scale factor 2— informally, by degrees on the Fahrenheit scale—though, again, those numbers are subject to a certain constraint (again, see the discussion of Lines 4-6 below).

- Lines 4-6 give a precise definition of how the values that constitute type TEMPERATURE are constrained. To be specific, TEMPERATURE values are (thanks to Lines 4 and 5) all and only those values that can possibly be represented by a decimal number CD with precision 5 and scale factor 2 such that $-100.00 \leq CD \leq +200.00$; equivalently (thanks to Line 6), they're all and only those values that can possibly be represented by a decimal number FD with precision 5 and scale factor 2 such that $-148.00 \leq FD \leq +392.00$.

Now let TX be an expression of type TEMPERATURE (in particular, it might just be a reference to—syntactically speaking, just the name of—a variable of that type). Then the expression THE_CD (TX) will return a NUMERIC (5,2) number *cd* denoting the corresponding temperature in degrees Celsius, and the expression THE_FD (TX) will return a NUMERIC (5,2) number *fd* denoting that same temperature in degrees Fahrenheit (and *fd* will be equal to $(9 \times cd) / 5 + 32$).[16] Similarly, if NX is an expression of type NUMERIC (5,2), then the expressions C (NX) and F $((9 \times NX) / 5 + 32)$ will both return the same TEMPERATURE value.

Aside: Consider the following. An individual degree Fahrenheit is 5/9 the size of an individual degree Celsius (in other words, the "granularity" of the Fahrenheit scale is 5/9 that of the Celsius scale). So let *dF* = 1.00. Then:

---

[16] The present discussion doesn't illustrate the point, but those operators THE_CD and THE_FD can also be used as what are called *pseudovariables*, thereby supporting certain update operations on variables of type TEMPERATURE in terms of Celsius and Fahrenheit measurements, respectively. See Chapter 8 for further explanation.

```
dF × 5           =  5.00
5.00 / 9         =  0.555555...
0.555555... × 9  =  4.999999...
4.999999... / 5  =  0.999999...
```

Mathematically speaking, of course, 0.999999... is equal to 1 (they're just two equally valid representations of the same number in decimal notation)—but what about computer arithmetic? As the foregoing thought experiment suggests, we might need to be a little careful in practice over rounding off the results of computations. More specifically (and with reference to the paragraph above beginning "Now let TX"), we might need to exercise some care if we want to guarantee that, e.g., *fd* is indeed equal to (9 × *cd* / 5) + 32 and that (by the same token) *cd* is indeed equal to 5 × (*fd* − 32) / 9. However, such matters are more properly the concern of computing in general, not of type theory in particular, and further consideration of them is beyond the scope of the present discussion. *End of aside*.

So what does all this mean in terms of the three numbered points in Celko's text as quoted above? Well, switching from Celsius to Fahrenheit or the other way around is just a question of using the appropriate "possrep." And if we wanted to switch to, say, Kelvin, we can easily add yet another possrep. So much for his first point.

As for his second point: Changing the data type of a possrep from, say, NUMERIC (5,2) to NUMERIC (7,2) is rather more than just a matter of "modifying a CHECK clause"—and the same is true in Celko's world, too, though he seems to be claiming it isn't. The problem is that certain expressions that were previously of type NUMERIC (5,2), or were required to be of that type, will now be, or will now be required to be, of type NUMERIC (7,2) instead. What the ramifications of this change are will depend on circumstances, however, and it's impossible to be more specific here.

Celko's third point has to do with changing the physical representation and is thus not relevant to this discussion.

I turn now to the question of operators—specifically, to the suggestion that (a) it makes no sense to add two temperatures together "by themselves," as it were, but that (b) it does make sense to add them together if we're going to go on and divide by two to find their average. (I limit my attention to the case of averaging just two temperatures for simplicity.) OK: Regarding point (a), we simply don't define any kind of ADD operator ("+") for temperatures as such. Regarding point (b), here's the code for finding the average of two temperatures:

```
OPERATOR AVG_TEMP ( T1 TEMPERATURE , T2 TEMPERATURE )
                                      RETURNS TEMPERATURE ;
     RETURN C ( ( THE_CD ( T1 ) + THE_CD ( T2 ) ) / 2 ) ;
END OPERATOR ;
```

Observe in particular that what this code doesn't do is add the temperatures T1 and T2 as such—instead, what it does is this:

- First it adds the corresponding Celsius measurements (which are just NUMERIC (5,2) values, or in other words numbers), to obtain a NUMERIC (6,2) value x, say (another number).

- Then it divides that value x by two, returning a NUMERIC (5,2) value y, say.

- The invocation C (y) then returns the temperature "possibly represented" by that value y, considered as a measurement on the Celsius scale.

And while I'm on the subject of operators, here's how I'd define (e.g.) "greater than" for temperatures:

```
OPERATOR ">" ( T1 TEMPERATURE , T2 TEMPERATURE )
                                 RETURNS BOOLEAN ;
     RETURN ( THE_CD ( T1 ) > THE_CD ( T2 ) ) ;
END OPERATOR ;
```

And here's how I'd handle that business of "fuzzy temperatures" ('hot', 'warm', etc.). First I'd define a data type, FUZZYTEMP say:

```
TYPE FUZZYTEMP
     POSSREP FZT ( Z CHAR )
     CONSTRAINT Z = 'hot'  OR
                Z = 'warm' OR
                Z = 'cool' OR
                Z = 'cold' ;
```

Then I'd define an operator for mapping exact temperatures to fuzzy temperatures, perhaps like this:

```
OPERATOR CORRESP_FZT ( T TEMPERATURE ) RETURNS FUZZYTEMP ;
    RETURN ( IF T > C ( 35.00 ) THEN FZT ( 'hot'  ) ELSE
             IF T > C ( 20.00 ) THEN FZT ( 'warm' ) ELSE
             IF T > C (  0.00 ) THEN FZT ( 'cool' ) ELSE
                                     FZT ( 'cold' ) ) ;
END OPERATOR ;
```

And here's the "hotter than" operator for type FUZZYTEMP:[17]

```
OPERATOR HOTTER_THAN ( Z1 FUZZYTEMP , Z2 FUZZYTEMP )
                                        RETURNS BOOLEAN ;
    RETURN
    ( IF Z1 = FZT ( 'hot' ) AND Z2 ≠ FZT ( 'hot' ) THEN TRUE
      ELSE IF Z1 = FZT ( 'warm' ) AND Z2 ≠ FZT ( 'hot' )
                           AND Z2 ≠ FZT ( 'warm' ) THEN TRUE
      ELSE IF Z1 = FZT ( 'cool' ) AND Z2 = FZT ( 'cold' )
                                                 THEN TRUE
      ELSE FALSE ) ;
END OPERATOR ;
```

POSTSCRIPT

Here again is that quote from Joe Celko's June 1995 column in *DBMS* magazine that I opened this chapter with:

> The part I don't agree with in *The Third Manifesto* is that simply defining a domain as having a data type and rules is not enough.

It occurs to me now that part of Celko's confusion here might perhaps have been due to the SQL standard. The standard does include something it calls a domain, and domains in the standard do "have data types and rules" (where—contrary to what I suggested in the body of the chapter—the term "rules" does refer to constraints and not to operators). As I've explained elsewhere, however, domains in the SQL standard have almost nothing to do with true relational domains![18] If it's indeed the case that Celko was confused by the standard, then that fact only serves to support my contention that it was a very bad idea to call that SQL standard construct a "domain" in the first place.

---

[17] "Hotter than or the same as" might be a little more useful, but "hotter than" is the operator specifically mentioned in Celko's October 1995 letter.

[18] See, e.g., my column "SQL Domains Aren't Domains" (*Database Programming & Design 8*, No. 10, October 1995), republished in my book *Relational Database Writings 1994-1997* (Addison-Wesley, 1998).

Chapter 11

Dropping ACID

He used to drop acid and now he loves God,
but he's still got that look in his eye

—Jim Ringer:
Still Got that Look (1981)

This chapter consists primarily of material repeated from various other
books of mine, including in particular (a) An Introduction to Database
Systems, 8th edition (Addison-Wesley, 2004) and (b) SQL and Relational
Theory: How to Write Accurate SQL Code, 3rd edition (O'Reilly, 2015).
The message is thus not new. But it's important, and it doesn't seem to
be much understood or appreciated in the computing community at
large, and so I've decided to say it all again—but to do it this time in a
self-contained chapter devoted to that topic, and that topic alone.

Here are some questions that any database professional should be able to answer almost without thinking:

1. What exactly is a database?

2. What's the most important thing about a database?

3. When should integrity constraints be checked?

4. What are the ACID properties of a transaction?

I claim, however, that there's more to these questions—or less, depending on your point of view!—than meets the eye. In fact, empirical evidence, gathered over many years, suggests rather strongly that a majority of database professionals are *not* able to give good answers to Questions 1, 2, or 3, even though they're quite happy to give a fairly lengthy response to Question 4. It's interesting to note, therefore, that the right answer to Question 4 depends rather crucially on the right answers to Questions 1, 2, and 3. What's more, the right answer to Question 4—at least, the one that seems right to me—isn't the one that's usually given; in fact, it's one that's somewhat at odds with conventional wisdom.

The aim of this chapter, then, is to explore these issues in detail. It begins by offering what I believe are the right answers to Questions 1, 2, and 3— answers that might appear novel to some readers. It then goes on to examine the so called ACID properties of transactions (Question 4) in the light of those answers, and concludes that, while ACID might be a nice acronym, the concepts it represents don't really stand up to close examination. To be more specific:

- The "A" property (*atomicity*) is only a weak approximation to what's really required.

- If the "C" property is *consistency*, it's trivial; if it's *correctness*, it's unenforceable (indeed, it's not really a property at all but merely a desideratum).

- The "I" property (*isolation*) is likewise merely a desideratum, because it too is unenforceable, even if all transactions execute at the maximum isolation level.

- By contrast, the "D" property (*durability*) can reasonably be described as a property as such; even so, however, it too needs some refinement.

These conclusions are clearly somewhat counter to orthodox opinion! Please note carefully, therefore, that they're not meant as an attack on the vast amount of excellent research that has been done on transaction management over the past 40 or 50 years, nor on the many elegant and useful results that have been obtained from that research. Rather, they're offered in an attempt to improve our understanding of certain issues that lie at the very foundation of the computing field in general and the database field in particular. Let's take a closer look.

WHAT'S A DATABASE?

First of all, I hope you agree that a database, whatever else it might be, is basically just a variable—probably a rather large and complicated variable, but a variable nonetheless. After all, databases are certainly updatable (even a "read only" database, meaning one that's used purely for lookup or reference purposes, has to be populated initially); and, by definition, to be updatable is to be a variable, and to be a variable is to be updatable. Logically, therefore, we ought really to distinguish between database variables as such, on the one hand, and database values, which are the values that can be assigned to a database variable, on the other. In fact, the distinction between database variables and database values is precisely analogous to the familiar distinction we already draw between relation variables (*aka* relvars) and relation values.[1]

Let's consider an example. Fig. 11.1 below shows a sample value for the familiar suppliers-and-parts database, consisting as usual of three relations, viz., a suppliers relation, a parts relation, and a shipments relation:

S

SNO	SNAME	STATUS	CITY
S1	Smith	20	London
S2	Jones	10	Paris
S3	Blake	30	Paris
S4	Clark	20	London
S5	Adams	30	Athens

P

PNO	PNAME	COLOR	WEIGHT	CITY
P1	Nut	Red	12.0	London
P2	Bolt	Green	17.0	Paris
P3	Screw	Blue	17.0	Oslo
P4	Screw	Red	14.0	London
P5	Cam	Blue	12.0	Paris
P6	Cog	Red	19.0	London

SP

SNO	PNO	QTY
S1	P1	300
S1	P2	200
S1	P3	400
S1	P4	200
S1	P5	100
S1	P6	100
S2	P1	300
S2	P2	400
S3	P2	200
S4	P2	200
S4	P4	300
S4	P5	400

Fig. 11.1: The suppliers-and-parts database—sample value

---

[1] At least, this latter distinction *ought* to be familiar. It's probably not as familiar as it should be.

Note that I use the unqualified term *relation* to mean a relation value specifically; thus, the three relations shown in the figure represent current values for the suppliers relvar S, the parts relvar P, and the shipments relvar SP, respectively.

Here now are some mutually interdependent definitions:

Definition (database variable): Loosely, a container for relvars; more accurately, a variable whose value at any given time is a database value, q.v. As already noted, there's a logical difference, analogous to that between relation values and relation variables, between database values and database variables; thus, what we usually call a "database" is really a variable, and updating that database has the effect of replacing one value of that variable by another such value, where the values in question are database values and the variable in question is a database variable.

Definition (database value): Either the actual—i.e., current—or some possible "state" for some database; in other words, a collection of relations, those relations being actual or possible values for the applicable relvars.

Definition (database): Strictly, a database value; in practice (and in this chapter in particular), more commonly used to refer to what would more accurately be called a database variable.

Aside: Of course, I'm assuming for the purposes of this chapter that databases are always relational. Be aware, however, that the term *database* is also used in nonrelational contexts to mean a variety of other things—for example, a collection of data as physically stored. It's also used, all too frequently, to mean a DBMS, but this particular usage is strongly deprecated. After all, if we call the DBMS a database, then what do we call the database? *End of aside.*

Consider Fig. 11.1 once again. The relations shown in that figure constitute the "state" of the suppliers-and-parts database that happens to be current at some particular time (which we can assume without loss of generality to be "the time right now"). But if we were to look at that database at some different time, we would probably see a different state; thus, the database is indeed really a variable—a database variable, that is, or in other words a variable whose values are database values. In fact, to be more precise about the matter, a database is really a *tuple* variable, where:

- The tuple variable in question contains one attribute for each relvar in the database in question, and no other attributes.[2]

- Each attribute of that tuple variable is relation valued.

In the case of the suppliers-and-parts database, for example, we're talking about a tuple variable, SPDB say, of (let's say) the following tuple type:

```
TUPLE { S   RELATION { SNO    CHAR ,
                       SNAME  CHAR ,
                       STATUS INTEGER ,
                       CITY   CHAR } ,
         P   RELATION { PNO    CHAR ,
                       PNAME  CHAR ,
                       COLOR  CHAR ,
                       WEIGHT RATIONAL ,
                       CITY   CHAR } ,
        SP RELATION { SNO    CHAR ,
                       PNO    CHAR ,
                       QTY    INTEGER } }
```

It follows that, e.g., the following relational update on the suppliers-and-parts database—

```
DELETE SP WHERE QTY < 150 ;
```

—is really shorthand for the following *tuple* update:[3]

```
UPDATE SPDB : { SP := SP WHERE NOT ( QTY < 150 ) } ;
```

And this tuple update in turn is shorthand for the following tuple assignment:

```
SPDB := TUPLE { S    ( S   FROM SPDB ) ,
                P    ( P   FROM SPDB ) ,
                SP ( ( SP FROM SPDB )
                     WHERE NOT ( QTY < 150 ) ) } ;
```

To summarize to this point, then:

---

[2] The phrase "each relvar" here ought really to be "each base relvar," but I'll assume for simplicity that all relvars mentioned in this chapter are base relvars specifically, barring explicit statements to the contrary.

[3] Actually this update (also the tuple assignment it's shorthand for) wouldn't be valid in **Tutorial D**, because there's no such thing as a database name in **Tutorial D**—but there could be.

■ The unqualified term *database* is usually taken to mean a database variable specifically.[4]

■ A database variable is really a tuple variable, and a database value is a tuple value, or just a tuple for short.

■ Let *t* be the tuple that's the current value of database *D*. Tuple *t* has one attribute for each relvar in *D*, and no other attributes.

■ Let *R* be an attribute of *t*. Attribute *R* has as its value the relation *r* that's the current value of the pertinent relvar (which is also called *R*) of database *D*.

■ Each tuple within relation *r* denotes a certain proposition, one that's understood by convention to evaluate to TRUE.

■ The current value of database *D*—which is to say, tuple *t*—can thus be understood, loosely, as a set of sets of true propositions.[5]

One last point to close this section: In practice, of course, a database isn't just a set of relvars; rather, it's a set of relvars *that are together subject to a certain constraint*: namely, the pertinent total database constraint, or in other words the logical AND of all integrity constraints that mention—i.e., apply to—any of the relvars in the database in question. And it seems reasonable to require that any given database be "fully connected" (and hence require it to form a coherent whole); that is, it seems reasonable to require the total database constraint to be such that every relvar in the database is logically connected, via that constraint, to every other (not necessarily directly, of course). The following definition is aimed toward formalizing this requirement.

---

[4] There's a slightly unfortunate asymmetry of terminology here. As I've said a couple of times already, the logical difference between database values and database variables is analogous to that between relation values and relation variables. Now, in the latter case, we take the unqualified term *relation* to mean a relation value specifically. In the former case, therefore, we ought by rights to take the unqualified term *database* to mean a database value specifically—but we usually don't, we take it to mean a database variable instead. Apologies if you find this state of affairs confusing, but it's sanctified by common usage.

[5] Of course, tuple *t* as such denotes just a single proposition, but the proposition in question is effectively a conjunction of conjunctions of finer grained propositions (as it were), one such "finer grained proposition" for each tuple in each relation in the current value of *D*.

Definition (fully connected): Let *DB* be a set of relvars, and let *C* be the logical AND of all integrity constraints that mention any relvar in *DB*. Assume without loss of generality that *C* is in conjunctive normal form.[6] Then:

- Let *A* and *B* be distinct relvars in *DB*. Then *A* and *B* are logically connected if and only if there exist relvars *R1, R2, ..., Rn* in *DB* ($n > 0$, *A* and *R1* not necessarily distinct, *Rn* and *B* not necessarily distinct) such that there's at least one conjunct in *C* that mentions both *A* and *R1*, at least one that mentions both *R1* and *R2*, ..., and at least one that mentions both *Rn* and *B*.

- *DB* is fully connected if and only if every relvar in *DB* is logically connected to every other.

It should be clear that if *DB* isn't fully connected in the foregoing sense, then the relvars it contains can be partitioned into two or more disjoint sets, each of which *is* fully connected in that same sense.

WHAT'S THE MOST IMPORTANT THING ABOUT A DATABASE?

I once asked someone I know very well—someone with no background in computers at all, who understands of a database only that it's something you keep information in, information you presumably therefore want to retrieve again at some later time—what she thought was the most important thing about a database. She thought for a moment and then said: "Well, I suppose it's making sure the information in there is correct." *Yes!* I couldn't have said it better myself. In other words, integrity constraints (constraints for short) are *absolutely fundamental*—and yet they seem to be widely underappreciated, if not completely misunderstood, in the database community at large.[7] As we all know, the emphasis, at least in the commercial environment, seems always to be on

---

[6] Any given logical expression is logically equivalent to one that's in conjunctive normal form (CNF), where a logical expression is in CNF if and only if it's of the form (*C1*) AND (*C2*) AND ... AND (*Cm*) and none of the conjuncts (*C1*), (*C2*), ..., (*Cm*) involves any ANDs. *Note:* The parentheses enclosing the subexpressions *C1, C2, ..., Cm* might not be needed in practice.

[7] Note the assumption here that enforcing integrity constraints is what's needed in order to "make sure the information is correct"! I'll be examining that assumption more carefully in a little while.

performance, performance, performance; other objectives, such as ease of use, data independence, and in particular data integrity, all seem to be sacrificed to, or at best take a back seat to, this overriding goal. But what's the point of a system running very fast if you can't be sure the information you're getting from it is correct? Frankly, I don't care how fast the system runs if I don't feel I can trust it to give me the right answers to my queries.

I'd like to take a moment to offer evidence in support of my contention that the database community in general seems not to have much understanding or appreciation of the fundamental nature and importance of integrity and integrity constraints.[8] A quick and admittedly not very scientific survey of a whole shelf load of database textbooks—37 in all, to be exact, including essentially all of the best known ones[9]—revealed the following:

- Only one book had an entire chapter devoted to the topic of integrity (and even there I had severe reservations about the treatment).

  Note: At first glance it looked as if there were three other books that had a whole chapter on the subject too, but closer examination quickly revealed that one was using the term to refer to normalization (?), while the other two were using it to refer not to integrity at all in its usual sense but rather to locking and concurrency control issues. *Caveat lector.*

- Most of the books I examined didn't even mention integrity in a chapter title at all, and those that did tended to bundle it with other topics in what seems to me a very haphazard fashion ("Integrity, Views, Security, and Catalogs" was a typical example).

- I couldn't find a *good* explanation or definition of the concept, let alone the kind of emphasis I think the concept deserves, in any of the books at all.

Note: In addition to all of these complaints on my part, I simply can't resist mentioning one particular book, on SQL specifically, which had a chapter called "Constraints, Assertions, and Referential Integrity." What would you think of a book on biology that had a chapter called "Birds, Feathered Bipeds, and Sparrows"? The parallel is exact. (Though in fairness I should add that SQL

---

[8] The discussion that follows is basically a repeat of material from Chapter 4, "Constraints and Predicates," from the book *Logic and Relational Theory: Thoughts and Essays on Database Matters* (Technics Publications, 2020).

[9] It wouldn't have been appropriate to include any of my own books in this survey, of course, and I didn't.

itself is partly to blame here, inasmuch as it uses the keyword CONSTRAINT in connection with some constraints and the keyword ASSERTION in connection with others. While most constraints can be expressed using either the CONSTRAINT style or the ASSERTION style, some are required to use the CONSTRAINT style and some the ASSERTION style. I have no idea why this is.)

So why exactly do I think constraints are so important? Well, of course, it all comes down to that business of making sure the information in the database is correct. Now, it's certainly true that if some constraint is violated, then the database is incorrect, in the sense that it—more precisely, its current value—can't possibly reflect the true state of affairs in the real world.[10] Sadly, however, the database can still be incorrect, even if all constraints are satisfied (and the goal of correctness is thus unachievable, at least at the 100% level). The fact is, the information in the database all derives ultimately from what some user asserts to be true (which the user does, in effect, by requesting the DBMS to perform some update operation). And the DBMS can't possibly know in general whether what the user asserts to be true actually is true! For example, suppose the user asserts (by requesting some update to be done) that there's a supplier S6 named Lopez with status 30 and city Madrid. Clearly, there's no way the DBMS can know whether that assertion is true; all it can do is check to make sure it doesn't cause any integrity constraint to be violated.[11] Assuming it doesn't, the DBMS will accept the assertion, will perform the requested update, *and will treat what the user said as true from that point forward* (that is, until the user tells the DBMS, by requesting another update, that it isn't true any more). In other words:

The DBMS can't enforce truth, only consistency.

Sadly, truth and consistency aren't the same thing. To be specific, if the database satisfies all constraints, then it's consistent by definition—that's what "consistent" means, in the database context—and if it's inconsistent, then it

---

[10] Of course, I'm assuming here that the integrity constraints themselves are correct, in the sense that they faithfully reflect some applicable "business rule" from the real world. See any of my books *SQL and Relational Theory: How to Write Accurate SQL Code* (3rd edition, O'Reilly, 2015); *Database Design and Relational Theory: Normal Forms and All That Jazz* (2nd edition, Apress, 2019); or especially *WHAT Not HOW: The Business Rules Approach to Application Development* (Addison-Wesley, 2000), for further discussion of business rules in general.

[11] Even if the assertion does violate some constraint, by the way, it doesn't follow that it must be false—there might already be something wrong somewhere else in the database.

violates at least one constraint. To say it again, however, the database can be consistent without being correct. Or to put it another way, *correct* implies *consistent* (but not the other way around), and *inconsistent* implies *incorrect* (but not the other way around)—where, to repeat, to say the database is correct is to say it faithfully reflects the true state of affairs in the real world.

WHEN SHOULD INTEGRITY CONSTRAINTS BE CHECKED?

Answer: Immediately! That is, constraints must be satisfied—meaning they must evaluate to TRUE, given the values currently appearing in the database—*at statement boundaries* (or, very informally, "at semicolons"); in other words, they must be checked at the end of any statement that might cause them to be violated. If any such check fails, changes to the database, if any, caused by the offending statement must be undone and an exception raised.

Now, the alternative to immediate checking is *deferred* checking, meaning the checks aren't done until the end of the pertinent transaction ("commit time"). Deferred checking is prescribed by the SQL standard—at least for some constraints, though not all—and is therefore supported by commercial SQL products as well. But it's logically incorrect. Why? Because, as I've shown elsewhere, we can *never* tolerate any inconsistencies in the database, not even within the bounds of a single transaction.[12] That is, while it might be true, thanks to the isolation property of transactions (which I'll be discussing in more detail in the section "The ACID Properties" below), that no more than one transaction ever sees any particular inconsistency, the fact remains that that particular transaction does see the inconsistency and can therefore produce wrong answers.

Now, I think this first argument is strong enough to stand on its own, but for completeness I'll give the other arguments as well. Second, then, I don't agree that any given inconsistency can be seen by only one transaction, anyway; that is, I don't really believe in the so called "isolation" property of transactions. Part of the problem here is that the word *isolation* doesn't mean quite the same in the world of transactions as it does in ordinary English. In particular, it doesn't mean that transactions can't communicate with one another. For if transaction *A* produces some result, in the database or elsewhere, that's subsequently seen by

---

[12] See in particular my book *SQL and Relational Theory: How to Write Accurate SQL Code*, 3rd edition (O'Reilly, 2015). *Note:* As we saw in Chapter 2, the fact that all integrity checking must be immediate is actually a logical consequence of **The Golden Rule**, which (to repeat from that chapter) can be stated thus: *No update operation must ever cause any database to acquire a value that makes its total database constraint evaluate to FALSE.*

transaction *B*, then *A* and *B* have certainly communicated, and so they aren't truly isolated from each other (and this remark applies regardless of whether *A* and *B* run concurrently or otherwise). In particular, therefore, if (a) *A* sees an inconsistent state of the database and as a consequence produces an incorrect result, and (b) that result is then seen by *B*, then (c) the inconsistency seen by *A* has effectively been propagated to *B*. In other words, it can't be guaranteed that a given inconsistency, if permitted, will be seen by just one transaction, anyway. *Note:* Similar remarks apply if some transaction (a) sees an inconsistency and as a consequence assigns an incorrect value to some local variable *V* and then (b) transmits the value of that variable *V* to some outside user (since local variables aren't, and can't possibly be, subject to the jurisdiction of the transaction management subsystem).

Third, we surely don't want every program (or other "code unit") to have to deal with the possibility that the database might be inconsistent when it's invoked. There's a severe loss of orthogonality if some piece of code that assumes consistency can't be used safely when constraint checking is deferred. In other words, we should be able to specify and write code units independently of whether they're to be executed as a transaction as such or just as one part of a transaction.

Fourth, there's a principle, *The Principle of Interchangeability*, that implies that the very same business rule in the real world might map to a single relvar constraint with one design for the database and a multirelvar constraint with another. (A single relvar constraint is a constraint that mentions just one relvar; a multirelvar constraint is one that mentions two or more.) Let me elaborate. First, the principle in question was defined in Chapter 2 as follows:

> **Definition (*The Principle of Interchangeability of Base Tables and Views*):** There should be no arbitrary and unnecessary distinctions between base tables and views; i.e., views should "look and feel" just like base tables so far as users are concerned.

By way of example, consider the suppliers-and-parts database once again. Suppose we define two virtual relvars, or views, of base relvar S from that database as follows (LS = London suppliers, NLS = non London suppliers):

```
VAR LS   VIRTUAL ( S WHERE CITY = 'London' ) ;
VAR NLS  VIRTUAL ( S WHERE CITY ≠ 'London' ) ;
```

These views are subject to the constraint that no supplier number appears in both. However, there's no need to state that constraint explicitly, because it's implied by the fact that every supplier has exactly one city—i.e., the functional dependency {SNO} → {CITY} holds in base relvar S—together with the fact that any given city is necessarily either London or not London. But suppose we were to design the database differently; suppose we made LS and NLS base relvars and then defined their union as a view called S. Then the constraint *would* have to be stated explicitly, perhaps as follows:

```
CONSTRAINT ...
    IS_EMPTY ( LS { SNO } JOIN NLS { SNO } ) ;
```

Now what was previously a single relvar constraint on base relvar S ("supplier numbers are unique") has become a multirelvar constraint instead.[13] Thus, if we agree (as most writers, and indeed most systems, certainly do) that single relvar constraints must be checked immediately, we must surely agree that multirelvar constraints must be checked immediately as well (because, logically, there's no real difference between the two, as the example demonstrates).

Fifth and last, there's an important optimization technique known as *semantic* optimization. By way of example, consider the following expression: (SP JOIN S){PNO}. Now, the join here is based on the correspondence between a foreign key in a referencing relvar (viz., relvar SP) and the target key in the referenced relvar (viz., relvar S). As a consequence, every SP tuple does join to some S tuple, and every SP tuple thus does contribute a part number to the projection that's the overall result. So there's no need to do the join!—the expression can be simplified to just SP{PNO}. Note carefully, however, that this transformation is valid *only* because of the semantics of the situation; with join in general, each operand will contain some tuples that have no counterpart in the other and so don't contribute to the overall result, and transformations such as the one just mentioned therefore won't be valid. But in the case at hand, every SP tuple necessarily does have a counterpart in S, because of the integrity constraint—actually a foreign key constraint—that says that every shipment must have a supplier, and so the transformation is valid after all. And a transformation that's valid only because a certain integrity constraint is in effect is called a

---

[13] Well, it could still be defined as a single relvar constraint with the revised design, but that single relvar constraint would be a single relvar constraint on a *view* (viz., view S), and that view in turn involves two distinct base relvars.

semantic transformation, and the resulting optimization is called a semantic optimization.

Now, in principle, any constraint whatsoever can be used in semantic optimization—we aren't limited to foreign key constraints as in the example. For example, suppose the suppliers-and-parts database is subject to the constraint "All red parts must be stored in London" (which is satisfied by the sample value shown in Fig. 11.1, please observe), and consider the query:

> *Get suppliers who supply only red parts and are located in the same city as at least one of the parts they supply.*

This is a fairly complex query! Thanks to the integrity constraint, however, we see it can be transformed—by the optimizer, I mean, not by the user[14]—into this much simpler one:

> *Get London suppliers who supply only red parts.*

We could easily be talking about several orders of magnitude improvement in performance here. And so, while commercial products do comparatively little in the way of semantic optimization at the time of writing (as far as I know), I certainly expect them to do more in the future, because the potential payoff is so dramatic.

To get back to the main thread of the discussion, I now observe that if a given constraint is to be usable in semantic optimization, then that constraint must be satisfied at all times (or rather, and more precisely, at statement boundaries), not just at transaction boundaries. Why? Because, as we've just seen, semantic optimization means using constraints to simplify queries in order to improve performance. Clearly, then, if some constraint is violated at some time, then any simplification based on that constraint won't be valid at that time, and query results based on that simplification will be wrong at that time (in general).[15]

---

[14] Though the transformation *could* (and perhaps should) be done by the user, of course, if the optimizer isn't smart enough to do it.

[15] Alternatively, we could adopt the weaker position that "deferred constraints" (meaning constraints for which the checking is deferred until commit time) can't be used in semantic optimization—but I think such a position would effectively just mean we've shot ourselves in the foot, that's all.

But Doesn't Some Integrity Checking Have to Be Deferred?

Note: This subsection is based in part on material from Chapter 2, Appendix A.

The foregoing arguments notwithstanding, conventional wisdom is that multirelvar constraint checking, at least, does have to be deferred, typically to commit time. By way of example, suppose the suppliers-and-parts database is subject to the following constraint:

```
CONSTRAINT ...
     COUNT ( ( S WHERE SNO = 'S1' ) { CITY }
              UNION
            ( P WHERE PNO = 'P1' ) { CITY } ) < 2 ;
```

This constraint says that supplier S1 and part P1 must never be in different cities. To elaborate: If relvars S and P contain tuples for supplier S1 and part P1, respectively, then those tuples must contain the same CITY value (if they didn't, the COUNT invocation would return the value two); however, it's legal for relvar S to contain no tuple for S1, or relvar P to contain no tuple for P1, or both (in which case the COUNT invocation will return either one or zero). Given this constraint, then, together with our usual sample values, each of the following SQL UPDATEs will fail under immediate checking:

```
UPDATE S
SET    CITY = 'Paris'
WHERE  SNO = 'S1' ;

UPDATE P
SET    CITY = 'Paris'
WHERE  PNO = 'P1' ;
```

Note: I show these UPDATEs in SQL rather than **Tutorial D** precisely because integrity checking *is* immediate in **Tutorial D** and the conventional solution to the problem therefore doesn't work in **Tutorial D** (nor is it needed, of course). What is that conventional solution? *Answer:* We arrange for integrity checking to be deferred to commit time,[16] and we make sure the two UPDATEs are part of the same transaction, as in this SQL code:

---

[16] For details of how that deferring is specified (and what happens if it is), see Chapter 2.

```
START TRANSACTION ;
UPDATE S SET CITY = 'Paris' WHERE SNO = 'S1' ;
UPDATE P SET CITY = 'Paris' WHERE PNO = 'P1' ;
COMMIT ;
```

In this conventional solution, the constraint is checked at the end of the transaction, and the database is inconsistent between the two UPDATEs. In particular, if we assume our usual sample values, then if the transaction were to ask the question "Are supplier S1 and part P1 in different cities?" between the two UPDATEs, it would get the answer *yes*; in other words, it would see the constraint being violated.

Multiple Assignment

A better solution to the foregoing problem is to support a *multiple* form of assignment, which allows any number of individual assignments to be performed "simultaneously," as it were. For example (switching back now to **Tutorial D**):

```
UPDATE S WHERE SNO = 'S1' : { CITY := 'Paris' } ,
UPDATE P WHERE PNO = 'P1' : { CITY := 'Paris' } ;
```

Explanation: First, note the comma separator, which means the two UPDATEs are part of the same overall statement. Second, UPDATE is really shorthand for a certain assignment, of course, and the foregoing "double UPDATE" is thus just shorthand for a double assignment of the following form:

```
S := ... , P := ... ;
```

This double assignment assigns one value to relvar S and another to relvar P, all as part of the same overall (and atomic, i.e., all or nothing) operation. In general, the semantics of multiple assignment are as follows:[17]

- First, all of the source expressions on the right sides of the individual assignments are evaluated.

- Second, those individual assignments (to the variables on the left sides) are executed.

---

[17] The definition that follows requires a slight refinement in the case where two or more of the individual assignments involve the same target variable, but that refinement needn't concern us here.

■   Third, all pertinent integrity constraints are checked.

Observe that, precisely because all of the source expressions are evaluated before any of the individual assignments are executed, none of those individual assignments can depend on the result of any other (and so the sequence in which they're executed is irrelevant; in fact, you can think of them as being executed in parallel, or "simultaneously"). Moreover, since multiple assignment is defined to be a semantically atomic operation, no integrity checking is performed "in the middle of" any such assignment; indeed, this fact is the major reason for supporting the operation in the first place. In the example, therefore, the double assignment succeeds where the two separate single assignments failed. Note in particular that there's now no way for the transaction to see an inconsistent state of the database between the two UPDATEs, because the notion of "between the two UPDATEs" now has no meaning. Note further that there's now no need for deferred checking at all.

As an aside, I observe that SQL has had some support for multiple assignment for many years. First of all, referential actions such as CASCADE imply, in effect, that a single DELETE or UPDATE statement can cause several base tables to be updated "simultaneously," as part of a single operation. Second, the ability to update (e.g.) certain join views implies the same thing. Third, FETCH INTO and SELECT INTO are both multiple assignment operations, of a kind. Fourth, SQL explicitly supports a multiple assignment form of the SET statement (indeed, that's exactly what SQL's "row assignment" is). And so on ... However, the one kind of multiple assignment that SQL doesn't currently support is an explicit "simultaneous" assignment to several different *tables*[18]—which is precisely the case illustrated by the foregoing example, and precisely what we need in order to avoid having to do deferred integrity checking.

One last point: Please understand that support for multiple assignment doesn't mean we can discard support for transactions. Transactions are still necessary for recovery and concurrency purposes, if nothing else. All I'm saying is that transactions aren't the "unit of integrity" they're usually supposed to be.

---

[18] I'm told, however, that this functionality might be provided in some future version of the standard.

THE ACID PROPERTIES

ACID is a well known acronym, standing for *atomicity – correctness – isolation – durability*, all of which are classically understood to be properties that transactions are supposed to possess. Just to review briefly:

- *Atomicity* means the given transaction is all or nothing—either it executes in its entirety or it's made as if it never executed at all.

- *Correctness* (usually called *consistency* in the literature) means the given transaction transforms a consistent state of the database into another such state, without necessarily preserving consistency at all intermediate points.

- *Isolation* means the given transaction's updates are concealed from all other transactions, until such time as the given transaction commits. (Another way of saying the same thing is that, for any two distinct transactions *A* and *B*, *A* might see *B*'s updates after *B* has committed or *B* might see *A*'s updates after *A* has committed, but not both.)

- *Durability* means that once the given transaction commits, its updates survive in the database, even if there's a subsequent system crash.

So ACID is a nice acronym—but do the concepts it represents really stand up to close examination? In this section, I present evidence to suggest that the answer to this question is, in general, *no*. However, it suits my purposes better to discuss those concepts in the order C – I – D – A.

Correctness

As I've already said, the literature usually refers to the "C" property as *consistency* rather than correctness. But *consistent* in this context merely means "satisfying all declared integrity constraints"—and if constraints are always checked immediately, the database is *always* consistent by definition, and transactions therefore *always* transform a consistent state of the database into another such state a fortiori. But consistency alone is not enough; what we really want is *correctness*, not mere consistency. By way of example, consider Fig. 11.2, which shows pseudocode for a transaction whose purpose is to transfer $100 from account 123 to account 456. As you can see, what's presumably intended to be a single atomic operation—"transfer $100 from one account to another"—in fact involves two separate updates on the database.[19] Moreover, the database is in an incorrect state between those two updates, in the sense that it doesn't reflect a valid state of affairs in the real world (clearly, a transfer from one account to another shouldn't affect the total number of dollars in the accounts concerned, but in the example the sum of $100 temporarily goes missing, as it were, between the two updates).

```
START TRANSACTION ;
UPDATE ACC 123 : { BALANCE := BALANCE - $100 } ;
   IF any error occurred THEN GO TO UNDO ; END IF ;
UPDATE ACC 456 : { BALANCE := BALANCE + $100 } ;
   IF any error occurred THEN GO TO UNDO ; END IF ;
COMMIT ;                          /* transfer succeeded */
GO TO FINISH ;
UNDO :
   ROLLBACK ;                     /* transfer failed    */
FINISH :
   RETURN ;
```

Fig. 11.2: A sample transaction (pseudocode)

In the example, then, we want the total number of dollars in accounts 123 and 456 taken together not to change. However, it would be unreasonable to declare an integrity constraint to that effect—why, exactly?—and so we can't expect the DBMS to enforce the requirement. Sadly, therefore, all we can do—and all the DBMS does do—is simply *assume* that transactions are correct, in the sense that they faithfully reflect just those real world operations they're supposed to. More precisely, we assume that if some arbitrary transaction transforms the database from some arbitrary state *D1* to some other state *D2*, and if *D1* is correct, then *D2* is correct as well. However, to say it again, this desirable property *can't be enforced by the DBMS* ("the DBMS can't enforce truth, only consistency," as I put it earlier).

Despite everything I've been saying, I now observe that, typically, the database world simply assumes that correctness and consistency are the same thing! For example, the book *Transaction Processing: Concepts and Techniques*, by Jim Gray and Andreas Reuter (Morgan Kaufmann, 1993)—generally regarded as the definitive work in this field—gives the following definitions:

---

[19] The example deliberately uses two separate UPDATE statements instead of making use of **Tutorial D**'s multiple assignment feature in order to make its point.

Consistent. Correct.

Consistency. A transaction is a correct transformation of the state. The actions taken as a group do not violate any of the integrity constraints associated with the state. This requires that the transaction be a correct program.

To say it again, however, if constraints are always checked immediately, the database is always consistent—not necessarily correct—and transactions therefore always transform a consistent state of the database into another consistent state a fortiori. So if the C in ACID stands for consistency, then the property is trivial,[20] and if it stands for correctness, then it's unenforceable. Either way, therefore, the property is essentially meaningless, at least from a formal standpoint. As already indicated, my own preference would be to say that the C stands for correctness; then we can go on to regard "the correctness property" not really as a property as such, but rather just as a desideratum.

Isolation

I turn now to the isolation property. As I've already indicated (in the section "When Should Integrity Constraints Be Checked?"), in my opinion this property too is somewhat suspect. First of all, the fact is that, as I've already explained, transactions simply aren't truly isolated from one another, even if they all operate at the maximum isolation level. Typically, however, they don't all operate at that maximum level anyway. Let me explain.

In essence, the idea behind isolation levels is this: The level of isolation that applies to a given transaction represents the amount of interference the transaction in question is prepared to tolerate on the part of concurrent transactions. At least five different levels can be defined,[21] of which the SQL standard supports four. Generally speaking, the higher the level, the less the interference and the lower the concurrency; the lower the level, the more the interference and the higher the concurrency.

---

[20] As a matter of fact, it would still be trivial even if constraints weren't checked immediately—the transaction would still be rolled back, and thus in effect never have executed, if it violated any constraint. In other words, it would still be the case that transactions have a lasting effect on the database only if they don't violate any constraints.

[21] See my book *An Introduction to Database Systems: Volume II* (Addison-Wesley, 1983).

Now, if correctness is to be guaranteed, the only amount of interference that can possibly be tolerated is obviously none at all.[22] To spell the point out: If transaction *A* permits interference (at any level), then it's *always* possible to define some other transaction *B* that, running concurrently with *A*, can cause *A* to produce an incorrect result. In my opinion, therefore, the isolation level should always be the maximum possible (which does effectively equate to "no interference at all"). Unfortunately, however, SQL products and the SQL standard both support various levels lower than the maximum—presumably on the grounds that insisting on complete isolation can have an undesirable effect on throughput, though I'm not aware that any such claim has ever been conclusively proved.

Note: The paper that introduced the concept[23] actually referred to levels of isolation as *degrees of consistency*!—not the happiest of names, in my opinion. Data is surely either consistent or it isn't. The notion that there might be "degrees" of consistency thus sounds like it might be subject to some dispute ... In fact, it seems to me (though I freely admit I'm speculating here) that what happened was that the theory behind "degrees of consistency" was developed before we had a clear notion of exactly what "consistency" meant or ought to mean, or—perhaps more crucially—of why data integrity was so fundamentally important.

Be that as it may, it should be clear that, like the correctness property, the isolation property of transactions is really much more of a desideratum than it is an ironclad guarantee. What's more, such would be the case even without the isolation level concept! Isolation levels lower than the maximum just make an already bad situation worse.

Durability

I turn now to the durability property. This property is reasonable, thanks to the system's recovery mechanism, *so long as there's no transaction nesting*—which is indeed typically the case, at least in SQL systems today. But suppose transaction nesting is supported. To be specific, suppose transaction *B* is nested inside transaction *A*, and the following sequence of events occurs:

---

[22] Note carefully that this sentence says *if*, not *if and only if*. That is, it's obvious that "no interference at all" is necessary in order to guarantee correctness, but it's equally obvious that it's not sufficient.

[23] J. N. Gray, R. A. Lorie, G. R. Putzolu, and I. L. Traiger: "Granularity of Locks and Degrees of Consistency in a Shared Data Base," in G. M. Nijssen (ed.), *Proc. IFIP TC-2 Working Conf. on Modelling in Data Base Management Systems* (Elsevier Science, 1976).

```
START TRANSACTION /* transaction A */ ;
   ...
   START TRANSACTION /* transaction B */ ;
      ...
   ... transaction B updates database D ;
      ...
   COMMIT /* transaction B */ ;
   ...
ROLLBACK /* transaction A */ ;
```

If *A*'s ROLLBACK is honored, then *B* is effectively rolled back too (because *B* is really part of *A*), and *B*'s effects on the database are thus not "durable"; in fact, *A*'s ROLLBACK causes database *D* to be restored to its pre *A* value.[24] In other words, the durability property can no longer be guaranteed, at least not for a transaction like *B* in the example that's nested inside some other transaction.

Now, you might object that my concerns in this connection are purely academic, given that (as I've said) systems today typically don't support the ability to nest transactions in the manner suggested. But many writers have argued that such nesting should be supported; indeed, the very first paper on what later evolved into the discipline of transaction management—viz., "Data Processing Spheres of Control," by C. T. Davies, Jr. (*IBM Systems Journal 17*, No. 2, 1978)—did so. So too does the paper "Concepts for Transaction Recovery in Nested Transactions," by Theo Härder and Kurt Rothermel (Proc. 1987 ACM SIGMOD International Conference on Management of Data (May 1987), which gives at least three reasons for wanting such support (viz., intratransaction parallelism, intratransaction recovery control, and system modularity). And as the example indicates, in a system with such support, COMMIT by an inner transaction will commit that transaction's updates, but only to the next outer level. (In effect, the outer transaction has veto power over the inner transaction's COMMIT—if the outer transaction does a rollback, the inner transaction is rolled back too.) In the example, *B*'s COMMIT is a COMMIT to *A* only, not to the outside world, and indeed that COMMIT is subsequently revoked (i.e., rolled back) by *A*.

As an aside, I note that nested transactions can be thought of as a generalization of savepoints (which *are* supported today, at least in some

---

[24] More precisely, *A*'s ROLLBACK causes that part of database *D* that has been updated by *A* to be restored to its pre *A* value. Of course, if other parts of *D* have been updated by separate and independent (but concurrent) transactions, *A*'s ROLLBACK will have no effect on them.

systems). Savepoints allow a transaction to be structured as a linear *sequence* of actions that are executed serially (one at a time), and rollback can occur at any time to the start of any earlier action in the sequence. Nesting, by contrast, allows a transaction to be structured, recursively, as a *hierarchy* of actions that are executed concurrently. In other words, transaction nesting implies that:

- START TRANSACTION is extended to support "subtransactions" (i.e., if START TRANSACTION is issued when a transaction is already running, it starts a *child* transaction).

- COMMIT does "commit" but only within the *parent scope* (if this transaction is a child).

- ROLLBACK undoes work, but only back to the start of the pertinent transaction (including child, grandchild, etc., transactions but not including the parent transaction, if any).

From all of the above it should be clear that the durability property of transactions does apply, but only at the outermost level (in other words, only to transactions not nested inside any other transaction). In other words, the durability property too is not an absolute, in general.

Atomicity

Finally I turn to the atomicity property. Like the durability property, this property is guaranteed by the system's recovery mechanism (even with nested transactions). My objections here are a little different. To be specific, I simply observe that if the system supported multiple assignment properly (as of course I believe it should), then there wouldn't be any need for transactions as such to have the atomicity property; rather, it would be sufficient for statements to do so (and then transactions would do so too, a fortiori).

CONCLUDING REMARKS

Transactions are frequently described in the literature as "a unit of work," and/or "a unit of recovery," and/or "a unit of concurrency," and/or "a unit of integrity."

To what extent are these descriptions justified, given everything discussed in this chapter prior to this point? Well, let's see:

- *Are transactions a unit of work?* Yes, but only if multiple assignment isn't supported; otherwise the multiple assignment statement might more aptly be so described.

- *Are they a unit of recovery?* Yes, but only if multiple assignment isn't supported; otherwise there's no reason why the multiple assignment statement couldn't be that unit.

- *Are they a unit of concurrency?* Same answer.

- *Are they a unit of integrity?* Yes, but only if "all constraint checking immediate" isn't supported; otherwise the assignment statement (multiple or otherwise) is that unit.

Overall, then, I conclude that the transaction concept is important more from a pragmatic (and perhaps historical) point of view than it is from a theoretical one. Please understand that this conclusion on my part isn't meant to be disparaging! As noted in the introduction to this chapter, I have nothing but respect for the many elegant and useful results obtained from well over 50 years of transaction management research. I'm merely observing that now we have a better understanding of some of the assumptions on which that research was based: a better understanding of the crucial role of integrity constraints in particular, plus a recognition of the need to support multiple assignment as a primitive operator. Indeed, it would be surprising if a change in assumptions did not lead to a change in conclusions.

APPENDIX A: DAVID McGOVERAN'S CRITICISMS

The material of this chapter first saw the light of day—not in as much detail, however—as Section 16.10 of my book *An Introduction to Database Systems* (8th edition, Addison-Wesley, 2004). Shortly after that book was published my friend and colleague David McGoveran sent me a draft of an article he planned to publish in the February 2004 issue of the magazine *Intelligent Enterprise*. That draft was titled "On ACID"—I believe the published version was called

"Getting Back on ACID"—and it consisted of a detailed and highly critical review of the aforesaid Section 16.10. The following text is taken from the abstract for David's article, which can be found (the abstract, that is) on the website *www.alternativetech.com*:

> In C. J. Date's *An Introduction to Database Systems* (8th edition), Date wrote a chapter titled "Dropping ACID" which recommended dropping the ACID requirements for transactions in a true relational database.[25] This article analyzes Date's arguments and concludes that the apparent recommendations of the chapter cannot and should not be followed.

Here are some extracts from David's draft (I give them in the form of a bullet list for clarity, though that's not how they appear in that draft):

- [*Introductory remarks:*] Now, the very foundations of transaction management are threatened with abandonment ... If Date is correct, then we may as well replace all the transaction managers with application controlled rollback mechanisms ... To the extent that one can treat the ACID properties and database systems idealistically, I agree with Date's pronouncement[s]. But since I do not make that mistake, I must respectfully disagree ... In my opinion, Date's attack on the ACID properties is full of logical error[s].

- [*Regarding consistency:*] Date mistakenly equates correctness with consistency ... The references he cites in equating consistency and correctness are clearly referring to computational completeness (which is enforceable despite Date's claims to the contrary). Date, however, seems to treat correctness as a synonym for faithfulness to reality ... and says consistency is trivial.

- [*Regarding isolation:*] Date claims that all integrity constraints should be checked immediately ... Date proposes relational operations be implemented with multiple assignment so there are no intermediate steps ... But reality intervenes and this hypothetical concept simply cannot be implemented ... "A transaction could write to a file that is read by another transaction." Nonsense! Either a resource manager has the isolation property or it does not. If it does, isolation applies to all I/O regarding state data! ... "Serialization protocols are unenforceable." False! ... "*The Principle of Interchangeability* means that the same constraint might be a relvar constraint in one design and ... a database constraint in another." This claim is merely word confusion ... Performing integrity checks earlier, even through some kind of multiple assignment, is an implementation specific *optimization!*

---

[25] It wasn't a chapter, it was one section of a chapter.

"[Semantic] optimization requires the database to be consistent at all times, not just at transaction boundaries." Actually, it requires merely that semantic optimization ... be performed at points of consistency ... [There] is no point at which an inconsistent state of the database is accessible for semantic optimization across transactions! ... Date argues that real world systems provide explicit mechanisms to violate isolation. This is a red herring and completely irrelevant.

■ [*Regarding durability:*] Date argues that transaction nesting destroys durability, and that it applies only to the outermost level ... [But] the inner transaction can only ... enforce durability within its scope—not globally ... Date seems to think of consistency as some kind of absolute truth ("correctness") rather than as a relative or "scoped" property.

■ [*Regarding atomicity:*] Date says that if the system supports multiple assignment ... then it is sufficient for atomicity to be a property of statements rather than transactions. However, reliance on multiple assignment is a red herring. No computer system implements arbitrarily complex statements ... as atomic operations. To do so would require that every possible multiple assignment be a primitive operation, a thoroughly unpractical idea.

■ [*From the conclusion:*] Date's arguments ... are vacuous ... I hope that Date will cancel the blank check he seems to give those who would prefer ad hoc approaches to transaction processing.

Gosh. Well ... as you can imagine, there were numerous things I would have liked to have said in response to all this, but (for reasons that aren't important now) I was forced to limit myself at the time to requesting that *Intelligent Enterprise* publish the following remarks following the subject article:

McGoveran—who, it's perhaps as well to state immediately, is a good friend of mine!—misrepresents my position. "If Date is correct, then we may as well replace all the transaction managers with application controlled rollback mechanisms." I didn't say this, and I don't believe it, and I find it extraordinary that anyone could think that what I wrote was suggesting any such thing. A more accurate representation of my position is as follows:

1. For a variety of reasons, we need support for an operation I call *multiple assignment*.

2.   If that operation were supported, then *statements* could (and logically should) replace transactions as the unit of recovery, concurrency, and integrity.[26]

I do not believe (nor have I ever believed) that "application level transaction management" is the right approach to the problem of transaction processing. Nor do I believe I have given a "blank check to those who would prefer ad hoc approaches" to that problem.

There are many points of detail in McGoveran's article that I would like to contest, but I will limit my attention here to just three:

■   McGoveran asserts that multiple assignment is a "hypothetical concept [that] simply cannot be implemented." I find this to be a very strong claim—especially in view of the fact that today's SQL products already implement multiple assignment to some degree, and the next version of the SQL standard [*or some future version, at any rate*] is likely to include greatly extended support for that operation.

■   "Date mistakenly equates consistency with correctness": I do nothing of the kind. *Au contraire*, I discuss the difference between the two at some length (see in particular pages 263-265 and 449 of my book [*i.e., An Introduction to Database Systems, 8th edition, Addison-Wesley, 2004*]).

■   "Serialization protocols are unenforceable": I never said this, and of course I know it isn't true.

For readers who are seriously interested in this subject, I respectfully request that you read my original text for yourself and form your own opinions (and draw your own conclusions), instead of accepting McGoveran's inaccurate characterizations of that text. Thank you.

Now, however, I'd like to take the opportunity to respond more thoroughly to some of the specific claims and criticisms in McGoveran's article. *Note:* Of course, McGoveran (or David, rather, as I'll refer to him throughout the remainder of this appendix) wasn't criticizing the present chapter as such, he was criticizing the earlier version that appeared as Section 16.10 of *An Introduction to Database Systems*, 8th edition. But there's no discrepancy between the two

---

[26] I do believe, strongly, that statements should be the unit of integrity. Whether they should also be the unit of recovery and the unit of concurrency is perhaps more open to debate. I don't see it as a big issue. (Footnote added in this rewritten form of my original remarks.)

versions on matters of substance—it's just that the present version gives a lot more by way of background, clarification, examples, and the like. That said, however, if a specific criticism applies to the earlier version and not to the new one, I'll indicate as much below.

- Date wrote a chapter titled "Dropping ACID" which recommended dropping the ACID requirements for transactions.

Well, I suppose that should teach me not to choose "clever" titles! I wasn't arguing that "the ACID requirements" as such should be dropped. What I was really doing was arguing as follows:

- *Atomicity:* It's my position that this property should be strengthened (not weakened, and certainly not dropped) to apply to statements instead of transactions.

- *Consistency / correctness:* It's my position that if the *C* stands for consistency, then it's trivial; if it stands for correctness, then it's merely an unenforceable desideratum.

- *Isolation:* It's my position that (a) this property should be strengthened (not weakened, and certainly not dropped), meaning that transactions should always operate at the maximum isolation level, but that (b) even if they do, true isolation, in the natural language sense of that word, is another unenforceable desideratum.

- *Durability:* It's my position that this property should be generalized (not weakened, and certainly not dropped) to allow for nested transactions.

What we might consider dropping, though, is the ACID acronym[27] ... Part of the problem, perhaps, is the acronym is so catchy and clever that it dulls the critical faculties. The brief summary above should serve to show why I believe we shouldn't regard the ACID properties is a single, monolithic, "take it or leave it" proposition.

---

[27] The source of that acronym (though not of the concepts the acronym represents, which date back to the early 1970s) is the paper "Principles of Transaction-Oriented Database Recovery," by Theo Härder and Andreas Reuter (*ACM Comp. Surv. 15,* No. 4, December 1983).

■   To the extent that one can treat the ACID properties and database systems idealistically, I agree with Date's pronouncement[s]. But since I do not make that mistake, I must respectfully disagree ... In my opinion, Date's attack on the ACID properties is full of logical error[s].

I find these remarks quite puzzling. David seems to be saying I'm right really, but wrong because we don't live in an ideal world. I don't see what living or not living in an ideal world has to do with the issue. At the same time he says my "attack" is full of logical errors, but I don't think he manages to demonstrate even one such on my part. And by the way, I never intended what I wrote, either then or now, to be taken as an "attack."

■   The references [Date] cites in equating consistency and correctness are clearly referring to computational completeness (which is enforceable despite Date's claims to the contrary). Date, however, seems to treat correctness as a synonym for faithfulness to reality ... and says consistency is trivial.

The references I cite don't have anything to do with computational completeness. Nor does the present chapter, and nor does the original text on which the present chapter is based. Nor have I ever claimed, in that original text or anywhere else, that computational completeness is unenforceable. Yes, I do take "correct" to mean "faithful to reality"; I draw a distinction, as some other writers do not, between "correct" and "consistent." And yes, consistency as I define the term is indeed trivial, as my original text and the present chapter both show. What's wrong with that?

■   Date proposes relational operations be implemented with multiple assignment so there are no intermediate steps ... But reality intervenes and this hypothetical concept simply cannot be implemented.

Well, I've already pointed out that SQL systems today already provide some support for "this hypothetical concept," so it can't be as hypothetical as all that. What's more, when Hugh Darwen and I first came up with the concept in the 1990s, we made a point of discussing it with Jim Gray (as our "go to guy" on transactions), and he gave it his blessing at the time. And what's more again, it's implemented in some of the prototype systems mentioned on the *Third Manifesto* website (*www.thethirdmanifesto.com*).

■   "A transaction could write to a file that is read by another transaction." Nonsense! Either a resource manager has the isolation property or it does not. If it does, isolation applies to all I/O regarding state data!

Here David is referring specifically to something I wrote in my original text in *An Introduction to Database Systems*:

> For example, if transaction A sees an inconsistent state of the database and so writes inconsistent data to some file F, and transaction B then reads that same information from file F, then A and B are not really isolated from each other (regardless of whether they run concurrently or otherwise).[28]

In the present chapter this text is replaced by the following:

> For if transaction A produces some result, in the database or elsewhere, that's subsequently seen by transaction B, then A and B have certainly communicated, and so they aren't truly isolated from each other (and this remark applies regardless of whether A and B run concurrently or otherwise). In particular, therefore, if (a) A sees an inconsistent state of the database and therefore produces an incorrect result, and (b) that result is then seen by B, then (c) the inconsistency seen by A has effectively been propagated to B.

Either way, however (i.e., whichever version of the text we consider), David's comment ("Nonsense!") simply misses the point. Note the remark in parentheses in my text, to the effect that A and B are in communication, and thus not totally isolated from each other, *regardless of whether they run concurrently*. The point is this: B could start after A has finished—but if it sees a result produced by A, then it's not "isolated" from A.

■   "*The Principle of Interchangeability* means that the same constraint might be a relvar constraint in one design and a database constraint in another." This claim is merely word confusion.

No, it isn't, it's 100 percent correct—though what I was referring to at the time as a relvar constraint I now prefer to call a *single* relvar constraint (for emphasis), and what I was referring to at the time as a database constraint I now prefer to call a *multirelvar* constraint.

---

[28] In fact the problem arises even if A doesn't see an inconsistent state of the database; it's still possible that A might write inconsistent data to some file that's subsequently read by B. (Footnote in the original.)

■ Performing integrity checks earlier, even through some kind of multiple assignment, is an implementation specific *optimization!*

No, it isn't, it's logically required—it's the *model*. (The model in *The Third Manifesto*, at any rate.)

■ "[Semantic] optimization requires the database to be consistent at all times, not just at transaction boundaries." Actually, it requires merely that semantic optimization ... be performed at points of consistency ... [There] is no point at which an inconsistent state of the database is accessible for semantic optimization across transactions!

Regarding "points of consistency," I note that David doesn't define the term, but I would say it's precisely part of my point that such "points of consistency" need to be statement boundaries. Regarding the final sentence in this quote, I wasn't talking about "semantic optimization across transactions"!—indeed, I find it hard to imagine what such a notion might consist of. Rather, I was talking about semantic optimization of relational expressions (which you might think of as "semantic optimization *within* transactions," I suppose, if you really want to).

■ Date argues that real world systems provide explicit mechanisms to violate isolation. This is a red herring and completely irrelevant.

I don't "argue" this point, I merely state it as a truism. Moreover, it's not a "red herring" and it's not "completely irrelevant"—at least not in the real world, which David seems to want to serve as a basis for his arguments (see his earlier remarks about agreeing with me "idealistically").

■ Date argues that transaction nesting destroys durability, and that it applies only to the outermost level ... [But] the inner transaction can only ... enforce durability within its scope—not globally ... Date seems to think of consistency as some kind of absolute truth ("correctness") rather than as a relative or "scoped" property.

Regarding the first two sentences here, I don't argue that transaction nesting "destroys" durability, I merely point out that such nesting requires a generalization of the durability notion—an observation that David seems to agree with (?). I can't make any sense of the third sentence.

■ Date says that if the system supports multiple assignment ... then it is sufficient for atomicity to be a property of statements rather than transactions. However, reliance on multiple assignment is a red herring. No computer system implements arbitrarily complex statements ... as atomic operations. To do so would require that every possible multiple assignment be a primitive operation, a thoroughly unpractical idea.

Yes, I do say that if the system supports multiple assignment, then it's sufficient for atomicity to be a property of statements rather than transactions. Reliance on multiple assignment is *not* a red herring! And it's not true, as I've already explained, that "no computer system implements arbitrarily complex [assignments] as atomic operations." And it's also not true, as I've also already explained, that the idea is "thoroughly unpractical." It's *implemented*.

■ Date's arguments are vacuous.

Well, please excuse me for thinking they're not vacuous in the least.

Chapter 12

Relational Trumpery

trump (n.) ... *an audible act of breaking wind*;
(v.i.) ... *[to] break wind audibly*
—Shorter Oxford English Dictionary

trumpery (n.) *showy and worthless stuff: rubbish: ritual foolery*
—Chambers Twentieth Century Dictionary
(which also says the word can be used as an adjective)

trumpery (adj.) *brummagem, cheap, flashy, grotty, meretricious,*
nasty, pinchbeck, rubbishy, shabby, shoddy, tawdry,
trashy, trifling, useless, valueless, worthless
—Chambers Twentieth Century Thesaurus
(which also gives as an antonym *first-rate*)

trump (n.) *an obstruction cast in one's way*;
(v.t.) *to deceive: to cast as an obstruction: to allege:*
to concoct and put forward unscrupulously
—Chambers Twentieth Century Dictionary

trumped-up (adj.) *concocted, contrived, cooked-up, fabricated,*
fake, faked, false, falsified, invented, made-up, phoney, spurious, untrue
—Chambers Twentieth Century Thesaurus
(which also gives as an antonym *genuine*)

Trumpery indeed ... This chapter consists of a collection of fairly appalling quotes from the database literature, with comments and analysis by myself. Here's the first one—it's the opening sentence of an article with the title "Object / Relational Grows Up," by W. Donald Frazer (*Data Base Programming & Design 11*, No. 1, January 1998), and in some ways it sets the tone for all of the others to come. It runs as follows:

Despite its many virtues, the relational data model is a poor fit for many types of data now common across the enterprise.

I'd like to offer the following parallel observation for readers to meditate on:

Despite its many virtues, the periodic table is a poor fit for many types of matter now common across the universe.

In my opinion, the two observations are just about equally sensible.

A few years ago I received the following request from a reader of one of my books:

I recently read an article by Jim Gray and Mark Compton titled "A Call to Arms" (*ACM Queue 3*, No. 3, April 2005). The authors seem to be quite critical of relational technology. Do you want to respond to any of their criticisms?

Yes, I most certainly do. Actually, I think the entire article merits a response, or detailed critique, much longer than it would be appropriate to include in a chapter such as this one; however, its conclusions and recommendations seem to be based on (among other things) a few explicitly stated, but mistaken, premises that I do think are worth addressing here. *Note:* Several of the premises in question derive from the all too common, but mistaken, assumption that relational technology and SQL technology are the same thing.

The bulleted quotes in what follows are all taken from the referenced article.

■ Traditional relational database constructs—always cumbersome at best—are now clearly at risk of collapsing altogether.

In my opinion, "traditional relational database constructs" are not now, nor were they ever, "cumbersome at best." First of all, I think the authors should define and defend their use of the word "cumbersome" in this context—with examples, please. Second, do they have a proposal for something to replace the relational model, something they can clearly prove is less "cumbersome"? If so, they need to tell us—in detail, please—just what it is, and demonstrate just how it's superior to, and in particular how it's less "cumbersome" than, the relational model. (Of course, if all they mean is that *today's SQL implementations* are cumbersome and in danger of imminent collapse, well, then they might have a point; but if so, then the point in question has nothing to do with "relational database constructs," and it isn't what they said.)

- Classic relational database architectures are slowly sagging to their knees.

According to Fred Brooks, in his classic book *The Mythical Man-Month* (20th anniversary edition, Addison-Wesley, 1995), the "architecture" of a system is "the complete and detailed specification of the user interface" to the system in question. For a relational database system, therefore, the architecture (at least at a certain level of abstraction) is clearly the relational model itself, and I would like to assure the authors that the relational model is very far from "sagging to its knees." Or do they perhaps think logic is "sagging to its knees"? Or mathematics?

Of course, if the authors want to argue that the "classic relational"[1] user interface isn't the relational model at all but is instead *the SQL language*, then I might agree it's sagging—but then I would also argue that (a) the SQL language isn't the relational model, and hence that (b) if SQL is sagging, then that fact has nothing to do with "relational database architectures." And if they want to argue that it's *today's SQL implementations* that are sagging, well, again they might have a point; but if so, the point in question has nothing to do with "relational database architectures," and it isn't what they said.

- Traditional relational databases [were] never ... designed to allow for the commingling of data and algorithms.

Stuff and nonsense! Well, perhaps I shouldn't be so short tempered and rude; but the fact is, this claim is just stupefyingly wrong. For consider:

1. Relations are defined over domains.

2. Domains are types.

---

[1] Or would-be relational, rather.

3. Values and variables of a given type can be operated upon solely by means of the operators defined in connection with that type.

4. The code that implements a given operator is, by definition, code that represents some algorithm.

5. Hence, data and algorithms are *and always were* "commingled" in the relational world. Q.E.D.

By the way, note the deprecated use of "databases" in the foregoing quote to mean (I think!) database management systems or DBMSs.

■   Data and procedures are being joined at long last ... The problem starts, of course, with Cobol, with its data division and procedure division.

The misrepresentations, misconceptions, and other errors in this extract are much too extensive and complicated to deal with adequately in a short response like this one. Suffice it to say that they have to do with (a) an apparent lack of recognition of the purpose of a database, (b) a mistaken perception of how to achieve data independence, and—if the authors are to be taken at their word—(c) the bizarre suggestion that, apparently, procedures can exist and operate without any data to operate on. PS: I love that *of course*, by the way (in the authors' sentence "The problem starts, of course," etc.).

■   Fields are objects (values or references); records are vectors of objects (fields); and tables are sequences of record objects. Databases ... are transforming into collections of tables.

Assuming the authors mean, by their use of the terms *fields*, *records*, and *tables*, what the relational model calls *attributes*, *tuples*, and *relations*, respectively, then I can assure them of the following:

1. "Fields" in the relational model are most certainly not "objects."

2. "Records" in the relational model are most certainly not "vectors" (not of "objects," and not of anything else, either).

3. "Tables" in the relational model are most certainly not "sequences" (not of "record objects," and not of anything else, either).

4. And databases in the relational model are most certainly not "transforming" into "collections of tables." Haven't the authors read Codd's papers?

But perhaps I should expand on these observations, instead of simply stating them baldly and claiming them as facts without offering any evidence to support such claims. All right, then, I will.

1. *"Fields" in the relational model are most certainly not "objects."*

    What the authors actually say is: "Fields are objects (values or references)." Now, there doesn't seem to be any consensus in the world of objects as to what exactly an object is; but most writings seem to suggest rather strongly that an object is basically just what in conventional programming languages would be called a *variable*.[2] And "fields" in the relational model most certainly aren't variables. More precisely (and switching now to accepted and conventional relational terminology):

    a. If r is a relation (i.e., a relation *value*) and A is an attribute of relation r and t is a tuple of relation r, then the value of attribute A within tuple t is just that, a value. It's certainly not a variable. Indeed, the suggestion that a value (viz., r) might somehow harbor a variable, nested inside itself as it were, is simply nonsense.

    b. If R is a relation *variable* (i.e., a relvar), then the value of R at any given time is some relation r. Since as we've just seen r can't possibly harbor a variable nested inside itself, it follows that R can't harbor a variable nested inside itself either. Indeed, the suggestion that a variable might somehow harbor another variable nested inside itself is also nonsense.
        Note: You might object here (pardon the pun) that I've argued previously—see Chapter 11—that (a) databases are variables and (b) databases contain relvars, which are also variables. So don't we

---

[2] Though the variable in question might be quite complicated; for example, a geometric program might involve a variable of type POLYGON. By the same token, a geometric database might involve relations with attributes of such a type. But this state of affairs still doesn't mean that "fields are objects."

have here an example of "variables containing variables"? Am I talking out of both sides of my mouth? No, I'm not. The fact is, relvars aren't really variables at all; rather, they're what elsewhere I've referred to as *pseudovariables*. Briefly, pseudovariables are just a syntactic shorthand that simplifies the task of formulating updates on a large, complicated variable (like a database) by making it possible to think of such updates as if they were directed at individual components of such a variable. But in the last analysis, that's all pseudovariables are—just shorthand. Highly convenient shorthand, I might add, but still just shorthand.

So much for "objects"; what about "references"? Well, by "references" the authors clearly mean object IDs, or in other words *pointers*—and (as is well known, and for very good reasons) the relational model doesn't allow pointers in relations in the database. (As an aside, I note that this talk of pointers lends weight to the claim—see above—that objects are really variables, because (a) pointer values are basically addresses and (b) values don't have addresses but variables do.)

Coming back to objects for a moment: It's possible that when the authors said "Fields are objects," what they might have meant is that relational attributes can have values of arbitrary complexity—in other words, that the type *T* of an attribute *A* might be arbitrarily complex. If that's what they meant, then I completely agree (see footnote 2). But it's not what they said.

2. *"Records" in the relational model are most certainly not "vectors" (not of "objects," and not of anything else, either).*

Given the context, I have to assume that what the authors mean by "records" is *tuples*; I also have to assume assume that what they mean by "vectors" is *one-dimensional arrays*. Well, there are at least two logical differences between tuples and such arrays (and I remind you that all logical differences are big differences[3]):

a. One-dimensional arrays have an ordering to their components, which tuples most certainly don't.

---

[3] This apothegm, which is due to Wittgenstein, is one of the guiding principles underlying both *The Third Manifesto* as such and everything to do with that *Manifesto*.

    b. The elements of an array (of any dimension) are all of the same type, which the components of a tuple don't have to be, and usually aren't.

3. *"Tables" in the relational model are most certainly not "sequences" (not of "record objects," and not of anything else, either).*

I'm not even going to try to guess exactly what "record objects" might be. But in any case there are at least two logical differences between "tables" (or relations, rather) and "sequences" (of "record objects" or anything else):

    a. Sequences have an ordering to their components (that's what "sequence" *means*!), which relations most certainly don't.

    b. Relations don't just contain tuples, they also have a *heading*, which sequences don't.

4. *And databases in the relational model are most certainly not "transforming" into "collections of tables." Haven't the authors read Codd's papers?*

I don't think I need to add anything to this one.

In conclusion, let me make it clear that I've always held Jim Gray in the highest regard, and I find it quite painful to see him attaching his name to a piece of writing as muddled and misleading as the subject article. It's particularly distressing to see him signing on to, and thereby helping to perpetuate, some of the same old confusions that have plagued the relational field ever since its inception.

The widespread lack of understanding of the relational model, among people who really ought to know better, continues to irk, dismay, and amaze me. Here's another example. This one is taken from a paper by Erik Meijer with the title "All Your Database Are Belong to Us," which appeared in *Communications of*

the ACM 55, No. 9 (September 2012).[4] The first two paragraphs of that paper read as follows:

> In the database world, the raw physical data model is at the center of the universe, and queries freely assume intimate details of the data representation (indexes, statistics, metadata). This closed world assumption and the resulting lack of abstraction have the pleasant effect of allowing the data to outlive the application. On the other hand, this makes it difficult to evolve the underlying model independently from the queries over the model.
>
> As the move to the cloud puts pressure on the closed world assumption of the database, exposing naked data and relying on declarative magic becomes a liability rather than an asset. In the cloud, the roles are reversed, and objects should hide their private data representation, exposing it only via well-defined behavioural interfaces.

And so on, and so on ... Well, David McGoveran and I wrote a joint letter in response to this nonsense, which was published, under the title "Not the Database World We Know," in *Communications of the ACM 55*, No. 12 (December 2012). I reproduce that letter verbatim below (except that I've broken up what were originally two very long opening paragraphs into bullet lists to improve readability).

> *Communications* readers have a right to expect accuracy. Sadly, accuracy isn't always what they get. The article "All Your Database ... ," by Erik Meijer (*CACM* 55, 9) contains so many inaccuracies, confusions, and errors regarding "the database world" that it's hard to criticize it coherently. The first paragraphs contain more egregious misstatements than most entire papers. For the record:
>
> ■ "The raw physical data model" is categorically not "at the center of the [relational database] universe."
>
> ■ Queries do not "assume intimate details of the data representation (indexes, statistics, metadata)."

---

[4] I deliberately omit here any explanation of the paper's absurd title. I do note, however, that (according to the paper in question) the author is, among other things, "part time professor of cloud programming at TUDelft [*i.e., Delft University of Technology, in the Netherlands*]." Well, don't you think that, given the nature of their job and the role they play in educating others, surely it's the responsibility of professors, perhaps even more than it is of the rest of us, to get their facts straight?

■ While database technology does rely on *The Closed World Assumption*, that assumption has nothing whatsoever to do with what the author apparently means when he uses that term.

■ "Exposing naked data and relying on declarative magic becomes a liability": Every phrase here relies on at least one counterfactual.

■ "Objects should hide their private data representation, exposing it only via well defined behavioral interfaces": But this is *exactly* what the relational model does!—except (unlike OO) it adopts an interface discipline that makes ad hoc query and the like possible.

■ "In the realm of [data] modelers, there is no notion of data abstraction": Astoundingly wrong.

■ "[Database technology necessarily involves] a computational model with a limited set of operations": False. Although the (very powerful, well defined, provably correct) *required* set of relational operations is small, the sky's the limit on derived relational operations or operations that define abstract data type / domain behavior.

The author's unfounded antipathy toward relational databases even dominates his application of CAP:[5]

■ "The problem with SQL databases …is the assumption that the data … meets a bunch of consistency constraints that is difficult to maintain in an open ["anything goes"?] distributed world." CAP does *not* eliminate this requirement.

■ "[The] hidden cost of forfeiting [system enforced] consistency…is the need [for the programmer] to know the system's invariants" [Eric Brewer, "CAP Twelve Years Later: How the 'Rules' Have Changed," *IEEE Computer 45*, No. 2, pp. 23-29]. Nor can programmers "… design their systems to be robust … to inconsistency." Once data inconsistency invades a computationally complete system, it isn't even, in general, detectable and all

---

[5] From Wikipedia: "The CAP theorem ... states that it is impossible for a distributed [database] to simultaneously provide more than two out of the following three guarantees: consistency (every read receives the most recent write or an error), availability (every request receives a ... response [,but] without the guarantee that it contains the most recent write), and partition tolerance (the system continues to operate despite an arbitrary number of messages being dropped or delayed by the network between nodes) ... Note that consistency as defined [here] is quite different from the consistency guaranteed in ACID database transactions." Well, I most certainly agree with the final sentence of this extract, regarding consistency! See Chapter 11.

bets are off! Consistency must be *enforced*, hence constraints. The author seems to equate detecting abnormal execution with enforcing logical data consistency. No wonder confusion abounds: CAP consistency is single copy consistency, a subset of what ACID databases provide, yet the Gilbert / Lynch CAP proof relies on linearizability, a more stringent requirement than the serializability ACID databases need or use.

And so on. Deconstructing the entire article properly would take more time than we care to devote, but the foregoing should suffice to demonstrate its fallaciousness. We hope the professor is not teaching these confusions, errors, and logical inconsistencies and fallacies.

It's hard to believe this article was peer reviewed. Indeed, it's truly distressing that the article does not demonstrate even minimal understanding of one of the most important contributions to computing: the relational model. We can only deplore *Communications'* role in promulgating that lack of understanding.

Meijer responded (in print) to our letter as follows:

The purpose of the article was not to criticize the relational model but to point out how building industrial strength systems using today's relational database systems requires leaving the ivory tower and dealing with a morass of ad hoc extensions to the clean mathematical basis of first-order predicate logic. Rather than depend on pure sets and relations, developers need to think in terms of (un)ordered multisets. For the sake of efficiency and lock contention avoidance, transactions allow for various isolation levels that clearly violate the ACID guarantees of Platonic transactions. The article also considered whether in the new world of the Cloud we should view as complementary computational models that fundamentally address loosely coupled distributed systems, like Carl Hewitt's Actors.

Well, I'll leave it to you to figure out exactly what Meijer means by this response, also to figure out whether it truly responds to the points in our letter. Meanwhile, the plot thickens ... The following month (January 2013), another, related letter was published in *Communications of the ACM*. This one was from Carl Hewitt,[6] and it appeared under the title "Relational Model Obsolete."

---

[6] According to Wikipedia, Carl Hewitt is "an American computer scientist who designed the Planner programming language for automated planning and the actor model of concurrent computation, which have been influential in the development of logic, functional, and object-oriented programming." I wonder who wrote this Wikipedia text.

Here's what it said, more or less (I've made a few very minor cosmetic adjustments, but otherwise it's quoted verbatim):

> I write to support and expand on Erik Meijer's article "All Your Database Are Belong to Us" (*CACM 55, 9*). Relational databases have been very useful in practice but are increasingly an obstacle to progress due to several limitations:
>
> - *Inexpressiveness:* Relational algebra cannot conveniently express negation or disjunction, much less the generalization / specialization connective required for ontologies.
>
> - *Inconsistency nonrobustness:* Inconsistency robustness is information system performance in the face of continually pervasive inconsistencies, a shift from the once dominant paradigms of inconsistency denial and inconsistency elimination attempting to sweep inconsistencies under the rug. In practice, it is impossible to meet the requirement of the Relational Model that all information be consistent, but the Relational Model does not process inconsistent information correctly. Attempting to use transactions to remove contradictions from, say, relational medical information is tantamount to a distributed-denial-of-service attack due to the locking required to prevent new inconsistencies even as contradictions are being removed in the presence of interdependencies.
>
> - *Information loss and lack of provenance:* Once information is known, it should be known thereafter. All information stored or derived should have provenance.
>
> - *Inadequate performance and modularity:* SQL lacks performance because it has parallelism but no concurrency abstraction. Needed are languages based on the Actor Model (*http://www.robust11.org*) to achieve performance, operational expressiveness, and inconsistency robustness. To promote modularity, a programming language type should be an interface that does not name its implementations contra to SQL, which requires taking dependencies on internals.
>
> There is no practical way to repair the Relational Model to remove these limitations. Information processing and storage in computers should apply inconsistency-robust theories(1) processed using the Actor Model (2) in order to use argumentation about known contradictions using inconsistency-robust reasoning that does not make mistakes due to the assumption of consistency. This way, expressivity, modularity, robustness, reliability, and performance beyond that of the obsolete Relational Model can be achieved because computing has changed

dramatically both in scale and form in the four decades since its development. As a first step, a vibrant community, with its own international scientific society, the International Society for Inconsistency Robustness (*http://www.isir.ws*), conducted a refereed international symposium at Stanford University in 2011 (*http://www.robust11.org*); a call for participation is open for the next symposium in the summer of 2014 (*http://www.ir14.org*).

David McGoveran and I responded to this letter, too. Our letter follows (this response was published under a title chosen by us[7]—"Relational Model Alive and Well, Thank You"—in *CACM 56*, No. 5, May 2013):

Carl Hewitt's letter (*CACM 56*, 1) betrays an extremely shallow and unfortunately all too common level of understanding of the relational model. Of the five specific claims he makes regarding "limitations" of the model, not one is valid. To respond briefly:

- *Inexpressiveness:* This one is simply wrong. Negation and disjunction are easily—in fact, almost trivially—expressible. Type generalization and specialization are easily expressible too, though to some extent this is more of an issue for the accompanying type system than it is for the relational model as such.

- *Inconsistency nonrobustness:* This one is both wrong and horribly confused. Space prohibits detailed discussion; suffice it to say that "*p* AND NOT *p*" is an inconsistency, but "Alice says *p* AND Bob says NOT *p*" is certainly not. Moreover, even if the database really does contain an inconsistency, the relational model as such will still function (so we're not talking about a problem with the model here); rather, the problem is with the database and with the consequent fact that you can't trust the answers the system gives you. Further, a query language based on logic that encourages logical contradictions is just nonsense.

- *Information loss:* Whether your updates "lose information" is entirely up to how you choose to use the model—it has nothing to do with the relational model as such. One of us was coauthor on a book[8] 100% devoted to use of the relational model to manage temporal data and thereby not "lose

---

[7] The title under which our previous letter was published, "Not the Database World We Know," was chosen not by us but by the *CACM* editor.

[8] C. J. Date, Hugh Darwen, and Nikos A. Lorentzos: *Temporal Data and the Relational Model* (Morgan Kaufmann, 2003). *Note:* This book has since been superseded by *Time and Relational Theory: Temporal Databases in the Relational Model and SQL* (Morgan Kaufmann, 2014), by the same authors.

information." For the record, the relational model requires *no* "correction," *no* "extension," and above all no *perversion*, in order for this desirable aim to be realized.

■ *Lack of provenance:* Again this point has to do not with the model as such but with how you use it. Note that "Alice says" and "Bob says" [*in the second bullet item*] above are provenance information. In fact, the relational model is ideally suited to recording such information and SQL DBMSs are widely used for that purpose.

■ *Inadequate performance and modularity:* Criticizing the relational model for having no concurrency abstraction is like criticizing a cat for not being a dog. (Hewitt actually says it's SQL that has no concurrency abstraction, but of course SQL and the relational model aren't the same thing; indeed, SQL has very little to do with the relational model.) As for "a ... type should be an interface that does not name its implementations": To the extent we understand this remark, we believe types in the relational model meet this criterion.

We would never dream of publishing a critique of (for example) Hewitt's Actor Model without understanding it well; why then does he feel he can publish a critique of the relational model, when he demonstrably doesn't understand it?

Perhaps not surprisingly, Hewitt responded to this letter, too. His response began as follows:

Unfortunately, Date and McGoveran make no good arguments against the limitations of the relational model, as outlined in my letter, partly because we are using incommensurable terminology (such as "negation," "disjunction," "concurrency," and "abstraction")[9] ...

Well, I'm sure I don't know how reasonable people could disagree on the meanings, in context, of the particular terms Hewitt mentions (negation, disjunction, concurrency, abstraction), but let that pass. This opening sentence was then followed by a lengthy puff piece for Hewitt's own "Actor Model" and

---

[9] *Incommensurable* means "having co common measure; disproportionate; not adequate." I don't really see how, e.g., negation or conjunction can sensibly be described as possessing any of these qualities. It's a small point, perhaps, but I've always felt that sloppy use of words is evidence of sloppy thinking—in the relational world above all, where precision is surely paramount.

for his language ActorScript "as a more appropriate foundation than SQL for a family of languages for information integration." And the letter finished up with:

> [The] relational model and SQL have become obsolete due to the limitations I've outlined here, and innovations like the actor model and ActorScript are required to address current and future needs.

Obsolete? Limitations? Frankly, there are so many detailed criticisms we could have made of Hewitt's original letter that we hardly knew where to begin. Let me just say say that I for one continue to find his claims and complaints regarding the relational model to be totally devoid of any merit whatsoever.

———— ♦ ♦ ♦ ♦ ————

Some 25 years ago or so I attended a conference on what was a fairly hot button issue at the time, "object / relational" technology (viz., the Miller Freeman Object / Relational Conference, October 7th-9th, 1996, Burlingame, Calif.). Recently, quite by chance, I rediscovered the trip report I wrote at the time. I give below a few lightly edited extracts from that trip report, partly just for interest, and partly to let you judge for yourself what kind of progress the industry has made over the past quarter of a century in improving its understanding of relational matters.

> *Overall:* The event overall was, I suppose, "successful"—there were some 200 attendees plus a few exhibitors (six or seven). But it all made me feel a little ill ... There's massive confusion out there, even, or perhaps especially, among those who ought to know better (I mean presenters, for the most part). One thing conspicuous by its absence was a clear definition of *object*. Ditto *object model*.

> *Rick Cattell, keynote* ("Future Database Architectures: Are We All Building the Same DBMS Now?"): Included a survey of the manifestos[10] and a survey of approaches to "marrying objects and relations" out in the marketplace. Appeared to use "architecture" to mean "implementation" (?)—e.g., a slide titled "Relational Architecture" was really about the internal structure of a typical SQL DBMS—and proceeded to criticize the relational model because it "requires" a two-level store

---

[10] "The Object-Oriented Database System Manifesto," by Malcolm Atkinson et al.; the "Third Generation Database System Manifesto," by Michael Stonebraker et al.; and *The Third Manifesto*, by Hugh Darwen and myself.

(*grrr*).[11] General logical vs. physical confusion, too; in fact, this same confusion permeated the entire conference, pretty much, and so did muddled thinking.

My own session ("A Relational View of the Objects vs. Relations Controversy"): Criticized ahead of time on the grounds that "None of the vendors are behind *The Third Manifesto*." I responded by saying we had a longer range vision ... we believed you had to get the foundation right, otherwise you're building castles on sand ... things built on bad foundations might work for a while but will ultimately collapse ... and none of the vendors were behind the relational model originally, either. I also invited people to consider the alternative—i.e., do nothing and just accept the status quo.[12] Many people I subsequently spoke to said *The Third Manifesto* made sense but felt "the horse was out of the barn." We'll see.

Dave DeWitt ("Combining Object / Relational and Parallel: Like Trying to Mix Oil and Water?"): Suggested that set valued attributes might have to map to separate stored tables under the covers (implying additional joins at the physical level), because otherwise you can get "data skew" (department D1 might have two employees and department D2 might have a hundred), which interferes with data distribution patterns and hence parallelism. Note that for years people have been saying exactly the opposite!—namely, that "dependent tables" might have to map to set valued attributes under the covers in order to avoid (physical) joins.

Jim Melton ("SQL3: Moving into the Future"):[13] OK, though far too much on aspects of SQL having little or nothing to do with either OO or O/R. But SQL3 still seems to have some logical / physical confusions. And Jim is still asking (rhetorically?) "Is this really OO support?" And REF types seem confused to me—what exactly do they reference? *Note:* In this connection, see the further remarks below regarding my conversation with Don Chamberlin.[14]

---

[11] It's true that SQL assumes a two-level store, but the relational model doesn't. My original proposals, when I worked on database matters for IBM, for extending the high level languages (primarily PL/I, but also COBOL and others) to include relational functionality very explicitly involved a single-level store. Of course, I received a lot of flak on that score at the time—but then IBM itself released its System/38, a computer with a built-in single-level store and a built-in (and more or less relational) DBMS, thereby, I felt, validating my position in this regard. *Note:* The System/38 subsequently evolved into the AS/400 and IBM then implemented SQL on top of it ("SQL/400"). The SQL/400 implementation thus involved simulating a two-level store on top of a single-level store. Isn't that wonderful?

[12] In retrospect, I should perhaps have quoted George Bernard Shaw here: "The reasonable man adapts himself to the world; the unreasonable one persists in trying to adapt the world to himself. Therefore all progress depends on the unreasonable man." But I didn't think of that at the time.

[13] SQL3 was the working name for what became the 1999 version of the SQL standard ("SQL:1999").

[14] See also Chapter 22 ("Inheritance in SQL") of my book *Type Inheritance and Relational Theory: Subtypes, Supertypes, and Substitutability* (O'Reilly, 2016).

David Maier ("Approaching Object / Relational from the OODBMS Side"): Confusing and (in my opinion) confused. His first example implied that an object was a value. His next implied that an object was a variable. So after his presentation I stopped him in the aisle and asked him what an object was ... A crowd began to gather. "Is an object a value?" "Not really." "Well, is it a variable?" "No, not really." "Well, perhaps I should back up and define my terms [*and here I gave my own definitions for value and variable*]. Do you agree with these definitions?" "No, not really." "Well, what do *you* think a variable is?" "Well, I suppose to me a variable is a binding between a name and a piece of state" (I'm quoting verbatim).

Clearly, nothing was resolved in this discussion, but I think the onlookers were well able to see that one of the leading OO proponents[15] was quite incapable of explaining some of the most fundamental concepts underlying his approach. And I hope they took the message to heart.

Maier did, however, say in his presentation that user defined types (UDTs) were "the one good thing about OO"! Wow! What an admission! He also made considerable use of the term "pointing to," which I thought OO folks didn't do (they insist that object IDs aren't pointers, don't they?). That's another paper I'm going to have to write soon ("Why Object IDs Are Pointers"): If it walks like a duck, looks like a duck, and quacks like a duck, then by God it's a duck.[16]

Maier also told me later that two program variables can have the very same object as their value—meaning that if a "state change" occurred in that object (so an object's a variable!) it would be visible instantly via both variables. So I said "You mean those two variables really contain pointers to the object?" "No." "No?" "Well, not explicitly." "But surely implicitly, at least—for otherwise how do you explain the semantics to the user?" "Well, yes, perhaps implicitly." "So the *model* is that program variables contain pointers to objects, and objects are variables of some more general kind?" "Well, yes, I suppose so." I rest my case.

Won Kim (for some reason I didn't record the title of Kim's presentation):[17] First slide: "Provide options to remove the major problems of ... RDB technology (no

---

[15] Maier was one of the authors of "The Object-Oriented Database System Manifesto."

[16] I did write that paper—I called it "Object Identifiers vs. Relational Keys," and you can find it in my book *Relational Database Writings 1994-1997* (Addison-Wesley, 1998).

[17] Kim was subsequently described, in a product presentation by a speaker from UniSQL, as "the father of object / relational database." By the way, that particular product presentation included one of those dreadfully dishonest "objects vs. relations" comparisons, contrasting an SQL query of many lines with an OO program of just two or three—but the OO program invoked a user defined method, the code for which wasn't shown. Mary Loomis's book *Object Databases: The Essentials* (Addison-Wesley, 1995) uses the same trick (pages 78-80).

repeating groups, no pointer chasing, limited data types)." Oh *dear* ... Re pointer chasing, Kim said: "It's not really *physical* pointer chasing I'm talking about, but *logical* pointer chasing." What *is* one to do with these people? (Anyway, I'm glad to see that Kim, at least, thinks that object IDs are pointers.) PS: My old friend Charley Bontempo told me later that this same muddle arose years ago over database keys in CODASYL ... "Are they logical pointers?" "No." "Well, are they physical pointers?" "No." "So what *are* they?" "Well, they're sort of in between."

Kim went on to say that "[the UniSQL] data model subsumes data models of all current and past generations of databases." Sounds like it's time to revive the old UDL onion layer arguments!—i.e., apply Occam's Razor.[18]

And he asked a truly bizarre (rhetorical?) question: "Should there be one inheritance hierarchy for views and classes?" I couldn't make any sense of this at all, and still can't.

Don Chamberlin ("Anatomy of an Object / Relational System"): Unfortunately I wasn't able to attend this session. But Don and I did have some subsequent conversation[19] ...

■ First of all, Don wanted to know what was wrong with having a REF type, according to which a relation could include a column whose values were references to rows somewhere else. Heresy! I didn't do a very good job of answering this question at the time. (As far as I was concerned it was right out of left field ... I mean, I thought Codd had answered it pretty well about a quarter of a century previously.) But what I did do was go away and write a paper—"Don't Mix Pointers and Relations!"—in which I tried to answer the question in detail. [*That paper was republished in my book Relational Database Writings 1994-1997 (Addison-Wesley, 1998).*]

---

[18] Regarding UDL in general, see "An Introduction to the Unified Database Language (UDL)," in my book *Relational Database: Selected Writings* (Addison-Wesley, 1986). But the point I'm alluding to here can be summed up very simply: (a) UDL supported all three of relations, hierarchies, and networks; (b) the features needed for relations were a proper subset of those needed for hierarchies, which in turn were a proper subset of those needed for networks; (c) the language thus had a kind of onion layer structure, with relational features at the center, hierarchic features as a layer surrounding that center, and network features as a layer surrounding that hierarchic layer; hence, (d) hierarchies and networks, though they didn't add any power (there's nothing useful that can be done with hierarchies and networks that can't be done with relations), certainly added a lot of extra, and unnecessary, language features and complexity.

[19] The substance of the first of the bullet items that follow also appears in Chapter 2 of my book *Fifty Years of Relational, and Other Database Writings: More Thoughts and Essays on Database Matters* (Technics Publications, 2020). I apologize for the duplication, but judged it better to include the material here anyway, in order not to interfere with the overall flow. By the way: If Kim can be described as "the father of object / relational database" (see footnote 17), then Chamberlin can be described—with, in my opinion, a great deal more justification—as "the father of SQL."

- Second, he wanted to know why we insisted on basing *The Third Manifesto* on relations instead of (say) lists, and why we didn't permit (say) lists as "first class objects" in the database. More left field questions as far as I was concerned, and more heresy! I don't think I did a very good job of answering these questions either.

- Third, I asked him why SQL had to have both "DISTINCT types" and "structured types." His answer was that (a) "DISTINCT types" have a more efficient implementation, since they're directly defined in terms of a single (system defined) base type, and (b) "DISTINCT types" are scalar types, while "structured types" are tuple types. (My terminology, not his—this is my interpretation of what he said.) I didn't point out the logical vs. physical confusions in this answer, and remain unconvinced as to the *logical* need for "DISTINCT types."[20]

———— ◆ ◆ ◆ ◆ ◆ ————

Following on from some of the foregoing discussions (i.e., at that object / relational conference), I'd like to say a little more about this business of object IDs. The argument—such as it is—in favor of object IDs goes something like this. Suppose we have a tuple *t* representing the facts that a certain employee has a certain employee number (ENO), a certain name (ENAME), a certain salary (SALARY), and a certain department (DNO). Now, in the relational world, we're allowed to update tuples on a component by component basis, and so we might change *every single component* of tuple *t*.[21] But if we do, then in what sense is that tuple still "tuple *t*"?[22]

The object aficionados define their way out of this "dilemma"—again, such as it is—by affixing an unchangeable ID to *t*, so that even if every

---

[20] Having now studied DISTINCT vs. structured types much more carefully and written about them in great detail—see Chapter 22, "Inheritance in SQL," of my book *Type Inheritance and Relational Theory: Subtypes, Supertypes, and Substitutability* (O'Reilly, 2016)—I find myself more unconvinced than ever.

[21] I'm speaking *very* loosely here, of course, as I hope the subsequent explanation makes clear. Do note, however, that I'm pretending for the sake of the argument that tuple *t* is just "stand alone," as it were. If it's supposed to be part of some relation (or some relvar) instead, then my explanation would need some rather careful rewording. (Recall my claim earlier to the effect that no variable can sensibly be considered part of either a value or another variable.) However, on the grounds that, as Bertrand Russell once said, "writing can be either readable or precise, but not at the same time," I decided, rightly or wrongly, not to attempt that "careful rewording" here. Apologies if you find my explanation a little confusing as a result.

[22] This question reminds me of the old philosophical puzzle: Is my car still the same car after I've replaced every part of it? (Of course, some might say it obviously wasn't a car in the first place, it was a lemon.)

component of *t* changes it still has the same ID and is thus still the same "object." (Incidentally, this scheme accounts for the remarks one occasionally hears, to the effect that relational systems are value based whereas object systems are identity based.) And then, given the availability of object IDs, we can obviously now have two distinct "objects" with the same value,[23] and we can also build arbitrarily complex data structures in the database, and so on and so forth.

Well, I hope the flaw in the foregoing is obvious; indeed, I believe the argument is fundamentally confused. It all has to do with that business of values vs. variables. The OO literature is permeated by an unrecognized, or at least unadmitted, confusion between these two concepts. Now, it's true that objects are sometimes classified into *mutable* and *immutable* categories; but as far as I'm concerned, a mutable object is just a variable and an immutable object is just a value. Moreover, I think the terms *variable* and *value* are vastly preferable—because they're familiar, well defined, and (I hope) well understood—and I see no need to talk in terms of objects at all. The argument I gave above "in favor of" object IDs simply fails to recognize the distinction between a tuple per se—that is, a tuple *value*—and a tuple *variable*. The "tuple *t*" mentioned in that argument was really a tuple variable: the same variable at all times, of course, but with different values at different times. Thus, the alleged "dilemma" was never a dilemma in the first place.

Further, I hope it's also obvious that:

a. Values or "immutable objects" don't need any kind of ID—they are, by definition, self-identifying.

b. By contrast, variables or "mutable objects" do need some kind of ID, and that ID is provided, precisely, by the variable's *name*.

> *Aside:* Point b. here is perhaps a little oversimplified. Object systems typically allow new "mutable objects" of a given "class" (i.e., type) to be created dynamically, in which case the objects in question might not have a conventional name—which is precisely why they have to be accessed via pointers. Indeed, an illuminating and fruitful analogy can be drawn between mutable objects as such and the "explicit dynamic variables" supported by certain conventional

---

[23] At the cost of having to deal with the complexity of supporting two different "=" operators, of course (viz., equal value vs. equal ID).

programming languages (PL/I's *based variables* are a case in point). For example, consider the following PL/I code fragment:

```
DECLARE 1 ABOBJ BASED ,
          2 A INTEGER ,
          2 B FLOAT ;

DECLARE P POINTER ;

ALLOCATE ABOBJ SET ( P ) ;

P -> ABOBJ.A = 3 ;
```

Observe the parallels between this PL/I code and conventional object code:

- The declaration of the based variable ABOBJ is akin to defining a new object class. Any number of individual objects (or variables) of that class can now be created in turn.

- Individual objects (or variables) of that class have two "public instance variables" called A and B, of types INTEGER and FLOAT, respectively. *Note:* In the OO context, A and B would probably contain pointers (i.e., "object IDs") rather than numbers, but this fact is irrelevant as far as the present argument is concerned.

- P is a program variable whose values are pointers (i.e., "object IDs").

- The ALLOCATE statement is akin to an object constructor function invocation: It creates a new object (or variable) of class ABOBJ, allocating storage for that object, and setting P to point to it.[24] Observe that this new object has no distinguishing name apart from its address—which (as previously indicated) is precisely why object IDs are necessary, in the object world.

- The assignment statement "mutates" the object that P points to by assigning the value three to its A instance variable.

And so on. *End of aside.*

---

[24] "Setting P to point to it" means, more precisely, assigning the address of the ABOBJ "instance" just created to the variable P, which is declared to be of type POINTER.

By way of further evidence in support of my contention that the object world is confused over values vs. variables, consider the following quotes, all of them taken from the paper "Object Query Standards," by Andrew E. Wade (*ACM SIGMOD Record 25*, No. 1, March 1996). The comments in italics are mine, of course.

■   Even if all the state information (all the attribute values) of the object changes ... [*so an object is a variable*].

■   [A] simple one-to-one relationship can be viewed as an object-valued attribute within each of the two related objects [*so an object is a value*].

■   [The] result of the query may be a scalar (including tuples), an object, or a collection of objects ... [*so again an object is a value, although "scalars (including tuples)" are apparently not objects, and neither are "collections"—not to mention the weird suggestion that tuples are scalars*].

■   Abstract Data Types [in SQL] ... have much the same functionality as OMG or ODMG objects ... [*so an object is a type!*].

■   ... individual objects [in] collections [comprise] various, possibly complex, data types, as well as objects [*I'm afraid I can't make head or tail of this one*].

All this, in a paper allegedly about *standards* ... !

Finally, I can't resist throwing in a couple of quotes from the book *Object-Oriented Databases*, by Setrag Khoshafian (Wiley, 1993):

■   This eliminates the need to use variable names that do not have the support of object identity, but it introduces some practical limitations. One limitation is that a single object may be accessed in different ways. Thus, an object may be bound to different variables that have no way of finding out whether they refer to the same object.

Some questions: What does it mean for a "variable name" to have "the support of object identity"? Or not to have it, come to that? When exactly is there a "need to use variable names" that either have or don't have such support? What are the "different ways" in which "a single object may be accessed"? Why is the fact that "a single object may be accessed in different ways" a "limitation"? What exactly is it that's being limited? Why exactly is it a "practical" limitation, as opposed to some other kind?

What other kinds might it be? Do I have to worry about them? What does it mean for an object to be "bound to" a variable? What does it mean for an object to be bound to "different variables"? What does it mean for variables to "find out whether they refer to the same object?" Or to different objects, come to that? In fact, what does it mean for a variable to "find out" anything at all? Why are trees cut down to print such stuff?

- In programming languages identity is realized through memory addresses. In databases identity is realized through identifier keys. User-specified names are used in both languages and databases to give unique names to objects. Each of these schemes compromises identity. In a complete object-oriented system each object is given an identity that will be permanently associated with the object immaterial of [*sic*] the object's structure or state transitions. The identity of an object is also independent of the location, or address, of the object. Object identity provides the most natural modeling primitive to allow the same object to be a subobject of multiple parent objects. With object identity, objects can contain or refer to other objects. Object identity clarifies, enhances, and extends the notions of pointers in conventional programming languages, foreign keys in databases, and file names in operating systems ... .

Do you understand all this? I for one most certainly don't.

This next item is an excerpt from an interview with a Very Famous Computing Person; the interview originally appeared in *DBMS Magazine*, and the excerpt in question had to do with a database product that the Very Famous Computing Person was planning to bring to market in the near future. Unfortunately I haven't been able to track the original interview down—all I have is a rather scruffy typescript—so I can't be more specific as to the actual source (though from internal evidence it's fairly clear that it must have been published in the mid to late 1980s). For such reasons I won't identify the Very Famous Computing Person here, though the typescript in fact does so. *Note:* I strongly suspect that many of the references in what follows to "databases" should more correctly be references to "DBMSs" (or maybe not; sometimes it's hard to tell).

DBMS: At some point, will [your product] go further and let the database engine enforce integrity, or at least referential integrity?

VFCP: The type of integrity we support in [our product] is far, far more general. Referential integrity is a small part of it. [Our product] allows arbitrary integrity checks, OK? Referential integrity, I mean ... I don't know if you really want to talk about that. I'm pretty sure there's nothing shipping that has it. I'm not sure that people reading this know or want to know what those words mean, I mean, unless you'd have a long article about it.

DBMS: We've talked about it in pieces of several articles, and we actually have a piece scheduled later in the year about it.

VFCP: The word referential integrity?

DBMS: Yes.

VFCP: The word referential integrity? I mean, you realize there are no relational databases. Did you write an article about that?

DBMS: It's come up in several articles.

VFCP: There never have been, and there never will be in the next decade, any relational databases.

DBMS: Do you think it's important to fully conform to Codd's rules and be a full relational database?

VFCP: No!

DBMS: Why not?

VFCP: What do you want me to do, go through it rule by rule?

DBMS: We actually went to the length of publishing Date's rules on what constitutes a distributed database[25] in our article on distributed databases ...

VFCP: Right, but that doesn't mean people understand them when you write that stuff down. You think I know what it means? I'll sit here and read this article.

DBMS: You don't have to read it now.

---

[25] C. J. Date: "Twelve Rules for a Distributed Database" (*Computerworld*, June 8th, 1987). An expanded version can be found (under the revised title "What Is a Distributed Database System?") in my book *Relational Database Writings 1985-1989* (Addison-Wesley, 1990).

VFCP: Do you think I have any sense about why I'd care?

DBMS: Well, I think that one role this magazine has is to talk about what the state of the art is, what the relational model lets you do, and why you should care about these things.

VFCP: The key issues have to do with, well, not having redundant data, not building into the data a big set way of querying the data. I mean, those are the big benefits, and in addition most databases labeled "relational" give you this arbitrary query language that operates with some efficiency. Actually you can have an arbitrary query language against any database, but they end up enumerating every record in the database to process the queries. Do some [SQL-style SELECT] against a hierarchical database that's not going down the hierarchy? The nice thing about relational databases is they let you do queries on a very ad hoc basis in an efficient fashion. Now, this notion of not having data redundancy requires someone who sets up that database to understand the entities and what's independent of what, and what's driven by what—it takes a little bit of expertise, and developers have gotten relatively good at that stuff. But I don't think you'll see the relational rules being the key competitive factor in the microcomputer world.

The arrogance is breathtaking. So is the ignorance.[26]

One particular piece of relational trumpery that I and numerous others have written about, and strongly criticized, many times over the years is the use of "nulls" and three-valued logic (3VL) as a basis for dealing with information that's missing for some reason.[27] Now, I certainly don't propose to rehash any of the usual tired old arguments here. However, I do want to make a point that,

---

[26] As a matter of fact I have an anecdote of my own concerning the VFCP ... My phone rang late one evening (this would have have been in the mid 1980s). A female voice said: "Hold the line for Mr VFCP" (so right away I'm annoyed; the guy can't even make his own phone calls). Anyway, Mr VFCP comes on the line. "I understand you teach relational database stuff." "Well, yes, I do." "We're planning to build a relational product, and I'd like you to come and educate my people." "OK, fine" ... and so we discussed possibilities for a while. Eventually, however, he turned me down because I was (according to him) "too expensive."

[27] Throughout the present discussion I use the term *null* (a trifle loosely) to mean either or both of the following: 1. nulls as supported in SQL; 2. nulls as introduced and added to the original relational model by Codd in his paper "Extending the Database Relational Model to Capture More Meaning," *ACM Transactions on Database Systems 4*, No. 4 (December 1979).

even if it's widely understood (which it might or might not be), I for one have never seen spelled out anywhere else. The point I want to make is this: Logic and philosophy are often said to be founded on certain "Laws of Thought." To quote Wikipedia:

> The laws of thought are fundamental axiomatic rules upon which rational discourse itself is often considered to be based.[28]

And in his book *Introduction to Logic* (6th edition, MacMillan, 1982), Irving M. Copi has this to say (I've edited his words very slightly):

> These [laws] have traditionally been called the Principle of Identity, the Principle of Noncontradiction, and the Principle of [the] Excluded Middle. There are alternative formulations of these principles, appropriate to different contexts.

The formulations that best suit my present purposes are as follows. Let *x* denote anything that's of interest for some reason—anything in the universe of discourse, as the logicians might say—and let $p(x)$ be understood to mean that *x* has property *p*. Then the following expressions all evaluate to TRUE:

Principle of Identity:
```
FORALL x ( x = x )
```

Principle of Noncontradiction:
```
NOT EXISTS x ( p ( x ) AND NOT p ( x ) )
```

Principle of Excluded Middle:[29]
```
FORALL x ( p ( x ) XOR NOT p ( x ) )
```

But if *x* happens to be null, then all three of these principles are violated!—and it seems to me that this state of affairs should have been sufficient to stop the entire misguided "nulls" idea dead in its tracks, before it ever became as ubiquitous as it sadly now is. *Sigh.*

---

[28] Bertrand Russell, in his 1912 book *The Problems of Philosophy*, adds that "What is important is not the fact that we think in accordance with these laws, but the fact that things behave in accordance with them; in other words, the fact that when we think in accordance with them we think *truly*."

[29] XOR here denotes exclusive OR.

———— ♦ ♦ ♦ ♦ ♦ ————

I was tempted to label this final item "Unclear on the Concept" ... The following text is taken verbatim[30] from the magazine *IBM Data Management 5*, No. 3 (2010). It's a sidebar, with the title "Look How You've Grown" (and I was very tempted to comment on that title, too, but resisted):

> When DB2 SQL was first introduced, you could practically count the functions [*sic*] on one hand. These days, there's a lot more to choose from:
>
> table expressions ♦ complex correlation ♦ global temporary tables ♦ CASE ♦ 100+ builtin functions ♦ limited FETCH ♦ scrollable cursors ♦ UNION everywhere ♦ MIN / MAX single index support ♦ self-referencing UPDATEs with subqueries ♦ sort avoidance for ORDER BY ♦ AND row expressions ♦ 2M statement length ♦ GROUP BY expression ♦ sequences ♦ scalar fullselect ♦ materialized query tables ♦ common table expressions ♦ recursive SQL ♦ CURRENT PACKAGE PATH ♦ volatile table support ♦ star join sparse index ♦ qualified column names ♦ multiple DISTINCT clauses ♦ IS NOT DISTINCT FROM ♦ ON COMMIT DROP ♦ transparent ROWID column ♦ GET DIAGNOSTICS ♦ Stage1 unlike data types ♦ multirow INSERT ♦ multirow FETCH ♦ dynamic scrollable cursors ♦ multiple CCSIDs per statement ♦ enhanced Unicode ♦ AND parallel sort ♦ TRUNCATE ♦ decimal FLOAT ♦ VARBINARY ♦ optimistic locking ♦ FETCH CONTINUE ♦ MERGE ♦ CALL from trigger ♦ statement isolation ♦ FOR READ ONLY KEEP UPDATE LOCKS ♦ SET CURRENT SCHEMA ♦ client special registers ♦ long SQL object names ♦ SELECT from INSERT ♦ UPDATE ♦ DELETE ♦ MERGE ♦ INSTEAD OF trigger ♦ native SQL procedure language ♦ BIGINT ♦ file reference variables ♦ XML ♦ FETCH FIRST & ORDER BY in subselect and fullselect ♦ caseless comparisons ♦ INTERSECT ♦ EXCEPT ♦ NOT LOGGED tables

———— ♦ ♦ ♦ ♦ ♦ ————

Well, that's enough for now. In my files I have many, many more examples of bizarre pronouncements on the relational model and related matters that I could comment on, but I'm getting tired, and I dare say you are too, so I'll stop. At least for the time being ...

---

[30] Except that the original is in all caps, and I've added the diamond separators (the original used commas).

Chapter 13

Leonardo Was Right

And I am right,
And you are right,
And all is right as right can be!

—W. S. Gilbert:
The Mikado (1885)

This chapter can be seen as a kind of coda to Chapter 12, and indeed to
the entire book, in a way. It was originally written in response to a
request from one of the trade publications for a short "popular" piece
that would help explain why people should still pay attention to
relational theory, but for various reasons it wasn't published at the time.

Here are some not entirely rhetorical questions:

1. Would you want to fly in an airplane that hadn't been constructed in accordance with solid principles of mechanical engineering and aeronautical science?

2. Would you want to live or work in a high rise building that hadn't been constructed in accordance with solid principles of architecture and material science?

3. Would you want to run your business on a database that hadn't been constructed in accordance with solid principles of computing and database science?

Well, your answer to the first two of these questions is surely *no*. But what about the third one? Clearly the answer to that one ought to be *no* as well. To judge from current practice, however, all too often it's *yes*. Why is this? What accounts for this state of affairs? Maybe the problem is that not too many people are aware that the pertinent principles and science even exist. By way of evidence for this suggestion, I offer the following quotes. They're all taken, with permission, from Fabian Pascal's website *www.dbdebunk.com*, but I've omitted the original sources in order to protect the guilty. (I've also taken the liberty of editing a few of them for reasons of readability—but only very slightly, and never in such a way as to change the sense.) My own comments appear interleaved with the quotes.

—————— ♦ ♦ ♦ ♦ ♦ ——————

I have done an Entity-Attribute-Value database design before. The big advantage is that much of your logical model is stored as data rather than as schema, so changes to the logical model can be made without changing the schema. And if you write your [stored procedures] correctly, you won't need to change them either. The drawback? VERY complicated SQL code. The main reason I used this was for a client that did not have a clear understanding of their own requirements, but needed a working application on a deadline.

First let me give some idea of what an entity-attribute-value design might look like. The following picture shows a sample value for a simple employees relvar that has been designed in accordance with such a scheme:

ENO	ATTRIBUTE	VALUE
E1	ENAME	Lopez
E1	DNO	D1
E1	SALARY	40K
E2	ENAME	Cheng
E2	DNO	D1
E2	SALARY	42K
E3	ENAME	Finzi
E3	DNO	D2
E3	SALARY	30K

Aside: Given such a design, the question of attribute data types is an interesting one. Presumably attribute ATTRIBUTE can be of type CHAR; but what about attribute VALUE? Almost certainly that attribute will have to be of type CHAR as well—implying that type conversions are going to be needed rather frequently, if (for example) there's any need to perform arithmetic on salaries. *End of aside.*

Well, it seems to me that if you're going to do such an entity-attribute-value design, there's very little point in using a relational DBMS in the first place. Certainly such a design means throwing away some of the most obvious, and most important, benefits of the relational approach. Among other things, ad hoc query becomes very difficult—probably beyond the abilities of the typical end user. Not to mention constraints! *Exercise:* Try writing a **Tutorial D** or SQL expression representing the query "For each department, get the department number and average salary for employees in that department," given the design illustrated above. Also try writing a **Tutorial D** or SQL expression representing the constraint "Every employee must be in a known department (and that department must be unique)."

What's more, I venture to suggest that "a client that doesn't have a clear understanding of their own requirements" (!) is definitely going to want to be able to do ad hoc queries sooner or later (probably sooner), if only to make up for their own unbelievable lack of foresight and planning. For example: "Get all employees not in exactly one known department."

———— ♦ ♦ ♦ ♦ ♦ ————

[In my opinion] databases are supposed to be dumb storage, they are intended to manage the storing of data, not business logic ... Let [the] database be dumb and [the] application smart, after all the application is a model of the business process, the database is just storage to support and expedite the data being pulled into business objects.

Good grief! This person shouldn't be allowed anywhere near a database, or database applications! The giveaway, of course, is in the last few words, where the writer refers to "the data being pulled into business objects." In other words, we're dealing here with an object person ... and in my admittedly limited experience, object people generally have little or no understanding of what databases are all about. All they want to do is keep their "business objects" in persistent storage so they don't go away when their program stops executing.

OK, that might be a legitimate requirement—but please don't call that persistent storage a database. You can call it that only if it does all the things a database system is supposed to do, including but not limited to things like ad hoc query and update, views, recovery and concurrency, security and integrity, and so on.

———— ◆ ◆ ◆ ◆ ◆ ————

[Data] is best kept closest to its natural source rather than at the intersection of a row and tuple of a database.

"The intersection of a row and a tuple"? Well, *tuple* is just the formal relational term for what SQL calls a row—so someone is confused here, and I don't think it's me. As for the overall sense of the quote … well, actually I don't think there is any overall sense. Which makes it difficult to comment any further.

———— ◆ ◆ ◆ ◆ ◆ ————

[The trouble with relational databases is that] you need to adapt the table structure every time you want more data …With RDF you can just pour data into your triple store, and then work with it immediately. This is much more agile.

RDF is basically just the "entity-attribute-value" approach by another name, and so I refer you to my comments on the first quote, earlier, in that connection. As for "This is much more agile," it looks to me as if we're dealing once again with someone who "doesn't have a clear understanding of their own requirements." Now, it's true that a relational design is much more flexible than older, prerelational designs (and relational DBMSs are likewise much more flexible than their prerelational counterparts, older or otherwise)—meaning that, when changes are required (and changes are always required, sooner or later)—then the changes in question are easier to apply. But none of this is an excuse for not doing proper planning in the first place. Databases and "agility," in the sense the writer here means it, just aren't a natural fit (and run away, fast, from anybody who tries to tell you otherwise).

———— ◆ ◆ ◆ ◆ ◆ ————

SQL is inadequate to the task of fully utilizing the RELATIONAL MODEL because it doesn't have any way to EXPRESS RELATIONSHIPS other than "table." Isn't this a limitation of the relational data model itself? I think only the entity-relationship model can distinguish between relationships and other data. Once you convert your model to the relational data model, you've lost that distinction. This is not an SQL-specific problem. At least this is what we learned at our university on a database course.

Assuming the writer's last sentence here is accurate, what an indictment of our education system! In fact, the whole paragraph could be taken as such an indictment …Note how it contradicts itself—"SQL can't fully utilize [*sic*] the relational model" vs. "This is a limitation of the relational model" (paraphrasing slightly). Perhaps more to the point: "The relational model can't distinguish entities and relationships" (paraphrasing again). Now, I'm prepared to concede this latter point for the sake of the argument.[1] But the point is, *the entity and relationship concepts aren't (and in my opinion can't be) precisely defined.* As I've written elsewhere, many times and in many different places, one person's entity is another person's relationship. (The classic example is marriages: A marriage can be regarded as a relationship between people, or—to a marriage registrar, for example—it can be regarded as an entity in its own right.) So any approach that attempts to draw a *formal* distinction between the two concepts—as the entity / relationship approach explicitly does, and as the relational model deliberately doesn't—is doomed to eventual failure.

I am a novice user of Microsoft Access. I typically do not use Primary Keys. Everything I read indicates that the primary key is used mainly to speed up the search of a database. I am currently just using two small tables which contain a common record ID. I am doing queries on these tables and I have not discovered any errors. Based on what I have seen I still obtain the correct information from my queries. Is it critical that I use a primary key or is [it just] a "nice to have" with large databases?

This one received an online response (not from me!):

---

[1] But *only* for the sake of the argument, please note.

Online response: **Establishing a primary key is never necessary even in a large database. There are advantages to having a primary key—mainly that Microsoft Access will make sure that the field will contain only unique values. This will stop a user from accidentally entering a duplicate record. [Microsoft] Access will also make sure that the primary key contains a value—again this is necessary to keep each record uniquely identified.**

There's so much wrong with the original question that it would take many, many pages to deconstruct it fully, and I'm not even going to try. Indeed, the only sentence that doesn't contain an obvious error (at least of understanding, if not of fact) is the very first!—which, from the evidence of the rest of the question, is probably accurate. As for the response: Well, with friends like that ...

———— ◆◆◆◆◆ ————

Relational databases are basically two-dimensional matrices with pointers ... high-class spreadsheets. Object and XML databases are more likely to accept the architectures and data models you're working with every day, and are more adaptable, flexible, and customizable: You'll be able to apply extreme programming principles and add fields as you go, connect to other systems and maintain focus on your data model and your project, not that of the database and the best possible model that fits into that database. Before choosing to ignore this suggestion and go back to relational databases, struggling to fit your designs into its data model, consider XML and object databases. Import / export from/to RDBMSs is straightforward, and has been set up in real time to truly garner the design / maintenance benefits of OODBMSs while retaining the atomicity and existing relational tools without sacrificing data quality and currency.

This is even worse than the previous one. What to say? Well, relational databases aren't two-dimensional—that's the first point. Second, they don't contain pointers! (Codd deliberately excluded pointers from the relational model, for all kinds of good reasons. I know object people like pointers, but as I've already said, object people typically don't understand databases. Evidence provided on request.) Object databases are like the old failed network (CODASYL) databases. Do you really want to go back 40 or 50 years? XML databases are like the old failed hierarchic databases. Again, do you want to go back 40 or 50 years? "More adaptable, flexible, and customizable"? Really?

Justify this very strong claim! I could say more (much more), but I think that's enough to be going on with.

I never had to have database design explained or taught to me. It was just so intuitive, so obvious, so simple, that there was no other way you could do it. That's my problem. My brain can't even comprehend the idea of any other database structure design. I'm really looking forward to learning something new [*viz., data warehouse*], whose fundamental concepts I can't even grasp right now...

Online response: **The first rule of data warehouse is: Forget everything you think you know about data modeling.**

Actually, the question here, as opposed to the response, isn't too unreasonable. Good database design often *is* intuitive (though not always). What's wrong is the online response, which is (sadly) all too typical. I've discussed this issue in detail elsewhere; suffice it to say that, just because data warehouses are typically used for analytic processing and are only rarely updated, it does *not* follow that the principles of relational design theory are therefore inapplicable. Quite the opposite, in fact.

To deliver great reports fast without having to have a team of PhD statisticians pulling all-nighters, [we] just had to do one trivial, minor, insignificant thing. Scrap the whole "the database is at the heart of everything we do" mentality. To quote [a certain] website: Stop architecting the database! Applications tied directly to relational databases are costly to develop and maintain and, while once considered state-of-the-art, are by today's standards notoriously lacking in sophistication and adaptability.

Let's be charitable here and assume the experience the writer is reporting on in his or her first two sentences was indeed as described. (I'd need to know a lot more about the specific database and the specific reports before I could be convinced of this state of affairs, but I'm willing to accept the point as stated for the sake of the argument.) But even if so, I don't think it could reasonably be advanced as sufficient evidence in favor of the very strong conclusions articulated in the last two sentences. Hasn't anybody, anywhere, ever had any success with relational databases?

———— ◆ ◆ ◆ ◆ ————

I could spend a long time deconstructing the foregoing quotes further, but I don't think that should be necessary; I think the overall message is pretty clear. To spell it out: There's a vast amount of ignorance of these matters out there in the industry. Indeed, I have one further quote that sums up my overall feelings in this area pretty well. It's from a letter in the July 2011 issue of *Communications of the ACM* (Volume 54, Number 7).[2] *Note:* The writer is referring specifically to "object / relational mappings" and (another currently fashionable piece of nonsense) "NoSQL systems," but I think his remarks are actually of wider applicability. The italics are mine.

> Object Relational Mappings and NoSQL systems attempt to solve (through technical means) a nontechnical problem: *reluctance of talented people to master the Relational Model*, and thus benefit from its data consistency and logical inferencing capabilities. Rather than exploit it and demand more relational functionality from DBMS vendors, they seek to avoid and replace it, unwittingly advocating a return to the fragile, unreliable, illogical systems of the 1960s, minus the greenbar fanfold paper.

The fact is, there's a great deal of good theoretical science available for addressing "the database problem," but there doesn't seem to be much evidence that it's widely used in practice. Indeed, many people deliberately seem to avoid that theory; there seems to be a widespread perception that if something is theoretical, then it can't be practical. ("Don't bother me with that theoretical stuff, I'm a practical person.") My own position is exactly the opposite: namely, if something isn't based on solid theory, it's likely to be very unpractical indeed (not least because it'll probably be hard to understand). And I'd like to close this brief survey with an appeal to Leonardo da Vinci, who wrote the following over 500 years ago (I've added the boldface):

---

[2] The letter was from James K. Lowden. I've quoted it before, in Chapter 2 of my book *Fifty Years of Relational, and Other Database Writings: More Thoughts and Essays on Database Matters* (Technics Publications, 2020).

Those who are enamored of practice without theory are like a pilot who goes into a ship without rudder or compass and never has any certainty where he is going. **Practice should always be based upon a sound knowledge of theory.**

Leonardo was right.

I n d e x

For alphabetization purposes, (a) differences in fonts and case are ignored; (b) quotation marks are ignored; (c) other punctuation symbols—hyphens, underscores, parentheses, etc.—are treated as blanks; (d) numerals precede letters; (e) blanks precede everything else.

www.ingramcontent.com/pod-product-compliance
Lightning Source LLC
Chambersburg PA
CBHW080607060326
40690CB00021B/4611